THE
WINE
ACCESS
BUYER'S
GUIDE

D0557483

As a purchaser of this book, you are entitled to a complimentary one-year subscription to WineAccess CellarNotes™. For more details on this special offer see page 11 or go to www.wineaccess.com/specialoffer.

THE
WINE
ACCESS
BUYER'S
GUIDE

THE WORLD'S BEST WINES
& WHERE TO FIND THEM

Stephen Tanzer

Sterling Publishing Co., Inc.
New York

Map artwork created by Jeffrey Ward

Design adapted by 3+Co. (www.threeandco.com)

2 4 6 8 10 9 7 5 3 1

Published by Sterling Publishing Co., Inc.
387 Park Avenue South, New York, NY 10016

© 2006 by Stephen Tanzer

Distributed in Canada by Sterling Publishing
c/o Canadian Manda Group, 165 Dufferin Street
Toronto, Ontario, Canada M6K 3H6

Distributed in the United Kingdom by GMC Distribution Services
Castle Place, 166 High Street, Lewes, East Sussex, England BN7 1XU

Distributed in Australia by Capricorn Link (Australia) Pty. Ltd.
P.O. Box 704, Windsor, NSW 2756, Australia

Manufactured in the United States of America
All rights reserved

Sterling ISBN-13: 978-1-4027-2816-7
ISBN-10: 1-4027-2816-6

For information about custom editions, special sales, premium and
corporate purchases, please contact Sterling Special Sales
Department at 800-805-5489 or specialsales@sterlingpub.com.

CONTENTS

ACKNOWLEDGMENTS

To paraphrase the comedian Steven Wright, "It's a small world, but I'd hate to have to taste it." Or, more accurately, I'd hate to have to taste it on my own. In fact, creating this book was far from a lonely effort: I had plenty of support.

I would like to thank Ian d'Agata and David Schildknecht for their substantial contributions to this project. For their valued opinions and insights, and for bringing wines to my attention that I might not otherwise have come to taste, I would like to single out the following people—most of them in the wine trade and all of them true professionals: Rory Callahan, Jeffrey Davies, Gerry Dawes, Joe Dressner, Luis Gutiérrez, Victor Honoré, Matt Kramer, Dan McCarthy, André Morgenthal, Peter Moser, Jeremy Oliver, Pierre Paillardon, Joel Payne, Neal Rosenthal, Bruce Schneider, David Strada, and Tim Wilson. Many of these names will be familiar to long-time readers of my bimonthly *International Wine Cellar*.

For his unflagging energy, tasting ability and steel-trap memory, and for his important contributions to this guide, I would like to give special thanks to Josh Raynolds, who is open-minded and enthusiastic, the antithesis of a wine snob. Heartfelt thanks, too, to my assistant Merrie-Louise Raynolds for her attention to detail and unflappable good humor.

Also, to my Internet partner and the founder of WineAccess, Jim Weinrott, special thanks for helping me bring this unique project to life.

I would like to dedicate this book my wife Amy Tucker, who has made everything possible.

NOTE FROM WINEACCESS
& A SPECIAL OFFER

I first read Stephen Tanzer's *International Wine Cellar* in the mid-1980s. The independent bimonthly journal contained about 20 pages of tasting notes on wines Tanzer had tasted in his dining room, as well as a detailed listing of where to find the best wines at the best prices in the most important New York City wine shops (at the time the publication was actually called *The New York Wine Cellar*). Apparently, every two months Tanzer made the rounds of the best wine shops in New York, clipboard in hand, and created an inventory of wines and their retail prices. While I found Tanzer's notes excellent and his writing impeccable, I couldn't help but question the accuracy of his pricing data. After all, the availability of wines constantly changes as the most sought-after items sell out and new vintages arrive. And of course Tanzer's universe at the time was limited to Manhattan wine shops.

By the mid-1990s, the Internet, as we know it today, was in its infancy. Fine wine consumption was on the rise. A few years earlier, *60 Minutes* had told the nation that red wine could retard heart disease. Whisky drinkers were switching to Cabernet. Baby boomers wanted to learn more and the industry just wasn't equipped to satisfy the hunger for wine knowledge.

I conjured up the first germ of the idea for WineAccess in 1996. I didn't know much about the Internet, but I knew quite a lot about wine and wine distribution. I determined that if one could create a master database of all the wines people were looking for, figure out how to grab inventories from stores all over the country, and match the wines in their inventories to the master database, one could create a very interesting shopping experience for the consumer. This had never been done before.

By the late 1990s, Steve had built quite an international reputation as a wine taster and journalist. While his renamed *International Wine Cellar* didn't contain pricing data from Manhattan wine shops, it had become a remarkably comprehensive wine journal. Published bi-monthly, it was the result of his tastings of 10,000 or more wines each year, both in his own home and during lengthy tasting trips to the greatest cellars in the most important wine regions of the world. By the late 1990s many connoisseurs inside and outside the wine trade considered Steve to be the most reliable wine taster on the planet.

A few months prior to the launch of WineAccess.com, I called Steve. I began by talking about my first experience with his writing back in the mid-1980s. We laughed about his efforts to create an accurate database of wine prices entirely manually. Then,

I told him about WineAccess and I asked him if he was interested in creating a new online version of the *International Wine Cellar* that could automate much of the pricing function he tried to include in his first publication, and expand it nationwide. Internationalwinecellar.com was launched in the Spring of 2000. Today the site enjoys a subscription base of thousands of wine enthusiasts in all 50 states and 34 countries.

In 2005, we hatched a new idea. You're looking at the first page of our invention: a wine buying guide that not only recommends the best wines to drink in every important category, but is also linked to a customized website where you can easily purchase these wines at the best prices from stores across the country. In most cases, the wines you desire can be shipped right to your door!

A SPECIAL OFFER. As a purchaser of this book, you are entitled to a complimentary one-year subscription to WineAccess CellarNotes™, an enhanced version of *The WineAccess Buyer's Guide* that will be continually updated as new wines arrive in the U.S. retail wine market. *CellarNotes* includes the contents of the book in easily searchable electronic form, including Stephen Tanzer's selections of top producers and wines to look for, and profiles of wine regions and specific types of wine. Over the course of your online subscription you will find ratings of new vintages as they become available in wine shops.

Best of all, *CellarNotes* links the wines recommended by Tanzer to the WineAccess database, which enables you to "purchase from the book" in just a couple of clicks. In the book, Tanzer guides you through the world of wine; CellarNotes offers you the best—and easiest—way to purchase and enjoy the distinctive wines recommended in the guide. You should never have to buy another bottle of mediocre wine again.

To sign up for your free one-year subscription to *CellarNotes*, just go to the Website www.wineaccess.com/specialoffer and follow the instructions.

—Jim Weinrott
Founder, WineAccess

WHY & HOW TO USE THIS GUIDE

I have tried to write the wine buyer's guide that I searched for in vain when I was developing a passion for wine more than a quarter-century ago. Back then, my goal was to gain a wine education—not to mention maximum drinking pleasure—by tasting as many of the most interesting wines of the world as I could afford to try. The problem was finding the information I needed.

Back in 1980, when it came to wine books the choices were limited. There were outsized coffee-table books and wine atlases, but these tomes rarely offered much in the way of specific information on the best wines to buy and sample. There were wine "encyclopedias," which were useful reference sources but were not meant to be page-turners and offered little in the way of explicit wine recommendations. And there were general wine guides, frequently earnest and dull, most of them covering more or less the same ground. The only real buyer's guide in those days came from the estimable English wine writer Hugh Johnson. But although his book offered vintage-specific information on the best wines of Bordeaux—as these wines historically had been the cornerstone of most great cellars in the British Isles—buying advice on other regions of the wine world was generally limited to a relative handful of the top producers and updated only sporadically.

Even today, buyer's guides rarely attempt to cover all of the important wine regions in a single volume. And while some guides attempt to list the best producers in a given area, they are rarely wine- and vintage-specific. In other words, very few guides go that critical last step: recommending currently available vintages of specific bottlings from specific producers. And even if they do, the information quickly grows old as new vintages are released. The result, almost invariably, is frustration on the part of the book user, a frustration that is typically compounded by the difficulty of actually finding recommended bottles in the marketplace.

HOW THE WINEACCESS GUIDE IS DIFFERENT. In *The WineAccess Buyer's Guide,* I name names: I recommend the best producers in all of the world's most important wine-producing areas, highlighting their consistently most interesting bottlings and offering a quality assessment of the vintage or vintages you are likely to find on retail shelves. And through my long-time association with WineAccess, a website that provides its users with the ability to learn about, search for, and buy wines from a network of wine shops around the U.S., this book goes an important step further: your purchase of the book entitles you to a free one-year subscription to a special electronic version of this guide, where new vintages of the wines featured in the book will be *updated continually* to stay abreast of new arrivals in the marketplace. In addition, new producers of merit will steadily be added to the collection of recommended wine sources. Thus, no matter when you purchase the book, you will be assured not only that the book is current, but that it will remain so for a full year. It's the guide that keeps on giving.

Equally important, the website created by WineAccess will enable you to find and purchase a sizable percentage of the wines recommended in the guide, at the most favorable prices. One of the major drawbacks associated with other wine buyer's guides is that readers motivated to try recommended bottles quickly become frustrated when they realize how hard it is to track down these desirable items, which by their very nature are made in limited quantities. *The WineAccess Buyer's Guide* not only is producer-, wine-, and vintage-specific, but it offers readers *real-time availability information on recommended bottles*. You simply follow a couple of electronic links from the item you would like to buy to the retail merchants who offer it.

HOW THE GUIDE WORKS. *The WineAccess Buyer's Guide* is not intended to be comprehensive or definitive: no book that you could actually lift could possibly include all the wines that are worthy of your attention. There are simply too many quality-conscious producers making too many different bottlings in too many countries around the world today. But the guide is designed to provide you with a wealth of choices in every important region, grape variety, and wine style, and at a range of price points. And through the link to the website, the guide is organic and constantly evolving.

In this book, I have singled out my personal favorites. The list of producers featured represents a combination of veteran stars and talented newcomers. Due to space constraints, numerous very good to excellent producers are simply listed at the end of the appropriate section. Similarly, a number of so-called "cult producers" are listed at the end, rather than being given full profiles, for the simple reason that their production is so limited that the typical wine shopper would have little hope of finding a bottle of their wines, even through the WineAccess network.

Under my brief profile of each featured estate or winery, I have listed one to four of the producer's signature wines—wines that are consistently successful and that you are likely to find in the marketplace. For each wine, I have indicated the approximate retail price by assigning it one to five dollar signs, as follows:

$	**$15.00 OR LESS**
$$	**$15.01 TO $30**
$$$	**$30.01 TO $60**
$$$$	**$60.01 TO $100**
$$$$$	**MORE THAN $100**

Key to Vintage Ratings		Key to Assessments of Specific Wines	
★★★★★	Outstanding	**03**	An excellent to outstanding example *of that wine*
★★★★	Excellent	03	A good to very good example *of that wine*
★★★	Good to very good	03	A disappointing effort (often due to a
★★	Fair to average		difficult vintage)
★	Poor		

I have avoided using an absolute scale to rate wines, such as the 100-point scale that I use in my own bimonthly *International Wine Cellar* publication. Rather, my intention has been to bring to your attention the best examples in virtually every important wine category—whether that category is *grand cru* white Burgundy or far less pricey Chardonnay from Chile. It must be emphasized that a good vintage from a producer featured in this guide will never be less than an interesting wine, one that's well worth trying.

THE SCOPE AND ORGANIZATION OF THE GUIDE. The heart of the guide is its hundreds of brief profiles of top producers, with recommended wines to try. Under each chapter heading and subsection, summary paragraphs provide a context for understanding the wines, discussing the geographic area, and the variety(ies) a wine is made from; the soil and the climate, where relevant; what the wine tastes like; how it stacks up as a value; and why it merits your interest. Where appropriate, I have also provided brief vintage charts that address the quality of the vintages likely to be available in the retail market. But keep in mind that vintage charts give only the most general overview of wine quality: the most talented and uncompromising producers routinely manage to make interesting wines even in so-so years, while underperformers can make disappointing wines in the most outstanding vintages.

The book is organized according to geography, simply because no other organizing principle offers the same degree of coherence. For exampe, organizing by style of wine (i.e., light whites, medium-bodied whites, full-bodied whites) is a risky proposition because even closely defined types of wines are frequently made in a range of styles. By the same token, organizing by variety does not work because so many interesting wines today, especially those from the Old World, are blends of two or more varieties. However, if you feel more comfortable searching for your favorite wines by variety, such as Chardonnays or Syrahs, you can refer to the short appendix entitled *Wines of the World by Key Variety*, which will send you to the appropriate sections of the book.

So the guide presents the world of wine by country or major region—or, in the case of the U.S., by state. If there's one thing you should know before buying wine, it's that in Europe, wines are generally labeled by appellation, or place name, while in the New World wines are typically labeled by variety, even if the wine's area of origin is also displayed on the label. So within each of the following chapters, information is normally presented by subregion, or major appellation, for European countries (such as Bordeaux in the chapter on France), and by grape variety for the New World (e.g., Cabernet Sauvignon).

My operating principle in this guide has been to attempt to include 90 percent of the wines of greatest interest to 90 percent of the readers of this book. This is why extremely small, high-quality producers have generally been listed rather than featured. Certain marginal wine regions have been omitted, not because the wines are not good but because they generally attract little interest in the U.S. and Canadian markets or have limited distribution (e.g., wines from Switzerland, Hungary, or Greece, or even wines from Canada's Okenagan Valley, which are difficult to find outside Canada and the Pacific Northwest). Certain less relevant categories of wine are mentioned only in passing. For example, white wines in the southern Rhône Valley and the Languedoc, two regions where reds account for the overwhelming majority of production and an even higher percentage of the wines of interest to export markets.

TODAY'S COMPLEX WINE MARKETPLACE. Twenty-five years ago the wine world was a far simpler place. Fewer wine producers shipped their bottles outside their local area, wineries offered fewer different bottlings, and fewer producers aspired to make wines of real concentration and character. Since then, profound improvements in grape growing, vinification, and *élevage* (the French term that describes the "raising," or aging, of the wine before it is bottled) have resulted in a vast increase in the number of wines that combine concentration, character, and an absence of technical flaws. Reduction of vine yields and better equipment (especially the ability to control the temperature of both fermentations and aging cellars) have enabled many Old World growing areas to revolutionize their wines. In some cases, regions that previously made rustic, hot-country wines consumed mostly in the local market (including a sizable portion of Spain, Portugal, and southern France) have exploded onto the world wine scene with full-flavored, technically sound, and often relatively inexpensive wines. At the same time, the primacy of French wines like Bordeaux and Burgundy has been challenged by regions like California, Oregon, Australia, New Zealand, and South Africa, where better vineyard techniques and increasingly sophisticated winemaking enable producers to make world-class wines. In the past decade or so, the wine world has literally been turned upside down. As recently as 1990, for example, wine-producing countries in the Southern Hemisphere (Australia, New Zealand, South Africa, Chile, and Argentina) accounted for less than ten percent of U.S. wine imports. Today they are closing in on 50 percent, and countries like Argentina, South Africa, and New Zealand are among the fastest-growing import categories in our market. Wine shops in the U.S. are now loaded with interesting wines you can afford to try, from places you may never have heard of.

So while this guide attempts to single out the best producers from Europe and America, it is also intended to bring to your attention a host of exciting wines from the rest of the world—and to help you track down bottles. I attempt to stay abreast of all of these developments in the course of publishing my bimonthly *International Wine Cellar* (www.internationalwinecellar.com), an independent newsletter read by wine lovers all over the world. In just the past couple of years I have visited top wineries in Argentina, South Africa, and New Zealand and tasted hundreds of additional new releases from those countries—this in addition to my regular visits to France, Italy, Spain, and America's West Coast. *The WineAccess Buyer's Guide* brings the fruits of these tastings to you.

Most casual North American wine drinkers stick to familiar varieties and feel more comfortable with labels in English. They sense that retail shelves are loaded with other wines of equal or higher quality, often at lower cost—if only they knew which ones to try. *The WineAccess Buyer's Guide* is designed to point you toward these wines. There have never more choices for the open-minded wine lover, and a world of exciting wine flavors awaits.

Cheers!

Stephen Tanzer

EUROPE

FRANCE

This guide begins with France and devotes considerable space to its wines because France is the fountainhead of the grape varieties most craved by North American wine drinkers: Cabernet Sauvignon, Merlot, Pinot Noir, Syrah, Chardonnay, and Sauvignon Blanc. In fact, these grapes are widely referred to as "international" varieties because they have been planted and imitated all over the world. Of course, one of the most exciting developments in wine over the past generation has been the growth of intriguing local styles of these varieties, such as Pinot Noir in Oregon and New Zealand, or Syrah in Australia, South Africa, and California. But most cosmopolitan wine-lovers—and even winemakers—would agree that France's versions are the archetypes.

France enjoys the perfect geographic position for the production of a wide range of fine wines. Its relatively northerly location ensures long hours of daylight during the summer months and an extended growing season, allowing for the slow and steady accumulation of flavor in the grapes. Although the country as a whole enjoys a temperate climate, conditions can vary significantly within a limited land mass: cool and Atlantic-influenced; continental, with very cold winters and hot summers; warm and Mediterranean, with wet winters and dry summers.

France began classifying its best wine-producing sites more than 200 years ago. Its detailed *appellation contrôlée* system, designed in the 1930s, has served as the model for classification systems adopted by other countries in Europe and elsewhere. *Appellation d'Origine Contrôlée* (often abbreviated to AOC), means "controlled place name" and is the consumer's assurance of the origin and authenticity of any wine whose label bears these words. AOC laws, administered by France's INAO (*Institut National des Appellations d'Origine*), establish the geographic limits of each appellation, permissable grape varieties and methods of production, minimum alcohol level, and maximum crop level (or yield) per hectare. Just beneath the highest category of *appellation contrôlée* is the comparatively tiny category of VDQS (Vins Délimités de Qualité Supérieure), wines which may eventually be promoted to AC status and which are most commonly found in the Loire Valley and the Southwest. The third category is *Vins de Pays*, or "country wines." This latter category gives producers, including some of France's more adventurous wine growers, an escape route from the straitjacket of AC regulation in terms of higher permitted yields and less restrictive geography, a wider range of legal grape varieties, and fewer restrictions as to method of production and minimum age of vines. Finally, at the bottom of the pyramid, there are *Vins de Table*, or simple "table wines."

And yet, despite France's illustrious wine history and the fact that it is still the world's leading producer of wine, the country is struggling to compete in the international market. Today, France faces fierce competition from New World wine producers. U.S. imports of French wines actually declined, in number of cases, between the end of 2002 and early 2006—this during a period when overall wine consumption in the U.S. grew by more than 50 percent. Today, the French government is agonizing over how to help its producers, who are also facing homegrown challenges such as changing domestic drinking habits and an aggressive anti-alcohol abuse program. Wine producers in some regions of France are coming to view the AC system itself as an obstacle to selling wines to North America and other important export markets. Among the changes being considered are loosening restrictions on what can be planted where and on how wines can be made, and allowing producers in certain areas to indicate the grape variety or varieties on their labels—rather than simply the place name, which is less meaningful to consumers in many of France's key export markets.

BORDEAUX

Bordeaux and its environs constitute this planet's largest source of fine wines. Bordeaux is the model for Cabernet Sauvignon—and Merlot-based wines around the globe. Its top bottles—called classified growths—are considered by many wine connoisseurs to be the world's greatest reds. About three-quarters of the region's wine is red, but excellent dry and sweet white wines are also made here, as the region's temperate climate and diverse soil types (gravel, clay, chalk, and limestone) are well suited to numerous grape varieties.

For centuries, red Bordeaux has been the cornerstone of nearly every great wine cellar. Its appeal for collectors is due not only to its slow development in bottle and uncanny longevity but to its track record for nearly inexorable price appreciation as well. Historically, English collectors, who have long used the term *claret* when referring to these dry, flavorful, medium-bodied and tannic red wines, sold off half of each vintage ten years later for twice what they paid for it and drank the other half for free. But if you're buying wine to savor soon rather than to lay down for years or resell, keep in mind that a good classified-growth claret really needs at least eight to ten years of aging before its tannins begin to subside, and a first growth from a great vintage may require 12 to 20 years to take on the velvety texture and suavity that connoisseurs prize.

The classic austerity of claret is one of the reasons Bordeaux is in a state of crisis today—that plus the fact that the region also produces a lot of mediocre wines. With a new generation of enophiles around the world seeking wines that offer suppler tannins and early gratification, and avoiding the stern, uncompromisingly dry wines of the past, it has become increasingly hard to sell wines that must be cellared for years before they become fun to drink. That is not to mention the difficulty winemakers have in selling wines from less-ripe vintages, which can be lean and herbal. At the same time, more and more money has

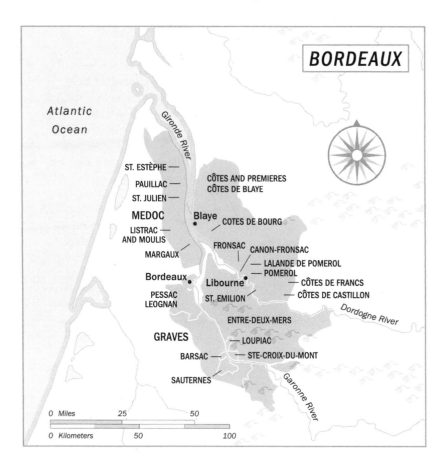

been chasing fewer and fewer wines—the first growths plus a handful of wines whose complexity, sweetness of fruit, and layered texture have garnered strong reviews from the wine press. The result: a few dozen wines have become increasingly expensive, while most of the thousands of other châteaux are struggling to sell their production.

The financially stable châteaux have been able to invest in a host of expensive and often labor-intensive measures in the vineyards and in the cellars to improve the quality of their wines. Some of these steps include: improvements in viticultural practices aimed at limiting vine yields and ensuring more concentrated grapes that reach adequate ripeness earlier; later and more precise harvesting for riper grape skins and thus suppler tannins; more careful sorting of grapes at the time of harvest to eliminate less-ripe fruit and grapes with damaged skins; fermentation in smaller lots to allow better control; and a more stringent

BORDEAUX GEOGRAPHY & WINE STYLE

The Atlantic-influenced Bordeaux region covers both banks of the Gironde estuary in southwest France, as well as the land bordering the Garonne and Dordogne rivers, which split off from the Gironde in the southern Médoc. Bordeaux's highest-quality—and most expensive—red wines generally come from seven major appellations: St. Éstèphe, Pauillac, St. Julien, and Margaux in the greater Médoc region, Graves to the south of the city of Bordeaux itself, and Pomerol and St. Emilion to the east (an area commonly referred to as the right bank, as it lies east of the Dordogne). The best dry whites come from the large Graves region, while the finest sweet wines are made in Sauternes and Barsac, enclaves within the southern reaches of the Graves appellation. In general, red wines from the left bank of the Gironde, particularly from the Médoc region, are based on Cabernet Sauvignon, with varying amounts of Merlot and Cabernet Franc, and sometimes bits of Malbec and Petit Verdot, included in the blends. These wines are dry and firm, with a solid tannic spine, and are often austere in their youth. They are among the longest-lived wines made anywhere. Red wines from the gravel and sand soils of the Graves often show a bit more texture early on, as well as more roasted notes of smoke, hot stones, and tobacco. Wines from Bordeaux's right bank, located mostly to the east of the town of Libourne, are blends based on the softer Merlot grape. They are generally fleshier and more pliant than wines from the Médoc, and are accessible earlier even though the best of them are capable of improving in bottle for decades.

selection of the components for the château's *grand vin*, or "flagship label." And of course global warming has allowed the region to ripen its fruit on a more consistent basis in recent years. Still, literally thousands of châteaux are not able to get a sufficiently high price for their wines to be able to afford making the improvements necessary to attract the attention of consumers. And caught in the middle are hundreds of properties that are making very good wine but must sell it for less than its intrinsic value. The CIVB (Conseil Interprofessional du Vin de Bordeaux) has said that fully 20 percent of Bordeaux's vines—representing an amount of wine greater than the combined production of the states of Washington and Oregon—will need to be pulled up to correct the current glut of wine.

RED WINES/MÉDOC

BANG FOR THE BUCK. The most famous names of Bordeaux are priced like collectible works of art, but they are the exceptions. The Médoc region in particular offers great value for open-minded consumers who know where to look.

2005 ★★★★★   2004 ★★★+   2003 ★★★★+   2002 ★★★+

2001 ★★★★−   2000 ★★★★★−

The Bordeaux Vineyard Hierarchy

All Bordeaux wines are entitled to the basic appellation Bordeaux. Bordeaux Supérieur is a slight step higher in quality. Bordeaux from districts known for special quality carry the name of their appellation on the label. While seven appellations—St. Estèphe, Pauillac, St. Julien, Margaux, Graves, Pomerol, and St. Émilion—are most familiar to wine lovers, lesser-known districts—such as Moulis and Listrac in the Médoc, and Fronsac, Canon-Fronsac, and Côtes de Castillon on the right bank can also produce excellent wines, generally at much lower prices. All of the best wines of Bordeaux also carry the name of the specific château, or estate. More than 200 of the finest châteaux of the Médoc, Graves, and St. Émilion (and Sauternes as well) have been awarded *cru classé*, or classified growth, status. The famous 1855 Classification, which officially ranked the best Bordeaux wines, established four *premiers crus*, or first growths—Lafite-Rothschild, Latour, Margaux, and Haut-Brion (in 1973, Mouton-Rothschild too was officially declared a first growth)—as well as a host of second through fifth growths.

Three right-bank wines—Pétrus, Cheval Blanc, and Ausone—are commonly considered to be equivalent in quality to the "official" first growths, and the right-bank appellations of St. Émilion has its own system of classification. In addition, there are hundreds of *crus bourgeoises* in the Médoc, as well as the lesser properties throughout the Bordeaux region that are commonly referred to as petits châteaux. If these thousands of so-called little wines have less pretension to importance, they are also, as a rule, easier to drink when young.

St. Estèphe

These chunky, earthy, slow-aging wines are characterized by solid tannins that tend to be less fine-grained than those of wines from Pauillac and St. Julien. St. Estèphes show notes of black fruits, black olive, fresh herbs, and pepper. While these wines do not often achieve the complexity or delicacy of wines from Pauillac or St. Julien, they are full-flavored and often quite powerful.

RECOMMENDED PRODUCERS

Château Calon-Ségur. The oldest property of St. Estèphe, relying on a high percentage of Cabernet Sauvignon to produce a rich, structured, concentrated wine marked by sweet, dark berry fruit, with an often wild, spicy-woodsy tone. Has a great track record for aging.

Calon-Ségur	04	**03**	02	$$$$

Château Cos d'Estournel. Among the handful of Bordeaux wines that can challenge the first growths for complexity and power. Current vintages are more accessible than before, displaying broad and often chocolaty-rich dark berry flavors and supple tannins.

Cos d'Estournel	04	**03**	**02**	$$$$

Château Lafon-Rochet. On the upswing since the mid-1990s, under ownership by the Tesseron family (see Pontet-Canet in Pauillac). A good percentage of new oak and a healthy addition of Merlot results in a rich, lush, meaty wine that's rarely austere in the early going.

Lafon-Rochet	04	**03**	02	$$$

Château Montrose. Long regarded as possessing one of the finest terroirs in the Bordeaux region, Montrose has been on fire since vintage 1989, and especially since 2000, rivaling the first growths for complexity and palate presence. Today's tannins are suppler than ever before, but this rather muscular, densely-packed wine must normally be laid down for a decade or more.

Montrose	**04**	**03**	02	$$$$

OTHER PRODUCERS TO LOOK FOR: Château Cos Labory, Château Haut-Marbuzet, Château Meyney, Château Les Ormes de Pez, Château de Pez, Château Phélan-Ségur.

Key to Vintage Ratings		Key to Assessments of Specific Wines	
★★★★★	Outstanding	**03**	An excellent to outstanding example *of that wine*
★★★★	Excellent	03	A good to very good example *of that wine*
★★★	Good to very good	03	A disappointing effort (often due to a
★★	Fair to average		difficult vintage)
★	Poor		

PAUILLAC

This is the most renowned region of Bordeaux, thanks to being home to three of the five first growths. Typically firmly tannic and uncompromisingly dry, Pauillacs offer aromas and flavors of black currant, lead pencil, cedar shavings, and tobacco leaf, and are generally considered to be the longest-lived of all Bordeaux. They are prized for the way they combine structure, power, and fairly full body with aromatic complexity and finesse.

RECOMMENDED PRODUCERS

Château Clerc-Milon. With its fairly substantial percentage of Merlot, this Pauillac often displays an exotic aromatic character, with rich if sometimes rather medicinal-scented fruit and smooth tannins. Closer in style to its big brother Mouton-Rothschild than to d'Armailhac, which is also owned by the Rothschild family.

| Clerc-Milon | 04 | 03 | 02 | $$$ |

Château Grand-Puy-Lacoste. Concentrated, polished wine, with classic Pauillac notes of dark berries, plum, spices, and earth. Extremely consistent in recent years.

| Grand-Puy-Lacoste | 04 | 03 | 02 | $$$ |

Château Lafite-Rothschild. Along with Latour, the most famous and prestigious property of Bordeaux. A wonderfully concentrated, supremely elegant wine with ineffable aromas of ripe berries, lead pencil, minerals, and flowers, plus outstanding cellaring potential. Never a heavy wine; in fact, some vintages of Lafite can appear deceptively light for their first decade or more in bottle.

| Lafite-Rothschild | 04 | **03** | 02 | $$$$$ |

Château Latour. If Lafite is renowned for elegance, Latour is prized for power. In recent years, there has been no finer wine made in Bordeaux, as Latour displays an uncanny combination of deep color; Cabernet-dominated flavors of dark berries, licorice, and minerals; the finest oak that money can buy; and great length on the aftertaste. As age worthy as Bordeaux gets, which means that the best vintages will develop in bottle for at least three or four decades.

| Latour | **04** | **03** | **02** | $$$$$ |

Château Lynch-Bages. A rich, powerful, full-bodied Pauillac capable of long life. Often dense, solid, and somewhat medicinal in the early years, the wine turns fleshier and more supple with a decade in bottle.

| Lynch-Bages | 04 | 03 | 02 | $$$ |

Château Mouton-Rothschild. Often the most exotic and perfumed wine of the Médoc, Mouton-Rothschild was promoted from second- to first-growth status in 1973, the only château to be so elevated since 1855. Its dramatic cassis and black cherry fruitiness, along with mineral and graphite notes, are complemented by nuances of smoke, char, coffee, and chocolate from the 100 percent new oak barrels.

| Mouton-Rothschild | 04 | **03** | **02** | $$$$$ |

Château Pichon-Longueville Baron. The Cabernet-dominated Pichon-Baron has staged a dramatic comeback since the late 1980s. Today's wines are deeply colored, dense, pliant, and deep, with layered flavors of dark fruits, chocolate, spices, and minerals and suave use of new oak.

Pichon-Baron   04 **03** 02 $$$$

Château Pichon-Longueville Comtesse de Lalande. Silky, stylish, spicy, and sweet, with a sizable dollop of Merlot frequently contributing an almost chocolaty richness. Perhaps second only to Lafite in Pauillac for the finesse of its tannins. More accessible early on than most top Pauillacs but built to age.

Pichon-Lalande   04 **03** **02** $$$$

Château Pontet-Canet. This property, located adjacent to Mouton, has been in top form in recent years and now routinely produces wines of near-first-growth class, with rich, concentrated cassis fruit and lush texture. Prices have yet to catch up with quality.

Pontet-Canet   **04** **03** 02 $$$

OTHER PRODUCERS TO LOOK FOR: Château d'Armailhac, Château Batailley, Château Duhart-Milon, Château Grand-Puy-Ducasse, Château Haut-Bages-Libéral, Château Haut-Batailley.

St. Julien

Although the smallest of Bordeaux's most important appellations in terms of acreage, St. Julien accounted for the lion's share of wines named in the Classification of 1855. The wines are elegant and of medium weight, with a cedary perfume, solid but rarely aggressive tannic structure, and considerable aging ability.

RECOMMENDED PRODUCERS

Château Branaire. A densely packed and rather powerful St. Julien that typically shows complex aromas and flavors of dark berries, exotic cocoa powder, smoky oak, and mint. Very good value.

Branaire   04 **03** 02 $$$

Château Ducru-Beaucaillou. Wonderfully fragrant, heavily Cabernet-influenced wine with superb cellaring potential. The best vintages offer dramatic perfume of black fruits, cedar, coconut, and flowers. As at so many other Médoc châteaux, recent vintages have been suppler than ever.

Ducru-Beaucaillou   04 03 02 $$$$

Château Gruaud-Larose. An earthy, leathery, densely packed wine that typically suggests an almost roasted ripeness. Can seem deceptively approachable early on owing to its sweet fruit, but the wine's major tannic clout generally calls for extended aging.

Gruaud-Larose   04 03 02 $$$

Château Lagrange. Fragrant, classically structured St. Julien that typically shows an almost medicinal austerity in the early going, with dominant notes of cassis, kirsch, menthol, and minerals. Very fairly priced.

| Lagrange | 04 | **03** | 02 | $$$ |

Château Léoville-Barton. Rich, densely concentrated wine with compelling fruit complexity, enticing inner-mouth perfume, and suave tannins. Capable of extended aging but rarely hard in its youth.

| Léoville-Barton | 04 | **03** | 02 | $$$$ |

Château Léoville-Las Cases. A powerful, rich, and classy St. Julien made with no compromises, often quite Pauillac-like in its black fruit and mineral character and firm tannic spine. Deeply colored, hugely concentrated, and generally in need of extended aging. The most expensive Médoc wine after the first growths, but many Bordeaux aficionados consider Las Cases to be at virtually the same level of quality.

| Léoville-Las Cases | 04 | **03** | **02** | $$$$$ |

Château Léoville-Poyferré. Based heavily on Cabernet, Poyferré is a classic, aromatically complex St. Julien with substantial tannins that normally require a decade of aging. Recent vintages have been broader and suppler than previous ones.

| Léoville-Poyferré | 04 | **03** | 02 | $$$$ |

OTHER PRODUCERS TO LOOK FOR: Château Beychevelle, Château Langoa-Barton, Château Talbot.

MARGAUX

Margaux is renowned for perfumed wines with sweet, silky, fruit flavors, supple tannins, and considerable delicacy, which is not to say that these wines are meager. As an appellation, Margaux was underperforming until the mid-1990s, but is far more consistent today.

RECOMMENDED PRODUCERS

Château Lascombes. After a couple of decades of fits and starts, this large property is back on form, with today's wines in a distinctly modern style: fragrant, rich, and sweet.

| Lascombes | 04 | **03** | 02 | $$$ |

Château Malescot St. Exupéry. A distinctly modern-style producer whose deeply colored wines are now routinely silky and sweet, if not downright voluptuous, with low acidity but plenty of ripe tannins for aging. Vastly improved over the past ten years.

| Malescot St. Exupéry | 04 | 03 | 02 | $$$ |

Château Margaux. The suavest and most graceful of the Bordeaux first growths, with an ineffable floral perfume, silky texture, and great persistence on the aftertaste. But describing this wine as elegant or feminine does not capture its superb concentration, structure, and aging potential.

| Margaux | 04 | **03** | 02 | $$$$$ |

Château Palmer. An intensely perfumed, impeccably balanced, and mellow wine in a quintessential Margaux style. Suave, seamless, and seductive, but with plenty of underlying muscle for aging.

Palmer   `04` `03` `02` $$$$

OTHER PRODUCERS TO LOOK FOR: Château d'Angludet, Château Boyd-Cantenac, Château Brane-Cantenac, Château Cantenac-Brown, Clos des Quatres Vents, Château Giscours, Château d'Issan, Château Kirwan, Château Labégorce-Zédé, Marojallia, Château Rauzan-Gassies, Château Rauzan-Ségla, Château du Tertre.

RED WINES/GRAVES

The greater Graves region begins literally in the city of Bordeaux and extends 25 miles to the southeast along the Garonne river. Virtually all the best wines (including the Bordeaux region's finest dry whites) come from the appellation of Pessac-Léognan. Pessac is in the southern outskirts of Bordeaux itself, while Léognan is essentially an area of woodlands several miles to the south. The deep gravel of Pessac produces some of the earthiest, most soil-driven wines of Bordeaux, and their sometimes wild notes of roasted meat, tobacco, leather, iron, and hot stones can be a bit of a shock to the uninitiated. These distinctive wines have plenty of tannins to support aging but are rarely austere in the early going.

2005 ★★★★-   **2004** ★★★+   **2003** ★★★★-   **2002** ★★★

2001 ★★★★-   **2000** ★★★★★-

RECOMMENDED PRODUCERS

Domaine de Chevalier. An emphatically traditional wine, often lean in its youth, with a restrained, Cabernet-dominated personality that requires cellaring to reveal its cedar, tobacco leaf, and mineral complexity.

Domaine de Chevalier   `04` `03` `02` $$$

Château Haut-Bailly. Classic aromatic Graves: balanced, understated, and graceful. Often deceptively open in its youth, Haut-Bailly has a long track record for positive development in bottle.

Haut-Bailly   `04` `03` `02` $$$

Château Haut-Brion. The most famous château of Graves and one of the great names in French wine history, dating back to the 16th century. (Haut-Brion was the only château outside the Médoc and Sauternes to be classified in 1855.) Among the first growths, this is the most soil-inflected wine, showing almost roasted berry and plum fruit complicated by notes of tobacco, hot stones, and minerals. While rarely hard in its youth, the wine ages at a glacial pace. Located within the city limits of Bordeaux, Haut-Brion has arguably been the most consistently outstanding Bordeaux red over the past 20 years.

Haut-Brion   `04` `03` `02` $$$$$

Château La Mission Haut-Brion. Adjacent to Haut-Brion, and often its former rival as the most profound wine of Graves, La Mission has been under the same ownership as Haut-Brion since 1983 but has retained its distinctive wilder identity: More powerful and more tannic, often displaying a meaty, truffley character with extended time in bottle.

La Mission Haut-Brion `04` `03` `02` $$$$

Château Pape-Clément. One of the oldest properties in Bordeaux (it was named after Pope Clement V in 1305), Pape Clément produces dense, full wines typically characterized by notes of raspberry, gravel, and exotic wood smoke. As this château is located within the warmer city limits of Bordeaux, it often does well in difficult years.

Pape Clément `04` `03` `02` $$$$

Château Smith Haut Lafitte. This old property has been totally renovated and transformed since being purchased by the Cathiard family in 1990. Today's wines are impressively concentrated and fairly full-bodied yet suave, in a modern style.

Smith Haut Lafitte `04` `03` `02` $$$

OTHER PRODUCERS TO LOOK FOR: Château Branon, Château Les Carmes Haut-Brion, Château de Fieuzal, Château Malartic-Lagravière, Château Olivier, Château La Tour Haut-Brion.

RED WINES/RIGHT BANK
POMEROL

Merlot rules in Pomerol, and nowhere in the world does this variety make more complete wines than on the flat, clay-rich plateau that lies at the heart of this appellation. As in neighboring St. Émilion, not to mention the surrounding satellite appellations of the right bank, vineyard size and scale of production in Pomerol are much smaller than on the grand estates of the Médoc: most Pomerol properties are châteaux in name only. Pomerols are characterized by extravagantly rich, sweet fruit and supple tannins. Not surprisingly, enophiles who prize wines that are accessible at an early age crave these wines.

BANG FOR THE BUCK. Due to the diminutive size of most Pomerol properties and strong worldwide demand for the wines from this very small appellation, Pomerol is expensive and real values are scarce. Thanks to the proliferation of new labels each year, St. Émilion offers the adventurous wine lover a wealth of opportunity to find satisfying bottles at very affordable prices.

2005 ★★★★– **2004** ★★★– **2003** ★★★– **2002** ★★★

2001 ★★★★– **2000** ★★★★+

RECOMMENDED PRODUCERS

Château L'Eglise-Clinet. Rich, classy wine from a high percentage of old Merlot vines planted on the Pomerol plateau. In spite of its often exotic aromas of black raspberry, mocha, and caramel, L'Eglise-Clinet is rarely a heavy wine and has the density and balance for extended aging.

L'Eglise-Clinet `04` `03` `02` $$$$

Château L'Evangile. This Merlot-dominated wine from an early-ripening site near Pomerol's border with St. Émilion typically offers compelling aromatic complexity and chocolaty ripeness, but possesses enough supple tannins for long aging.

L'Evangile `04` `03` `02` $$$$

Château Pétrus. This legendary and extravagantly priced wine, from a prime vineyard on well-drained clay soil atop the Pomerol plateau, has for decades stood as the greatest example of Merlot in the world. The wine is extraordinarily creamy and thick but with the substantial tannic underpinning to ensure decades of development in bottle. The panoply of exotic aromas and flavors typically encompasses black raspberry, mulberry, iron, cocoa powder, truffle, and expensive, new oak.

Pétrus `04` **`03`** `02` $$$$$

Château Trotanoy. Trotanoy can be among the most aromatically complex, fascinating, and refined wines of Pomerol. Beneath its velvety texture and expressive aromas of ripe fruits, iron, game, nuts, spices, and minerals is a supple but serious tannic structure that requires at least five to ten years of bottle aging.

Trotanoy `04` `03` `02` $$$$

Vieux Château Certan. The wonderfully aromatic VCC, as the wine is referred to by its fans, has always been a rather atypical Pomerol thanks to its unusually high percentage of Cabernet Franc, as well as some Cabernet Sauvignon. Although the Cabernet component often makes for a reticent and very firm wine in the early going, some recent vintages have been more Merlot-dominant and thus more open and sweet in their youth, even if they possess the structure for long aging.

Vieux Château Certan **`04`** 03 `02` $$$$

OTHER PRODUCERS TO LOOK FOR: Château Beauregard, Château Le Bon Pasteur, Château Certan de May, Château Clinet, Château Clos L'Eglise, Château La Conseillante, Château La Fleur-Pétrus, Château Le Gay, Château Gazin, Château Hosanna, Château Latour à Pomerol, Château Lafleur, Château Nenin, Château Petit Village, Château Le Pin, Château Rouget.

St. Émilion

This huge appellation around the gorgeous medieval hill town of St. Émilion is the most fascinating of Bordeaux, with more than 12,000 acres broken down among a dizzying number of mostly small châteaux. Cabernet Franc has long been the favored grape in most of the region, but the percentage of Merlot, particularly on soils rich in clay, is sizable and growing. Styles vary tremendously within this large area, depending on soil, blend of varieties, vinification, and aging of the wines. Many of the finest wines come from two very different areas within the appellation: a limestone-rich escarpment around the town of St. Émilion (the Côtes; some of the best are Ausone and Pavie), and a sand and gravel plateau adjacent to Pomerol (the Graves; includes Cheval Blanc and Figeac). The list of recommended properties below represents just the tip of the iceberg, as new and intriguing wines emerge every year in St. Émilion.

RECOMMENDED PRODUCERS

Château Angélus. As extroverted as Bordeaux gets, with saturated dark ruby color, considerable power and richness, and huge but ripe tannins. A sizable Cabernet Franc component typically adds aromatic complexity and freshness to this decidedly modern-style wine.

Angélus   **`04`** **`03`** `02` $$$$

Château Ausone. Ausone and Cheval Blanc are the only first growths of St. Émilion. In recent vintages Ausone has been as intensely flavored, nuanced and profound as any made in the Bordeaux region. The secrets to greatness here are the perfectionist proprietor Alain Vauthier's obsession with quality and the limestone hillside on which the estate's old Merlot and Cabernet Franc vines are planted.

Ausone   **`04`** **`03`** **`02`** $$$$$

Château Cheval Blanc. The other first growth (see Ausone) of St. Émilion, Cheval Blanc can be wound-up, even tough, in the early going due to its strong Cabernet Franc component, but in the best vintages shows a distinctly Pomerol-like lushness of texture with maturity, evolving into one of the region's most decadent and velvety elixirs, with a stunning bouquet of spicy, dark fruits, flowers, bitter chocolate, tobacco, licorice, and game.

Cheval Blanc   **`04`** `03` `02` $$$$$

Château Pavie. After underperforming for years, Pavie was purchased in 1998 by the *hypermarché* ("superstore") owner Gérard Perse, who invested heavily to realize the great potential of this remarkable south-facing hillside site. Today, Pavie is one of the deepest, ripest, most palate-saturating and lushly tannic wines of Bordeaux, as well as one of the most controversial, with detractors saying that it more closely resembles a California cult wine than Bordeaux from limestone-rich soil. But in blind tastings it frequently blows its colleagues off the table.

Pavie   **`04`** `03` `02` $$$$

Château Le Tertre-Rôteboeuf. Iconoclast proprietor François Mitjavile makes one of the Bordeaux region's most flamboyantly full-blown wines from low-acid grapes harvested at the point of overripeness for maximum maturity of tannins. Tertre Rôteboeuf typically shows explosive, liqueur-like fruit flavors with exotic notes of bitter chocolate, Cuban tobacco, and game.

Le Tertre-Rôteboeuf   `04` **`03`** `02` $$$$

Château Troplong-Mondot. An exotic, flashy example of modern St. Émilion, Troplong-Mondot is one of the most dramatic wines of its appellation, from "cold," late-ripening soils on the limestone plateau east of the town. While it possesses more than enough stuffing and structure for extended cellaring, the wine's depth of fruit and supple tannins rarely get in the way of early drinkability.

Troplong-Mondot   `04` **`03`** `02` $$$$

OTHER PRODUCERS TO LOOK FOR: Château Barde-Haut, Château Beau-Séjour Bécot, Château Beauséjour-Duffau, Château Bellefont-Belcier, Château Bellevue-Mondotte, Château Berliquet, Château Canon, Château Canon La Gaffelière, Château Clos Fourtet, Château Le Dôme, Château Figeac, Château Fleur Cardinale, Château La Gomerie, Château Gracia, Château Jean Faure, Château Larcis-Ducasse, Château Magrez-Fombrauge, Château Grand Mayne, Château La Mondotte, Château Monbousquet, Château Moulin St. Georges, Château Pavie Decesse, Château Pavie Macquin, Château Quinault L'Enclos, Château Rol Valentin, Château Valandraud.

OTHER RED WINES OF BORDEAUX

Not all claret is made by and for Rothschilds. Alongside the swankier addresses, there are literally hundreds of crus bourgeoises and petits châteaux—not to mention a host of lesser-known wines from satellite appellations surrounding the principal, and far tonier, districts of the Médoc, Graves, St. Émilion, and Pomerol. Often lower in acidity and less rigorously tannic, these more obscure wines are generally far more conducive to early consumption. Although some of these wines with lesser pedigree command steep prices due to consistently high quality and brisk demand, the overwhelming majority are remarkably affordable. Still, while today's Bordeaux is not especially pricey once you look past the big names and limited-production cult wines, there's still an ocean of mediocre wine made in this region. The list below is just a small sampling of the best "other red wines" of Bordeaux.

BANG FOR THE BUCK. Bordeaux's "other wines" are where the value-conscious Bordeaux drinker—as opposed to the investment-minded label-fondler—looks first.

OTHER RECOMMENDED PRODUCERS

Château Charmail. A deeply colored, lush, and distinctly modern-style wine made just north of the St. Estèphe appellation.

| Charmail | `04` | **`03`** | `02` | $$ |

Château Fontenil. An intense, supple, black fruit-flavored wine from a Fronsac property owned by globe-trotting enologist Michel Rolland.

| Fontenil | `04` | `03` | `02` | $$ |

Château Poujeaux. A Merlot-based wine from Moulis that combines definition and verve with firm underlying spine.

| Poujeaux | `04` | `03` | `02` | $$ |

Château de Reignac. A sweet, chocolaty-rich wine from perfectionist proprietor Yves Vatelot.

| Reignac | **`04`** | **`03`** | `02` | $$ |

Château Sociando-Mallet. A complex, rich, structured, and age-worthy blend of Cabernet and Merlot that is still underpriced for its consistently high quality. Makes the perfect ringer in a blind tasting of classified growths from the Médoc.

Sociando-Mallet `04` `03` `02` $$$

SECOND LABELS ARE ANOTHER PLACE TO LOOK FOR VALUE IN BORDEAUX. Today, most classified growths use second labels for those components deemed not quite strong enough to go into their grand vin. The best of these second labels offer some of the character and quality of the premium offering at a fraction of the price. Another important advantage of these wines is that they typically provide earlier accessibility. Every bottle of declassified juice represents a significant financial sacrifice for a château owner but a potential opportunity for the alert consumer, as the typical second label commands a price between one-fifth and one-third that of the estate's flagship wine. Some consistent standouts, not surprisingly, come from the first growths: Carruades de Lafite, Les Forts de Latour, Pavillon Rouge du Château Margaux, Bahans-Haut-Brion, Le Petit Cheval (Cheval Blanc), and Chapelle d'Ausone. Considerably less expensive are Les Pagodes de Cos (Cos d'Estournel), Les Hauts de Pontet (Pontet-Canet), Les Tourelles de Longueville (Pichon-Baron), La Dame de Montrose, and Réserve de la Comtesse (Pichon-Lalande). The Clos du Marquis of Château Léoville-Las Cases, widely considered to be one of the best second labels of all, is technically a separate wine, rather than a lesser version of the grand vin. Look for second labels in the successful, ripe years; in cooler vintages these wines can be repositories for a château's underripe fruit.

DRY WHITE WINES

Bordeaux's dry white wines, the most important of which come from Pessac-Léognan, generally consist of Sauvignon Blanc and Sémillon, sometimes with a bit of Muscadelle. A relative handful of white Graves are superconcentrated, minerally, uncompromisingly dry wines that evolve very slowly in bottle and are capable of lasting for decades. These examples—the most famous of which are Haut-Brion Blanc, Laville Haut-Brion and Domaine de Chevalier Blanc—are rare and expensive and often stubbornly closed in their youth. But the majority of today's Graves whites are made in a distinctly modern, fruit-driven style, aged with their lees, or dregs, in barrel to give them more texture, fat, and early appeal. There can be a great sameness to many of these wines, which are frequently more about varietal fruit character, new oak, and lees than about the soil from which they come. Sadly, the racy, crisp style of white Bordeaux that was based largely on Sauvignon Blanc and did not rely on new oak barrels for its flavor has become rare.

BANG FOR THE BUCK. Bordeaux's white wines are tricky to buy, as the elite examples are scarce and breathtakingly expensive, while too many moderately priced wines show a boring sameness of texture and flavor.

2005 ★★★★+ **2004** ★★★★− **2003** ★★★− **2002** ★★★+

RECOMMENDED PRODUCERS

Château Couhins-Lurton. A 100 percent Sauvignon Blanc wine that's typically dominated by the citrus fruit character of its variety early on but which deepens with several years in the bottle to show more complex, minerally soil character.

Couhins-Lurton   04 03 02 $$$

Domaine de Chevalier. The third of the "big three" white Graves, with Haut-Brion and Laville Haut-Brion, Domaine de Chevalier blanc, aged a full 18 months in barrel, is uncommonly elegant and age worthy, offering an exhilarating blend of fruits, flowers, and minerals with extended time in bottle.

Domaine de Chevalier Blanc   **04** 03 02 $$$$

Château de Fieuzal. This roughly 50/50 blend of Sémillon and Sauvignon Blanc, often with an exotic oaky element, has been among the deepest and most concentrated dry whites of Bordeaux in recent years.

Fieuzal Blanc   04 03 02 $$$

Château Haut-Brion. The ultimate white Graves, a hugely rich, complex, and expensive wine with as much flavor authority, opulence, and personality as the greatest white Burgundy, and capable of developing in bottle for decades.

Haut-Brion Blanc   **04** **03** 02 $$$$$

Château Laville Haut-Brion. A Sémillon-based white Graves that can begin life quite tight, even deceptively lean, but develops an extraordinarily complex waxy, honeyed character and great richness with a decade or more of bottle aging.

Laville Haut-Brion   **04** 03 02 $$$$$

Château La Louvière. For the past two decades, proprietor André Lurton has offered a stylish, fresh, aromatically precise and very reasonably priced wine from mostly Sauvignon Blanc, typically accessible early but capable of some further development in bottle.

La Louvière Blanc   04 03 02 $$

Château Smith Haut Lafitte. In just the last few years, the Cathiard family has elevated their white wine, made almost entirely from Sauvignon Blanc, to the level of the top dry whites of Bordeaux. Today's wines combine exhilarating fruits, musky minerality, and an opulent, creamy texture rare for Sauvignon.

Smith Haut Lafitte Blanc   **04** 03 **02** $$$

OTHER PRODUCERS TO LOOK FOR: Château Carbonnieux, Château Les Charmes-Godard, Clos Floridène, Pavillon Blanc du Château Margaux, Château Pape-Clément, Château Latour-Martillac.

SWEET WINES

The wines made in Sauternes, neighboring Barsac, and three other adjacent communes, are the most renowned of all the world's late-harvest sweet wines, and are among the only ones made in commercially serious quantities. They are usually affected to some extent by botrytis, or "noble rot," a beneficent fungus that increases glycerol and concentrates sugars and acids by dehydrating and shriveling the grapes. However, in years that don't offer the right climatic conditions (i.e., alternating humidity and dry heat), destructive gray rot, noble rot's evil twin, may ruin the grapes. Or, if there's no rot at all, an estate may merely be able to make a sweet wine that misses out on the nectar-like complexity and texture of classic Sauternes. Making great Sauternes is always a financially risky venture, as waiting for ideal botrytis runs the risk of encountering rain or frost, which could ruin a season's crop.

Most of these sweet wines are based on the Sémillon variety, which is prone to botrytis and yields rich, broad wines, often with a honeyed character. A percentage of Sauvignon Blanc is used to add acidity and freshness to most Sauternes, while some estates also like to blend in a bit of aromatic Muscadelle. The richness and unctuous quality of the best Sauternes belie an often high acid content, which, along with elevated alcohol levels, provides Sauternes with the structure to age remarkably well, in some instances for several decades. Not surprisingly, styles of Sauternes vary significantly by varietal makeup, the quality of the site, the seriousness of work in the vineyards, and approaches to vinification and aging.

BANG FOR THE BUCK. Because classic Sauternes can normally be made only four or five times a decade, and because harvesting typically requires multiple labor-intensive passes through the vineyards to pick botrytis-affected clusters and even individual berries, Sauternes is never cheap. But except for highly touted years like 2001, prices have barely kept up with the rate of inflation since the late 1980s.

2004 ★★★–   2003 ★★★★+   2002 ★★★+   2001 ★★★★★

RECOMMENDED PRODUCERS

Château Climens. This Barsac is often the most elegant sweet wine of the Bordeaux region and capable of developing great complexity with bottle aging. Never fat or weighty, Climens offers a particularly complex combination of citrus and pit fruits, honey and toasty oak, as well as uncanny clarity and definition in the mouth.

| Climens | 04 | 03 | 02 | $$$$$ |

Château de Fargues. The home property of the Lur-Saluces family, formerly owners of Château d'Yquem, Fargues produces extraordinarily unctuous, honeyed wines from tiny vine yields. As exotic as this wine can be, it has a long history of aging for decades in bottle.

| Fargues | 03 | 02 | $$$$ |

Château Guiraud. A distinctly restrained style of Sauternes that emphasizes the pungent, firmer quality of Sauvignon Blanc rather than the more exotic tones of Sémillon. But recent vintages have been especially rich.

Guiraud   04 03 02 $$$

Château Lafaurie-Peyraguey. Wonderfully rich, honeyed, tropical-fruity Sauternes with lovely balance and precision of flavor. In the good vintages, this wine is an exceptional value in the context of Sauternes.

Lafaurie-Peyraguey   04 03 02 $$$

Château Nairac. A focused, elegant wine that showcases the fresh, lively style of Barsac. Typically more citric and spicy than unctuous and honeyed.

Nairac   04 03 02 $$$

Château Rieussec. Consistently among the most concentrated and viscous wines of the region, with exotic apricot, spice, and honey character and great depth of flavor. Better than ever since it was purchased by the owners of Château Lafite-Rothschild in the mid-1980s.

Rieussec   03 02 $$$$

Château Suduiraut. At its best, Suduiraut produces a deeply colored, honeyed wine of great richness and complexity. Although among the fattest wines of Sauternes, recent vintages of Suduiraut have also been almost magically light on their feet.

Suduiraut   04 03 02 $$$$

Château La Tour Blanche. One of the sweetest and most opulent wines in Sauternes, La Tour Blanche is owned by France's Ministry of Agriculture and made at the local Ecole de Viticulture et Oenologie. Recent vintages have shown compelling peachy fruit with firm underlying acid spine.

La Tour Blanche   04 03 02 $$$

Château d'Yquem. For centuries, Yquem has been unchallenged as the finest example of Sauternes and the most famous sweet wine in the world. A dramatically rich wine of dizzying complexity and extravagant depth, it is capable of aging effortlessly for several decades. Vine yields are tiny, with perfectly botrytized grapes harvested in a number of labor-intensive passes through the vineyard, and the wine undergoes three years or more of aging in new oak barrels. In 2004, the majority shareholder LVMH/Moët Hennessey installed Pierre Lurton, director of Château Cheval Blanc, as manager of the estate.

Yquem   02 01 99 $$$$$

OTHER PRODUCERS TO LOOK FOR: Château d'Arche, Château Clos Haut-Peyraguey, Château Coutet, Château Doisy-Daëne, Château Doisy-Dubroca, Château Doisy-Védrines, Château de Malle, Château Rabaud-Promis, Château Raymond-Lafon, Château de Rayne-Vigneau, Château Sigalas-Rabaud.

BURGUNDY

The finest red and white wines of Burgundy set the standard for Pinot Noir and Chardonnay. At their best, they are the world's most aromatically complex, silky, and seductive wines, thanks to their ineffable combination of fruits, flowers, minerals, and earth, and their ability to project flavor authority without excess weight. But first-rate Burgundies are produced in limited quantities. Burgundy is a minefield for the casual wine lover, as there is still far too much mediocre and grossly overpriced wine. The problem in a nutshell is that ownership of a single small premier cru vineyard may be carved up among a dozen or more owners, and the wines produced—even though they sell for roughly the same price at the cellar door—can range from the sublime to the undrinkable, depending on the talent and commitment of the producer.

Historically, the production and distribution of Burgundy wines was dominated by *négociants*, well-capitalized merchants whose wines could come from purchased grapes (or unfermented juice) or from finished wines bought from small growers. Today, as intense competition for the best grapes has made ownership of land more important than ever, many of these négociants have also become major vineyard owners. At the same time, the past generation has witnessed a proliferation of small grower labels as numerous *vignerons* (literally, "wine growers") who previously sold most, if not all, of their production to the large merchants have chosen to bottle their own product. To a great extent this is because a younger and more cosmopolitan generation has seen the value of their family vineyards—as well as the prices of Burgundy wines in general—skyrocket. The best of these new producers have radically reduced vine yields and have taken a number of additional measures in the vineyards and in the winery to create a luxury product that can command, and merit, a very high price.

The Côte d'Or, or "golden slope," is the heart of Burgundy, a 30-mile-long ribbon of vineyards stretching from just south of Dijon to Chagny. But the greater Burgundy region also encompasses Chablis in its extreme north, and the Côte Chalonnaise and Mâconnais regions located to the south of the Côte d'Or. Beaujolais, at the extreme southern end of Burgundy, virtually reaches the outskirts of Lyon.

Key to Vintage Ratings		Key to Assessments of Specific Wines	
★★★★★	Outstanding	**03**	An excellent to outstanding example *of that wine*
★★★★	Excellent	03	A good to very good example *of that wine*
★★★	Good to very good	03	A disappointing effort (often due to a
★★	Fair to average		difficult vintage)
★	Poor		

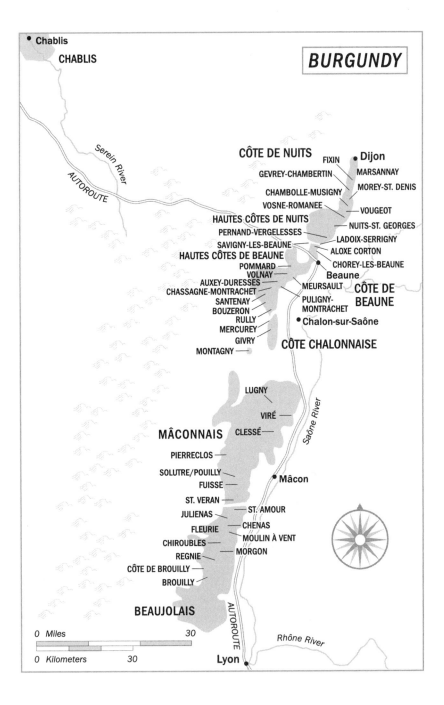

CHABLIS

Wine lovers who have come to think of Chardonnay as weighty and thick will find Chablis a revelation. When grown in the coo, clay-and-chalk soils around the sleepy town of Chablis, at the northern reach of Burgundy, Chardonnay is transformed into one of the world's most cerebral and distinctive white wines. With its brisk citrus character, floral lift, and incisive minerality, Chablis is at once sharper and more delicate than white Burgundy from the Côte d'Or nearly 100 miles to the southeast— and potentially at least as long-lived. And Chablis is about as far removed from fruit- and oak-driven New World Chardonnay as a white wine can be.

The growing season in Chablis is shorter and cooler than that of the Côte d'Or. The deposits of limestone and chalk here, which give energy to the wines, have the same origin as those found in the Loire Valley and Champagne. Chablis is crisp and minerally, and is generally higher in acidity than wines of the Côte d'Or, which tend to have more body, weight, and alcoholic strength. Wines from lesser vineyards or lesser producers can be downright meager, with excessive production levels and widespread machine harvesting frequently leading to skinny wines with little flesh or ripeness. But the best grand cru and premier cru Chablis bottlings from the top estates display an uncanny combination of concentration and finesse. While they can seldom match their cousins from the Côte d'Or for sheer power or heft, they are unequaled for precision, balance, and verve. The majority of Chablis producers emphasize the brightness and clarity of their wines by raising them in stainless steel or neutral oak vessels, although some producers continue to make extensive use of small and frequently new oak barrels.

BANG FOR THE BUCK. At prices typically one-third to one-half lower than those for wines of similar pedigree (i.e., village level, premier cru and grand cru; see box on page 41) from the Côte d'Or, Chablis can offer excellent value in high-class Chardonnay.

2004 ★★★+   2003 ★★   2002 ★★★★

RECOMMENDED PRODUCERS

Domaine Billaud-Simon. Crisp, sharply focused, mineral-driven Chablis, among the finest examples of the nonoaked school.

Chablis Tête d'Or	04	03	$$
Chablis Montée de Tonnerre	04	03	$$$
Chablis Les Clos	04	03	$$$$$

Domaine Vincent Dauvissat. At the top of the Chablis hierarchy for decades, the Dauvissat wines, made using a small percentage of new oak *barriques*, are concentrated, broad, minerally, and deep, unfolding impressively with bottle aging.

Chablis	04	03	$$$
Chablis La Forest	04	03	$$$
Chablis Les Clos	04	03	$$$$

Domaine Jean-Paul & Benoît Droin. Under the direction of Benoît Droin, these wines are now much less marked by the aromas and flavors of oak than the wines made by his father, Jean-Paul. The Droins benefit from an extensive array of premier and grand cru vineyard holdings.

Chablis Mont de Milieu	04	03	$$$
Chablis Montée de Tonnerre	04	03	$$$
Chablis Grenouille	04	03	$$$$

Domaine William Fèvre. One of the most exciting developments in Chablis of the past 20 years, this house, with substantial vineyard holdings, has been utterly transformed under ownership by the Henriot family of Champagne, which also owns Bouchard Père et Fils in Beaune. The wines are rich, deep, and powerful, with outstanding purity of flavor and expressive vineyard character. Prices are very reasonable for the high quality.

Chablis Montée de Tonnerre	04	03	$$$
Chablis Fourchaume Vignoble de Vaulorent	04	03	$$$
Chablis Bougros	04	03	$$$$

Domaine Louis Michel. Unoaked, pure, restrained wines that display an almost metallic minerality. For years a paradigm of the stainless steel school of Chablis. Time in bottle generally brings more texture and richness.

Chablis Montée de Tonnerre	04	03	$$$
Chablis Les Clos	04	03	$$$$

Domaine Christian Moreau Père et Fils. These richly flavored yet precise examples of Chablis, some of which spend some time in oak, strike a near-perfect balance between traditional and modern.

Chablis Vaillons	04	03	$$$
Chablis Les Clos	04	03	$$$$

Domaine François Raveneau. For many Burgundy fans, Raveneau stands above the rest of Chablis, and the estate's strong cult following means that prices are high and bottles scarce in the retail market. Raised in neutral oak, the wines are deep, chewy, and multi-faceted, with their taut minerality requiring—and repaying—extended bottle aging.

Chablis Butteaux	04	03	$$$$
Chablis Montée de Tonnerre	04	03	$$$$
Chablis Clos	04	03	$$$$$

Verget. The Mâconnais-based négociant Jean-Marie Guffens has made a major investment in the Chablis region and now vinifies a large quantity of Chablis. The wines are pure and precise, and are less marked by oak than the Verget wines from the Côte d'Or. They are also widely available in the market and frequently offer great value.

Chablis Terroir de Chablis	04	03	$$
Chablis Vaillons Vieilles Vignes de Minots	04	03	$$$
Chablis Montée de Tonnerre	04	03	$$$
Chablis Bougros	04	03	$$$$

OTHER PRODUCERS TO LOOK FOR: Domaine Jean-Marc Brocard, La Chablisienne, Domaine de Chantemerle, Domaine Jean Collet, Domaine Jean & Sébastien Dauvissat, Domaine Daniel-Etienne Defaix, Maison Joseph Drouhin, Domaine Gérard Duplessis, Domaine Grossot, Domaine Laroche, Domaine Pinson Frères, Domaine Servin, Domaine Gérard Tremblay, Domaine Laurent Tribut, Domaine Vocoret.

THE CLASSIFICATION OF BURGUNDY

The wines of the Côte d'Or are classified into five categories based upon the quality of their *terroir* (see box on page 45), a hierarchy of vineyard sites that has been established over literally hundreds of years. At the base of the quality pyramid is generic Burgundy (the label simply says Bourgogne), which may come from any vineyard in Burgundy. Next is a special category of generic wines entitled to use a regional appellation (for example, Côte de Nuits-Villages) on the label. The third category of Burgundy, popularly referred to as village wine, comes from vineyards located entirely within the boundaries of a group of favored villages, or communes; the label normally lists only the name of the village—e.g., Chambolle-Musigny, although sometimes additional place names *(lieux-dit)* are appended.

Next in rank in the Burgundy pecking order are the first growths (premiers crus), specially designated vineyards with particularly favorable soil and exposition. The name of the premier cru is appended to the village name on the label (such as Chambolle-Musigny Les Amoureuses), and the words premier cru appear on the label. Finally, at the apex of the Burgundy pyramid are the grands crus, those ideally situated hillside vineyards that over the centuries have consistently produced the region's greatest wines. These grand crus (e.g., Chambertin, Musigny) have become so well known that their labels need not make reference to the villages in which they are located. In fact, in the 19th century several villages capitalized on the reputations of their most famous vineyards by appending the name of the grand cru to their own. Unfortunately, this can cloud the important distinction between a vineyard (Musigny) and the village in which it is located (Chambolle-Musigny).

Why Burgundy Is So Tricky To Buy

The history factor. A small dose of history is necessary to explain the jigsaw puzzle that is the typical Burgundy cru, or growth. Following the French Revolution, vineyards previously owned by the Catholic Church and the aristocracy were confiscated and auctioned off, mostly to wealthy speculators who in turn subdivided and resold them. The parceling of vineyards was accelerated by the French laws of inheritance established by the Napoleonic code, which ended primogeniture and required property to be equally divided among all heirs. The result is that today's typical vineyard is carved up among multiple owners. Thus, there's really no single wine called Vosne-Romanée Les Suchots: 20 or more growers and négociants offer this first growth.

The climate factor. The great wines of Burgundy are made from a single grape variety (either Pinot Noir or Chardonnay) grown in a closely defined site, rather than a blend of varieties from multiple sites. This means that grape growers do not have the luxury of being able to increase the proportion of a particular grape that fared better (as they can in Bordeaux) or to favor a site that did relatively well. Whereas grapes in warmer areas reach reasonable levels of ripeness almost every year, vintage variation is much more of a factor in Burgundy than it is in many other wine-growing regions. For starters, Pinot Noir buds early and is particularly vulnerable to spring frosts. Highly localized summer hailstorms can decimate a parcel of vines in a matter of minutes. Cold weather in September can prevent proper ripening and result in tart, undernourished wines. Rain just before or during the harvest can swell the grapes with water or bring on rot, always a risk with the relatively thin-skinned, tight-clustered Pinot Noir grapes. While underripeness has historically been the more common problem in Burgundy, uncharacteristically hot and dry years, like 2003, can produce excessively alcoholic and tannic wines with inadequate acidity or a cooked-fruit character. Some vintages produce such copious crop loads that unless growers take active steps to hold down yields, they are doomed to produce dilute wines. Unfortunately, with the high prices Burgundy fetches in today's marketplace, and with numerous major markets all clamoring for limited quantities of the best wines, there is little financial incentive to limit production.

A Burgundy's label will tell you the wine's vintage and appellation, but it won't tell you whether the grapes were ripe enough or whether the producer overproduced or cut corners during vinification. While Burgundy snobs gravitate toward the most famous grand cru vineyards and undervalue lesser sites, more liberated pinot fans know that the producer's name on the label is easily as important as the wine's origin.

CÔTE D'OR

The fragile Pinot Noir grape reaches its apotheosis along Burgundy's Côte d'Or, especially in the northern portion of the Côte d'Or known as the Côte de Nuits, which is planted almost exclusively to Pinot. The Côte de Nuits is home to virtually all the most famous names in red Burgundy: Chambertin, Musigny, and Romanée-Conti, to name just a few. This is the most expensive wine real estate on earth and hallowed ground for lovers of Pinot Noir. All but a handful of Burgundy's grand cru vineyards are in the Côte de Nuits. The Côte de Beaune, which comprises the southern half of the Côte d'Or, is the source of the most famous names in white Burgundy. It also produces outstanding red Burgundies, even if Pinot Noir here rarely possesses quite the stuffing, complexity, and longevity of the better examples from the Côte de Nuits.

White Burgundies from the villages of Meursault, Puligny-Montrachet, and Chassagne-Montrachet—plus the grand cru Corton-Charlemagne—are, along with the best examples from Chablis, as transcendently fine as Chardonnay gets. Few New World Chardonnays can consistently match the better white Burgundies for aromatic complexity, flavor intensity, precision, lift, and cellaring potential. On the other hand, it's tempting to say that not enough white Burgundies do. In their youth, most white Burgundies are dominated by primary fruits, flowers, and minerals, and often the aromas of new oak barrels. With time in bottle, more complex fruit notes emerge, along with subtle earthy elements and nuances of smoked meat, butter, and toasted nuts. Recent vintages in Burgundy have been warm, with the result that white Burgundies (and reds as well) have been riper, richer, and more substantial than ever before.

BANG FOR THE BUCK. Burgundies worth buying are expensive, sometimes extravagantly so, but there are relative values to be found in less-hallowed villages like Marsannay and Savigny-lès-Beaune for red wine and St. Aubin for white. Burgundies not worth buying are some of the most overpriced wines made anywhere. Why are they all expensive? The typical small grower may own tiny slices of a half-dozen premier and grand cru vineyards, and make five or six barrels of wine from each—that's a piddling 1,500 to 1,800 bottles of each wine, or 125 to 150 cases, for the world. Compare that to a Bordeaux first growth like Château Lafite-Rothschild, which releases 20,000 to 30,000 cases in a typical year, and you may wonder why the most sought-after Burgundies are not even more expensive.

Red Burgundy: 2004 ★★★+   **2003** ★★★+   **2002** ★★★★

White Burgundy: 2005 ★★★★+   **2004** ★★★★–   **2003** ★★+   **2002** ★★★★

RECOMMENDED RED BURGUNDY PRODUCERS

Domaine Marquis d'Angerville. Pure, fragrant, silky, and eminently age-worthy wines that have long been at the summit of the Volnay hierarchy. The late Marquis Jacques d'Angerville was one of the first estate owners to bottle his own wine and export it to America.

Volnay Champans	04	03	$$$
Volnay Clos des Ducs	04	03	$$$$

Domaine Robert Arnoux. Sweetly oaky, supple Burgundies that combine aromatic complexity with deep fruit and lush textures. Rarely hard in the early going.

Nuits-St. Georges Les Poisets	04	03	$$$$
Vosne-Romanée Les Suchots	**04**	03	$$$$$

Domaine Ghislaine Barthod. Ghislaine Barthod offers an impressive array of premiers crus from the village of Chambolle-Musigny, each reflecting its distinct site character. The style here favors elegance and precision over sheer power.

Chambolle-Musigny Charmes	04	03	$$$$
Chambolle-Musigny Veroilles	**04**	03	$$$$

Bouchard Père et Fils. This major producer (a négociant as well as the largest owner of premier and grand cru vineyards in the Côte d'Or) offers a broad range of consistently excellent wines that display superb freshness and purity of fruit as well as considerable aging potential.

Beaune Grèves Vigne de l'Enfant Jésus	04	**03**	$$$
Le Corton	04	**03**	$$$$
Vosne-Romanee Aux Reignots	**04**	**03**	$$$$$

Domaine Robert Chevillon. Along with Henri Gouges, the Chevillon family is one of the top two producers in the village of Nuits-St. Georges. The Chevillons offer a slew of premiers crus: supple, fruit-driven, impeccably balanced, and rarely hard in their youth.

Nuits-St. Georges Les Pruliers	04	03	$$$$
Nuits-St. Georges Les Cailles	04	03	$$$$
Nuits-St. Georges Les St. Georges	04	**03**	$$$$

Domaine de Courcel. Concentrated, generous wines made from fruit harvested very late for maximum ripeness. While they possess the sweetness to give early pleasure, they also have the structure and stuffing to age.

Pommard Grand Clos des Epenots	04	**03**	$$$
Pommard Les Rugiens	04	**03**	$$$

Domaine Joseph Drouhin. This leading négociant and vineyard owner is prized for gentle, perfumed wines that impress more for their elegance and aromatic complexity than for their size or brute strength.

Beaune Clos des Mouches		03	$$$$
Chambolle-Musigny Les Amoureuses	04	03	$$$$$
Bonnes-Mares	04	03	$$$$$

THE CONCEPT OF TERROIR

Terroir is a French concept incorporating everything that contributes to the distinctiveness of a particular vineyard site: its soil and subsoil, drainage, slope and elevation, and its microclimate, which in turn includes temperature and precipitation, exposure to the sun, and the like. The concept of terroir is essential to a variety like Pinot Noir because this grape is hypersensitive to its environment, reflecting the slightest nuances of soil and climate in its tastes and textures. Whereas the great majority of wines made from Cabernet Sauvignon, for example, will demonstrate that grape's characteristic deep color, black-currant flavor, and firmly tannic structure with regional variations on this theme, the Pinot Noir is chameleon-like, and, not suprisingly, a far less adaptable international traveler. If the climate is too cool, the wines tend to be weedy and pale; if too warm, they can turn out roasted, even pruney, or overly tannic. Too-rich soils can produce excessive crop loads or ponderous wines devoid of nuance. Vineyards literally 100 yards apart can yield completely different styles of wine.

The concept of terroir is especially relevant where wines are made from a single variety grown in a highly specific vineyard site, in a region where vintages vary substantially in quality and style—like Pinot Noir in Burgundy, Chardonnay in Chablis, Riesling in Germany, or the great Nebbiolo wines Barolo and Barbaresco in Italy's Piedmont region.

Domaine Dujac. Elegant, perfumed, oak-spicy wines that are almost deceptively sweet in the early going but have a track record for extended aging. Under the direction of the young Jeremy Seysses, the estate appears to be moving toward a somewhat richer, fuller style.

Morey-St. Denis	04	03	$$$$
Clos de la Roche	04	03	$$$$$

Domaine Fourrier. The young but wise Jean-Marie Fourrier makes perfumed, aromatically precise Burgundies in a traditional fashion, using limited new oak and bottling his wines later than most of his neighbors. The estate benefits from a high percentage of very old vines.

Gevrey-Chambertin	04	03	$$$
Gevrey-Chambertin Champeaux	04	03	$$$$
Gevrey-Chambertin Clos Saint Jacques	04	03	$$$$$

Domaine Henri Gouges. For decades the leader in the village of Nuits-St. Georges, this was one of the first estates in Burgundy to bottle its own wines rather than send production off to the local merchants. Following a dip in quality in the 1980s, today's wines are once again at the top of their appellation: concentrated, solidly structured, and generally in need of aging.

Nuits-St. Georges Les Pruliers	04	03	$$$$
Nuits-St. Georges Les Vaucrains	04	**03**	$$$$$
Nuits-St. Georges Les Saint-Georges	**04**	**03**	$$$$$

Domaine Jean Grivot. Dark berry- and mineral-scented wines that combine elegance and intensity, consistently among the stars of their respective vintages in recent years. Etienne Grivot is unusually flexible both in his choice of when to harvest and in his approach to vinifying each year's grapes.

Nuits-St. Georges Les Boudots	04	03	$$$$
Vosne-Romanée Les Beaumonts	04	**03**	$$$$
Echézeaux	04	**03**	$$$$

Maison Louis Jadot. This major merchant and vineyard owner, which was purchased by its American importer Kobrand in the mid-1980s, has long been noted for traditionally made, firmly structured wines that require and reward extended cellaring. Under the direction of the brilliant enologist Jacques Lardière for more than 25 years, the Jadot wines admirably reflect their individual site character.

Beaune Clos des Ursules	04	03	$$$
Gevrey-Chambertin Clos St. Jacques	04	**03**	$$$$
Bonnes-Mares	04	**03**	$$$$$

Domaine Jayer-Gilles. Flamboyant, fleshy wines marked by ripe, sweet fruit, and lavish, spicy new oak. The estate's Côte de Nuits-Villages is always a perfect ringer in a blind tasting with Burgundies of higher pedigree.

Hautes Côtes de Nuits	04	03	$$$
Côte de Nuits-Villages	04	**03**	$$$
Echézeaux	04	**03**	$$$$

Domaine Michel Lafarge. Quintessentially elegant, sweet, well-delineated Volnays that are approachable in their youth but improve with cellaring. A benchmark domaine in this village for decades.

Volnay Vendanges Sélectionnées	04	03	$$$
Volnay Clos du Château des Ducs	04	03	$$$$
Volnay Clos des Chênes	04	**03**	$$$$

Domaine Hubert Lignier. Rich, deeply flavored, consistently age-worthy wines that favor purity and balance over weight and thickness. The Clos de la Roche is the king of the cellar.

Morey-Saint-Denis 1er Cru Vieilles Vignes	04	03	$$$$
Clos de la Roche	04	**03**	$$$$$

Domaine Méo-Camuzet. Flamboyantly aromatic Burgundies that offer sweet fruit and abundant oak spice character along with deep, velvety texture. The domain's very scarce Vosne-Romanée Cros Parantoux bottling is from a vineyard made famous by the most esteemed Burgundy winemaker of the last half-century, Henri Jayer.

	04	03	
Vosne-Romanée	04	03	$$$$
Nuits-St. Georges Les Boudots	04	03	$$$$$
Vosne-Romanée Aux Brûlées	04	**03**	$$$$$

Domaine Hubert de Montille. Known for decades for their austerity, firm acid, lowish alcohol, and slow development in bottle, this estate's wines are now a bit suppler and less forbidding in their youth under the direction of Etienne de Montille, without loss of purity of fruit or soil character.

	04	03	
Volnay Les Mitans	04	03	$$$$
Volnay Les Taillepieds	04	**03**	$$$$
Pommard Les Rugiens	**04**	**03**	$$$$$

Domaine Georges Mugneret/Mugneret-Gibourg. Remarkably elegant, pure wines with a long track record of aging gracefully.

	04	03	
Vosne-Romanée	04	03	$$$
Nuits-St. Georges Les Chaignots	**04**	03	$$$$
Clos Vougeot	04	**03**	$$$$$

Domaine Jacques-Frédéric Mugnier. A top-notch source for elegant, silky wines that perfectly capture the sappy red berry and mineral character of Chambolle-Musigny.

	04	03	
Chambolle-Musigny	04	03	$$$
Chambolle-Musigny Les Amoureuses	**04**	03	$$$$$
Musigny	**04**	03	$$$$$

Domaine Jean-Marc Pavelot. Pure, concentrated, fruit-driven wines with enticing sweetness and excellent balance. Arguably the top estate in the underappreciated village of Savigny-lès-Beaune, which means that these wines frequently offer terrific value by the standards of Burgundy.

	04	03	
Savigny-lès-Beaune Les Guettes	04	03	$$
Savigny-lès-Beaune Aux Gravains	04	03	$$$
Savigny-lès-Beaune La Dominode	**04**	03	$$$

Domaine Perrot-Minot. In the late 1990s Christophe Perrot-Minot made the marketing decision to cut yields drastically and offer superconcentrated, deeply colored, no-compromise wines at a substantial price premium over those of his neighbors. After a couple of heavily extracted, new-oaky vintages, today's wines are still extravagantly rich but velvety, finer, and better-balanced.

	04	03	
Morey-Saint-Denis En La Rue de Vergy	04	03	$$$
Chambolle-Musigny La Combe d'Orveaux Vieilles Vignes	**04**	03	$$$$$
Mazoyères-Chambertin	04	**03**	$$$$$

Domaine de la Romanée-Conti. Despite this fabled domain's steep prices, its superb bottles are difficult to obtain as collectors all over the world battle for bottles. DRC's wines are flamboyantly rich and concentrated yet never heavy, with a spicy, minerally complexity that pinots from outside Burgundy simply have not yet achieved.

Grands-Echézeaux	04	**03**	$$$$$
La Tâche	**04**	**03**	$$$$$

Domaine Roumier. One of Burgundy's most reliable and sought-after producers, thanks to its deeply flavored, highly perfumed wines with the tangy mineral, red berry, and spice character that makes the best Burgundies so exhilarating. Two of Roumier's top wines, the Chambolle-Musigny Les Amoureuses and Musigny, are made in extremely limited quantities.

Chambolle-Musigny	04	03	$$$
Morey-St. Denis Clos de la Bussière	04	03	$$$
Bonnes-Mares	**04**	**03**	$$$$$

Domaine Christian Sérafin. Concentrated, balanced wines that are loaded with sweet, spicy fruit and enticing, toasty oak.

Gevrey-Chambertin Vieilles Vignes	04	03	$$$
Gevrey-Chambertin Le Fonteny	04	**03**	$$$$
Gevrey-Chambertin Les Cazetiers	04	**03**	$$$$

Domaine Comte Georges de Vogüé. A legendary producer that owns nearly three-quarters of the grand cru Musigny, arguably the greatest vineyard in the world. The wines are powerful, dense, rich, and expensive, requiring extensive cellaring to display their inherent complexity. If there's a value here, it's the Chambolle-Musigny premier cru, made from young vines in Musigny.

Chambolle-Musigny	04	03	$$$
Chambolle-Musigny 1er Cru	04	03	$$$$$
Musigny Vieilles Vignes	04	03	$$$$$

OTHER PRODUCERS TO LOOK FOR: Domaine Amiot-Servelle, Domaine du Comte Armand, Domaine Denis Bachelet, Domaine Bertagna, Domaine Jean-Marc Boillot, Domaine Henri Boillot, Domaine Simon Bize, Domaine Alain Burguet, Domaine Sylvain Cathiard, Domaine Chandon de Briailles, Domaine Philippe Charlopin-Parizot, Domaine Jean Chauvenet, Domaine Bruno Clair, Domaine Bruno Clavelier, Domaine du Clos des Lambrays, Domaine du Clos de Tart, Domaine Jean-Jacques Confuron, Domaine Edmond Cornu, Domaine Maurice Ecard, Domaine Sylvie Esmonin, Domaine Faiveley, Domaine Forey Père et Fils, Domaine Geantet-Pansiot, Domaine Robert Groffier, Domaine Anne Gros, Domaine Gros Frère et Soeur, Domaine Hudelot-Noëllat, Domaine des Comtes Lafon, Dominique Laurent, Domaine Fernand Lécheneaut et Fils, Lucien Lemoine, Frédéric Magnien, Domaine Michel Magnien, Domaine Albert Morot, Domaine Denis Mortet, Nicolas Potel, Domaine de la Pousse d'Or, Domaine Jacques Prieur, Domaine Daniel Rion, Domaine Joseph Roty, Domaine Armand Rousseau, Domaine Emmanuel Rouget, Domaine Tollot-Beaut, Domaine Jean & Jean-Louis Trapet.

SCARCE BUT WORTH THE SEARCH: Domaine Claude Dugat, Domaine Dugat-Py, Domaine Leroy.

RECOMMENDED WHITE BURGUNDY PRODUCERS

Domaine Jean Boillot/Henri Boillot. Intensely flavored, layered, and aromatically complex wines made with impeccable use of new oak. In recent vintages these have been among the finest examples of white Burgundy.

Puligny-Montrachet	**05**	04	03	$$$
Puligny-Montrachet Clos de la Mouchère		05	04	$$$$
Corton-Charlemagne		05	04	$$$$$

Bouchard Père et Fils. This huge producer makes excellent white wines as well as reds, working with some of the greatest sites in Burgundy. The wines are intensely flavored and vibrant, never heavy or over the top.

Beaune du Château	05	04	$$$
Meursault Genevrières	05	04	$$$$
Chevalier-Montrachet	05	04	$$$$$

Domaine Louis Carillon & Fils. Pure, elegant, understated wines that are textbook examples of Puligny finesse and complexity—concentrated, minerally, and impeccably balanced rather than weighty.

Puligny-Montrachet	05	04	$$$
Puligny-Montrachet Les Perrières	05	04	$$$$
Puligny-Montrachet Les Referts	05	04	$$$$

Domaine/Maison Vincent Girardin. This dynamic young producer has sharply cut back on his red wine operation in favor of his consistently strong, densely packed, and vibrant whites, which feature expressive fruit and solid underlying minerality.

Meursault Genevrières	05	04	$$$$
Puligny-Montrachet Folatières	05	04	$$$$

Maison Louis Jadot. Elegant, steely, soil-driven wines that need time to unwind and gain in flesh and flavor. The malolactic fermentations typically are at least partially blocked to retain acid spine and ensure freshness.

Chassagne-Montrachet	04	03	$$$
Chassagne-Montrachet Abbaye de Morgeot	04	03	$$$
Corton-Charlemagne	04	03	$$$$$

Domaine des Comtes Lafon. Complex, creamy-rich, multilayered wines that showcase the nutty, citrusy, and mineral character of Meursault. Among the most sought-after white wines of Burgundy and quite expensive.

Meursault Clos de la Barre	05	04	$$$$$
Meursault Charmes	05	04	$$$$$

Domaine Leflaive. A legendary domaine that has consistently been among the two or three best in the village of Puligny-Montrachet. The wines are impeccably steely and fresh, with deeply concentrated fruit and mineral flavors and excellent cellaring potential. Prices are high.

Puligny-Montrachet	05	04	$$$$
Puligny-Montrachet Les Pucelles	05	**04**	$$$$$
Batard-Montrachet	05	**04**	$$$$$

Château de la Maltroye. This large domaine in the middle of the village of Chassagne-Montrachet has been elevated in recent years to the top ranks by Jean-Pierre Cournut, whose wines are vibrant, minerally, and light on their feet, with judicious use of oak.

Chassagne-Montrachet		**04**	$$$
Chassagne-Montrachet Clos du Château de la Maltroye	05	**04**	$$$$
Chassagne-Montrachet Dent de Chien	**05**	**04**	$$$$$

Domaine Matrot. Thierry Matrot makes stylish, precise, and exceptionally food-friendly wines without the makeup provided by new oak barrels.

Meursault	05	04	$$$
Meursault Perrières	05	**04**	$$$

Jean-Marc Pillot. Since the late 1990s this producer has been a consistently excellent source for concentrated, full-flavored wines notable for their abundant fruit and complex soil tones.

Chassagne-Montrachet		**04**	$$$
Chassagne-Montrachet Les Vergers	05	04	$$$$
Chassagne Montrachet Les Caillerets	**05**	**04**	$$$$

Domaine Ramonet. Highly individual wines with strong soil character and excellent thrust. Often quite taut and unforthcoming in their youth, they have a track record for developing slowly and well in bottle.

St. Aubin Les Charmois	04	03	$$$
Chassagne-Montrachet Les Ruchottes	04	**03**	$$$$
Batard-Montrachet	04	03	$$$$$

Domaine Guy Roulot. Supple, lush Meursaults that display the classic citrus fruit, butter, and hazelnut characteristics of the village's wines.

Meursault Meix Chavaux	**05**	04	$$$$
Meursault Tessons	05	04	$$$$
Meursault Perrières	**05**	**04**	$$$$$

Domaine Sauzet. Rich and rather powerful wines that can be a bit unyielding in their youth but round out and gain texture with medium-term cellaring. Sauzet has been a leading producer of white Burgundy for decades.

Puligny-Montrachet	05	04	$$$$
Puligny-Montrachet Champ-Canet	**05**	**04**	$$$$$
Puligny-Montrachet Les Combettes	**05**	04	$$$$$

OTHER PRODUCERS TO LOOK FOR: Domaine Guy Amiot, Domaine Robert Ampeau, Domaine Bitouzet-Prieur, Domaine Jean-Marc Boillot, Domaine Bonneau du Martray, Domaine Boyer-Martenot, Domaine Bruno Colin, Domaine Marc Colin, Philippe Colin, Domaine Michel Colin-Déleger, Michel Coutoux, Deux Montilles, Domaine Arnaud Ente, Domaine Jean-Philippe Fichet, Domaine Fontaine-Gagnard, Domaine Patrick Javillier, Domaine François Jobard, Domaine Rémi Jobard, Domaine Latour-Giraud, Domaine Hubert de Montille, Bernard Morey et Fils, Domaine Jean-Marc Morey, Domaine Marc Morey, Domaine Pierre Morey, Domaine Michel Niellon, Domaine Paul Pernot, Domaine Paul Pillot, Domaine Jacques Prieur, Château de Puligny-Montrachet, Verget.

SCARCE BUT WORTH THE SEARCH: Domaine d'Auvenay, Domaine Jean-François Coche-Dury.

CÔTE CHALONNAISE

Compared to the wines of the Côte d'Or just to the north, Côte Chalonnaise wines are less refined, even a bit rustic, especially in the case of the whites. But prices in this region are also substantially lower, with even the best wines usually selling for less than simple *village* examples from the high-rent neighborhoods of the Côte d'Or.

The top villages of the appellation are Rully (mostly white wines), Mercurey (both red and white wines), Givry (mostly reds), Montagny (exclusively whites), plus Bouzeron, which has its own appellation for wines from the white grape Aligoté. Red wines from the Côte Chalonnaise are typically less fruity and suave than those from the Côte d'Or, but a new generation of producers is making wines that are smoother, more lush, and less tannic than their predecessors. Most red wines, especially those from Mercurey, benefit from at least a couple years of bottle aging, but the whites are generally best consumed by their third or fourth birthday.

2004 ★★★   **2003** ★★+

RECOMMENDED PRODUCERS

Domaine Dureil-Janthial. Concentrated, deeply fruity wines, the whites strong in mineral character and less rustic than most Chardonnays from the area, and the reds sweet and supple, with both early appeal and ageability.

Rully Blanc Le Meix Cadot	`04`	`03`	$$
Rully Vielles Vignes	`04`	`03`	$$

Domaine Joblot. Jean-Marc Joblot's rich, layered, oaky red wines offer an almost exotic expression of fruit that's rare for the Côte Chalonnaise. The whites are rich and earthy.

Givry Clos de la Servoisine	`04`	`03`	$$$
Givry Clos du Cellier aux Moines	`04`	`03`	$$$

Domaine du Meix-Foulot. Agnes de Launay, with input from her father, Paul, produces concentrated, structured red wines that often require, and reward, aging—from some of the best-located, highest-elevation vineyards in Mercurey.

Mercurey Meix Foulot	03	$$
Mercurey Clos du Château de Montaigu	03	$$$

Domaine A. et P. de Villaine. This is the home estate of Aubert de Villaine, co-owner of the fabled Domaine de la Romanée-Conti in Vosne-Romanée. Villaine's Aligoté is widely considered the archetype of the variety, impressively deep and complex without losing the variety's delicacy or vivacity. The red wines offer suave texture and lush, berry flavors.

Aligoté de Bouzeron	04	$$
Bourgogne Blanc Les Clous	04	$$
Rully Blanc Les St. Jacques	04	$$$

OTHER PRODUCERS TO LOOK FOR: Domaine Stéphane Aladame, Domaine Faiveley, Domaine Henri et Paul Jacquesson, Domaine Michel Juillot, Domaine François Raquillet, Maison Antonin Rodet (Château de Chamirey and Château de Rully).

MÂCONNAIS

The vast Mâconnais region of southern Burgundy is a particularly rich source for reasonably priced Chardonnays. Most of this area is somewhat warmer than the Côte d'Or, and thus the vines here usually enjoy a longer season and achieve greater ripeness. Some of the best growers intentionally harvest late for maximum ripeness. You'll find everything from lush, tropical-fruity examples that can out-California California Chardonnay at half the price to more serious wines that can rival examples from the Côte d'Or at a fraction of the cost. (And of course at the level of many producers not featured here, there is also a sea of uncomplicated and sometimes dilute or underripe wines, made from excessively high vine yields and harvested by machine.) There is very little red wine of note made in the Mâconnais: Pinot Noir here must be labeled simply Bourgogne and the wine called Mâcon *rouge* is made from Gamay.

The most basic wines of the region, labeled Mâcon or Mâcon-Villages, are usually made in stainless steel tanks and bottled quickly to preserve their bright, crisp fruit. These wines are generally best suited for drinking within a few years after their release. In theory, Mâcon-Villages is the appellation used to signify higher-quality wines from the region's favored villages. As a general rule, sites on the first slopes near the Saône River are best. Wines made from fruit from a single village (out of nearly four dozen that have a right to the Mâcon-Villages appellation) generally append their name to Mâcon on the label (i.e., Mâcon-Fuissé, Mâcon-Vergisson, Mâcon-Davayé); wines that are blends from two or more of these villages are typically bottled as Mâcon-Villages. In the northern portion of the large Mâconnais area a new appellation contrôlée, Viré-Clessé, was created in 1999, originally for dry wines only, but now including wines with residual sugar too—from a large delimited area around the towns of Viré and Clessé. The harvest here takes place a good week to ten days later than in vineyards farther to the south, leaving open the possibility of extra ripeness and the incidence of botrytis.

The Pouilly-Fuissé appellation, spread over a series of limestone-rich hills west and slightly south of the city of Mâcon, has long been the source of the Mâconnais region's best and most expensive white wines. The wines from vineyards at higher elevation show minerality, vibrancy, and grip from chalky soil, while warmer sites facing south and southeast often yield rounder wines with more tropical aromas of soft citrus fruits, apricot, and honey. The best Pouilly-Fuissés are typically the most age-worthy, dry white wines of the Mâconnais region, improving in bottle for 12 to 15 years in vintages with sound acidity. Pouilly-Vinzelles and Pouilly-Loché, at the warm eastern edge of Pouilly-Fuissé, can be almost as good. St. Véran is a rather odd, bifurcated appellation for Chardonnay, covering land both south and north of Pouilly-Fuissé.

2005 ★★★★+   2004 ★★★+   2003 ★★

RECOMMENDED PRODUCERS

Domaine Daniel Barraud. Balanced, rich, mostly barrique-aged wines from a vigneron who is quite willing to harvest late for thorough ripeness.

St. Véran Les Pommards	04	$$
Pouilly-Fuissé La Roche	04	$$$
Pouilly-Fuissé Les Crays Vieilles Vignes	04	$$$

Domaine André Bonhomme. This reliable estate produces elegant, lively wines with sound acidity and penetrating minerality. Prices are extremely reasonable.

Viré-Clessé	04	03	$$
Viré-Clessé Vieilles Vignes		02	$$

Domaine Cordier Père et Fils. An excellent source of rich wines made from thoroughly ripe fruit, often lush and high in alcohol but always juicy and minerally. Some of Cordier's wines, such as the St. Véran Clos à La Côte, are made in 100 percent new oak.

St. Véran Clos à La Côte	04	$$
Pouilly-Fuissé Vignes Blanches	04	$$$

Domaine Corsin. A very good source for rich, full-bodied Mâconnais wines with structure and power reminiscent of more exalted examples from the Côte d'Or.

St. Véran	04	03	$$
Pouilly-Fuissé	04	03	$$

Château Fuissé. This old family domain, with choice vineyard parcels in Pouilly-Fuissé, harvests late for maximum ripeness, then often blocks the malolactic fermentation to ensure a firm acid backbone. Their prime holding is Le Clos, a chalk-and-limestone vineyard that includes some vines dating back to 1920.

Pouilly-Fuissé Vieilles Vignes	04	$$$
Pouilly-Fuissé Le Clos	04	$$$

Domaine Guffens-Heynen. This is the tiny family estate of Jean-Marie Guffens, owner of the Verget négociant operation, and his wife, Maine Guffens-Heynen. Here the wines are more minerally, taut, and classically made, requiring some time in bottle to unwind and flesh out. Also look for exotic, densely packed Pouilly-Fuissé.

Mâcon-Pierreclos	04	$$$
Mâcon-Pierreclos Le Chavigne	04	$$$
Pouilly-Fuissé La Roche	04	$$$$

Domaine Jean Manciat. Precise, understated, food-friendly wines. The Franclieu, made in stainless steel, offers a flinty minerality, while the Vieilles Vignes is aged in a significant percentage of new oak.

Mâcon-Charnay Franclieu	05	04	$$
Mâcon-Charnay Vieilles Vignes	04	03	$$

Domaine Robert-Dénogent. Highly concentrated, stylish, and complex wines aged in barrel and bottled late, without fining or filtration.

Pouilly-Fuissé Cuvée Claude Dénogent	03	$$$
Pouilly-Fuissé Les Carrons	03	$$$

Domaine la Soufrandière/Bret Brothers. Tactile, minerally estate and négociant wines from old vines, made with almost no new oak and vinified to showcase their site character.

Viré-Clessé la Verchère	04	$$$
Pouilly-Vinzelles Les Quarts	04	$$$

Domaine de la Bongran/Domaine de Roally. Jean Thévenet's highly individual wines under these two labels come from grapes picked at the outer limits of ripeness and beyond. His sweet wines from Chardonnay—including the partly botrytized Levrouté and the exotic, full-blown Cuvée Botrytis, made in years when autumn conditions bring noble rot—are dramatic and different, and are favorites of top restaurants across France.

Domaine de Roally Mâcon-Montbellet	03	$$
Domaine de la Bongran Mâcon-Villages Tradition	02	$$$

Maison Verget. Capitalizing on his intimate knowledge of the region's best sites and old vines, Jean-Marie Guffens offers a mindboggling array of négociant bottlings from the Mâconnais. The wines are consistently intense, ripe and flavorful, and generally offer considerable early appeal.

St. Véran Terres Noires	04	$$
Mâcon-Vergisson La Roche	04	$$
Pouilly-Fuissé Terroirs de Vergisson La Roche	04	$$$

OTHER PRODUCERS TO LOOK FOR: Domaine J. A. Ferret, Domaine Guillemot-Michel, Les Heritiers des Comtes Lafon, Domaine Roger Lassarat, Olivier Merlin, Jean Rijckaert, Château des Rontets, Domaine St. Denis, Domaine Saumaize-Michelin, Domaine Thibert Père et Fils, Domaine Valette, Domaine des Vieilles Pierres.

BEAUJOLAIS

Made from the Gamay grape, the red wines of Beaujolais are mostly exuberantly fruity and brisk wines that are often served lightly chilled for added refreshment. There is also a small amount of white Beaujolais, made from Chardonnay, but little of this is exported to the U.S. Today, the overwhelming majority of Beaujolais production is controlled by négociants, of whom Georges Duboeuf is the undisputed king.

The fruit-dominated aromas and flavors of so many Beaujolais are due in part to fermentation via carbonic maceration, in which the whole bunches go into the vat unbroken and some or most of the fermentation takes place within the uncrushed berries. By minimizing contact between the juice and the skins, carbonic maceration brings much lower tannin levels and emphasizes the fruity character of the Gamay variety. This is not a bad thing, as most wine lovers view Beaujolais as a simple, care-free wine to be drunk young with straightforward or strongly flavored dishes and in warmer weather. In wine bars in Lyon, Beaujolais is most commonly served as a quaffing wine or with the *charcuterie* and other strongly flavored foods of the region.

The widespread use of enzymes and certain commercial yeasts, as well as high yields and heavy chaptalization (the addition of sugar during fermentation to increase a wine's alcoholic strength), tend to produce bland wines of limited concentration and character, sometimes exaggeratedly candied. But there are also far more serious, intense, and even structured wines produced by fiercely dedicated and usually small estates that exert more effort in the vineyards and follow traditional wine-making practices. These artisanal wines bear comparison to lesser Burgundies and can become increasingly Pinot-like with bottle aging.

Ten villages in the northern end of the Beaujolais region—Brouilly, Chénas, Chiroubles, Côte de Brouilly, Fleurie, Juliénas, Morgon, Moulin à Vent, Regnié, and St. Amour—are allowed to show their names on the label. These crus, most of which feature soils rich in granite, have proven to be the best sites for producing wines with greater complexity and character. Beaujolais-Villages is made from a few dozen additional villages that are felt to offer somewhat lower potential quality, while wines simply labeled Beaujolais are generally less serious and intended for drinking young. Beaujolais Nouveau, which can legally be released the third Thursday of November, barely two months after the harvest, is a very fresh wine that provides cash flow for its producers and instant gratification for consumers. But way too much Beaujolais Nouveau is overchaptalized or overprocessed.

BANG FOR THE BUCK. Beaujolais remains quite inexpensive, with simple négociant offerings often barely $10 a bottle. In fact, prices are so low today that many Beaujolais estates are for sale. The best artisanal examples hover around the $20 mark but many can be found for under $15, making them exceptional value.

2005 ★★★★+ **2004** ★★★+ **2003** ★★★

RECOMMENDED PRODUCERS

Domaine des Terres Dorées: Naturally made wines with low alcohol and great purity of fruit, from one of the only top producers at the southern end of the Beaujolais region, where limestone rather than granite dominates. In addition to deliciously light nouveau, there is also a vibrant Beaujolais blanc that displays excellent minerality and cut.

Beaujolais L'Ancien	04	03	$

Domaine de la Voûte des Crozes. Côte de Brouilly at its most succulent, lush, and spicy, favoring pure red berry fruit.

Côte de Brouilly	03	$$

Domaine Louis-Claude Desvignes. The Desvignes family owns land in the best sites of Morgon, one of the most age-worthy crus of Beaujolais. These are serious Beaujolais bottlings, sappy and red-fruity, with Pinot-like finesse and firm backbone.

Morgon Côte du Py	03	$$
Morgon Javernières	04	$$

Georges Duboeuf. No other wine region of France is so dominated by a single firm as is Beaujolais by Duboeuf. The dozens of bottlings each year emphasize sweetness and supple textures, and prices are extremely reasonable. Duboeuf's top grower-designated bottlings tend to be a bit more serious.

Morgon Jean Descombes	05	04	$$
Fleurie Domaine des Quatre Vents	05	04	$$
Moulin à Vent Domaine des Rosiers		04	$$

Domaine Jean Foillard. A complex, fragrant, naturally made wine from an outstanding site that displays creamy cherry, berry, and mineral flavors and the palate presence of a serious red Burgundy.

Morgon Côte du Py	04	03	$$

Domaine Pascal Granger. Crisp, elegant wines with lively fruit character and silky texture. There is also a delicious Chénas as well as reserve bottlings in better vintages.

Juliénas	04	03	$$

Domaine Marcel Lapierre. Deeply concentrated and unusually powerful Morgon made, like those of Jean Foillard, in noninterventionist fashion, without sulfur additions. Working in the village that boasts the greatest number of serious producers in Beaujolais, Lapierre is arguably the best.

Morgon	05	04	03	$$

Clos de la Roilette. Frequently the most concentrated and weighty wines of Fleurie, with sappy red and black fruits, complex soil tones, and the ability to age and improve in bottle for up to a decade. In the top years there is also a reserve bottling called Cuvée Tardive.

Fleurie			04	03		$$

Château Thivin. This historic estate produces suave, balanced wines with noteworthy concentration.

Côte de Brouilly		05	04	03		$$

Trenel Fils. A fastidious, quality-driven négociant whose best Beaujolais bottlings combine brightness and cut with unusual richness of texture.

Beaujolais-Villages				04		$
Juliénas				03		$$
Moulin à Vent Domaine de la Tour du Bief			04	03		$$

Domaine du Vissoux. Some of the most natural and wild Beaujolais of all, made without chaptalization, commercial yeasts, or filtration. Vissoux's Moulin à Vent bottling has uncanny structure for Beaujolais.

Beaujolais Cuvée Traditionelle			04		$$
Fleurie Poncié			04		$$
Moulin à Vent Rochegrès			04		$$

ALSACE

Alsace has been almost pathologically ignored by the American wine-drinking public for generations—a real mystery in light of the great number of juicy, pure wines produced in this picture-postcard region of northeastern France. Virtually all of Alsace's best wines are white, and they are particularly food-friendly thanks to their fresh fruit flavors unobscured by oak. While the majority of the region's most important wines are Riesling, Pinot Gris, and Gewürztraminer, other grapes—especially Pinot Blanc and Muscat—account for some of Alsace's best values.

Comparisons to German wines are common, and this has confused the identity of Alsace for many American wine lovers. Over the centuries, Alsace has bounced back and forth between French and German possession, and the rich cuisine here leans more to Germany than to France. Vineyard names on the labels are distinctly Germanic, and the wines of Alsace are bottled in the traditional *flute* that is also used in Germany. To the current generation of North American wine drinkers, a tall, thin bottle usually signifies a wine with at least some sweetness. But the vast majority of Alsace wine is dry, or at least it was until recent years. Here's the final source of

DECODING THE ALSACE WINE LABEL

Unlike most other French wines, Alsace's bottles are labeled according to their grape variety. That's the good news for consumers. The bad news is that you'll find lots of other terms on the label, including some that have no legal meaning (such as Cuvée Particulière), proprietary names such as Cuvée Laurence, and the names of the villages or specific vineyards from which the wines were made. Wines labeled Vendange Tardive (late harvest) are made from late-picked, very ripe fruit and normally carry 13 percent to 15 percent alcohol, or more; these heady, powerful releases range from completely dry to moderately sweet. The rare and pricey wines called Sélection de Grains Nobles (SGN) come from even riper grapes, usually heavily affected by the "noble rot" botrytis, and are very sweet, even nectar-like. Many Alsace labels also show the name of a grand cru vineyard (e.g., Schlossberg, Schoenenbourg).

fusion for the poor consumer: Over the past 15 years it has gotten harder and harder to find truly dry Alsace wines, while in Germany more dry wine is made today than in previous years. At the same time, it must be noted that, thanks to their healthy levels of natural acidity, even Alsace wines with moderate residual sugar come across as no sweeter than the typical California Chardonnay.

The distinctly continental Alsace region is sheltered from inclement weather out of the west by the Vosges mountain range and bounded by the Rhine River, the border with Germany, to the east. Surprisingly, in light of its northerly location, the town of Colmar, in the center of Alsace, is one of the driest cities in France, so grape growers in this region are able to pick healthy grapes deep into autumn. Slow ripening allows the fruit to develop intensity of flavor while retaining sound acidity. No doubt global warming has largely been responsible for ever-riper grapes in recent years and finished wines with more residual sweetness.

RIESLING

Riesling is the king of Alsace wines. It is the most demanding and the most age worthy of the region's varieties. Prized more for their intensity of flavor and elegance than for sheer power or weight, the Rieslings of Alsace nonetheless tend to be rounder and more substantial than those of Germany, with somewhat lower acidity owing to Alsace's warmer climate. With the notable exceptions of wines from many of Alsace's grand cru vineyards—i.e., favored sites offering the best soil and ripening conditions—Alsace Riesling typically leads with its fresh fruit, with mineral, floral, and earthy notes adding layers of complexity. But the most serious grand cru Rieslings can be quite austere in their youth and are capable of developing in bottle for a decade or two.

Note that in the following listing of top sources, individual grand cru wines from Riesling, Pinot Gris, and Gewürztraminer may be bottled as Vendange Tardive in the ripest years.

BANG FOR THE BUCK. Top examples from grand cru vineyards are typically in the $30 to $60 range, and sometimes higher, but entry-level Rieslings can offer very good value, not to mention immediate drinkability.

2004 ★★★★   2003 ★★   2002 ★★★+   2001 ★★★★–

RECOMMENDED PRODUCERS

Domaine Léon Beyer. This producer has resisted the trend in Alsace toward wines with increasing residual sugar: the Beyer wines are drier than the norm in every category. Best here are Riesling (and Gewürztraminer) bottlings at the réserve level and higher.

Riesling Les Ecaillers		`02`	`01`	$$
Riesling Comtes d'Eguisheim	`02`	`01`	`00`	$$$

Domaine Paul Blanck. The Blanck family's grand crus are serious, minerally wines, released later than most and meant for aging. They are also reasonably priced by Alsace standards.

Riesling Schlossberg	`02`	$$$
Riesling Furstentum	`04`	$$$

Domaine Albert Boxler. Structured, concentrated, mineral-driven Rieslings with texture, weight, and cellaring potential. The Boxlers benefit from holdings in two of the region's best grand crus for Riesling.

Riesling Brand	`02`	$$$
Riesling Sommerberg	`02`	$$$

Domaine Marcel Deiss. Jean-Michel Deiss is attempting to resurrect the original style of Alsace winemaking by introducing field blends, labeled only by the name of the site, that he believes can best communicate the personality of each vineyard. Specificity of site and soil is everything for this uncompromising winemaker, but his basic, communal bottlings are wonderfully pure, complex examples of their varieties. Prices here are generally high.

Riesling St. Hippolyte	`02`	$$$
Grasberg	`02`	$$$$

Domaine Dirler-Cadé. Dry, classically structured, mineral-rich wines made in the warmer southern end of the region. Dirler's slow-developing wines are typically suggestive of citrus and orchard fruits but also display stronger soil tones than most in the region.

Riesling Bollenberg	`02`	$$
Riesling Saering	`02`	$$$

Josmeyer. Proprietor Jean Meyer is a well-known gourmand whose wines are among the most food-friendly of Alsace: vibrant, crisp, and light on their feet. The Rieslings here are minerally, focused, on the dry side, and capable of aging, especially at the upper end of the price range.

Riesling Le Kottabe		04	$
Riesling Les Pierrets	02	01	$$
Riesling Hengst		02	$$$

Domaine Marc Kreydenweiss. Round, textured wines, from an estate that has been farmed biodynamically for more than a decade; the mineral-driven Rieslings are the standouts here. Kreydenweiss encourages his wines to go through malolactic fermentation because he believes that lactic acidity is easier on the head and stomach than malic, and that it is more conducive to digestion.

Riesling Wiebelsberg	04	$$
Riesling Kastelberg	04	$$$

Domaine Albert Mann. While most of the Barthelmé brothers' other wines are fat, round, and at least moderately sweet, their Rieslings are vibrant and minerally, offering excellent cut and clarity. The estate's classic example from the granite soil of Schlossberg is typically austere in its youth.

Riesling Furstentum	03 02	$$
Riesling Schlossberg	03 02	$$$

Domaine René Muré/Clos St. Landelin. A source of rich, succulent, sometimes exotically fruity wines from the relatively warm grand cru Vorbourg. Owner René Muré's section of this vineyard, the Clos St. Landelin, is planted with the full range of Alsace grapes and produces fat, broad, and satisfying wines.

Riesling Vorbourg Clos St. Landelin	02	$$$

Domaine Schoffit. Modernist Bernard Schoffit is a reliable source for creamy-rich and often high-alcohol Rieslings with considerable weight. Even the dry bottlings here normally have significant residual sugar.

Riesling Sommerberg	02	$$$
Riesling Rangen Clos St. Théobald	02	$$$

Trimbach. The standard-bearer in the region for tightly wound, focused, and truly dry wines, especially Riesling. Trimbach's great Clos Ste. Hune from a parcel within the Rosacker grand cru, is widely considered to be one of the greatest expressions of Rieslings in the world. Their Frédéric Émile bottling, true to the sappy, stony house style, sells for a fraction of the price of the Clos St. Hune.

Riesling		03 02	$
Riesling Cuvée Frédéric Émile	03	02 01	$$$

Domaine Weinbach. The Faller family offers an extensive range of pure, highly expressive wines that exhibit strong soil tones and complex, well-delineated flavors. Their concentrated, densely packed Rieslings combine fruity and stony elements in a particularly exhilarating way.

Riesling Réserve Personnelle	04	$$
Riesling Cuvée Ste. Catherine	04	$$$
Riesling Schlossberg Cuvée Ste. Catherine	04	$$$

Domaine Zind-Humbrecht. Olivier Humbrecht's supremely rich, complex, and concentrated wines are controversial owing to their overwhelming power, often considerable residual sugar and flamboyant personalities. But this is one of the world's great producers of white wine, with no corners cut in the vines or winery. It's hard to choose a favorite variety here, as Humbrecht excels with Riesling, Gewürztraminer, Pinot Gris, Muscat, and Pinot Blanc. Vendange Tardive wines here are as rich as most producers' SGNs.

Riesling Turckheim	04	$$$
Riesling Herrenweg	04	$$$
Riesling Brand	02	$$$$
Riesling Rangen Clos St. Urbain	04	$$$$

OTHER PRODUCERS TO LOOK FOR: Domaine André Kientzler, Domaine Barmes Buecher, Domaine Léon Beyer, Domaine Ernest Burn, Hugel et Fils, Domaine Mittnacht-Klack, Domaine Ostertag.

GEWÜRZTRAMINER

One of the wine world's love-it-or-hate-it grapes, Gewürztraminer is for many wine lovers the signature variety of Alsace. Its highly perfumed aromas of rose petal, smoked meat, lichee, grapefruit, and spices are immediate and captivating, although some examples lack refinement and seem a bit blowzy owing to low acidity and high alcohol. The variety is as unlike the steelier, more aristocratic Riesling as a white grape can be. No other region of the world has been able to produce significant quantities of Gewürztraminer that even approach the decadent richness and exotic fruit qualities that the best producers in Alsace achieve. Still, other than late-harvest versions, Gewürztraminer is normally a dry wine in Alsace, despite smelling like a sweet one. Gewürztraminer marries beautifully with rich, fatty dishes like pork and goose or ripe cheeses, as well as with the exotic spices of Moroccan, Indian, and Far Eastern cuisines.

BANG FOR THE BUCK. As with Alsace Riesling and Pinot Gris, scarce late-harvest and grand cru Gewürztraminers are fully priced, but sharp-eyed shoppers can find very good examples at reasonable prices.

2004 ★★★–   2003 ★★★   2002 ★★+

RECOMMENDED PRODUCERS

Domaine Barmés Buecher. A completely biodynamic estate producing clean, vibrant wines that display very good detail and focus. Numerous small cuvées from some of Alsace's best grands crus are bottled individually and the overall quality standard is consistently high.

Gewürztraminer Herrenweg	02	$$
Gewürztraminer Pfersigberg	02	$$$

Domaine Ernest Burn. Powerful, weighty, dense wines with sometimes flamboyant bouquets, usually slightly off-dry. The estate has an admirable holding in Goldert, one of Alsace's greatest grand cru sites for the Gewürztraminer variety.

Gewürztraminer Goldert Clos St. Imer	`02`	$$$

Josmeyer. Jean Meyer has been known to pair six or seven of his Gewürztraminer bottlings with multiple courses at a single meal to show the flexibility of his wines with food.

Gewürztraminer Les Folastries	`04`	$$$
Gewürztraminer Hengst	`02`	$$$$

Domaine Trimbach. The spicy, smoked-meaty, age-worthy Seigneurs de Ribeaupierre is frequently one of the elite Gewürztraminers of Alsace, which is to say of the world.

Gewürztraminer Réserve	`03`	`02`	$$
Gewürztraminer Seigneurs de Ribeaupierre	`03`	`02`	$$$

Domaine Zind-Humbrecht. Boldly flavored, hugely rich Gewürztraminers from sugar-laden grapes, often very high in alcohol.

Gewürztraminer Herrenweg	`04`	$$$
Gewürztraminer Clos Windsbuhl	`04`	$$$$
Gewürztraminer Hengst	`02`	$$$$

Domaine Weinbach. Winemaker Laurence Faller crafts Gewürztraminers that showcase the variety's extravagant richness and exotic perfume, but with precision of aromas and flavors.

Gewürztraminer Cuvée Théo	`04`	$$$
Gewürztraminer Cuvée Laurence	`04`	$$$
Gewürztraminer Altenbourg Cuvée Laurence	`04`	$$$$

OTHER PRODUCERS TO LOOK FOR: Léon Beyer, Domaine Bott-Geyl, Domaine Marcel Deiss, Domaine Meyer-Fonné, Domaine Dirler-Cadé, Domaine Kuentz-Bas, Domaine Albert Mann, Domaine Ostertag, Domaine Schoffit, Domaine Bruno Sorg.

PINOT GRIS

The third grape in Alsace's holy trinity, Pinot Gris is far more likely to produce a fat, oily, even viscous wine than a racy, high-pitched drink. Pinot Gris is characterized by rather exotic aromas and flavors of peach and apricot, tropical fruits, orange peel, butter, nut oil, smoked meat, spices, earth, and honey. As with Gewürztraminer, traditional versions are dry or just off-dry, with alcohol in the 13+ percent range, giving them substantial body and impact on the palate. In texture and weight, the better Pinot Gris are reminiscent of ripe Chardonnay. In the hands of some producers, they are among the richest white wines of France. Pinot Gris is a versatile food wine well matched to the rich cuisine of the region—it's frequently paired not only with patés and foie gras, rich fish preparations and white meats, but even with red meat dishes.

Most bottles one encounters are still labeled Tokay-Pinot Gris, as the wine was historically known as Tokay d'Alsace in deference to the long-maintained belief that the grape had its origins in the Tokaj wine-growing region of Hungary. It is now clear that the grape is almost surely a transplant from Burgundy, where it is known as Pinot Beurot and seldom grown any longer.

BANG FOR THE BUCK. There are few outright bargains here, least of all at the grand cru level.

2004 ★★★+   2003 ★★★−   2002 ★★★−

RECOMMENDED PRODUCERS

Domaine Bott-Geyl. Jean-Christophe Bott, who recently took the family domaine into the biodynamic camp, produces a vast array of essentially supple, easygoing wines. His basic releases are classically built, minerally, and focused while his grand cru and Vendange Tardive bottlings are flashy, weightier, and more exotic.

Pinot Gris Furstentum		02	$$$
Pinot Gris Sonnenglanz		02	$$$

Hugel et Fils. The Hugel style emphasizes minerality and precision and the wines are typically made dry, except for the collection of superb late-harvest wines that have made this ancient domaine famous. Hugel's Pinot Gris bottlings are tensile and firm, with very good aromatic expression.

Pinot Gris Tradition		02	$$
Pinot Gris Jubilee	01	00	$$$

Domaine Ostertag. Long controversial for his aging of Pinot Gris and Pinot Blanc in barrel, the young and restless André Ostertag is best known for his rich but mostly dry Pinot Gris bottlings.

Pinot Gris Zellberg		04	$$$
Pinot Gris Fronholz		04	$$$

Domaine Schoffit. Bernard Schoffit is a reliable source for creamy-rich and often high-alcohol wines with considerable weight. Even the dry bottlings here normally carry significant residual sugar.

Tokay-Pinot Gris Tradition		02	$$
Tokay-Pinot Gris Rangen Clos St. Théobald		02	$$$

Domaine Zind-Humbrecht. Like his Rieslings and Gewürztraminers, Olivier Humbrecht's Pinot Gris bottlings are among the most complex and powerful of Alsace. They frequently have the sweetness and size of Vendange Tardive wines even if they don't say it on the label.

Tokay-Pinot Gris Clos Jebsal		02	$$$$
Tokay-Pinot Gris Rotenberg		02	$$$$
Tokay-Pinot Gris Rangen Clos St. Urbain		04	$$$$

OTHER PRODUCERS TO LOOK FOR: Domaine Barmés-Buecher, Domaine Paul Blanck, Domaine Boxler, Domaine Ernest Burn, Domaine Marcel Deiss, Josmeyer, Domaine André Kientzler, Domaine Kuentz-Bas, Domaine Albert Mann, Domaine Meyer-Fonné, Domaine René Muré/Clos St. Landelin, Domaine Weinbach.

OTHER WINES OF ALSACE

Virtually every producer in Alsace makes a broad range of wines from varieties other than Riesling, Gewürztraminer, and Pinot Gris, and the better ones offer some of the best values in Alsace wines. Pinot Blanc is made in some form by all wineries and can be an outstanding value. Muscat is a pungently aromatic wine that's commonly served in Alsace with two fearsome wine killers, asparagus and artichokes. Traditional Sylvaner and Chasselas wines are made less often today as growers tear out older vines, especially in the best sites, and replace them with more noble varieties. Very little Alsace Pinot Noir makes it outside the local market, but the best ones, made from lower-yielding vines, can be elegant, lighter examples of the variety with considerable flexibility at the dinner table. Occasionally, one encounters Edelswicker, a traditional wine made from a blend of grape varieties, often from younger or lesser vines. Crémant d'Alsace is a cheap alternative to Champagne that has long been popular in Europe. Much of Alsace's overproduction of Sylvaner and Pinot Noir ends up in these sparkling wines, especially now that the export market for Edelswicker is virtually nonexistent.

BANG FOR THE BUCK. Alsace's "other wines" are the obvious place to look for the best values from this region.

RECOMMENDED PRODUCERS

Domaine Ernest Burn. An unusually powerful Muscat with serious heft.

Muscat Goldert Clos St. Imer	`02`	$$$

Domaine Marcel Deiss. This producer makes two different and very good Pinot Blanc bottlings, the spicy, exotic Bennwihr and the more penetrating, stony Bergheim. Deiss also makes a deeply colored, intense, and serious Pinot Noir now simply labeled by its vineyard, Burlenberg.

Pinot Blanc Bergheim	`03`	`02`	$$
Burlenberg		`01`	$$

Domaine Pierre Frick. This biodynamic producer makes one of Alsace's densest and most concentrated examples of Sylvaner from old vines.

Sylvaner Vieilles Vignes	`02`	$

OTHER WHITE GRAPES OF ALSACE

Chasselas: In France today, Chasselas is grown almost exclusively for use as a table grape. But those producers in Alsace who have old vines make rich, creamy wines that can bear comparison to Pinot Blanc.

Muscat: Highly aromatic wines that are normally more refined than Gewürztraminer, and almost always vinified dry. One of the few wines with a prayer of standing up to asparagus. Expect to find notes of ripe peach and apricot, lime oil, flowers, mint, and fresh herbs.

Pinot Blanc: Confusingly, two different grapes can be bottled as Pinot Blanc in Alsace. Klevner makes a minerally, citrus-toned wine with generally firm acidity, while Auxerrois, with origins in Burgundy, yields rich, sometimes tropical, smoky wines with lower acidity and a more glyceral character. When folks refer to Alsace Pinot Blanc as the poor man's Chardonnay—and certainly many of these wines are fresher and more distinctive than California Chardonnay but half the price—they're usually talking about Auxerrois.

Sylvaner: Most examples are thin and mean, with modest bouquet and fruit character and little to recommend them save that they are wet and cheap. The very best examples, though, are bright, minerally, and food-friendly and show vibrant citrus character.

Domaine Marc Kreydenweiss. This estate's Klevner Kritt is dry, firm, and racy, with focused mineral and citrus notes.

Klevner Kritt	04	$$

Domaine Albert Mann. Auxerrois in a regular and an old-vines version, both rich and full-bodied, sometimes reminiscent of Pinot Gris in weight and texture.

Pinot Blanc	04	$
Auxerrois Vieilles Vignes	04	$$

Domaine Schoffit. Powerful, thick, and weighty Pinot Blanc made in the style of Pinot Gris, with plenty of smoky, tropical fruit and chewy texture.

Pinot Blanc-Auxerrois Vieilles Vignes	02	$$

Domaine Zind-Humbrecht. The Z-H Muscat from the grand cru Goldert is rich, concentrated, and packed with exotic fruits and flowers.

Muscat Goldert	02	$$$

OTHER PRODUCERS TO LOOK FOR: Josmeyer (Pinot Auxerrois), Marc Kreydenweiss (Pinot Blanc), Domaine René Muré/Clos St. Landelin (Crémant d'Alsace, Sylvaner, Pinot Noir), Rolly-Gassman (Muscat, Pinot Auxerrois), Bernard Schoffit (Chasselas), Albert Seltz (Muscat, Sylvaner), Bruno Sorg (Muscat), Pierre Sparr (Cémant, Chasselas).

CHAMPAGNE

No other wine region of France—indeed, the world—is as strongly associated with festivity, extravagance, and excess as Champagne. From launching boats to commemorating weddings, birthdays, or sports victories, Champagne exemplifies celebration and the high life. What's lost on most people, though, especially those for whom Champagne might be the only wine they ever drink, is that these are *real* wines, not just expensive bubbles. Note that numerous countries may produce sparkling wines using the Champagne method, but if the fruit is not from the Champagne district in the north of France, it's not Champagne.

Champagne making is the highly refined art of blending base wines into a whole that is greater than the sum of its parts. These component wines come from different grape varieties (the white grape Chardonnay and the red varieties Pinot Noir and Pinot Meunier) and from different villages and vineyards (grands crus, premiers crus, and a host of lesser sites). And because only four or five harvests per decade in this marginal climate northeast of Paris provide the raw materials to make balanced, complete wines—that is, vintage-designated Champagnes, which must be entirely from the year indicated on the label—most Champagnes also combine juice from two or more vintages. For example, a relatively lean, high-acid vintage can be softened by the addition of some mellower, riper wine. Or, wine from a hot, sunny growing season can be given needed backbone and vibrancy through the judicious introduction of some "greener" juice.

Blending across vintages is the way producers are able to maintain the house styles their customers have come to expect. As nonvintage wine accounts for about four-fifths of total Champagne production, it is hardly surprising that the reputations of most major houses hinge on the quality and consistency of their nonvintage blends. Not only that, but the better nonvintage Champagnes on the market today are often every bit as satisfying as the typical vintage bottling—and a lot cheaper to boot.

Champagne is big business: in an average year about a quarter billion bottles are produced. There are more than 20,000 growers in Champagne, of whom around 2,000 make wines from the produce of their own vineyards. Another 3,000 are members of co-ops, which sell their production either in bulk or in generically labeled bottles. The remaining 15,000 sell their production to a few dozen large houses, most of which are owned by large multinational companies and which account for more than 75 percent of total Champagne production.

BANG FOR THE BUCK. Champagne is never cheap, but then few sparkling wines made anywhere else can match Champagne's intensity, complexity, and subtlety of flavor. Still, smart shoppers can find relative bargains by snapping up the best nonvintage *brut* bottlings during the busy late fall season, when these wines are often discounted by distributors and retailers in major metropolitan markets.

2002 ★★★★   **2001** ★+   **2000** ★★★   **1999** ★★★   **1998** ★★★+

1997 ★★★+   **1996** ★★★★★   **1995** ★★★★

RECOMMENDED PRODUCERS

Billecart-Salmon. For many Champagne lovers, this is the house for rosé. While Billecart-Salmon is deservedly renowned for this delicate, impeccably balanced bottling, the house's other cuvées also emphasize purity and precision of flavor, with an emphasis on Chardonnay.

NV Brut Réserve		$$$
NV Brut Rosé		$$$
Cuvée Nicolas François Billecart	96	$$$$

Bollinger. Bollinger epitomizes what is often referred to as the British style: full-bodied, powerful, and rich, more appropriate at the dinner table than as an aperitif, and dominated by Pinot Noir. The house's basic Special Cuvée, which is typically austere on release, features mature notes of toffee and toasted bread due to the fact that a portion of the wine is fermented in cask and to the inclusion of older reserve wines in the blend. In the best vintages, a portion of the Grande Année is set aside for later disgorgement and released as R.D., for "recently disgorged."

NV Brut Special Cuvée			$$$
Grande Année	97	96	$$$$

Charles Heidsieck. Based largely on Pinot Noir and Pinot Meunier, these are rich, deep, complex Champagnes that, in the case of the nonvintage brut, benefit from the sizable percentage of older wines in the blend. The house style is rather full-bodied, but without excess weight or at the expense of fruit or finesse. Fortunately, prices have not caught up to quality here.

NV Brut Réserve		$$$
Blanc de Millénaires Brut	95	$$$$

CHAMPAGNE GEOGRAPHY, PRODUCTION, GRAPES & STYLES

Two districts of Champagne are considered best for high-quality grapes: the Côte des Blancs, whose chalk-and-limestone soils are ideal for Chardonnay, and the Montagne de Reims, which is ideally situated for growing the red grapes Pinot Noir and Pinot Meunier. The Vallée de la Marne, which stretches in a narrow band across most of the region and is planted to both red and white grapes, is the largest area aside from the lesser Aube district, which lies far to the south.

Champagne making is extremely labor-intensive, even if many producers have largely mechanized what were formerly manual processes. After the winemaker creates what is referred to as the base wine from a blend of still wines, sugar and yeast are added to induce a second fermentation that takes place in the bottle. The carbon dioxide that forms during this secondary fermentation eventually dissolves in the wine in the form of tiny bubbles, which remain in the bottle until you pop the cork. Champagne gains in texture and complexity by remaining in contact with its dead yeast cells after this secondary fermentation occurs for between two and six years, and sometimes even longer. Shortly before the wine is to be sent to market, it is disgorged; that is, the sediment is frozen in the neck of the upside-down bottle and popped out by hand. At this point, the wine is bone-dry, with high acidity and an effervescence that would make it too harsh for most consumers. So the producer adds a small amount of sugar dissolved in wine, known as the *liqueur d'expédition*, before the permanent cork is inserted in the bottle. The amount of this dosage is consistent with the house style. Even the category called brut, which technically means "raw," can in practice range from fairly dry to bone-dry, depending on the producer (and in some cases the particular export market).

Virtually all Champagnes fall into one of the following categories: brut, rosé, blanc de blancs, and blanc de noirs (all of which are typically dry), and slightly sweet to moderately sweet (labeled extra-sec—or "extra dry"—sec, demi-sec, and *doux*, in roughly ascending order of sweetness). The overwhelming majority of Champagnes are brut. Rosé Champagne, which comes in varying shades of pink, is most often made by adding a small percentage of red wine to the clear juice. Blanc de blancs Champagne is made entirely from Chardonnay, while the much rarer blanc de noirs is made from only "black" (that is, red) grapes.

Champagne bottlings can also be categorized as nonvintage, vintage, and deluxe. Deluxe bottlings include wines like Moët & Chandon's Dom Pérignon and Roederer's Cristal, and are usually but not always vintage-designated. These always expensive prestige cuvées are typically made from the best grapes, benefit from labor-intensive traditional methods at every step of the winemaking process, and are aged longer before being put on the market. And they are always expensive, some selling for $200 or more for a standard 750 ml. bottle.

Delamotte. Chardonnay-dominated wines that display focus and finesse. This is essentially the second label of Salon (see page 71), but the styles are different, with the Delamotte wines more graceful and delicate, and ideal as aperitifs. The blanc de blancs are dominated by Chardonnay from the favored village of Le Mesnil-sur-Oger.

NV Brut			$$$
NV Brut Blanc de Blancs			$$$
Blanc de Blancs Millésime	`99`	`97`	$$$$

Diebolt-Vallois. A small, high-quality estate renowned for pure, bright 100 percent-Chardonnay Champagnes from their own vines, the majority in the grand cru Cramant. The house style favors elegance, precision, and intensity of flavor over sheer power.

NV Blanc de Blancs Brut				$$$
NV Prestige Brut				$$$
Fleur de Passion Blanc de Blancs	`99`	`98`	`96`	$$$$

Pierre Gimonnet et Fils. All of Gimonnet's crisp, minerally, lively wines are made from Chardonnay from the Côte des Blancs.

Blanc de Blancs Gastronome Brut	`00`	$$$
Brut Special Club	`98`	$$$$

Gosset. Rich, full-bodied, rather robust Champagnes. This venerable house's blends make use of a large percentage of older reserve wines, with the top wines partly fermented and aged in oak barrels.

NV Brut Grande Réserve			$$$$
Grand Millésime	`96`	`95`	$$$$

Henriot. The Henriot Champagnes are deeply flavored, smoky, and powerful, with a majority of the raw material coming from the house's important holdings in the Côte de Blancs. Quality here has risen rapidly in recent years.

NV Souverain Brut			$$$
NV Blanc Souverain			$$$
Millésime Brut	`96`	`95`	$$$$

Jacquesson. Creamy-rich, spicy, nuanced wines, given added complexity by some aging in large oak casks. Look for the grand cru bottlings too.

NV Perfection Brut		$$$
Signature Extra Brut	`95`	$$$$

Guy Larmandier. Racy, elegant, Chardonnay-based Champagnes that receive minimal or even no *dosage*. The estate's holdings in Vertus and Cramant in the Côte de Blancs ensure wines with excellent delineation, finesse, and intensity of flavor.

NV Cramant Grand Cru	$$$
NV Rosé	$$$

Krug. To many Champagne aficionados, Krug stands in a category by itself. Krug is the only large house that ferments all its wines in small barrels, and its unfiltered Champagnes are rich, toasty, and dense. The basic blend (Krug calls it multivintage rather than nonvintage) includes a high percentage of reserve wine, sometimes from vintages up to 20 years old, and literally dozens of component wines, with the result that is a benchmark for the region. The very pale-colored rosé, which also includes older wine, is more often like a great red Burgundy than a Champagne in aromatic character as well as in body. Krug's breathtakingly expensive Clos de Mesnil is an essence of Mesnil Chardonnay.

NV Brut Grande Cuvée		$$$$$
NV Rosé		$$$$$
Brut Vintage	90	$$$$$

Laurent-Perrier. This house's rich, red-fruity rosé is made via some skin contact with 100 percent Pinot Noir grapes, rather than being a white wine to which a quantity of red wine has been added. The house's prestige cuvée, Grand Siècle, is a blend of three vintages and a distinct step up in complexity and class.

NV Rosé	$$$$
NV Grande Siècle Brut	$$$$$

Moët & Chandon. The largest producer and vineyard owner in Champagne, and one of the most famous wine brands in the world. Their Brut Imperial, the largest-selling nonvintage cuvée of Champagne is of average quality, but the house's prestige Cuvée Dom Pérignon is remarkably suave, consistent, and age worthy, particularly for a luxury bottling made in large quantities.

NV Millésime Blanc		99	$$$
Cuvée Dom Pérignon	98	96	$$$$$

Perrier-Jouët. Lighter-bodied Champagnes that emphasize balance and elegance, with fragrance and very good fruit. P-J's Grand Brut has consistently been among the best examples of basic nonvintage Champagne for the past decade.

NV Grand Brut			$$$
Fleur de Champagne Brut	98	97	$$$$

Pierre Peters. Elegant, racy Champagnes, from 100 percent Chardonnay, a sizable percentage of which is in the best sites of Mesnil, arguably the best village for this variety in the region. The wines offer an often-exotic combination of soft citrus fruits; penetrating minerality; and nutty, toasty, and spicy nuances. Downright cheap for their quality.

NV Cuvée de Réserve Blanc de Blancs			$$$
Cuvée Spéciale Blanc de Blancs	98	96	$$$$

Pol Roger. The style here combines richness and body with great finesse, with a consistently high level of quality across their range of wines that's virtually unmatched in the region. Their blanc de blancs Brut Chardonnay is a superb example of the genre.

NV Brut			$$$
Brut Chardonnay	96	95	$$$$
Cuvée Sir Winston Churchill		95	$$$$$

Roederer. Of all the best large Champagne houses, Roederer draws most heavily from its own vineyard holdings, the majority of which are in grand cru sites. Older wines are liberally used in the rich, complex nonvintage blend. Roederer's superexpensive prestige cuvée, Cristal, is remarkably dense and powerful; the house's vintage blanc de blancs is consistently excellent and far more affordable.

NV Brut Premier			$$$
Blanc de Blancs Brut	97	96	$$$
Cristal Brut		97	$$$$$

Salon. Salon is one of Champagne's true cult wines. There's just one wine here, an all-Chardonnay vintage brut made in only the best years from old vines in Mesnil and released only when the house deems it ready to drink, which is normally a good decade after the vintage. Very long aging on the yeasts gives this full-bodied, rich but penetrating wine extraordinary complexity and structure, with nutty and toasty notes characteristic of Mesnil.

Blanc de Blancs Brut	96	95	90	$$$$$

Jacques Selosse. Idiosyncratic, almost painfully intense, soil-driven blanc de blancs that demand aging. Often extraordinarily tactile and bracing, and not for the faint of heart. Only the house's powerful and scarce rosé includes a bit of Pinot Noir.

NV Substance Blanc de Blancs Brut	$$$$$

Taittinger. Noted for its aristocratic, graceful wines, Taittinger is among the best producers of aperitif-styled Champagnes. Though lighter in body, Taittinger's Champagnes are consistently full-flavored, with orchard fruit and floral notes and an essential pliancy of texture. The pair of Comtes de Champagne bottlings is superb, with the blanc de blancs typically creamy and seductive and the rosé one of Champagne's finest.

NV Brut Réserve			$$$
Comtes de Champagne Blanc de Blancs	96	95	$$$$$
Comtes de Champagne Rosé	99	96	$$$$$

Veuve Clicquot. Known for full-bodied, toasty, deep, Pinot-based wines, often with a moderate *dosage* (reportedly higher for the American market) that accentuates the impression of size. The *tête de cuvée* Grande Dame is especially dense and powerful, best suited to matching with foods, as one would a white Burgundy.

NV Brut			$$$
La Grande Dame Brut	96	95	$$$$$

Vilmart. These flamboyantly idiosyncratic wines, which are fermented in large oak casks and do not go through malolactic fermentation, are creamy, leesy, and tactile yet bracing, often with exotic suggestions of orange blossom and brown spices. The Coeur de Cuvée is a selection of the best juice vinified in small new barriques. Fine rosé too.

NV Grand Cellier Brut		$$$$
Coeur de Cuvée Brut	97	$$$$

RELIABLE LARGE PRODUCERS: Cattier, Demoiselle, Deutz, Drappier, Duval-Leroy, Nicolas Feuillatte, Heidsieck & Co. Monopole, Lanson, A. R. Lenoble, Mumm, Philipponnat, Pommery, Ruinart.

SMALLER PRODUCERS TO SEEK OUT: L. Aubry Fils, Paul Bara, Henri Billiot, Chartogne-Taillet, DeSousa, Egly-Ouriet, Pascal Doquet, Gaston-Chiquet, Gatinois, René Geoffroy, Laherte Frères, Jean Lallement, Larmandier-Bernier, J. Lassalle, R. & L. Legras, Lilbert, Margaine, Jean Milan, Pierre Moncuit, Ployez-Jacquemart, A. Soutiran, Tarlant, Varnier-Fannière.

LOIRE VALLEY

With the exception of Sancerre, which has been a hot wine in the U.S. market in recent years, Loire Valley wines are among the most underappreciated of France. The wines made from vineyards alongside France's longest river are aromatic, brisk, and generally well suited for early drinking; what they sometimes lack in flesh and complexity they more than make up for in sheer vibrancy and food-friendliness. The majority of this region's production is white, and white wine accounts for most Loire Valley wine shipped to the U.S.

Virtually all of the Loire Valley's best bottles come from four grape varieties. The Sauvignon Blanc grape, which makes the perfect summertime white wine—refreshingly brisk and dry—finds its greatest expression in Sancerre and Pouilly-Fumé. Chenin Blanc, a white grape grown in a variety of sites from Vouvray to Savenniéres, yields wines that range in style from austere, minerally, and bone-dry to lusciously sweet. There is even a sparkling wine made from Chenin Blanc. The chief red grape of the region is Cabernet Franc, which makes a fragrant, juicy, light- to-medium-bodied wine in reasonably ripe years but can be rather green, if not downright underripe, in cooler vintages. Recent vintages, happily, have shown more consistent ripeness, owing in equal part to global warming and to a variety of viticultural improvements aimed at reducing yields, increasing grape sugars, and lowering acid levels. And of course there's Muscadet, the ultimate oyster wine, made from the Melon de Bourgogne grape in a cool, ocean-influenced climate where the Loire Valley reaches the Atlantic. Most Loire Valley wines are made without the influence of new oak barrels; what they offer, first and foremost, are the flavors of fresh fruit and an expression of minerality.

SAUVIGNON BLANC

Sauvignon Blanc is most famous as the grape responsible for Sancerre and Pouilly-Fumé, two of the most popular and energizing white wines of France. In the eastern portion of the Loire Valley, Sauvignon Blanc (which is often simply referred to here as Sauvignon) produces bracing, aromatically pungent wines with strong citrus and

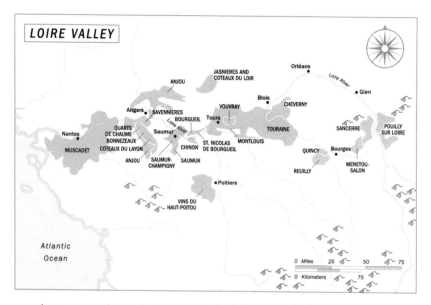

gooseberry tones along with grassy and herbal notes, which in extreme cases or underripe vintages can cross over to green or herbaceous. A whiff of what the French call *pipi de chat* (cat pee) is also present in many Loire Valley Sauvignons; while this element can add a note of complexity in small doses, it can easily become overbearing. The best examples from the Loire Valley display clear mineral nuances and a distinctly dry chalkiness resulting from the limestone-dominated soil.

Most high-quality Loire Sauvignon Blanc is fermented in temperature-controlled stainless steel tanks or in glass- or enamel-lined concrete tanks to preserve the vibrant, nervy quality of the wines. But some producers like to experiment with barrel fermentation and aging in small, sometimes new barriques—with mixed and occasionally disastrous results. No other wine-producing region on earth can quite match the Loire Valley for the pungent citric/minerally/grassy style of Sauvignon (New Zealand comes closest), but many have mimicked the oaky style, and much of this latter type of wine seems to miss the point of the variety.

SANCERRE: Classic Sancerre has always been characterized by vibrancy, steeliness, minerality, and pronounced Sauvignon pungency. Its fruit profile tends to the citric, evoking lemon, lime, and grapefruit. In riper years, or in the hands of some modernist producers, the wines are riper and rounder, more suggestive of orchard fruits like pear, quince, and apple. Whichever style one prefers, most aficionados agree that Sancerre should always be a wine of elegance, precision, and focus rather than volume and weight.

Most of the best producers are based in the villages of Bué and Verdigny. Chavignol, the other village with exceptional vineyards and a large number of quality-minded producers, is actually an appellation unto itself, and the wines are sometimes labeled as Chavignol rather than Sancerre. Broadly speaking, the wines of Chavignol are more powerful and intense while those of Bué and to a lesser extent Verdigny are more elegant and racy, with a subtle minerality. With rare exceptions, even the best Sancerres benefit only slightly from cellaring and are best drunk within three years of the vintage.

POUILLY-FUMÉ: Compared to the wines of their more exalted neighbor Sancerre, Pouilly-Fumé tends to be richer and a bit fuller-bodied, with greater aromatic pungency. The vineyards here feature more flint in the soil, producing wines that are typically broad, meaty, and less delicate than Sancerre. The most prized vineyards are especially rich in flint, or *silex*, which the locals claim is responsible for the smoky gunflint aroma that marks classic examples of Pouilly-Fumé. As with Sancerre, Pouilly-Fumé is usually best consumed during the two or three years following the vintage, before the vibrant fruit begins to fade. Broadly speaking, and with the prominent exception of the wines from cult producer Didier Dagueneau, Pouilly-Fumé tends to be priced in the North American market at about 20 percent less than most Sancerre, as it does not enjoy quite the same popularity.

MÉNÉTOU-SALON, QUINCY, REUILLY & TOURAINE: Ménétou-Salon, located just southwest of Sancerre, yields firm-edged and very dry wines from limestone-rich soil that tend to be a bit more herbaceous and more solid than Sancerre but often represent good value. (There are also red and rosé wines made here from Pinot Noir, as there are in Sancerre, but little is sold into the North American market.) The somewhat warmer Quincy appellation has historically produced rounder, more alcoholic, and less assertively citric wines than Sancerre, but a new generation of growers here is working at making more vibrant, racy wines. The same can be said about Reuilly's white wines from Sauvignon Blanc; this appellation also produces rosé and Pinot Noir, most of it consumed in the local market. Farther to the west, the appellation of Touraine, surrounding the city of Tours, is a growing source of competently made and inexpensive Sauvignon (as well as red wines from Gamay, Cot, and Cabernet Franc, and whites from Chenin Blanc).

BANG FOR THE BUCK. While never dirt-cheap, prices for Sancerre and Pouilly-Fumé have risen at a very modest rate over the past decade, so there are still great values to be found. Consumers are often surprised to discover just how affordable Loire Valley Sauvignon Blanc can be—especially from outside Sancerre and Pouilly-Fumé.

2005 ★★★★+   2004 ★★★

RECOMMENDED PRODUCERS

Domaine du Carrou. Dominique Roger, whose family has been making Sancerre in Bué since the 17th century, produces vibrant, minerally, sharply focused wines from limestone-rich soils.

Sancerre	04	03	$$
Sancerre La Jouline Vieilles Vignes		04	$$

Clos Roche Blanche. Pure, vibrant, mineral-driven wines made by organic methods—and with excellent value. The estate's red wines are also worth seeking out.

Touraine Sauvignon Blanc	04	$

Domaine François Cotat. The Cotat domaine in Chavignol, perhaps the most famous in the Sancerre area, is now divided between cousins François and Pascal, who work in two different facilities. Winemaking is virtually identical in both Cotat cellars but the wines from François are sometimes a bit more high-toned and racy than those of his cousin Pascal.

Chavignol Culs de Beaujeu	04	03	$$$
Chavignol La Grande Côte	04	03	$$$
Chavignol Montes Damnés	04	03	$$$

Domaine Pascal Cotat. Pascal tends to harvest later than his cousin, François; his wines usually display a rounder character, as well as more weight and richness. But virtually all of the Cotat wines have the necessary structure and concentration to reward cellaring, a rare exception in Loire Sauvignon.

Chavignol La Grande Côte	04	03	$$$
Chavignol Montes Damnés	04	03	$$$

Domaine Patient Cottat. Round, exuberantly fruity wines that will appeal to tasters who are put off by an excess of the grassiness or cat pee that characterizes much Loire Sauvignon. Flavors tend toward orchard rather than citrus fruits, and acids are generally ripe.

Sancerre Vieilles Vignes	04	03	$$

Domaine Lucien Crochet. Quintessential Bué style of Sancerre: sharply focused, bright, and minerally, with notes of pink grapefruit, chalk, and pink peppercorn. The estate also offers a small quantity of lively rosé and a classic Sancerre Pinot Noir.

Sancerre Le Chêne	04	03	$$
Sancerre La Croix du Roy	04	03	$

Domaine Didier Dagueneau. Tiny yields, brutal selection, and unflagging attention to detail result in densely concentrated and powerful wines of compelling originality. The most expensive wines of the appellation, from the cult producer of the Loire Valley

Blanc Fumé de Pouilly	04	$$$
Pouilly-Fumé Pur Sang	03	$$$$
Pouilly-Fumé Silex	03	$$$$

Domaine Serge Dagueneau et Filles. Classically proportioned, mineral-driven Pouilly-Fumés with textbook flint and citrus fruit character.

Pouilly-Fumé		04	$$
Pouilly-Fumé Les Pentes	**04**	03	$$

Domaine Marc Deschamps. Tightly wound, pungent Pouilly-Fumés from the limestone-rich commune of Les Loges. The style here is bright, assertive, and citric, sometimes a bit hard-edged. The old-vines Champs de Cri bottling is especially dense and powerful.

Pouilly-Fumé Vignes de Berge	04	03	$
Pouilly-Fumé Les Champs de Cri	04	03	$

Pascal Jolivet. Fruity, clean, suave négociant wines that are relatively supple and less pungent than many.

Sancerre	**05**	04	$$
Sancerre La Grande Cuvée		03	$$$
Pouilly-Fumé	**05**	04	$$
Pouilly-Fumé La Grande Cuvée		03	$$

Baron de Ladoucette. A huge and historically significant estate that's also a major buyer of grapes for their Pouilly-Fumé and Comte Lafond Sancerre. The style here is bright and focused but not austere, more suggestive of apples and pears than grapefruits. The barrel-fermented luxury bottling Baron de L is toasty, rich, exotic, and age worthy.

Pouilly-Fumé de Ladoucette	03	$$
Pouilly-Fumé Baron de L	**00**	$$$

Domaine Mardon. Bracing, even bitingly fresh wine with pronounced citric and mineral character. A more affordable alternative to Sancerre.

Quincy Très Vieilles Vignes	04	03	$

Alphonse Mellot. Historically important producer of taut, sharply focused Sancerres with emphatic mineral and citrus aromas and flavors.

Sancerre La Moussière	04	03	$$

Domaine André Neveu. Supple wines with noteworthy density of texture and soil character, and very reasonably priced.

Sancerre Le Manoir	**05**	04	$$
Sancerre Le Grand Fricambault	**05**	04	$$

Domaine Henry Pellé. The largest and best producer of Ménétou-Salon, crafting delicate, focused wines with strong citrus character.

Ménétou-Salon	04	03	$
Ménétou-Salon Morogues		**03**	$$

Domaine Philippe Portier. Excellent producer of brisk, elegant, refreshing Quincy.

Quincy	**05**	04	$

Domaine Hippolyte Reverdy. Steely, tangy Sancerre with strong citrus notes and lip-smacking acidity—real wine-class Loire Valley Sauvignon.

Sancerre	04		$$

Domaine Jean Thomas. Verdigny-based grower producing supple, juicy wines that emphasize orchard fruits and softer citrus fruits over herbal qualities.

Sancerre Clos de la Crèle	04	03	$$

Domaine Thomas-Labaille. Among the top producers in Chavignol, Jean-Paul Labaille is a reliable source of concentrated but balanced and pure Sancerres, with admirable minerality and focus even in riper years.

Sancerre Les Monts Damnés	04		$$

Domaine Vacheron. Lush, fruit-driven wines that retain the classic Sancerre qualities of brightness, balance, and focus. An extremely reliable producer, even in the most difficult vintages. Look also for the estate's rich but tangy Sancerre rouge, made from Pinot Noir.

Sancerre	04	03	$$

OTHER PRODUCERS TO LOOK FOR: Domaine Bailly-Reverdy (Sancerre), Domaine Claude Lafond, Domaine Jean-Paul Balland (Sancerre), Domaine A. Cailbourdin (Pouilly-Fumé), Domaine de la Charmoise (Touraine), Domaine Girard (Sancerre), Domaine Vincent Pinard (Sancerre), Domaine Michel Redde (Sancerre), Domaine Jean Reverdy et Fils (Sancerre), Domaine Hervé Séguin (Pouilly-Fumé), Jean-Michel Sorbe (Quincy), Domaine Tinel-Blondelet (Pouilly-Fumé), Château de Tracy (Pouilly-Fumé), Domaine Edmond Vatan (Sancerre).

CHENIN BLANC

Known in the Anjou and Touraine districts of the Loire Valley as the Pineau de la Loire, the Chenin Blanc grape lends itself to an extraordinary range of styles, from bracing, bone-dry Savennières and Vouvrays (there is also a sparkling version), to medium-dry, or demi-sec, wines, to some of the world's most staggeringly rich late-harvest wines made in years that benefit from the arrival of botrytis. General characteristics of Chenin include citrus fruits, peach, pear, apple, and quince; spring flowers and honeysuckle; occasionally a lanolin/wet wool element; and assertive mineral and earthy notes, sometimes reminiscent of fresh, sweet mushrooms.

Chenin Blancs in both dry and sweet styles are noted for their longevity—especially those from Vouvray. The very sweetest bottlings from Chenin Blanc are among the longest-lived nonfortified wines in the world. Note that, compared to Sauternes for example, sweet wines from the Loire Valley are lower in alcohol, higher in acidity, and dominated by the aromas and flavors of fruit rather than oak barrels.

BANG FOR THE BUCK. As Chenin Blanc is far from fashionable, few wines are over-priced, although the finest sweet wines from the best vintages are rare and expensive. Montlouis can be an exceptional value, often less than half the price of Vouvray. But even Vouvray is generally priced quite reasonably.

Classic dry Chenin Blanc: 2004 ★★★+ 2003 ★★★★+
Chenin Blanc with significant residual sugar: 2004 ★★★ 2003 ★★★★+

RECOMMENDED PRODUCERS

Domaine des Aubuisières. Bernard Fouquet produces rich, deep wines that show strong mineral qualities and sound structure. They are often distinctly opulent, with a tendency toward sweetness. Pricing is friendly.

Vouvray Cuvée de Silex	04	03	$$
Vouvray Le Bouchet		02	$$
Vouvray Le Marigny		02	$$

Domaine des Baumard. The Baumard house style emphasizes ripe, round fruit over the more earthy, mineral qualities of most other Savennières, and the Baumard wines are enjoyable sooner than most. Baumard's sweet wines are round and lush; though approachable early, they have an admirable track record for aging.

Savennières Clos du Papillon	03	$$
Savennières Trie Spéciale	03	$$
Coteaux du Layon Clos de Ste. Cathérine	03	$$$

Domaine Champalou. A user-friendly, fruit-dominated style of Vouvray, typically with sound but not especially bracing acidity.

Vouvray	05	04	$

Domaine François Chidaine. Perfumed, nuanced, soil-driven wines with excellent mineral cut and subtle orchard fruit notes. The dry versions are arguably the most impressive.

Montlouis Les Choisilles Sec	04	$$
Montlouis Clos des Tuffeaux	04	$$

Domaine du Closel. Long a leader of the appellation, with a sizable holding in the prized Clos du Papillon. Very low yields result in concentrated, deep, powerful wines that are often simultaneously dry and exotic.

Savennières La Jalousie	04	03	$$
Savennières Clos du Papillon	04	03	$$

Clos Baudoin. This historic estate in Vouvray, previously owned by Prince Poniatowski, a descendant of the last royal family of Poland, is now under the control of François Chidaine, of Montlouis fame, who is reviving the estate after years of neglect. The wines are once again pure, vivid expressions of Vouvray minerality.

Vouvray Clos Baudoin	04	03	$$
Vouvray Moelleux		03	$$$

CHENIN BLANC IN ITS MANY MANIFESTATIONS

- **Vouvray:** Depending on the site, the weather and the winemaker's proclivities, Vouvray may be dry (sec), off-dry (demi-sec), medium sweet (*moelleux*), or luscious beyond all reason (*doux, liquoreux*, or a variety of proprietary names). Underripe Vouvray grapes and those from lesser vineyards are often turned into sparkling wine, as this grape can be tooth-rattlingly austere in lesser vintages. The best dry Vouvrays are approachable when young, though high in acidity, and gain in complexity for a decade or more. Deposits of *tuffeau* (soft limestone) under some of the best hillside sites are partly responsible for the unique minerally, earthy character of many Vouvrays.
- **Montlouis:** Vouvray's less-exalted cousin on the opposite bank of the Loire produces more easygoing, rapidly maturing wines than typical Vouvray.
- **Savennières:** Mineral-dominated, steely examples of Loire Valley Chenin Blanc. Savennières is challenging, soil-driven, uncompromising, and even austere in its youth. Classic examples demand up to a decade in the cellar before revealing much in the way of fruit but can be exceptionally rewarding for patient collectors. With age, a honeyed, nutty richness emerges to accompany the citrus, pith, chalk, and earth tones.
- **Coteaux du Layon:** The largest of the exclusively sweet wine appellations of the Loire Valley. Classic versions are round, mellow, and often gentle compared to Quarts du Chaume and Bonnezeaux.
- **Bonnezeaux:** Bonnezeaux are Chenin Blanc's velvety-sweet elixirs from freakishly ripe grapes, the best of which retain Chenin Blanc's firm acidity. These wines are honeyed, tropical-fruity, and usually heavily botrytized; they rank among the most dramatic sweet wines of France, as AOC law dictates that they must contain at least 230 grams of residual sugar per liter, the highest of all Loire appellations.
- **Quarts de Chaume:** Any wine labeled Quarts de Chaume is sweet. These wines are dense and exotically fruity, heavily marked by botrytis, and worthy of cellaring, even if they typically offer considerable early appeal.
- **Anjou:** This appellation is used for dry white, rosé, and red wines made by producers throughout the region surrounding Angers. Anjou blanc is an often interesting but rather austere wine with a firm acid structure and notes of nuts, earth, and dried fruits; it demands to be served with food. The rosés are typically straightforward and simple. In most cases, the reds (made from Cabernets Franc and Sauvignon, like the rosés) are tough and hard-edged.

Domaine du Clos Naudin. Classically structured wines marked by firm acidity and solid structure in even the ripest vintages. The Foreau family has an excellent track record for producing aromatically complex, unmanipulated, long-lasting wines that benefit from cellaring.

Vouvray Sec		02	$$
Vouvray Demi-Sec	03	02	$$
Vouvray Moelleux	03	02	$$$

Domaine Deletang. Opulently fruity, even exotic wines whose fine mineral qualities and healthy acidity give them elegance. These compare favorably to most Vouvrays, and they're far cheaper.

Montlouis Sec	02	$
Montlouis Les Batisses	02	$$

Château d'Epiré. Traditional, understated, tightly wound, and often austere wines that require cellaring but open with age to reveal floral, nutty, and honeyed notes.

Savennières	04	03	$$

Domaine Huet. Along with Foreau, the standard-bearer of the Vouvray appellation for decades, producing deeply concentrated wines of superb clarity, power, and longevity. The late-harvested Cuvée Constance, made only in the best years, can be one of the greatest sweet wines in the world.

Vouvray Le Haut Lieu Sec		04	$$
Vouvray Le Mont Sec	03	02	$$
Vouvray Clos du Bourg Demi-Sec	04	03	$$$
Vouvray Le Haut Lieu Demi-Sec	03	02	$$$

Nicolas Joly/Coulée de Serrant. Idiosyncratic, wild, earthy wines from the godfather of the biodynamic movement. As Joly's policy is strictly hands-off, the wines vary dramatically from vintage to vintage—one year lean, wiry, and austere, the next honeyed and off-dry, the next in a distinctly oxidative style. Approach these wines with an open mind (and wallet). The Coulée de Serrant actually has its own appellation.

Savennières Becherelle		01	$$$
Savennières Clos de la Bergerie	03	02	$$$
Savennières Clos de la Coulée de Serrant	03	02	$$$$

Château Pierre-Bise. Opulent, soil-inflected wines that frequently combine strong mineral nuances with the exotic honey and tropical fruit notes that come from strong noble rot influence.

Quarts de Chaume	04	03	$$$
Coteau du Layon Beaulieu L'Anclaie	04	03	$$$
Coteau du Layon Beaulieu Les Rouannières	04	03	$$$

Domaine de la Sansonnière. Marc Angeli's version is far removed from standard-issue Anjou blanc. His wines from top sites in Coteaux du Layon and Bonnezeaux are rich and dense but dry, displaying the opulent, even exotic fruit qualities one expects to find in moelleux bottlings.

Anjou Blanc La Lune	04	03	$$$

Château Soucherie. Stylish, restrained wines with good balance and structure, offering a pleasing interplay of minerals, earth and pear, apple and peach. Acidities are sound but rarely intrusive.

Coteaux du Layon	`03`	`02`	$$
Coteaux du Layon-Chaume	`03`	`02`	$$$

OTHER PRODUCERS TO LOOK FOR: Marc Bredif (Vouvray), Château Bellerive (Quarts de Chaume), Domaine Cady (Coteaux du Layon), Domaine Philippe Delesvaux (Coteaux du Layon), Château de Fesles (Bonnezeaux), Domaine Dominique Moyer (Montlouis), Domaine Vincent Ogereau (Anjou), Domaine François Pinon (Vouvray), Domaine Pierre Soulez (Savennières), Domaine René Renou (Bonnezeaux).

MUSCADET

There are actually four Muscadet appellations—Muscadet, Muscadet Sèvre et Maine, Muscadet Coteaux de la Loire, and Muscadet Côtes de Grandlieu—located around the city of Nantes at the Atlantic end of the Loire. Although all four make wine from the Melon grape, which originated in Burgundy, nearly all the best producers are in the Muscadet Sèvre et Maine area. The top examples of Muscadet are lean, penetrating, and firmly structured, with mouthwatering acidity and pronounced mineral and citrus character. But too many examples are simply thin, watery, and shrill, from overcropped vines harvested by machine. Look for wines designated *sûr lie*; these have been aged on their lees, which generally adds richness and complexity, and occasionally a slight fizziness. Muscadet is perhaps the ultimate oyster wine, as French diners have known for years. With very few exceptions, Muscadet is best drunk as soon after release as possible, while it is bright and racy.

BANG FOR THE BUCK. The world's greatest value in bracing, shellfish-friendly white wine with cut.

2005 ★★★★+ 2004 ★★★★+ 2003 ★★★

RECOMMENDED PRODUCERS

Domaine de L'Ecu. Guy Bossard, who was a Loire pioneer of both organic and biodynamic farming, is a firm proponent of the primacy of terroir. He produces three different bottlings from the distinctive soil types that make up the Muscadet *vignoble*, all of which are classic in style, emphasizing bright citrus fruits, firm minerality, and bracing acidity.

Muscadet Sèvre et Maine Expression de Gneiss	`05`	`04`	$$
Muscadet Sèvre et Maine Expression de Orthogneiss		`05`	$$
Muscadet Sèvre et Maine Expression de Granit		`05`	$$

Domaine de la Louvetrie. Jo Landron has emerged as a leading producer of Muscadet, fashioning crisp, soil-driven wines from fastidiously farmed vineyards. These are especially food-friendly.

Muscadet Sèvre et Maine Amphibolite Nature	04	03	$
Muscadet Sèvre et Maine Hermine d'Or	04	03	$

Domaine Luneau-Papin. Exuberant, tangy, characterful wines made with minimal intervention, often bottled with a touch of spritz. The estate benefits from a high percentage of old vines.

Muscadet Sèvre et Maine Pierre de la Grange	04	03	$
Muscadet Sèvre et Maine Clos des Allées	04	03	$

Domaine de la Pépière. Marc Ollivier produces some of the most exciting wines of the Loire region. These are impeccably balanced, firmly structured, and very pure Muscadets that actually improve with some time in bottle. For the quality, they are absolute steals.

Muscadet Sèvre et Maine		05	$
Muscadet Sèvre et Maine Clos des Briords Cuvée Vieilles Vignes 05	04		$

Domaine de la Quilla. Racy, minerally Muscadet, aged on its lees without any loss of exuberance or freshness.

Muscadet Sèvre et Maine	04	03	$

Château de la Ragotière. Elegant, true-to-type Muscadet, with vibrant lemon and mineral notes. Great value, too.

Muscadet Sèvre et Maine	05	04	$

OTHER PRODUCERS TO LOOK FOR: Domaine Michel Bregeon, Château de Chasseloir, Chereau-Carré, Domaine de la Borne, Louis Metaireau.

CABERNET FRANC

The Loire Valley's most renowned red wines, Bourgueil and Chinon, are made from Cabernet Franc, as are the mostly lighter, friendlier wines of Anjou and the somewhat more serious wines of Saumur-Champigny. Until recently, the aroma and flavor profile of Cabernet Franc had been decidedly out of step with the tastes of modern wine drinkers: herbal and peppery, with notes of tobacco leaf, menthol, and licorice, and often rather dry-edged tannins. But thanks to a recent string of favorable growing seasons, and to considerable work in the vineyards to reduce vine yields and promote greater ripeness of the grapes, today's Loire Valley Cabernet Francs possess more flesh and sweetness of fruit than ever before. These wines are also wonderfully flexible at the table. (Incidentally, when it was discovered that a compound called resveratrol, which is found in the skins of many red grapes, offers cardiovascular and anticarcinogenic benefits, the Cabernet Franc variety was found to be particularly high in this substance.) Cabernet Sauvignon is making inroads lately in the Loire Valley, and up to 25 percent is now allowed in Chinon as well as Bourgueil, much to the consternation of purists.

BANG FOR THE BUCK. Prices for Loire Valley Cabernet Franc are generally reasonable, and there are many values to be found.

2004 ★★★+   2003 ★★★★★–   2002 ★★★★–

IMPORTANT APPELLATIONS FOR CABERNET FRANC

- **Chinon:** Two types of wine are made in Chinon. Those from sandy soils along the river tend to be elegant, refreshing, and relatively straightforward examples of Loire Cabernet Franc, while wines made from the best hillside vineyards are potentially denser, richer, and more powerful. Lighter versions of Cabernet Franc are quintessential bistro wines, enjoyed for their acidity and refreshingly bitter bite (not unlike the refreshing quality of Campari). The more serious versions are eminently age worthy, shedding their tannin and acid structure over the years and developing smoky, meaty, dark fruit qualities akin to those of Bordeaux.

- **Bourgueil and St. Nicolas de Bourgueil:** Along with Chinon, Bourgueil is where one finds the most serious and age-worthy red wines of the Loire Valley. Still, the majority of these wines, especially from cooler growing seasons in which the grapes reach only moderate ripeness levels, are light and easygoing and meant to be drunk within a year or two after release.

- **Saumur-Champigny:** Potentially dense, structured wines that improve slowly in bottle; the most serious producers here make deep wines that belong on the same table as the best examples from Chinon and Bourgueil. But there's also an ocean of accessible lighter wine valued more for early quaffing than for contemplation. Saumur-Champigny tends to be more fruit-driven and less herbal than Chinon and Bourgueil.

- **Anjou:** Mostly Cabernet Franc wines for early drinking, but the appellation also produces some reds from Cabernet Sauvignon and Gamay. Classic examples are characterized by red fruits and early drinkability; they are simple but satisfying wines that complement bistro cuisine.

RECOMMENDED PRODUCERS

Domaine Philippe Alliet. Serious, powerful Chinons that demand cellaring. These age along a curve that would be the envy of many modern Bordeaux wines.

Chinon Vieilles Vignes	`03`	`02`	$$
Chinon Coteau de Noiré	`03`	`02`	$$$

Domaine Bernard Baudry. Firmly structured, vibrant wines with juicy, red berry fruit and supple, fine tannins. These wines are deceptively easy to drink on release but develop with time in bottle—especially the old-vines Grézeaux, which is from a limestone-rich hillside.

Chinon Les Granges	`05`	**`04`**	**`03`**	$$
Chinon Les Grézeaux			**`03`**	$$

Domaine Breton. Vibrant wines that are quite literally alive. Pierre Breton is a hands-off, organic winemaker whose unmanipulated bottlings are often slightly earthy and funky but undeniably reflect their soil.

Bourgueil Les Galichets	**`04`**	**`03`**	$$
Bourgueil Clos Sénéchal		**`02`**	$$

Domaine Filliatreau. Elegant, deeply fruity wines with excellent focus and structure. The Grande Vignolle offers very good cellaring potential, while the Saumur Château Fouquet is a superb value.

Saumur Château Fouquet	**`04`**	`03`	$
Saumur-Champigny La Grande Vignolle	**`04`**	**`03`**	$$

Domaine Charles Joguet. The reference point for Chinon for many wine lovers: deeply fruity and often powerful wines that are rarely hard in their youth but nearly always repay cellaring.

Chinon Cuvée Terroir	04	`03`	$$
Chinon Clos du Chêne Vert	04	**`03`**	$$$
Chinon Clos de la Dioterie	04	**`03`**	$$$

Domaine Olga Raffault. Traditional, solid wines from old vines in top sites. Densely packed, honest and unadorned, tending more to black fruits than red, austere at the outset, and built for aging.

Chinon La Poplinière	04	**`03`**	$$
Chinon Les Picasses		`02`	$$

Clos Rougeard. Organically made wines from low-yielding old vines. The Foucault brothers ferment their wines in barrel and give them extended aging in oak to tame the Cabernet Franc tannins. These deep, structured, and age-worthy wines, typically released later than most, are made in small quantities and have achieved near-cult status in France.

Saumur-Champigny Le Bourg	**`02`**	$$$$
Saumur-Champigny Les Poyeux	**`02`**	$$$

Domaine Joël Taluau. Elegant, bright wines with vibrant berry fruit accented by violet and pepper. The top producer in St. Nicolas de Bourgueil.

St. Nicolas de Bourgueil	`03`	$$
St. Nicolas de Bourgueil Vieilles Vignes	`03`	$$

OTHER PRODUCERS TO LOOK FOR: Domaine Yannick Amirault (Bourgueil), Domaine Clos Roche Blanche (Touraine), Domaine Couly-Dutheil (Chinon), Domaine Pierre-Jacques Druet (Bourgueil), Domaine Olek-Mery (Chinon), Domaine des Roches Neuves (Saumur-Champigny), Château de Villeneuve (Saumur-Champigny).

RHÔNE VALLEY

Along with Bordeaux and Burgundy, the Rhône Valley is the source of some of the world's greatest red wines. But keep in mind that the Rhône Valley is really two distinct regions. The northern Rhône produces powerful, aromatically complex, and age-worthy red wines, generally in very limited quantities, from the noble Syrah grape. Traditionally, most northern Rhône red wines have carried alcohol in the moderate 12 to 13 percent range, but recent warm growing seasons like 1997, 1999, and especially 2003 have yielded considerably richer, more powerful, and more alcoholic examples.

The southern Rhône is a nearly bottomless source of somewhat more rustic and often even richer blends based on the high-alcohol Grenache grape, in a style that can only be described as warmer and more "southern" in flavor—that is, offering a richer mouth feel, a more roasted and sometimes liqueur-like fruit character, and notes of wild herbs and spices. Alcohol levels of 15 percent or higher are not uncommon in the ripest vintages. More than 90 percent of the Rhône Valley's total production comes from the South, and this area is one of the world's great sources of red wine value.

The northern Rhône Valley also produces the apotheosis of Viognier, an exotically scented white variety that has been widely planted on several continents in recent years by growers hoping to capitalize on strong worldwide demand. I have a hard time working up much enthusiasm, though, for the other white wines from the Rhône Valley, most of which are blends based on Marsanne and Roussanne in the north, and Grenache Blanc and less distinguished indigenous varieties in the south. Most of these wines are characterized by notes of honey, earth, and minerals more than by real freshness of fruit; too often they show more texture and alcoholic warmth than flavor. This style can be rough going for a new generation of drinkers who insist on succulence and vibrancy in their white wines. While there are some notable exceptions to this vast generalization (Chave's Hermitage Blanc and a few other white Hermitages, and Château de Beaucastel's Roussanne Vieilles Vignes, are at the top of this list), white wines other than Viogniers are not covered in this chapter.

CÔTE-RÔTIE & ST. JOSEPH

Syrah that is grown on the steeply terraced vineyards of Côte-Rôtie, which date back to Roman times, yields perfumed, seductive, sappy wines that typically show notes of raspberry, violet, black pepper, bacon fat, smoked meat, and spices. Modern-style producers tend to age a good percentage of their wines in barriques (the small 225-liter barrels routinely used in Bordeaux and Burgundy)—often including a high percentage of new oak—while the traditionalists use older and frequently much larger barrels customary to this region. In style, Côte-Rôtie is usually more delicate and scented, like Burgundy, than the brooding, slower-to-unfold Hermitage. Producers in Côte-Rôtie are legally entitled to add up to 20 percent Viognier to their blends (this variety can add aromatic lift and perfume), but few use more than five percent, for fear of compromising the ageability of their wines.

I think of St. Joseph as Côte-Rôtie's less sophisticated little brother: smaller-scaled, less complex, and less refined. The St. Joseph appellation covers a much larger area, stretching from just south of Côte-Rôtie virtually to Hermitage, along the western bank of the Rhône River. Because these wines generally sell for a fraction of the price of Côte-Rôtie and the economics of production rarely permit the use of much new oak, St. Joseph typically comes across as less sweet, more *sauvage* (wilder) and more old-fashioned—and sometimes offputtingly raw and austere to consumers who believe that Syrah should be a fruit bomb. But these wines are closer to my idea of classic Syrah than the overwhelming majority of superripe, high-alcohol monsters made in California, Australia, and elsewhere.

Côte-Rôties are normally at their best eight to fifteen years after the vintage, although very few wines will hurt your teeth if you consume them in their youth. St. Josephs are typically best from age three to ten. Top wines from the strongest vintages can offer longer aging potential.

BANG FOR THE BUCK. Côte-Rôtie is made in very limited quantities: total acreage under vine in this appellation is roughly equivalent to that of the three great Bordeaux first growths, Châteaux Lafite-Rothschild, Mouton-Rothschild, and Latour. Older vintages of the top examples are rarely sighted on retail shelves. Not surprisingly, prices have skyrocketed in recent years: today most of these wines sell for $50 to $100, with some considerably higher. St. Joseph, less pursued by collectors, remains reasonably priced (most often $20 to $40), and the best examples offer excellent value in pure, Old World Syrah.

2004 ★★★★+   2003 ★★★★–

RECOMMENDED PRODUCERS

J.-L. Chave Sélection. Gérard Chave's son Jean-Louis has developed a highly successful négociant offering of St. Joseph in recent years.

St. Joseph Offerus   `04` `03` $$

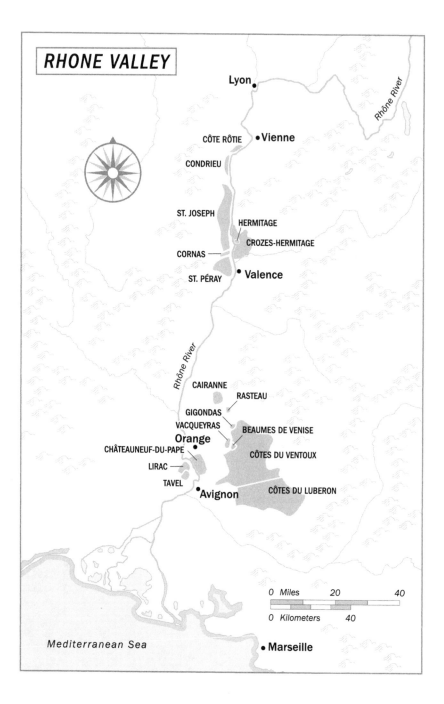

RHONE VALLEY

Lyon

CÔTE RÔTIE • Vienne

CONDRIEU

ST. JOSEPH

HERMITAGE

CROZES-HERMITAGE

CORNAS

ST. PÉRAY • Valence

Rhône River

CAIRANNE

RASTEAU

GIGONDAS

VACQUEYRAS

BEAUMES DE VENISE

Orange

CHÂTEAUNEUF-DU-PAPE

CÔTES DU VENTOUX

LIRAC

TAVEL

Avignon

CÔTES DU LUBERON

0   Miles   20   40

0   Kilometers   40

Mediterranean Sea

• Marseille

Rhône River

Domaine Coursodon. Updated traditional wines of concentration, purity, and perfume, from an old family estate with a high percentage of old vines planted on granite.

St. Joseph		`04`	$$$
St. Joseph L'Olivaie		`04`	$$$
St. Joseph Le Paradis St. Pierre		`04`	$$$

Domaine Yves Cuilleron. This Condrieu specialist also makes Côte-Rôtie and old-vines St. Joseph in a modern, oaky style.

St. Joseph L'Amarybelle	`04`	`03`	$$$
St. Joseph Les Serines	`04`	`03`	$$$$

Domaine Jean-Marc Gerin. Densely fruity, spicy, modern-style Côte-Rôties aged in mostly new barriques.

Côte-Rôtie Champin Le Seigneur	`04`	`03`	$$$$
Côte-Rôtie La Landonne	`04`	`03`	$$$$$
Côte-Rôtie Les Grandes Places	`04`	`03`	$$$$$

E. Guigal. The locomotive of the Northern Rhône Valley, Guigal is by a wide margin the largest producer of Côte-Rôtie. Guigal's limited and costly single-vineyard "La-La" wines— La Mouline, La Landonne, and La Turque—are among the most coveted red wines in the world, with extraordinary aromatic complexity, depth of flavor, and longevity. The good news is that Guigal's basic Côte-Rôtie Brune et Blonde bottling is made in relatively large quantities and is remarkably consistent in quality. Recent purchases of vineyards have enabled Guigal to offer first-rate St. Joseph as well.

Côte-Rôtie Brune et Blonde		`03`	$$$
Côte-Rôtie Château d'Ampuis		`01`	$$$$$
St. Joseph	`03`	`01`	$$
St. Joseph Lieu-Dit St. Joseph	`04`	`03`	$$$

Domaine Jean-Luc & Jean-Paul Jamet. Powerfully rich, complex, age-worthy Côte-Rôtie with a noble rusticity; typically become more refined with a decade of bottle aging.

Côte-Rôtie	`04`	`03`	$$$$

Domaine Michel & Stephane Ogier. This excellent domaine has been taken to the next level by young Stephane, who is making richer, more powerful wines without sacrificing the elegance and purity of his father's style. Stephane also offers a négociant bottling, Les Embruns, from purchased fruit.

Côte-Rôtie	`04`	`03`	$$$$
Côte-Rôtie Les Embruns		`03`	$$$$$
Côte-Rôtie Lancement		`04`	$$$$$

Domaine René Rostaing. Rostaing has become an important vineyard owner in Côte-Rôtie, thanks in large part to superb parcels of old vines inherited from his uncles Marius Gentaz-Dervieux and Albert Dervieux-Thaize. These are aromatically complex, rich, spicy wines that can be among the most flamboyant representatives of their appellation.

Côte-Rôtie	04	03	$$$$
Côte-Rôtie La Landonne	04	03	$$$$$
Côte-Rôtie Côte Blonde	04	03	$$$$$

OTHER PRODUCERS TO LOOK FOR: Domaine Gilles Barge, Domaine Christophe & Patrick Bonnefond, Domaine Bernard Burgaud, Domaine Jean-Louis Chave, Domaine Clusel-Roch, Domaine Courbis, Domaine Edmond Duclaux, Domaine Pierre Gaillard, Domaine Mathilde et Yves Gangloff, Domaine Bernard Gripa, Domaine Jasmin, Domaine Bernard Levet, Domaine du Monteillet, Tardieu-Laurent, Domaine François Villard, Les Vins de Vienne.

HERMITAGE & CROZES-HERMITAGE

Hermitage, historically referred to as France's "manliest" wine due to its deep ruby color and massive structure, is produced 30 miles south of Côte-Rôtie on a south-facing, granite-rich hillside overlooking the town of Tain l'Hermitage. A classic Hermitage offers a deep, saturated color; aromas of black currant, plum, meat, gunflint, tobacco, and spices; and a solid acid/tannin backbone. Though full-bodied and mouth-filling, Hermitage should not be heavy or coarse. Hermitage is typically at its best between 10 and 20 years after the vintage, but the greatest examples from the strongest years can go on for several decades. Think of Crozes-Hermitage, which comes from a wide variety of vineyard sites north and south of Tain, as a junior version of Hermitage—with less concentration, character, and aging potential but at a fraction of the price. Hermitage is the ultimate red meat and game wine, traditionally served with robust, full-flavored fare like T-bone steak, wild boar, or saddle of hare, which can take the edge off the tannic bite of these wines.

BANG FOR THE BUCK. As with Côte-Rôtie, the production of Hermitage is extremely limited and prices are high, with the top wines hotly pursued by collectors who have cool cellars and considerable patience. Expect to pay $60 to $125 for these wines, and even more for some examples. On the other hand, Crozes-Hermitage can offer very good value in the $20 to $35 range.

2004 ★★★★+   2003 ★★★★

RECOMMENDED PRODUCERS

Domaine Albert Belle. A highly consistent producer of nobly rustic pepper- and-black-fruited wines sweetened by the use of some new oak.

	04	03	Price
Crozes-Hermitage Les Pierrelles		03	$$
Crozes-Hermitage Cuvée Louis Belle		03	$$$

Maison Chapoutier. Under the single-minded leadership of Michel Chapoutier, this old family-owned, Hermitage-based merchant firm has returned to prominence since the late 1980s. Chapoutier's *cuvées parcellaires* ("single-vineyard wines"), made in very small quantities and extremely expensive, are their best wines by a wide margin.

	04	03	Price
Hermitage La Sizeranne		03	$$$$
Ermitage Pavillon		03	$$$$$

Domaine Jean-Louis Chave. The Chave family has been making wine in the Rhône Valley since 1481, and Gérard and son Jean-Louis remain at the top of the heap on the Hermitage hill. Their flagship red is a full-bodied and assertive yet refined blend from their multiple vineyard holdings all over the appellation. (In the best years a tiny quantity of the special Cuvée Cathelin is also offered.)

	04	03	Price
Hermitage	04	03	$$$$$

Delas Frères. Another old northern Rhône merchant firm that has been thoroughly resuscitated in recent years under the strong leadership of Jacques Grange. Special vineyard-designated wines are best here, but there are distinctive and interesting wines throughout the lineup of red wines.

	04	03	Price
Crozes-Hermitage Tour d'Albon	04	03	$$
Hermitage Marquise de la Tourette	04	03	$$$$
Hermitage Les Bessards	04	03	$$$$$

Domaine Alain Graillot. The quietly competent Graillot produces accurate, typical, food-friendly red wines that are dependable restaurant favorites.

	04	03	Price
Crozes-Hermitage	04	03	$$
Crozes-Hermitage La Guiraude	04	03	$$$

E. Guigal. Guigal has for years offered a consistently rich, classic Hermitage from purchased fruit. With the 2001 vintage, there will also be a stupendously rich Ex-Voto offering, from vines Guigal acquired in the late 1990s.

	04	03	Price
Crozes-Hermitage	04	03	$$
Hermitage		03	$$$$

Paul Jaboulet Aîné. A major vineyard owner in Hermitage and Crozes-Hermitage, with extensive merchant offerings from all over the Rhône Valley. Jaboulet's Hermitage La Chapelle has historically ranked with Chave's Hermitage as one of the monuments of the appellation—and one of the world's great age-worthy red wines—and the Crozes-Hermitage Thalabert has similarly been a yardstick for its appellation. Quality at this formerly family-owned firm is finally recovering from the slump in the mid-1990s following the death of Gérard Jaboulet.

	04	03	Price
Crozes-Hermitage Domaine de Thalabert	04	03	$$
Hermitage La Chapelle	04	03	$$$$$

Domaine des Remizières. Philippe Desmeure has rehabilitated this previously underperforming estate over the last decade and now makes rich, fresh, and age-worthy wines in a modern style, using a high percentage of new barrels.

Crozes-Hermitage Cuvée Christophe	04	03	$$$
Hermitage Cuvée Emilie	04	03	$$$$

OTHER PRODUCERS TO LOOK FOR: Domaine Yann Chave, Domaine du Colombier, Domaine Bernard Faurie, Domaine Marc Sorrel.

CORNAS

Twenty years ago, Cornas was a meaty, rustic wine whose typically coarse tannins routinely required a good decade of bottle aging. The wines were denser and chunkier than Crozes-Hermitage and St. Joseph and rougher in their youth. They were also cheap. Today, Cornas is just as dense and meaty but a lot more expensive, and generally a bit cleaner than previously, with many wines offering earlier accessibility. Aromas and flavors typically include dark fruits, smoked meat, leather, violet, licorice, and black olive.

BANG FOR THE BUCK. Cornas, a $12 to $15 wine 20 years ago, now routinely sells for $40 to $80—a questionable value.

2004 ★★★★+   2003 ★★★★–

RECOMMENDED PRODUCERS

Domaine Thierry Allemand. A top source for rich, vibrant, aromatically complex Cornas from mostly very old vines. These are complete and satisfying examples with flamboyant Cornas character, made with minimal intervention.

Cornas	04	03	$$$$

Domaine Clape. One of the long-time benchmarks of the appellation, this strict traditionalist makes his flagship Cornas by blending several parcels that have been vinified and aged separately according to the position of the vines on the hillside and the age of the vines.

Cornas	04	03	$$$$

Jean-Luc Colombo. Modern, barrique-aged Cornas from the home domaine of a talented enologist who makes wines for clients and for his own négociant label across much of southern France.

Cornas La Louvée	04	03	$$$$
Cornas Les Ruchets	04	03	$$$$

Domaine Courbis. The 2004s are the classiest set of wines yet produced by this estate. Courbis recently supplemented his Cornas holdings by purchasing some prime old vines from retiring producer Noël Verset.

Cornas Champelrose	04	03	$$$
Cornas La Sabarotte	04	03	$$$$

Domaine Alain Voge. Powerful, structured age-worthy Cornas that rarely carries excessive alcohol and is nicely sweetened by a bit of new oak.

Cornas Cuvée Vieilles Vignes	04	03	$$$$
Cornas Les Vieilles Fontaines	04	03	$$$$

OTHER PRODUCERS TO LOOK FOR: Domaine Eric & Joël Durand, Paul Jaboulet Aîné, Domaine Robert Michel, Domaine Vincent Paris, Tardieu-Laurent, Domaine du Tunnel.

CONDRIEU

The finest rendition of Viognier comes from the small appellation of Condrieu, where the best wines from steep, granite-rich slopes show an exotic perfume of peach, apricot, pear, spring flowers, and honeysuckle; a rich but normally dry middle palate; and an overall sense of delicacy. A growing number of wines are being made with substantial residual sugar, but the trend to increasing use of new oak, which often muffles the variety's delicate fruits and flowers, happily has peaked. Condrieu is generally best in the first year or two after release for its seductive aromatic qualities, but a few of the more classic, mineral-driven examples, especially from Château Grillet, are notable exceptions to this rule. Viognier planted in southern France, California, and elsewhere tends to be far less nuanced and delineated, more obviously warm with alcohol, and even shorter-lived.

BANG FOR THE BUCK. Condrieu is very expensive due to its scarcity more than to its consistently high quality. Expect to pay $50 to $80 for the better examples. As a general rule, stick to producers who specialize in Condrieu, rather than estates in Côte-Rôtie that are best known for their red wines.

2004 ★★★★+ 2003 ★★+

RECOMMENDED PRODUCERS

Domaine Yves Cuilleron. Boldly flavored, lush, round Condrieus, sometimes with a bit of residual sugar. Cuilleron has been backing away from the use of new oak in recent years.

Condrieu La Petite Côte	04	$$$
Condrieu Les Chaillets	04	$$$$

Domaine François Villard. Rich, spicy, fruit-salady Condrieus, often with a bit of residual sugar.

Condrieu Les Terrasses du Palat	04	$$$$
Condrieu Le Grand Vallon	04	$$$$
Condrieu de Poncins	04	$$$$

E. Guigal. Guigal offers superb Condrieu in two very different styles: a classic rich-but-dry basic bottling done partly in stainless steel, and the more exotic, floral La Doriane, made entirely in new barriques.

Condrieu	04	03	$$$
Condrieu La Doriane	04	03	$$$$

Domaine Georges Vernay. Founder Georges Vernay was responsible for replanting much of the Condrieu hillside after decades of neglect. His daughter Christine now makes concentrated, rich, minerally wines in a similar style, from top-notch holdings of old vines planted on steep south-facing terraces.

Condrieu Les Chaillées de l'Enfer	04	03	$$$$
Condrieu Coteau de Vernon	04	03	$$$$

OTHER PRODUCERS TO LOOK FOR: Château Grillet, Domaine Mouton.

CHÂTEAUNEUF-DU-PAPE

Châteauneuf-du-Pape has been one of the hottest categories of the new millennium in the North American market, thanks in equal part to the nearly candied ripeness and full-bodied, chewy texture of these wines and to an unprecedented string of four consecutive very good to outstanding vintages between 1998 and 2001. Châteauneuf-du-Pape comes in a variety of styles, from restrained midweights to extravagantly rich, roasted, low-acid headspinners with alcohol commonly in the 15+ percent range. The most rabid buying interest is concentrated on the latter category. Look for bold, liqueur-like aromas and flavors of cherry and raspberry complicated by game, leather, chocolate, earth, and roasted herbs and spices; lush, tactile mouth feel; and ripe, sweet tannins.

Although 13 grape varieties, including five white grapes, are permitted to go into Châteauneuf blends, the typical wine is based on 75 to 80 percent Grenache, a classic hot-climate grape that produces robust, full-bodied wines with high alcohol, low acidity, and a tendency to oxidize quickly. Small but increasing percentages of Syrah and Mourvèdre are frequently included to add color, aromatic complexity, spiciness, acidity, and structure.

BANG FOR THE BUCK. Châteauneuf-du-Pape, not too long ago a glorified hot-country wine from the south of France, even if the most important wine in this category, has skyrocketed in price since the late 1990s. Expect to pay $30 to $50 for most standard releases, but two to four times that much for limited special bottlings. Although the top

Châteauneufs rarely offer the finesse, vibrancy, or longevity of the best Burgundies at similar prices, they are wonderfully rich, satisfying, full-flavored wines. Detractors say that Châteauneuf-du-Pape is only glorified Côtes du Rhône, and that this appellation on a label routinely raises the price of the wine by $30—or sometimes by much more. Budget-conscious wine lovers looking for immediate gratification will be better off buying the best Côtes du Rhône bottlings at a fraction of the price of Châteauneuf.

2004 ★★★★+   **2003** ★★★+

RECOMMENDED PRODUCERS

Château de Beaucastel. Perhaps the most famous estate in the southern Rhône Valley, producing wild, complex, and age-worthy Châteauneufs that sometimes include all 13 permitted grape varieties. With their animal, vegetal, and mineral aspects, these wines can seem virtually to be alive. The estate's special and extremely limited Hommage à Jacques Perrin bottling, made in the best years, can be the most spectacular, and expensive, Châteauneuf-du-Pape of all.

Châteauneuf-du-Pape	**04**	**03**	$$$$

Les Cailloux. Very suave, silky, refined wines that combine aromatic complexity with uncommon richness on the palate. The special Cuvée Centenaire, offered in the best years, is worth a special search.

Châteauneuf-du-Pape	**04**	**03**	$$$

Domaine Charvin. Superripe, lush wines that combine compelling mid-palate fleshiness and solid underlying spine. An excellent source of Côtes du Rhône.

Châteauneuf-du-Pape	**04**	**03**	$$$$

Clos du Caillou. Very rich, fruit-driven wines with added sweetness and sex appeal from the use of some new oak. Clos du Caillou also offers unusually fresh Côtes du Rhône and Côtes du Rhônes-Villages bottlings. Grenache dominates here.

Châteauneuf-du-Pape	**04**	**03**	$$$
Châteauneuf-du-Pape Les Quarts	**04**	**03**	$$$$

Clos des Papes. A classic, brooding, structured style of Châteauneuf, less showy in its youth than most because of its sizable Mourvèdre component and its licorice and underbrush character, but built to age.

Châteauneuf-du-Pape	**04**	**03**	$$$

Domaine de la Janasse. A range of distinctive Châteauneufs that combine fresh fruit and inner-mouth vibrancy with substantial alcoholic richness. Look, too, for Sabon's fine, if pricey, Côtes du Rhône bottlings.

Châteauneuf-du-Pape	**04**	03	$$$
Châteauneuf-du-Pape Chaupin	**04**	**03**	$$$$
Châteauneuf-du-Pape Vieilles Vignes	**04**	**03**	$$$$$

Domaine de Marcoux. A biodynamically farmed estate making hugely ripe, Grenache-dominated Châteauneufs, frequently as rich as liqueur. Marcoux's Vieilles Vignes bottling ranks among the most sought-after wines of the appellation.

Châteauneuf-du-Pape	04	03	$$$
Châteauneuf-du-Pape Vieilles Vignes	04	03	$$$$$

Clos du Mont-Olivet. Restrained, traditionally made, age-worthy Châteauneufs that emphasize structure and restraint over early accessibility and flash. The old-vines Cuvée du Papet is densely packed, earthy, and particularly complex, with recent vintages featuring increasing percentages of Mourvèdre and Syrah. Look also for this estate's Côtes du Rhône-Villages Vieilles Vignes bottling.

Châteauneuf-du-Pape	04	03	$$$

Domaine du Pegau. A staunch traditionalist making extravagantly rich wines in huge, old wood ovals. Rustic, very high in alcohol, and often downright exotic, the Pegau wines have a track record of aging well on their sheer density of material.

Châteauneuf-du-Pape Cuvée Réservée	04	03	$$$

Château Rayas. Historically cited as the exception that proves that a 100 percent-Grenache wine can be capable of long aging (tiny crop levels and the right soil and site are as important here as vinification and aging of the wine), Rayas has for decades been treasured for its unique combination of almost Burgundian red berry perfume and extraordinary liqueur-like ripeness and mouthfilling richness. Long-time fans of this estate are not yet convinced that today's wines have the dimension and depth of flavor of those made by Jacques Reynaud before his death in 1996, but quality is once again on the rise.

Châteauneuf-du-Pape	03	$$$$$
Pignan Châteauneuf-du-Pape	03	$$$$

Domaine Pierre Usseglio & Fils. Following a generational change in the mid-1990s, this estate has produced a succession of round, enticing, superripe wines made from very low yields and long maceration of the grapes. The Cuvée du Mon Aïeul is particularly lush and thick.

Châteauneuf-du-Pape	04	03	$$$
Châteauneuf-du-Pape Cuvée de Mon Aïeul	04	03	$$$$$

Le Vieux Donjon. A traditional estate that produces a single quintessentially typical Châteauneuf-du-Pape—fleshy, silky, peppery, and flamboyantly ripe—of consistently high quality.

Châteauneuf-du-Pape	04	03	$$$

OTHER PRODUCERS TO LOOK FOR: Domaine Paul Autard, Domaine de Beaurénard, Bosquet des Papes, Domaine Font de Michelle, Château Fortia, Domaine Grand Veneur, Domaine Monpertuis, Château La Nerthe, Domaine de la Mordorée, Domaine Roger Sabon, Domaine Raymond Usseglio, Domaine du Vieux Télégraphe.

SCARCE BUT WORTH THE SEARCH: Domaine Henri Bonneau.

GIGONDAS & VACQUEYRAS

The village of Gigondas, a few miles to the northeast of Châteauneuf at the foot of the Dentelles de Montmirail, was the first Côtes du Rhône-Villages wine to win its own appellation, with nearby Vacqueyras the second to be so recognized. Like Châteauneuf-du-Pape, red wines from both of these villages are blends based on Grenache. Gigondas is typically more fruity and more supple than Châteauneuf-du-Pape, with wines from favored sites at the base of the hillside often showing a vibrant stony character. Vacqueyras is typically a more rustic variation on the Gigondas theme—chunkier and less aromatically complex but satisfyingly spicy, peppery, and ripe in the best years.

BANG FOR THE BUCK. Gigondas, generally less hotly pursued by collectors than Châteauneuf-du-Pape, is usually $25 to $40 and can offer good value. Vacqueyras in the $20 range can be a steal.

2004 ★★★★+   2003 ★★–

RECOMMENDED PRODUCERS

Domaine des Amouriers. Superripe, gamey wines with exceptional aromatic complexity. The special cuvée, Les Genestes, features an unusually high percentage of Syrah.

	04	03	
Vacqueyras		03	$$
Vacqueyras Les Genestes		03	$$

Domaine La Bouïssèire. Big, rich, complex wines that are also uncommonly detailed and age worthy. From some of the highest-altitude vineyards in the southern Rhône.

	04	03	
Vacqueyras La Ponché	04	03	$$
Gigondas	04	03	$$
Gigondas La Font de Tonin	04	03	$$$

Domaine Brusset. Very suave, creamy wines that are explosively aromatic and stuffed with sweet berry fruit. Look also for Cairanne and old-vines Côtes du Rhône-Villages.

	04	03	
Gigondas Le Grand Montmirail	04	03	$$
Gigondas Les Hauts de Montmirail	04	03	$$$

Domaine du Cayron. Traditionally made, solidly structured Gigondas that can be overlooked in early comparative tastings but has a history of mellowing and gaining in complexity with bottle aging.

	04	03	
Gigondas	04	03	$$$

Domaine Les Pallières. Now co-owned by the Châteauneuf-du-Pape estate Vieux Telegraphe and American importer Kermit Lynch, Pallires offers midweight wines that combine early appeal and the structure for aging.

	04	03	
Gigondas	04	03	$$

Domaine Raspail-Ay. Generous, classically made wines that can be youthfully unforth-coming on their release but age well.

Gigondas	04	03	$$

Château de St. Cosme. Precise, scented, modern-style Gigondas from a producer work-ing in a somewhat cooler, later-ripening corner of the appellation. Louis Barruol ages his Grenache like Pinot Noir, with minimal racking, and gets more structure from the inclusion of about 20 percent Syrah.

Gigondas	04	03	$$
Gigondas Cuvée Valbelle	04	03	$$$

Domaine Santa-Duc. Dramatically ripe, superconcentrated Gigondas, often with exotic berry liqueur and chocolate flavors, made from extremely ripe fruit and very long fermentations.

Gigondas		04	$$
Gigondas Les Hautes Garrigues	04	03	$$$

OTHER PRODUCERS TO LOOK FOR: Domaine du Gour de Chaulé, Domaine St. Damien, Château du Trignon.

OTHER CÔTES DU RHÔNE REDS

The entire Rhône Valley is frequently referred to as the Côtes du Rhône, but this is also the name of the generic appellation that covers more than 100 communes in the region north of Avignon. Wines simply labeled Côtes du Rhône may rank at the bottom of the hierarchy, but the best of them are immediate and satisfying, with lush flavors of black pepper, roasted herbs, cherry, cassis, and raspberry. (Côtes du Ventoux is very much like Côtes du Rhône, but a bit lighter in body and even less expensive.) A number of villages have the right to call their wines Côtes du Rhône-Villages, or to append the actual name of the village (e.g., Rasteau, Cairanne). Wines designated *Villages* are generally a step up in quality and price ($15 to $20, vs. $12 to $15 for basic Côtes du Rhône), as they must possess a higher minimum alcoholic strength (i.e., the grapes must be picked riper), and come from vines producing lower yields. Large cooperatives still control a majority of the region's production, but their wines generally offer limited concen-tration and personality.

BANG FOR THE BUCK. The southern Rhône provides a sea of wine, and this area remains one of the world's great sources of full-flavored red wine in the $15 range.

RECOMMENDED PRODUCERS

Domaine Daniel & Denis Alary. Classic plump, round, immediately appealing southern Rhône blends with soft tannins.

Cairanne Côtes du Rhône-Villages	04	03	$
Cairanne Côtes du Rhône-Villages Le Jean de Verde	04	03	$$

Domaine de Fondrèche. A large producer with a wide range of offerings, from the basic, fruity Cuvée Fayard to the more serious, concentrated and spicy Cuvée Nadal. Look also for this estate's delightful, aggressively priced rosé.

Côtes du Ventoux Cuvée Fayard	04	03	$
Côtes du Ventoux Cuvée Nadal	04	03	$$

Domaine Grand Veneur. Friendly, sweet, soft wines, typically excellent value. The Champauvins bottling is from a vineyard adjacent to Châteauneuf-du-Pape, and it shows.

Côtes du Rhône	04	03	$
Côtes du Rhône-Villages Les Champauvins	04	03	$

E. Guigal. This five-star producer of northern Rhône wine also makes a vast quantity of négociant Côtes du Rhône, typically with a high percentage of Syrah giving the wine unusual definition and spine (Guigal's white Côtes du Rhône is also very reliable). This is one of the world's best and most consistent wine values.

Côtes du Rhône		03	$

Domaine de l'Oratoire St. Martin. Spicy, low-acid, fruit-dominated wines in a crowd-pleasing style.

Cairanne Côtes du Rhône-Villages Réserve des Seigneurs	04	03	$$
Cairanne Côtes du Rhône-Villages Haut-Coustias		03	$$

Château Pesquié. Explosively fruity wines from old, mostly Grenache vines. Even La Quintessence, from old vines and a high percentage of Syrah, is best enjoyed in its youth.

Côtes du Ventoux Les Terraces	04	03	$
Côtes du Ventoux Cuvée Quintessence	04	03	$$

Domaine La Soumade. Dense, powerful wines with dark berry and chocolate flavors, sometimes with almost raisiny ripeness. For sheer power, these can often stand up to Châteauneuf-du-Pape.

Rasteau Côtes du Rhône-Villages Confiance	04	03	$$
Rasteau Côtes du Rhône-Villages Prestige	04	03	$$

Château de Segriés. A large, reliable producer of aromatic, lavishly fruity wines from mostly Grenache, with the more serious Clos de l'Hermitage from an almost equal blend of Grenache, Syrah, and Mourvèdre.

Côtes du Rhône	04	03	$
Côtes du Rhône Clos de l'Hermitage	04	03	$$

Tardieu-Laurent. The talented Michel Tardieu purchases superb old-vines material up and down the Rhône Valley and turns out rich, fresh, superconcentrated wines with added sweetness from new oak barrels. While his Côtes du Rhône offerings may be easiest to find, don't hesitate to snap up any Rhône Valley wine from Tardieu-Laurent.

Côtes du Rhône Les Becs Fins	04	03	$
Côtes du Rhône Guy Louis	04	03	$$

OTHER PRODUCERS TO LOOK FOR: Domaine des Bernardins, Domaine de Durban, Domaine de Espigouette, Domaine de Fenouillet, Domaine Gourt de Mautens, Domaine de Mourchon.

LANGUEDOC-ROUSSILLON

You may have read references to Europe's "wine lake"—that bottomless pool of oversupply that in recent years has caused the European Union to try to force grape growers to replace grapevines with more financially viable crops. The Languedoc-Roussillon region of France is this lake's deepest point, where the wine is most plentiful. Until about 20 years ago, the wines of the region were mostly rustic, roasted, and dirt-cheap, of little interest to export markets. But wine production in this sun-drenched, crescent-shaped region hugging the Mediterranean from the Rhône delta to the Spanish border has undergone a sea change in recent years. Today the Languedoc-Roussillon offers wine lovers more ripe, textured red wine for under $20—and sometimes for closer to $10—than just about any other grape-growing zone on the planet.

Most Languedoc-Roussillon reds are blends of two or more varieties. For years, the indigenous and ubiquitous Carignane grape (Carignan in France), which at high production levels tastes roughly like nothing at all, was widely complemented or replaced by more "noble" varieties like Syrah and Cabernet Sauvignon, along with Mourvèdre and even Merlot, but today Carignane is beginning to make a comeback. Cinsaut (Cinsault in France), which has a long history in this region, remains prominent in the entry-level bottlings of many producers. As a rule, though, today's top Languedoc wines, with their generally higher content of Syrah, Grenache, and Mourvèdre, are darker, more vibrant, and more refined than ever. Produced from

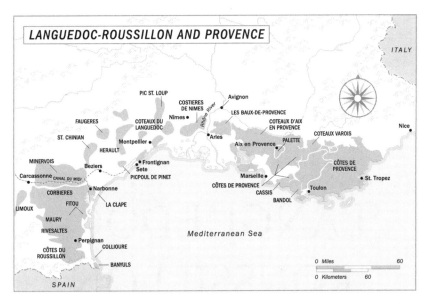

LANGUEDOC-ROUSSILLON AND PROVENCE

ITALY

PIC ST. LOUP

COSTIERES
DE NIMES

Avignon

LES BAUX-DE-PROVENCE

FAUGERES

COTEAUX DU
LANGUEDOC

Nîmes

COTEAUX D'AIX
EN PROVENCE

Nice

ST. CHINIAN

Montpellier

HERAULT

Arles

Aix en Provence

COTEAUX VAROIS

PALETTE

MINERVOIS

Béziers

Frontignan
Sete

CÔTES DE
PROVENCE

Carcassonne CANAL DU MIDI

PICPOUL DE PINET

Marseille

St. Tropez

CORBIERES

Narbonne

CÔTES DE PROVENCE

Toulon

LIMOUX

FITOU

LA CLAPE

CASSIS

BANDOL

MAURY

RIVESALTES

Mediterranean Sea

Perpignan

COLLIOURE

CÔTES DU
ROUSSILLON

0 Miles   60

BANYULS

0 Kilometers   60

SPAIN

riper fruit and at lower yields, and made in more hygienic cellar conditions, modern Languedoc-Roussillon wines are cleaner and much more stable in the bottle than the wines of just 15 years ago.

To a great degree, however, this region has been a victim of its own success, as rising prices for the better wines have convinced many consumers to look elsewhere for value. But even shipments of new vintages of inexpensive wines to the U.S. have slowed significantly, and some of the wines featured in this chapter will be difficult to find. A couple of the very best producers of the Languedoc, Domaine L'Aiguelière and Domaine Peyre Rose, have not been brought into the U.S. for some time, as their importers did not think their customers would accept the current prices for these wines.

While the Languedoc and Roussillon appellations are usually lumped together, wines made in these two areas are typically quite distinct in style. The Languedoc, located closer to the Rhône Valley, produces everything from juicy, Beaujolais-like fruit bombs meant for immediate pleasure to more serious, full-bodied, and structured wines that can call to mind the best examples from the southern, or even northern, Rhône Valley. Roussillon, on the other hand, is an essentially Catalan

Key to Vintage Ratings		Key to Assessments of Specific Wines	
★★★★★	Outstanding	**03**	An excellent to outstanding example *of that wine*
★★★★	Excellent	03	A good to very good example *of that wine*
★★★	Good to very good	03	A disappointing effort (often due to a
★★	Fair to average		difficult vintage)
★	Poor		

region near France's border with Spain, producing distinctly warm wines of near-roasted ripeness—so ripe, in fact, that most consumers are familiar only with the late-harvest and fortified wines of the region. One aromatic element that infuses many of the red wines from across this far-flung region is that of *garrigue*, the wild and pungently herbal/spicy brush that dots rocks and hillsides along France's Mediterranean coast. With relatively few exceptions, Languedoc wines communicate a distinctly warm, southern flavor.

COTEAUX DU LANGUEDOC

The vast Languedoc region is by far the most prolific wine-producing region of France, responsible for more wine than all of Australia. Much of this production can be best described as industrial in quality, but the Languedoc is also home to a growing collection of producers who are intent on making wines to rival the best of the Rhône Valley, often at a fraction of the price.

The Coteaux du Languedoc appellation covers a range of geography and microclimates. At the base of the quality pyramid, the majority of the region's wines are simply labeled as table wine—most frequently the generic Vin de Pays d'Oc—while others can lay claim to the Coteaux du Languedoc *appellation contrôlée*. Many of the best Languedoc sites (see box on page 102) are on limestone-rich soil along a line of hills roughly paralleling the coast, stretching from La Livinière (the favored appellation in the Minervois) in the southwest corner of the Languedoc, through St. Chinian, Faugères, and Montpeyroux, to Pic St. Loup, north of Montpellier. All of these favored spots lie considerably inland from the Mediterranean, and frequently benefit in summer from cooling northerly breezes off the Cévennes Mountains. These areas, along with others like La Clape and La Méjanelle, are allowed to put their names on labels. Faugères, St. Chinian, Minervois, and also Corbières can stand alone, while others (such as La Clape and Pic St. Loup) can append their name to Coteaux du Languedoc. Most of the best Coteaux du Languedoc wines rely on Syrah, Mourvèdre, and Grenache, but a handful of producers make characterful and concentrated wines from very old plantings of Carignane and Cinsaut. It is worth noting, however, that two of the top estates of the region, Mas de Daumas Gassac and Domaine de la Grange des Pères, eschew the Coteaux du Languedoc appellation in favor of the more mundane Vin de Pays de l'Hérault. Forfeiting the name of the appellation, while theoretically risking a lower selling price, allows these producers to transcend what they see as the constraints of the AOC system—most notably, limitations on permitted grape varieties.

Red wine rules in the Languedoc, as in Roussillon, accounting for well over 80 percent of production. Until recently too many white wines were tired, if not

SOME FAVORED LANGUEDOC SITES

La Clape: One of the oldest wine-producing areas of the entire Languedoc, thanks to its proximity to the earliest Roman settlements of Mediterranean France. The arid climate and rocky soils yield powerful wines with dark fruit flavors and surprisingly silky tannins.

Faugères: The vineyards here are dominated by dark soils rich in schist, which, in theory at least, gives the wines more perfume, finesse, and complexity. The appellation's inland location at higher altitude, where day-night temperature variation is more pronounced, also contributes to the delicacy of the wines.

La Méjanelle: The same large, round stones found in Châteauneuf-du-Pape dominate the landscape of La Méjanelle, part of which actually lies within the city limits of Montpellier. While some wines show similarities to Châteauneuf, those that rely more on Syrah are rich and intense, with a dark fruit character more suggestive of the black pepper and olive scents of northern Rhône wines. As with St. Drézéry and a few other villages, wines from La Méjanelle are now labeled under the rubric Grès de Montpellier.

Montpeyroux: Consists mostly of hillside vineyards on limestone and clay soil in a hot inland area with less influence from the Mediterranean. Wines here tend to be powerful, dense, and cellar worthy, with emphatic dark berry tones. Montpeyroux is one of a number of villages that has recently been grouped under the new name Terrasses du Larzac.

Pic St. Loup: Stony, limestone-dominated soils dominate this inland area, situated in the shadow of two mountains, the Pic St. Loup and the Montagne de l'Hortus. Regulations here are the strictest of the Languedoc, requiring vineyards to be planted to at least 90 percent Grenache, Syrah, and/or Mourvèdre. Cool nights and constant air movement prolong the growing season, resulting in wines with a perfumed character, sometimes reminiscent of the northern Rhône, sometimes even of Burgundy.

St. Chinian: Effectively a northern extension of Faugères with similar soils but generally higher-altitude plantings on hillsides. The wines are firm and meaty, with a serious tannic structure, and generally require at least a year or two of bottle aging. The vineyards must be planted to a mix of at least 60 percent Grenache, Syrah, and/or Mourvèdre.

dized, as few wineries had the equipment to control temperature from vinification all the way through to bottle storage. These wines were more likely to be characterized by aromas of white chocolate and honey than fresh fruit. A movement away from traditional varieties like Grenache Blanc, Bourboulenc, Terret, and Clairette and toward more fashionable white grapes like Viognier, Marsanne, and Roussanne is beginning to result in more vibrant white wines.

BANG FOR THE BUCK. Although the number of expensive limited bottlings from the Languedoc has skyrocketed in recent years, this category remains one of the world's deepest sources of bargains in full-flavored, user-friendly red wine.

2004 ★★★+   2003 ★★★   2002 ★★+   2001 ★★★★+

RECOMMENDED PRODUCERS

Domaine d'Aupilhac. Sylvain Fadat makes full use of some of the best old Carignane vines in southern France, producing wines that are explosively fruity but balanced to develop in bottle. The top bottling, Le Clos, a blend of Carignane, Mourvèdre, and Syrah, is more powerful, oaky, and age worthy.

Coteaux du Languedoc Montpeyroux	03	$$
Coteaux du Languedoc Les Cocalières	04	$$$

Domaine Léon Barral. Very naturally made wines, with low levels of sulfur dioxide. The Jadis bottling is a blend based on Syrah.

Faugères	03	$$
Faugères Jadis	03	$$

Château de Cazeneuve. The basic Terres Rouges bottling is an exuberant tank-fermented wine with considerable early appeal while the more serious, barrel-aged Roc des Mates is a brooding, Syrah-based monster that mimics Hermitage at a fraction the cost. Superb values here.

Coteaux du Languedoc Pic Saint Loup Les Terres Rouges	03	$$
Coteaux du Languedoc Pic Saint Loup Le Roc des Mates	03	$$

Domaine Clavel. Pierre Clavel is a quality leader of the Méjanelle area, producing vibrant wines with intense black fruit and pepper flavors. The flagship Copa Santa bottling is mostly Syrah with a bit of Grenache.

Coteaux du Languedoc Le Mas	03	$
Coteaux du Languedoc Méjanelle Copa Santa	03	$

Château des Estanilles. Modern-style, vivaciously fruity, and sometimes exotic wines based heavily on Syrah. Widely seen in top restaurants in southern France.

Faugères	03	$$
Faugères Cuvée Prestige	03	$$

Domaine de la Grange des Pères. Laurent Vaillé offers a single estate red wine, a superrich, layered, and flamboyantly ripe blend of Syrah, Mourvèdre, and Cabernet from hillside vineyards dotted with *garrigue*. His barrel-fermented white wine, made mostly from Roussanne, is a cult wine in the local market.

Vin de Pays de l'Hérault Blanc		`04`	$$$$
Vin de Pays de l'Hérault Rouge		`03`	$$$$

Domaine de l'Hortus. One of the pioneers of the Pic Saint Loup area, Jean Orliac makes serious, dense, but perfumed wines from Syrah, Grenache, and Mourvèdre vines farmed in a wind-blown site. Very good value here.

Coteaux du Languedoc Pic-Saint Loup Bergerie de L'Hortus	`03`	$
Coteaux du Languedoc Pic-Saint Loup Grand Cuvée	`03`	$$

Mas Champart. A relatively new property that produces sturdy wines meant for the cellar, with an emphasis on Mourvèdre and Syrah. These are quite cheap for their quality and seriousness.

Coteaux du Languedoc	`03`	$
St. Chinian Clos de la Simonette	`03`	$$

Mas de Daumas Gassac. Pioneering proprietor Aimé Guibert, working in a superb site with legendary Bordeaux professor and consultant Émile Peynaud, proved in the late 1970s that world-class wines could be made in the Languedoc. The estate's flagship red, based heavily on Cabernet Sauvignon, can be forbiddingly tannic and austere in its youth and normally benefits from a decade of bottle aging. (The estate's highly distinctive white wine is an unusual but successful amalgam of disparate varieties.) Guibert uses the simple Vin de Pays appellation but his red wine has been described as the only grand cru of the Languedoc.

Vin de Pays de L'Hérault	`03`	$$$

Château de la Négly. This estate is best known for its full-bodied, powerful, and staggeringly expensive La Porte du Ciel and Clos des Truffiers bottlings, Syrah wines designed to compete with the most exalted examples from the Rhône Valley (Clos des Truffiers is from very old vines in St. Pargoire, but is fermented and aged at Château de la Négly). The estate's basic bottling, La Côte, is focused and fruity, and an excellent value.

Coteaux du Languedoc La Côte	`04`	`03`	$
Coteaux du Languedoc La Falaise		`03`	$$
Coteaux du Languedoc La Porte du Ciel		`03`	$$$$
Coteaux du Languedoc Clos des Truffiers		`03`	$$$$

Prieuré de St. Jean de Bébian. A pioneer of high-quality wine production in the Languedoc, with Syrah, Mourvèdre, and Grenache introduced to supplement the old Carignane and Cinsaut vines already at the site. Following a change of ownership in 1994, attention to quality has increased, with the emphasis on complexity and finesse over raw power.

Coteaux du Languedoc La Chapelle de Bébian	`03`	$$
Coteaux du Languedoc	`03`	$$$

Château La Roque. A well-situated property producing sappy, dense, aromatic wines from Mourvèdre, Syrah, and Grenache. Vines have been cultivated on this site for nearly 1,000 years.

Coteaux du Languedoc Pic Saint Loup Cupa Numismae	`03`	$$

Château St. Martin de la Garrigue. Intensely fruity wines that are drinkable on release but also built to last. At their best, like poor man's Châteauneuf-du-Pape.

Coteaux du Languedoc Cuvée Bronzinelle		03	$
Coteaux du Languedoc Cuvée Tradition	04	03	$
Coteaux du Languedoc Cuvée St. Martin		03	$$

OTHER PRODUCERS TO LOOK FOR: Domaine Alquier, Clos Bagatelle, Clos Marie, Château de Flaugergues, Domaine Foulaquier, Château de Lancyre, Château de Lascaux, Mas d'Auzières, Mas Bruguiȷere, Mas Cal Demoura, Mas Jullien, Domaine Mas de Mortiès, Domaine de Montpezat, Château Puech-Haut, Château Pech-Redon.

SCARCE BUT WORTH THE SEARCH: Domaine L'Aiguelière, Domaine Peyre Rose.

CORBIÈRES & MINERVOIS

The two major appellations of the western Languedoc, Corbières and Minervois traditionally relied on Carignane, Cinsaut, and some Grenache, which made for pleasant, easy-drinking, fruity wines with a distinctly wild character and no great consequence. Today, as elsewhere in the Languedoc, rising percentages of Syrah and Mourvèdre are contributing freshness, aromatic complexity, and backbone to what were previously more rustic wines. The region of Minervois lies farther from the heat of the Mediterranean coast than most of Corbières, and its wines are typically less roasted and more refined. The village of La Livinière, a particularly favored spot thanks to its terraced vineyards and clay-limestone soils, has earned its own subappellation. Minervois is often a bit lower in alcohol and less solid than Corbières, but its freshness of fruit and aromatic character can make it more flexible at the dinner table. But the similarities between the wines of these two appellations outweigh the differences.

BANG FOR THE BUCK. Prices for the better Corbières and Minervois—rarely higher than $15—are still extremely low for their quality, making these bottlings some of the world's top values in red wine.

2004 ★★★+   2003 ★★★

RECOMMENDED PRODUCERS

Domaine d'Aussières. Domaines Barons de Rothschild, of Bordeaux fame, purchased this vast Corbières estate in 1999. These are powerful, deeply flavored, spicy wines featuring a good dose of Syrah. The "A" is the estate's second wine.

Corbières "A" d'Aussières	03	$$
Corbières Château d'Aussières	03	$$

Domaine Borie de Maurel. Full-bodied Minervois from La Livinière, made in a powerful style that will reward cellaring. The top bottlings are heavy on Syrah, which ensures solid structure and spicy, peppery, berry flavor.

Minervois Esprit d'Automne	03	$
Minervois Cuvée Sylla	03	$$

Castelmaure. Noted Rhône Valley négociant Michel Tardieu consults for this small Corbières cooperative, which is made up of growers focused more on quality than quantity. The usual local varieties are used here, with the particularly powerful and ripe top bottlings emphasizing Syrah.

Corbières Col des Vents	04	03	$
Corbières Grande Cuvée	04	03	$$

Château Etang des Colombes. A producer of classic blends of the appellation's permitted varieties, from the generously fruity Tradition to the more powerful and age-worthy Le Bois des Dames.

Corbières	03	$
Corbières Bois des Dames	03	$$

Domaine Faillenc Ste. Marie. Meaty, dense, distinctly wild Syrah-dominated wines that reveal their sweet blackberry and cassis fruit with a couple of years of bottle aging. The estate also makes a delightful and food-friendly rosé, finished with a bit of residual sugar.

Corbières	04	03	$

Domaine de Fontsainte. Well-balanced, vibrant wines that are elegant and perfumed by Corbières standards, with the Demoiselle repaying aging. The rosé, labeled Gris de Gris, is an excellent value.

Corbières	04	03	$
Corbières Réserve La Demoiselle	04	03	$$

Château de Gourgazaud. Wines based heavily on Syrah, from vines in the favored sub-appellation La Livinière. Great value.

Minervois-La Livinière	03	$

Château Mansenoble. Deep, powerful blends combining almost claret-like dark berry fruits with wilder game and leather notes. The réserve features more Syrah and Mourvèdre, while the basic bottling has a higher percentage of Carignane.

Corbières	03	$
Corbières Réserve du Château Mansenoble	03	$$

Château Maris. Fruit-forward but reasonably age-worthy wines from vines in La Livinière.

Minervois	03	$
Minervois-La Liviniére Vieilles Vignes	03	$$

Château d'Oupia. A high-quality producer of classically styled, berry-flavored Minervois from old hillside vines, ranging from the exuberant entry-level Vin de Pays Les Héretiques to the deeper and more concentrated top cuvées, which show some suave oak notes.

Minervois	`04`	`03`	$
Minervois Les Barons		`03`	$$

Domaine l'Oustal Blanc. A new project in Minervois overseen by noted Châteauneuf-du-Pape enologist Philippe Cambie. The wines are rich and concentrated, with lush but precise fruit and a degree of freshness rare for the region. There are also some exotic, powerful white wines.

Minervois	`03`	$$
Vin de Table de France Maestoso	`03`	$$$

Domaine Piccinini. Serious, dense wines that are heavy on Syrah, with the concentrated cherry and cassis fruit to support their new oak component.

Minervois	`03`	$
Minervois La Livinière Line et Laetitia	`03`	$$

Château Tour Boisée. Sweet, supple Minervois, with an emphasis on lush berry fruit, made from a blend of Carignane, Grenache, and Syrah. Accessible early but with sufficient structure to reward short-term bottle aging.

Minervois	`03`	$
Minervois Cuvée à Marie-Claude	`03`	$$

Val d'Orbieu. One of the most important cooperatives of the Languedoc/Roussillon region, offering estate bottlings (the co-op comprises member growers in St. Chinian, Minervois, and Corbières) as well as its own brands and private labels.

Réserve St. Martin Syrah Vin de Pays d'Oc		`04`	`03`	$
Les Deux Rives Corbières	`05`	`04`	`03`	$
La Cuvée Mythique Vin de Pays d'Oc			`03`	$$

OTHER PRODUCERS TO LOOK FOR: Domaine des Aires Hautes, Domaine Domergue, Clos de l'Escandil, Château La Voulte-Gasparets.

OTHER RED WINES OF LANGUEDOC-ROUSSILLON

The Costières de Nîmes, on the Languedoc's eastern border with Provence and the southern Rhône, features the oldest vineyards of the region, as Nîmes was the first Roman settlement in the Languedoc. As is the case in much of the rest of the Languedoc, high-quality wines with international appeal are a relatively recent phenomenon here. Carignane is the principal grape, with Syrah and Grenache making inroads. As in the neighboring Côtes de Provence, there is also a good bit of

Cabernet Sauvignon and Merlot. Still, most of the area's wines are best drunk before their third or fourth birthday for their exuberant fruit.

At the opposite end of the Languedoc, on France's border with Spain, lies Roussillon, a source of some aggressively priced dry red wines featuring blends not unlike Corbières. The extremely hot and dry vineyards of this dramatic landscape on the eastern edge of the Pyrenees are best known for Vins Doux Naturels (VDN), made by the addition of alcohol to partly fermented grape juice, which results in a wine with high alcohol and considerable sweetness. The VDNs of Rivesaltes include some distinctly rustic and often vaguely oxidized curiosities made from Muscat, and chocolaty-sweet and firmly tannic reds based on Grenache. Banyuls is another VDN, made from hugely ripe, mostly Grenache grapes in France's southernmost appellation, on the Mediterranean just north of the Spanish border. Dry reds from this area are labeled as Collioure.

BANG FOR THE BUCK. The "other red wines" of the Languedoc-Roussillon are a rich source of value, even if prices have inched higher in recent years.

RECOMMENDED PRODUCERS

Château de Campuget. Some astounding values in generously fruity, supple wines with medium weight and light tannins. There are also some very fresh, modern-style white wines made here, especially Viognier.

Costières de Nîmes Tradition de Campuget	03	$
Costières de Nîmes Prestige de Campuget	03	$

Domaine Gauby. The long-time standard-bearer of the Côtes de Roussillon appellation. Old vines, biodynamic viticulture, and attention to detail in the cellar make for wines of real depth and character—as well as surprising aging potential.

Côtes du Roussillon	03	$
Côtes du Roussillon Vieilles Vignes	03	$$$

Château Grande Cassagne. Seriously structured wines for their gentle price tags, the best bottlings relying heavily on Syrah. The rosé is also a consistent winner.

Costières de Nîmes G.S.	05	$
Costières de Nîmes Syrah Hippolyte	03	$$

Domaine du Mas Blanc. Better-known by the name of its founder, Dr. (André) Parcé, who helped to create the Collioure appellation. The estate's dry reds, made mostly from Syrah, Grenache, and Mourvèdre, are rich, dense, and powerful, in a superripe southern Rhône style, while the Grenache-dominated Banyuls—roasted, sweet red wines made from late-harvested grapes—have a rabid cult following in Europe.

Collioure Cuvée Cosprons Levants	03	$$
Banyuls Rimage La Coume	01	$$$

Mas des Bressades. Modern, fruit-driven wines with enticing dark fruit and spice flavors and considerable density and concentration. Appealing on release and perfectly suited to those who favor clean, New World wines. Mas des Bressades also makes an unusually fresh Roussanne-Viognier blend.

Costières de Nîmes Cuvée d'Excellence		03	$
Vin de Pays du Gard Cabernet/Syrah	04	03	$
Vin de Pays du Gard Grenache/Syrah		05	$

Domaine du Mas Cremat. Structured, brisk, focused wines with more emphasis on red fruits than most examples of its appellation. Made for the dinner table as well as for the cellar.

Côtes du Roussillon-Villages	03	$

Château Mourgues du Grès. Dense, powerful wines with a strong emphasis on Syrah. The most serious modern producer of the appellation, attempting to compete with top wines from the Rhône Valley.

Costières de Nîmes Les Galets Rouges	03	$
Costières de Nîmes Capitelles des Mourgues	03	$$

Château de Peña. Modern, fruit-forward, immediately appealing wines marked by a suave use of oak barrels. The "C" is for Carignane and the "S" for Syrah.

Côtes du Roussillon-Villages Réserve "C"	03	$$
Cotes du Roussillon-Villages Réserve "S"	03	$$

Domaine de la Petite Cassagne. Clean, vibrantly fruity wines made for early drinking, plus a delightful and very inexpensive rosé.

Costières de Nîmes	04	03	$

OTHER PRODUCERS TO LOOK FOR: Domaine Bertrand-Bergé, Mas Amiel, Domaine Maria Fita, Domaine de la Rectorie, Domaine Sarda-Malet.

PROVENCE

The Provence region of Mediterranean France, which stretches from Nîmes to Nice, is best known as one of the world's most popular tourist destinations and a bottomless source of pink wine. Indeed, across much of this sprawling region, red grapes are mostly turned into rosés, the majority of which offer more alcohol than real flavor. But across the region, numerous individual appellations produce highly distinctive red wines that express multiple variations on a ripe, southern theme. The most famous of these is Bandol, which has long been noted for powerful game- and earth-scented red wines based on the sturdy, late-ripening Mourvèdre grape. Coteaux d'Aix en Provence also produces predominantly red wines, as do the somewhat cooler Les Baux de Provence and Coteaux Varois. The Côtes du Luberon, which lies farther inland, has emerged as an area with potential for finer white wines as well as for more delicate reds, thanks to its higher elevation and extended growing season.

Most red wine producers in Provence offer at least one rosé. And most of the rosés that are pumped out of the local cooperatives are simple, refreshing wines not to be taken seriously. But the best examples, especially those made in Bandol, are truly distinctive, thirst-quenching numbers with real depth, richness, and complexity.

Outside of the Mourvèdre-heavy Bandol, the red wines of Provence feature varying percentages of Grenache, Mourvèdre, Syrah, Cabernet Sauvignon, Cinsaut, and Carignane. Unlike in other regions of southern France, Cabernet is not a recent arrival in Provence, having been planted here as far back as the mid-19th century. Provençal reds are usually boldly flavored, solidly built wines of at least medium body, with moderate to pronounced tannic structure. They pair well with the assertively flavored meat and game dishes of the region, especially lamb and venison. Provence, incidentally, is a center of organic viticulture, as the warm, dry growing season and Mistral wind normally prevent rot, mildew, and other vine maladies that would normally call for chemical treatments.

White wines from Provence, which are exported to North America in limited quantities, are based on the Ugni Blanc (called Trebbiano in Italy), Rolle (Vermentino in Italy), Sémillon, and the Rhône varieties Grenache Blanc, Marsanne, and Clairette. Viognier has begun to make inroads, as has Roussanne. With rare exceptions these are simple, straightforward, regional curiosities that should be drunk as soon as possible following release, as these varieties have a tendency to oxidize rapidly. The best versions, those that are raised in temperature-controlled stainless steel vats to preserve freshness, are excellent when matched with the seafood-based cuisine of the Mediterranean coast, as well as with the spices and herbs used so liberally in Provençal cuisine. Some of the most compelling whites are made in Cassis, but, due largely to strong local demand for these vibrant, floral wines, only a tiny amount makes its way into export channels.

BANDOL

Bandol, grown in vineyards virtually on the Mediterranean, is Provence's most important and age-worthy wine. Bandols can be fiercely tannic on release, owing to their high percentage of Mourvèdre (some of the best examples are 100 percent Mourvèdre), and typically demand upward of six to eight years of cellaring. But these meaty, musky, minerally, spicy, herbal wines can achieve added nuance and even grace with proper cellaring. Grenache is often blended in to give Bandol more flesh and sweetness, but the addition of this relatively oxidative variety can compromise the longevity of these wines.

BANG FOR THE BUCK. As the longest-lived wine of France's Mediterranean coast, Bandol commands a price premium.

2004 ★★★★– **2003** ★★★★

RECOMMENDED PRODUCERS

Domaine La Bastide Blanche. Firmly structured wines that display earthy and meaty qualities early on but evolve slowly to develop great tobacco- and cherry-laced aromatic complexity.

Bandol	03	$$
Bandol Estagnol	03	$$$

Château de Pibarnon. The most modern of the top Bandol estates, producing a single densely fruity red in the style of a Mourvèdre-based Châteauneuf-du-Pape. Château de Pibarnon's wine is bottled and released earlier than most Bandols.

Bandol	04	03	$$$

Château Pradeaux. Seriously structured, tannic wines made almost exclusively from Mourvèdre and released as much as four years after the harvest. With bottle aging come complex notes of dark berries, flowers, and game.

Bandol	01	$$$
Bandol Cuvée Longue Garde	01	$$$

Domaine Tempier. The leading Bandol name for decades: the Peyraud family almost single-handedly brought the wine world's attention to the Bandol appellation. Their wines have always been rich and powerful, but recent vintages have been sweeter and fleshier.

Bandol	04	03	$$$
Bandol La Tourtine	04	03	$$$$
Bandol Migoua	04	03	$$$$

OTHER PRODUCERS TO LOOK FOR: Château Ste. Anne, Domaine Sorin, Domaine de la Tour du Bon, Château Vannières.

OTHER RED WINES OF PROVENCE

Typical examples of Provençal red wine are ripe and medium to full in body, often with a slightly *sauvage*, or wild, character. They normally show some combination of dark berries and cherry fruit; gamey character; and pepper and herbal nuances, often like the *garrigue* notes found in the Languedoc. Less-expensive examples with little pretension are great for immediate consumption, while the more serious reds of the region, particularly from Les Baux de Provence, can be cellared.

BANG FOR THE BUCK. Thanks to the millions of tourists who flock to this destination, Provençal wines are often artificially expensive in view of their overall quality.

2004 ★★★★ **2003** ★★★

RECOMMENDED PRODUCERS

Château Calissanne. This large estate in Coteaux d'Aix en Provence produces a range of modern-style wines that emphasize sweet fruit and gentle tannins but also offer classic regional qualities. These are some of the better values in Provençal wine.

Coteaux d'Aix en Provence Cuvée du Château		03	$
Coteaux d'Aix en Provence Cuvée Prestige		03	$$

Mas de Gourgonnier. This completely organic estate produces consistently good red berry-flavored wines with enticing gamey sweetness and pungent floral and herbal character.

Les Baux de Provence	04	03	$
Les Baux de Provence Réserve du Mas		03	$$

Château Revelette. The German-born Peter Fischer's wines, based heavily on Syrah and Cabernet Sauvignon, are typically ripe, plumy, and loaded with dense, sweet fruit, with little of the rusticity that marks many wines of the Provence region.

Coteaux d'Aix en Provence Rouge	03	$$
Coteaux d'Aix en Provence Le Grand Rouge de Revelette	02	$$

Château Routas. A modernist producer of rich, supple wines often marked by oak spice. While deeply flavored, even powerful, these wines seldom show the gamey character of more traditional versions.

Coteaux Varois Cyrano	01	$$
Coteaux Varois Agrippa	02	$$

Château Simone. For all practical purposes, the sole producer in the tiny appellation of Palette. The estate red is a firmly structured, persistent wine reminiscent of Bandol, but without the forbidding tannins.

Palette Rouge	01	$$$

Domaine de Trévallon. Along with Mas de Daumas Gassac in the Languedoc, Trévallon was a pioneer for Cabernet Sauvignon-based wines in southern France in the 1970s. The estate's structured, serious, and highly age-worthy red is a near-equal blend of Cabernet and Syrah, with dark berry, leather, and tobacco tones complicated by spicy and peppery nuances. Even though it's in Les Baux, the wine is simply labeled Vin de Table due to the fact that the percentage of Cabernet is over the allowable maximum.

Vin de Pays des Bouches du Rhône	03	$$$

OTHER PRODUCERS TO LOOK FOR: Jean-Luc Colombo, Domaine de la Courtade, Domaine Hauvette, Domaine Richeaume, Château Romanin, Domaine Sorin, Mas de la Dame.

ROSÉS

More than 50 percent of all French rosé is produced in Provence. The same grapes used in the production of red wines are used to make rosés, which are usually blends fermented in stainless steel or concrete vats and bottled in early spring following the harvest to ensure freshness. There is of course far too much industrial-scale rosé. The better examples come in a range of styles, with lighter, crisper versions ideally suited as aperitifs and more substantial, structured, and still adamantly dry examples offering remarkable flexibility with food. In the south of France, these wines are routinely served with garlicky, salty, or oily fish preparations; grilled poultry; and *salade niçoise*. Provençal rosé has been a hot category in North America in recent years, especially in restaurants during the summer months. With few exceptions, rosés should be consumed by the time the next vintage is released.

BANG FOR THE BUCK. Provençal rosés are usually either mediocre and cheap or serious and overpriced, particularly next to rosés of nearly similar quality from other parts of southern France and Spain. But there are values to be found.

2005 ★★★★– **2004** ★★★★+

RECOMMENDED PRODUCERS

Commanderie de la Bargemone. Classic, vibrant, spicy rosé with scents of flowers and wild herbs.

Coteaux d'Aix en Provence Rosé	`05`	$

Commanderie de Peyrassol. An enormous estate, producing a full range of reds, whites, and rosés. The most intriguing are the bracing, floral, minerally rosés.

Côtes de Provence Rosé Château de Peyrassol	`05`	`04`	$$

Mas de Gourgonnier. Quintessential Provence rosé, with exuberant red berry and herbal aromas and flavors and fairly full body.

Les Baux de Provence Rosé	`05`	`04`	$

Domaines Ott. The most prestigious and often most expensive rosés of Provence, with fairly full body and a wide range of red fruit, citrus, spicy, and herbal flavors.

Côtes de Provence Rosé Château de Romassan	`04`	$$
Côtes de Provence Rosé Château de Selle	`04`	$$$

Château de Pibarnon. Fleshy, fruit-driven rosé with the body to stand up to hearty food. Like most Bandol rosé, not for casual sipping.

Bandol Rosé	`05`	`04`	$$

Château Pradeaux. Powerful, structured, very dry Bandol rosé that approaches red wine in body and complexity. Capable of aging.

Bandol Rosé	`05`	`04`	$$

Domaine Tempier. An earthy, dense rosé with the texture of a red wine. A distinctly powerful style of rosé that matches well with grilled meats and hearty fish courses. Not a carefree quaffing wine.

Bandol Rosé	`05`	`04`	$$$

ITALY

Like France, Italy offers a world of wine styles within a single country: dry whites ranging from lively and minerally to powerful and full-bodied; cheap and cheerful reds in both a cooler, northern style and a richer, warmer southern style; structured, powerful reds capable of long aging in bottle; sparkling wines; sweet wines and dessert wines. Most of Italy enjoys a relatively warm climate—and the southern portion of the country can be particularly hot in the summer months. However, Italy's Apennine mountain chain, which traverses the country from north to south, provides an almost infinite number of soil types and exposures, as well as favored hillside sites in virtually every region, where vines can be cultivated at higher, cooler altitudes. Mountainous terrain has also resulted in the segregation of many small wine regions, enabling dozens of indigenous grape varieties to survive in near isolation. Here, Italy markedly differs from most of the wine world, which is becoming increasingly international in nature.

But Italian wine, as most North Americans know it, is a fairly recent phenomenon. Prior to the 1950s, only a tiny proportion of Italy's wines were even bottled by the farmer who grew the grapes. Most Italian wine was consumed by the local market. The Italian government's DOC system (Denominazione di Origine Controllata), created in the 1960s, imposed more explicit standards and thereby improved wine quality while at the same clarifying the labeling of wines and thus making it far easier for Italian producers to ship their wines abroad. (Today DOCG—Controllata e Garantita—is theoretically the highest level in the quality pyramid of Italian wine, with this special status more recently granted to such historically important Italian wine areas as Barolo, Barbaresco, Brunello di Montalcino and others—areas that had previously enjoyed DOC status for at least five years.)

Of course, some of Italy's most innovative winemakers quickly began to look for ways to escape the restrictions of this system. They believed that DOC laws actually prevented them from making the best possible wines—for example, by proscribing the use of certain grape varieties or by requiring them to age their wines in wood barrels longer than they believed was beneficial in some years. Those with a more independent bent essentially opted out of the system, instead producing wines that were simply classified as Vini da Tavola (table wines) but that in a number of cases surpassed the "official" best Italian wines in quality and price. (A new law passed in 1992 created the IGT category, or Indicazione Geografica Tipica, for the innovative Vini da Tavola for which DOCs were not yet created.) These trailblazers have revolutionized Italian wine over a period in which French wines have merely "evolutionized."

NORTHWEST ITALY

Sheltered by the Alps to the north and west, and by the Mediterranean Sea to the south, Italy's Piedmont region has a continental climate, with cold winters and very warm, dry summers, as well as frequent heavy fog in the autumn. A majority of the most renowned Piedmont wines come from the Alba area, in south-central Piedmont, and from the areas of Asti and Alessandria a bit farther north and east. Other interesting wines come from the cooler northern part of the Piedmont region, in the foothills of the Alps that separate Northwest Italy from France and Switzerland.

Piedmont is the ancestral home to the Nebbiolo grape, which is responsible for two of Italy's greatest red wines, Barolo and Barbaresco. The best Barolos and Barbarescos are made in limited quantities on a series of mostly south-facing ridges perched above the frequent October fog (nebbia) in the Langhe hills around Alba, Italy's white truffle capital. The far less expensive and more user-friendly reds Dolcetto and Barbera have attracted widespread interest in export markets over the past decade, due partly to the soaring prices of Barolo and Barbaresco. But the growing popularity of Piemontese cuisine in North America and other countries has also helped stimulate interest in these wines. The natural acidity and taut structure of Piedmont wines provide a refreshing foil to the hearty meat dishes of the region, and their complex floral/earthy character works wonderfully with that other notable local product, the truffle.

White wines are secondary to reds in the Piedmont but are important in the neighboring region of Lombardy, whose greatest contribution to Italy's infinite range of wines is Franciacorta, a Champagne-method sparkling wine that is arguably the finest made outside Champagne. Valtellina, in the hilly alpine north of Lombardy, not far from the border with Switzerland, makes a rather austere, high-acid Nebbiolo in a climate that can be too extreme for this variety in some years.

BAROLO & BARBARESCO

For most of the past century, Barolo was an austere, powerful, and often rustic wine whose fierce tannins and pronounced acidity made it virtually unapproachable in the first decade of its life in bottle. But wines, like fashions, change with the times: today's Barolos and Barbarescos are coveted by mainstream wine lovers around the world. Two developments have accounted for this surge in popularity: a revolution in winemaking techniques that has produced wines that are more accessible in their youth, and an exciting proliferation of vineyard-designated bottlings, which enables connoisseurs to compare wines from different villages and sites the way Burgundy lovers can compare the wines of Chambolle-Musigny with those of Vosne-Romanée.

Barbaresco, located just north of Alba (Barolo is just to the southwest), is quite similar to Barolo in aromas and flavors, which can include cherry, plum, raspberry, licorice, truffle, mushroom, dried rose, road tar, leather, marzipan, underbrush, and menthol. Barbaresco is normally a somewhat more elegant wine with a bit less body and tannic grip, but the similarities between the wines far outweigh the differences. In fact, a Barbaresco from a traditional producer like Bruno Giacosa may be as powerful as, and require more aging than, many "new-wave" examples of Barolo—and can be capable of 20 years or more of positive evolution in bottle.

Piedmont resembles Burgundy in its scale of production. Many family estates own small fragments of multiple vineyards—as opposed to the grander estates of Tuscany and Bordeaux, which are more likely to consist of a single large parcel of land and where vinification is carried out on a much larger scale. Because it is common for a Barolo or Barbaresco producer to offer multiple single-site wines, as in Burgundy, quantities of the best wines are very limited and prices often very high.

BANG FOR THE BUCK. Thanks to limited production and strong international demand, prices soared for the most collectible Barolos and Barbarescos through the turn of the new century. But, ironically, the unprecedented string of very good to outstanding vintages from 1995 through 2001 flooded the market with wines, and consumers who were accustomed to buying a strong vintage and then skipping one or two lesser years seemed to freeze in the face of an embarrassment of riches, and cut back on their buying. Since then, the escalation of prices has cooled somewhat. Still, expect to pay at least $40 or $50 for "basic" bottlings and often more than $100 for the most sought-after vineyard-designated releases from the best producers.

2003 ★★★   2002 ★★–   2001 ★★★★+   2000 ★★★★–

RECOMMENDED PRODUCERS

Elio Altare. Among the best examples of the modernist school of Piedmont wine, Altare's Barolos get short, gentle fermentations and are raised in small French barrels. These densely packed wines boast almost Burgundian lushness of texture and sweet fruit. Although rarely austere in their youth, they also have a track record for improving in bottle.

Barolo	01	00	$$$$
Barolo Brunate	01	00	$$$$$
Barolo Vigneto Arborina	01	00	$$$$$

Fratelli Brovia. The Brovia family makes rich, pliant but firmly structured wines that strike a balance between old school and new. The Brovias eschew barriques but have nonetheless begun to use somewhat smaller casks than in the past. Today's wines are more approachable in their youth, but still appear to be capable of long aging in bottle.

Barolo Garblet Sué	01	00	$$$
Barolo Ca' Mia	01	00	$$$$

New vs. Old Style, &
the State of Today's Market

Modern-style Barolos and Barbarescos are made to be drinkable sooner than those made in the past. This mission is accomplished via such techniques as shorter fermentation and wood aging, and the use of smaller French oak barriques in place of *botti*, the large Slavonian oak casks that have traditionally been used in the Piedmont to age wines very slowly. Until the 1980s, wines were typically bottled after five to eight years of aging, sometimes even longer, and were so tannic and austere that they still required another 12 to 15 years of aging in bottle before they became civilized. And those were the successful examples! Too often, long aging in large old barrels introduced notes of oxidation, and barrels that were not kept sufficiently clean produced rustic wines with offputting leather or barnyard notes.

But today's new generation of wine drinkers are commonly an impatient lot and intolerant of what they perceive to be wine flaws. They have gravitated toward winemakers whose techniques include less energetic extraction of harsh tannins through shorter fermentation and maceration of the grape skins as well as shorter aging in smaller barrels, in which the wines develop more quickly and often take on more of an oaky character. These "new-wave" techniques privilege the fresh fruit character of the Nebbiolo—the notes of cherry, raspberry, and strawberry and the dried flower nuances—while minimizing the hard, dry tannins that might otherwise overwhelm the fruit. Today's modern-style Barolos are still powerful, rich, medium- to-full-bodied wines capable of at least a decade of positive development in bottle, if not much more, but they are far more accessible in their youth.

In recent years, however, the distinctions between old-style and new-wave have been blurred. Some modernists have cut back on their use of stainless steel rotofermenters, in which color is extracted quickly and the fermentation can be completed in as little as a few days, as well as of barriques, especially new ones. At the same time, all but the most uncompromising conservatives have shortened their fermentations and barrel aging, adopted more modern vinification equipment, or hired consulting enologists, who tend to be obsessed with cleanliness and suppler tannins.

Pio Cesare. This is one of Piedmont's historic estates, now run by Pio Boffa, great-grandson of founder Cesare Pio. For generations, this house worked with purchased fruit, but today its best wines come from estate vineyards in both Barolo and Barbaresco. The wines are aromatically fresh and slow to evolve. The most expensive wines, Barolo Ornato and the Barbaresco Il Bricco, are aged in a high percentage of small barrels, while the basic bottlings, more widely available and consistently strong, show much less barrique influence.

Barbaresco		**01** **00**	$$$
Barolo		**01** **00**	$$$
Barolo Ornato	**01**	**00** **99**	$$$$

Domenico Clerico. A relatively new producer (1976) of modern-style wines, Clerico does a gentle extraction using rotofermenters and then ages his wines in barriques. The wines are plump, lush, and loaded with sweet, sappy, red fruits, but have good tannic support. (Clerico's barrique-aged blend of Nebbiolo and Barbera, called Arte, was the original "Super-Piedmont" wine.)

Barolo	**01** **00**	$$$
Barolo Ciabot Mentin Ginestra	**01** **00**	$$$$

Aldo Conterno. One of two sons of the legendary Giacomo Conterno, Aldo set up his own property in the late 1960s and quickly ascended to the top ranks of Barolo. An enlightened traditionalist, Conterno allows his own sons to experiment with barriques in the estate's Barbera and Langhe Rosso bottlings, but believes that small barrels would impart too much flavor of oak to Barolo.

Barolo Bussia Soprano	**01** **00**	$$$$
Barolo Cicala	**01** **00**	$$$$$
Barolo Colonnello	**01** **00**	$$$$$

Giacomo Conterno. The late Giovanni Conterno's son Roberto is now in charge at this great estate in Monforte d'Alba, long known for making some of Barolo's most powerful, profound, and traditional wines. The monumental, ineffably perfumed Monfortino Riserva normally spends at least six years in large casks before being bottled and then can gain in nuance in the bottle for another two decades.

Barolo Cascina Francia		**01** **00**	$$$$
Monfortino Riserva	**01**	**00** **99**	$$$$$

Conterno-Fantino. Guido Fantino crafts deeply colored, glossy, modern-style wines that combine Nebbiolo perfume and sweet tannins. Year in and year out, his Sorì Ginestra bottling manages to be minerally and gripping while remaining seamless and velvety in texture.

Barolo Vigna del Gris	**01** **00**	$$$$
Barolo Sorì Ginestra	**01** **00**	$$$$

Angelo Gaja. Unashamedly modern in style and breathtakingly expensive, Angelo Gaja's wines are flamboyant, intense, and suave, like their maker. Gaja now labels his former single-vineyard Barbarescos and Barolos simply as Nebbiolo Langhe Rosso (along with the proprietary names known to well-heeled clients around the world), as he wanted to be free to include a small percentage of Barbera in his wines in years with low acidity. Gaja also makes a superb and rare-for-the-region Cabernet Sauvignon called Darmagi, not to mention a rich, multidimensional Chardonnay called Gaia & Rey.

Barbaresco	02	01	$$$$$
Sorì San Lorenzo Nebbiolo Langhe	01	00	$$$$$
Sorì Tildìn Nebbiolo Langhev	01	00	$$$$$
Sperss Nebbiolo Langhe	01	00	$$$$$

Elio Grasso. From their beautiful estate in the hills behind Monforte, the Grasso family offers three single-vineyard Barolos, purer and more complex today than ever. The Vigna Chiniera and the Case Maté are made in a more traditional style while the powerful Runcot is aged for 30 months in all new barriques.

Barolo Gavarini Vigna Chiniera	01	00	$$$
Barolo Ginestra Vigna Case Maté	01	00	$$$
Barolo Runcot (2001, 2000)	01	00	$$$$

Bruno Giacosa. This ultratraditionalist, who until recently produced most of his Barolos and Barbarescos from purchased fruit, has a long track record for making superconcentrated, wonderfully aromatic wines with uncompromising structure and impressive longevity. They are among the most sought-after wines of Italy. In the best vintages, he bottles some wines as *riserva*, with a deep burgundy-colored label.

Barbaresco Santo Stefano	01	00	$$$$$
Barolo Falletto di Serralunga	01	00	$$$$$
Barolo Le Rocche del Falletto di Serralunga	01	00	$$$$$

Bartolo Mascarello. It remains to be seen if these wines will be modernized following the death of Bartolo Mascarello, who described himself as "the last of the Mohicans." Mascarello's philosophy was to offer only a single blended wine from multiple sites, in the old style, and always poked fun at cru bottlings and Barolos with "fantasy" names. These are brooding, serious, distinctly old-fashioned wines with classic Barolo aromas of camphor and dried flowers.

Barolo	01	00	$$$$$

Giuseppe Mascarello & Figlio. Renowned for his fastidious vineyard work and attention to detail, Mauro Mascarello makes structured, slow-aging wines with sweet fruit and considerable finesse. His prime holding in the great Monprivato vineyard in Castiglione Falletto yields a powerful, structured wine with ineffable floral and red fruit perfume that calls to mind great Burgundy. Mascarello has trademarked the name of this vineyard (he owns 95 percent of it) and is now the only producer to so label his wine.

Barolo Santo Stefano di Perno		01	00	$$$$
Barolo Monprivato	01	00	99	$$$$

Moccagatta. There's something here for everyone, as Francesco and Sergio Minuto make three very different Barbaresco bottlings: the suave, velvety-rich Bric Balin; the sharply defined, stylish Basarin; and the powerful, tannic, and rather Barolo-like Colé.

Barbaresco Bric Balin	01		$$$
Barbaresco Basarin	01		$$$$
Barbaresco Vigneto Colé	01		$$$$

E. Pira & Figli. Chiara Boschis has reduced yields and practiced more careful selection in recent vintages to make consistently elegant wines with staying power.

Barolo Via Nuova	01	00	$$$$
Barolo Cannubi	01	00	$$$$$

Luigi Pira. Pira owns parcels in three of the Serralunga area's top crus: Margheria, Marenca, and Rionda. The powerful and slightly rustic Margheria generally needs extra bottle aging, while the floral Vigna Rionda, rather gentle for a wine from Serralunga, is aged in all new barriques.

Barolo Marenca	01		$$$$$
Barolo Margheria	01		$$$$
Barolo Vigna Rionda	01		$$$$$

Produttori del Barbaresco. One of the most respected wine cooperatives, the Produttori is also one of the best remaining sources of value in high-quality Barbaresco. Working with fruit supplied by more than 60 member growers, the Produttori makes multiple vineyard-designated bottlings that showcase the differences among the area's top sites. These wines undergo extended aging in larger barrels, including traditional large casks from Slavonian oak, and are labeled as riserva. The co-op also produces a bargain-priced regular Barbaresco.

Barbaresco	01	00	$$$
Barbaresco Montestefano	01	00	$$$
Barbaresco Asili	01	00	$$$

Prunotto. Under ownership by the Antinori empire, Prunotto continues to make glossy, aromatically complex wines from both Barolo and Barbaresco. Their most important holding is in the Barolo Bussia. Look also for the consistently suave, captivating Nebbiolo d'Alba Occhetti, always an excellent example of the variety in an immediately approachable form.

Nebbiolo d'Alba Occhetti	02	01	$$
Barolo	01	00	$$$
Barolo Bussia	01	00	$$$$

Giuseppe Rinaldi. Ultratraditionalist Rinaldi makes serious, dense, youthfully austere Barolos the old-fashioned way, aging his wines in leisurely fashion in large old casks. Rinaldi prefers severe—as opposed to fruity—Barolo and believes that the most noble Barolo perfume comes from long aging in barrel and in bottle.

Barolo Brunate-Le Coste	01	00	$$$

Luciano Sandrone. One of the pioneers of the modern school of Barolo, Sandrone's wines today manage to avoid the obvious oak tones and candied fruit shown by so many wines of the new school. But the suave, seamless texture and depth of flavor of these Barolos makes them some of the most sought-after wines of the region.

Barolo Le Vigne	01	00	$$$$$
Barolo Cannubi Boschis	01	00	$$$$$

Paolo Scavino. Modernist Scavino has actually cut back somewhat on his use of small barrels and lengthened his fermentations in order to make firmer wines with more tannic support. His wines are silky and fresh, and can show an almost exotic sweetness in the ripest years without losing their elegance.

Barolo	01	00	$$$
Barolo Bric dël Fiasc	01	00	$$$$$

La Spinetta. Giorgio Rivetti, who now also owns an estate in Tuscany, makes some of the flashiest and most popular modern, barrique-aged Barbarescos, as well as a Barolo from his holding just south of Alba, where he has constructed an airy, modern winery at the foot of his vineyard.

Barbaresco Vigneto Gallina	01	00	$$$$$
Barbaresco Vigneto Starderi	01	00	$$$$$

Cantina Vietti. Updated traditional wines that use a combination of barriques and larger barrels to make wines of great class and depth. The Barolo Villero and Rocche bottlings here undergo the longest fermentations and are the estate's most serious, long-aging wines. The 2001s here were brilliant.

Barolo Castiglione	01	00	$$$
Barolo Brunate	01	00	$$$$
Barolo Rocche	01	00	$$$$

Roberto Voerzio. Flamboyantly rich, dark, and expensive modern-style wines from low-yielding old vines in some of the best vineyards of La Morra.

Barolo Brunate	01	$$$$$
Barolo Cerequio	01	$$$$$
Barolo Rocche dell' Annunziata Torriglione	01	$$$$$

OTHER PRODUCERS TO LOOK FOR: Tenutta Carreta, Ceretto, Fratelli Cigliutti, Cordero di Montezemolo, Giovanni Corino, Damilano, Silvio Grasso, Marcarini, Marchesi di Gresy, Massolino, Mauro Molino, Andrea Oberto, Oddero, Paitin di Pasquero, Armando Parusso, Pelissero, Renato Ratti, Fratelli Revello, Albino Rocca, Podere Rocche dei Manzoni, Fratelli Seghesio, Sottimano, Mauro Veglio, Gianni Voerzio.

OTHER NEBBIOLO WINES

Nebbiolo-based wines made outside the Langhe hills are often lost in the commotion over Barolo and Barbaresco. The provinces of Vercelli and Novarra in the northern reaches of the Piedmont area are home to wines like Carema, Ghemme, and Gattinara. The latter two wines are mostly Nebbiolo, which has traditionally been blended with small percentages of other grapes native to this cool, mountainous region. (Nebbiolo is generally called Spanna in Ghemme and Gattinara.) Gattinara in particular has a long history of producing high-quality wines. The wines here tend to be lighter and more graceful than their cousins to the south, though seldom displaying the complexity or concentration of flavor achieved in the Langhe. But fans of traditional Piedmont wines that are free of modern artifice and new oak notes will find plenty of interest in these often gripping and very food-friendly wines. Note that vintages here do not exactly track those of the Langhe. In a hot summer like 2003, when Nebbiolo in Barolo and Barbaresco often lost some of its verve and spine as acidity levels plunged, many vineyards in the hillier northern reaches of Northwest Italy achieved near-perfect ripeness, providing fuller wines than usual without loss of balance or backbone.

Relatively unknown to North Americans are the wines of Valtellina, in the far north of Lombardy, at the foot of the Alps near the Swiss border. These steeply sloped, terraced vineyards were originally home to a host of indigenous varieties but today the wines made here are almost universally based on Nebbiolo (called Chiavennasca here). As might be expected from a relatively cool area, the wines are brighter and more vivacious than their Piedmont counterparts, with less weight and alcoholic richness. Sfursat is a wine made in Valtellina from dried Nebbiolo grapes, à la Amarone.

Of course, some of the best Nebbiolos come from the Alba area. These wines may be partly or entirely declassified Barolo and Barbaresco (i.e., juice from young vines or lots that are not up to the producer's standards for its flagship bottlings), or they may come from vineyards outside the closely delimited Barolo and Barbaresco zones. In either case, they are bottled and released much earlier and are suitable for drinking young. Consistently good and often surprisingly affordable Nebbiolos come from producers like Elio Altare, Aldo Conterno, Paolo Conterno, Bruno Giacosa, Elio Grasso, Prunotto and Produttori del Barbaresco, to name just a few.

BANG FOR THE BUCK. Compared to Barolo and Barbaresco, prices asked for better Nebbiolo wines from the northern Piedmont are generally reasonable. Nebbiolos offered by producers in the Langhe can also offer excellent value, and have the advantage of immediate drinkability. Prices for some Valtellinas can be on the high side owing to the small size of most of the top producers in this area.

2003 ★★★− **2002** ★+ **2001** ★★★★+ **2000** ★★★★−

RECOMMENDED PRODUCERS

Antoniolo. Producer of densely packed, rich Gattinaras with greater-than-normal floral and mineral complexity. The Castelle is aged in barriques.

Gattinara Vigneto San Francesco	01	00	$$$
Gattinara Vigneto Castelle	01	00	$$$
Gattinara Osso San Grato	01	00	$$$

Cantalupo. Elegant, old-style wines made from mineral-rich, alluvial glacial deposits—as good as it gets in Ghemme. These precise wines, raised in large Slavonian oak casks, have the balance and concentration for cellaring.

Ghemme	`01`	`00`	$$
Ghemme Collis Breclemae		`99`	$$$

Dessilani. Dessilani produces very good Gattinara and small amounts of Ghemme in a traditional style. The wines typically offer attractive balance and good fruit concentration and represent solid value.

Gattinara Reserva	`00`	$$

Luigi Ferrando. Aside from the local cooperative, Ferrando is the sole producer of Carema. The Ferrando wines are finely etched, never powerful or thick, but have a track record for extended aging in bottle. The Black Label, or Etichetta Nera, which is only produced in the best vintages, has the power and concentration of many Barbarescos and Barolos.

Carema	`01`	`00`	$$$
Carema Black Label	`01`	`00`	$$$$

Nino Negri. Elegantly styled, complex Valtellinas that convey the perfumed character of Nebbiolo in an easier-drinking, more immediately approachable style than Barolo or Barbaresco. Inferno refers to the sun-baked slopes on which the vineyards are planted within this cool alpine region. Negri's Sfursat 5 Stelle is one of Italy's top wines in virtually every vintage it is offered.

Valtellina Superiore Inferno	`02`	`01`	$
Valtellina Superiore Inferno Mazér	`02`	`00`	$$
Valtellina Sfursat 5 Stelle	`02`	`00`	$$$$

Travaglini. The largest producer, by far, in Gattinara and consistently good in recent vintages. The wines, which undergo a short, modern-style vinification but are aged mostly in larger oak barrels, are medium-bodied and elegant, with spicy, smoky Nebbiolo character, fresh acidity, and firm structure. Their ability to age is admirable, even if their lopsided bottles (inspired by old, hand-blown glass) make it tricky to lay them down in the cellar.

Gattinara	`00`	`99`	$$
Gattinara Tre Vigne		`98`	$$$

Vallana. Situated in the tiny DOC of Boca in Novara, this fabled estate has a long history of producing elegant, fragrant, age-worthy wines. They call their wine simply Spanna but don't be misled by the understatement as these are consistently first-rate examples of finely tuned, suave Nebbiolo.

Spanna	`00`	$$

OTHER PRODUCERS TO LOOK FOR: Sandro Fay (Valtellina), Nera (Valtellina), Aldo Rainoldi (Valtellina), Enologica Valtellinese (Valtellina).

DOLCETTO & BARBERA

Dolcetto and Barbera are the wines that the locals drink on an everyday basis, reserving the more serious and expensive Nebbiolo wines for special occasions. Dolcetto and Barbera are among the most flexible, food-friendly reds made anywhere, complementing everything from pizzas and tomato-based pastas to richer meat dishes to salty cheeses.

Dolcetto is generally a supple, intensely fruity, medium-bodied, low-acid wine with solid tannic support. Because Dolcetto is normally inexpensive and destined for early drinking, most examples are made in tank or in larger, neutral barrels; only a few are aged in French barriques. Barbera is typically leaner and more penetrating, relying almost entirely on its acidity, rather than its tannins, for structure. Its cherry and berry flavors are often complicated by spice notes and more obvious suggestions of soil. But it's also a more serious wine than Dolcetto, with the best examples possessing good density and the ability to gain in complexity with a few years of bottle aging.

Competition among quality-conscious estates and brisk demand for their wines have motivated producers to reduce Barbera crop levels in order to make riper, more concentrated wines. Stronger raw materials, in turn, have allowed an increasing number of producers to age these wines in small French oak barrels, which can intensify the natural spicy character of this variety and provide tannic grip. The sweetness of the wood also helps buffer Barbera's brisk acidity. These fleshier, deeper wines have found fans among those who view older-style Barberas as too lean and sharp. But where the underlying material is limited, the result of barrique aging can often be chocolaty, tarry, and sometimes bitter wine in which the oak overwhelms and dries the fruit.

Although a majority of the Dolcetto and Barbera bottlings most popular among North American wine lovers come from the top Barolo and Barbaresco estates in the Alba area, neighboring appellations are also good sources for these wines. Dolcettos from hilly sites in adjacent Dogliani are concentrated, fresh, and comparatively powerful, while Barberas from Asti, just north of Alba, can be especially smooth, soil-inflected, and long-lived. Keep in mind that in the Langhe the very best hillside vineyards are normally reserved for Nebbiolo, but in neighboring appellations where Barolo and Barbaresco cannot be made and where Barbera and Dolcetto have traditionally been more important, it's these varieties that enjoy pride of place.

BANG FOR THE BUCK. Although prices for some special Barbera bottlings aged in expensive French oak are high, Dolcetto and Barbera are generally moderately priced wines—and excellent values.

2004 ★★★★   2003 ★★★★   2002 ★+

RECOMMENDED PRODUCERS

Claudio Alario. Deeply fruity, pure, smooth Dolcettos from Diano d'Alba, an area between the Barolo and Barbaresco zones where many of the top vineyard locations are devoted to Dolcetto. The Costafiore generally needs a bit more time in bottle than the more quickly approachable Montegrillo.

Dolcetto di Diano d'Alba Montegrillo	04	03	$$
Dolcetto di Diano d'Alba Costafiore	04	03	$$

Elio Altare. Deeply colored, focused Barbera and Dolcetto with compelling sweetness and pliancy.

Dolcetto d'Alba	04	03	$$
Barbera d'Alba	04	03	$$

Braida. In the early 1980s the late Giacomo Bologna essentially invented the idea of making a rich world-class red wine by aging Barbera in small oak barrels, putting Asti's Barberas on the map in the process. His family's estate offers three barrique-aged Barberas, all deeply colored, juicy, and penetrating, loaded with dark fruits and spices. The Ai Suma, made in the best years from a vineyard harvested late for maximum ripeness, generally needs time in bottle to absorb its oak element.

Barbera d'Asti Bricco dell' Uccellone		03	$$$
Barbera d'Asti Ai Suma	03	01	$$$$

Francesco Boschis. A specialist in Dolcetto, producing clean, rich, rather powerful examples from south-facing slopes at a range of price points.

Dolcetto di Dogliani Sorì San Martino	04	03	$
Dolcetto di Dogliani Vigna dei Prey	04	03	$$

Fratelli Brovia. Intensely fruity, structured wines that, like the Barolos made here, strike a balance between complex earth tones and fresh, lively fruit. The high-end Dolcetto, Solatio, offered only in the best years, transcends the category with its penetrating fruit and power.

Dolcetto d'Alba Vignavillej	03	02	$$
Dolcetto d'Alba Solatio	03	00	$$$
Barbera d'Alba Brea (2003, 2002)	03	02	$$

Domenico Clerico. This superstar producer of Barolo also offers sturdy, substantial Dolcetto with some chocolaty, oak tones, and a spicy, intense Barbera aged in a high percentage of small barrels.

Dolcetto d'Alba Visadì	04	03	$$
Barbera d'Alba Trevigne		03	$$

Luigi Einaudi. In addition to making aromatically complex, stylish, firmly tannic Barolos, this estate in Dogliani offers serious Dolcetto bottlings. The Vigna Tecc is chewy, structured, and tannic, while I Filari shows more aromatic richness and obvious soil tones of flowers and earth.

Dolcetto di Dogliani Vigna Tecc	04	03	$$
Dolcetto di Dogliani I Filari	04	03	$$

Marcarini. A portion of Marcarini's consistently vibrant, complex, penetrating Dolcetto Boschi di Berri comes from vines that predate phylloxera; some may be up to 150 years old. The Fontanazza is a fruit bomb by comparison.

Dolcetto d'Alba Fontanazza	04	03	$
Dolcetto d'Alba Boschi di Berri	04	03	$$

Franco M. Martinetti. The juicy, bright, unoaked Bric dei Banditi is always a fruit bomb of a Barbera, while the Montruc is aged in new barriques. (Look, too, for Martinetti's Sul Bric Monferrato Rosso, a 50/50 blend of Barbera and Cabernet that is not overwhelmingly modern in style.)

Barbera d'Asti Bric dei Banditi	04	03	$$
Barbera d'Asti Montruc		03	$$$

Albino Rocca. Consistently excellent Dolcetto done in stainless steel and an often out-sized Barbera from ideally situated 50-year-old vines, aged in a combination of barriques and larger casks.

Dolcetto d'Alba Vignalunga	04	03	$$
Barbera d'Alba Gepin	03	02	$$

Luciano Sandrone. Sandrone's Dolcetto is vibrant, pure, and loaded with intense, ripe berry flavors, very much in keeping with the Barolos made here. His lusty, powerfully fruity Barbera is also worth seeking out.

Dolcetto d'Alba	04	03	$$
Barbera d'Alba	04	03	$$

La Spinetta. The house style of big, rich, densely flavored wines is on full display with Rivetti's Barbera lineup. The Ca'di Pian is a reasonably priced introduction to the house style and less influenced by new oak than the upper-tier bottlings.

Barbera d'Asti Ca'di Pian	04	03	$
Barbera d'Alba Gallina		03	$$$
Barbera d'Asti Superiore		03	$$$

Vietti. The Currado family's entry-level Tre Vigne Barbera is concentrated and penetrating, while their Scarrone comes from expensive Barolo soil near the Vietti winery. The barrique-aged wine labeled La Crena comes from vines in the Asti area that were planted in the 1930s.

Barbera d'Alba Tre Vigne	04	03	$$
Barbera d'Asti La Crena		03	$$
Barbera d'Alba Scarrone		03	$$$

OTHER PRODUCERS TO LOOK FOR: Pio Cesare (Barbera), Giacomo Conterno (Barbera), Conterno-Fantino (Barbera), Coppo (Barbera), Cordero di Montezemolo (Barbera), Giovanni Corino (Dolcetto and Barbera), Bruno Giacosa (Barbera and Dolcetto), Elio Grasso (Barbera), Giuseppe Mascarello (Barbera and Dolcetto), Prunotto (Dolcetto and Barbera), Fratelli Revello (Barbera), Bruno Rocca (Dolcetto and Barbera), Paulo Scavino (Dolcetto and Barbera), Sottimano (Dolcetto and Barbera).

WHITE WINES

The Piedmont's Arneis, which was once called Barolo Bianco, has emerged in the last decade as a trendy, insider's white wine, but production is limited and the wines are not widely seen in North America. This rather delicate pear- and-almond-scented wine, often with a refreshingly bitter, herbal edge, is ideal as an aperitif and is best consumed in the year or two following the vintage. Many of the better Barolo and Barbaresco producers offer an Arneis, normally made in stainless steel to preserve freshness.

Moscato d'Asti, which is bottled within months of the harvest at a very low alcohol level (sometimes below five percent) and with retained carbon dioxide, is an utterly delightful, if not downright addictive, sweet, lightly bubbly wine. It is also increasingly popular, with wide distribution. The exuberant peach, apricot, and pear fruit flavors and frothy texture diminish quickly in the bottle, so the wines are best drunk before the release of the next vintage. Moscato d'Asti is usually served as an aperitif or with fresh fruit desserts.

Gavi, the most popular Piedmont white wine and the most widely distributed in North America, is made mostly or completely from the Cortese variety planted in the extreme south of Piedmont, in the province of Alessandria. Wines labeled Gavi di Gavi come from vineyards around the favored town of Gavi. The vast majority of these wines are simply very dry whites of modest concentration and complexity, crisp at their best but often lacking verve and grip, and best consumed young. Gavi tends to have a pale straw color; subtle if not somewhat neutral aromas of citrus fruits, apple, flowers, minerals, and honey, and high acidity. The best examples are fruity, balanced, and persistent—and excellent accompaniments to fish dishes.

Although Piedmont dominates wine production in Northwest Italy, Lombardy is important for producing Italy's finest sparkling wines, using the Champagne method. The best are from Franciacorta, east of Milan, which earned its DOCG status only in 1995. These wines are made from Chardonnay and Pinot Bianco (Pinot Blanc), often with some Pinot Nero (Pinot Noir) blended in. Another subzone known for sparkling wines is Oltrepó Pavese, which also makes still red, white, and rosé wines that rarely achieve any special heights and provide the Milanese with much of their everyday drinking wine. Lugana, on the south shore of Lake Garda, produces dry, fruity, medium-bodied white wines from a local version of Trebbiano.

BANG FOR THE BUCK. There are few bargains in white wine from Northwest Italy, with the exception of Moscato d'Asti. The best Franciacorta bottlings are expensive.

2005 ★★★+   **2004** ★★★★   **2003** ★★

RECOMMENDED PRODUCERS

Bellavista. This is a large, quality-obsessed producer, utilizing almost completely organic vineyard practices and producing low vine yields. The wines are creamy and ample, but also balanced and detailed, with noteworthy finesse for the category.

NV Franciacorta Cuvée Brut			$$$
NV Franciacorta Gran Cuvée Satèn			$$$
Franciacorta Gran Cuvée Brut		01	$$$

Broglia. Classically bright, minerally Gavis with more concentration and personality than most renditions.

Gavi del Comune di Gavi La Meirana		04	$$
Gavi del Comune di Gavi Bruno Broglia		04	$$$

Ca' del Bosco. This major pacesetting producer, with a state-of-the-art vinification and aging facility, is considered by many to make the best Franciacortas. (There are very good table wines made here as well.) Founder Maurizio Zanella put Franciacorta on the map in the 1970s by crafting powerful, ripe wines with more body and heft than most Champagnes. The top-of-the-line Annamaria bottling is aged for six months in new barriques and then gets several years of aging on its lees, like a top prestige Champagne.

NV Franciacorta Brut			$$$
Franciacorta Vintage Brut	01	99	$$$$
Franciacorta Annamaria Clementi		99	$$$$$

Ca' dei Frati. A leading producer of Lombardy white table wines, especially known for white wines made from the often bland Trebbiano. The Bianco Lugana is fresh, elegant, and minerally while the partially barrel-fermented Brolettino is made in an international style, with more obvious body and richness.

Bianco Lugana I Frati	04	03	$$
Bianco Brolettino Lugana	04	03	$$

Bruno Giacosa. Intensely flavored, highly scented, classically dry Arneis, with notes of fruit, sage, and acacia blossom and excellent vinosity—perhaps the most serious example of this variety produced in Piedmont. (Giacosa also offers a rich, refreshing, vintage-dated sparkling wine, or spumante, in most good vintages.)

Arneis Roero	05	04	$$

Saracco. Fresh, bright, racy Moscato, among the most delicate and filigreed examples made, with wonderful elegance, balance, and pristine fruit flavor.

Moscato d'Asti	05	$$

La Spinetta. Giorgio Rivetti's Moscato d'Asti bottlings offer delicacy and power as well as abundant fruit. The Bricco Quaglia bottling has the structure to support its sweetness.

Moscato d'Asti Bricco Quaglia	05	$$

OTHER PRODUCERS TO LOOK FOR: Almondo (Arneis), Fratelli Berlucchi (Franciacorta), Castellino (Franciacorta), Cavalleri (Franciacorta), Contadi Castaldi (Franciacorta), Coppo (Moscato), La Giustiniana (Gavi), La Morandina (Moscato).

NORTHEAST ITALY

While far better known for its red wines than for its whites, Italy now makes very good white wines in virtually every region. The best ones come from Alto Adige and Friuli-Venezia-Giulia (FVG). These two regions, along with Veneto and Trentino, make up what is generally referred to as Italy's northeast, situated roughly between Austria in the north and part of Slovenia (part of the former

Yugoslavia) in the east. Friuli-Venezia-Giulia is where high-quality, fresh Italian white wines were born back in the early 1970s, thanks to pioneers like Mario Schiopetto and Livio Felluga. But although this part of Italy is best known for its whites, many interesting reds are also produced there, and the best of them are worth seeking out by wine lovers looking for new and different taste sensations.

Despite the high quality of the best wines of these four regions of Italy, they tend to be known outside Italy only by serious enophiles, due to a combination of factors. Most important is the generally poor image of wines like Soave and Pinot Grigio, which are still among the top-selling imported wines in North America, despite the fact that most are quite lackluster and made in industrial quantities. Moreover, the better wines of Northeast Italy are rarely cheap, as this is the part of the country with the highest costs associated with growing grapes and making wine. Yet each region has something special to offer.

WHITE WINES

Alto Adige is a prime source for excellent white wines from both native and international grapes. Because this region was part of the Austro-Hungarian Empire until 1917, you will find many Germanic grape varieties here, such as Riesling and Gewürztraminer. Alto Adige's Sauvignons and Pinot Grigios can be world-class, but its Chardonnays, like those from other parts of Italy, are generally less distinctive. Friuli-Venezia-Giulia produces very good Sauvignons, Pinot Grigios, and Pinot Biancos, as well as some delightful—and sometimes more serious—whites from native grapes like Ribolla, Malvasia, and Tocai (see box on page 133). The best wines of this region are made on the hilly slopes of subzones called Collio, Colli Orientali del Friuli, and Carso, as well as, strangely enough, the flat riverbed plain of the Isonzo valley. Trentino (along with Lombardy's Franciacorta) is where Italy's best sparkling wines are made, using the Champagne method and usually referred to as Talento. As a rule, they are more fruity and less yeasty than their counterparts from Champagne and Franciacorta. Trentino's still white wines can be good, but are generally less interesting than those of the other regions of Northeast Italy.

Last but not least, the northeast is where Italy's finest sweet white wines are made. Among the best are Recioto di Soave from Veneto; Picolit and Verduzzo from FVG; various versions of Passito, made in Alto Adige from aromatic grape varieties such as Riesling, Yellow Muscat, and Gewürztraminer; and Vin Santo from Trentino, made in small quantities but often of very high quality. Passito wines are dessert wines made by air-drying grapes on straw mats or plastic shelves for weeks or months before they are pressed, in order to concentrate sugars and other flavor molecules as the water evaporates. Vin Santos are very rich, sweet wines made from grapes that have been left to air-dry for up to four months and are typically bottled several years after the harvest.

DISTINCTIVE WHITE GRAPES OF NORTHEAST ITALY

- **Sylvaner:** Sylvaner grows in Valle Isarco, the coldest portion of Alto Adige, where the grape yields delicate, racy wines with hints of green apple, lemon drop, white flowers, and gin.
- **Müller-Thurgau:** A hybrid of Riesling and Chasselas, this is one of those grapes that gives dreadful results when not cared for properly, but it excels in Trentino and especially Alto Adige. With its fragrant notes of green apple, white pepper, and cinnamon, Müller-Thurgau goes perfectly with Indian and East Asian cuisines.
- **Gewürztraminer:** Similar to examples made in Alsace, the version from Alto Adige tends to be floral rather than fruity and is nearly always drier.
- **Pinot Bianco:** The ubiquitous Pinot Bianco, with its notes of honeysuckle, apple, and pear, is excellent as an aperitif or with simpler fish preparations. Some producers make it in oak to obtain a deeper, richer wine reminiscent of Chardonnay.
- **Pinot Grigio:** Well-made versions, with delightful apple, pear, and apricot aromas; firm minerality; and lively acidity, have nothing in common with the industrially made, taste-free wines with which most North American consumers are familiar.
- **Ribolla Gialla:** White flowers and citrus fruits are the hallmarks of this variety. Those done in oak are rarely as successful as the simpler, fresher examples aged in stainless steel.
- **Malvasia Istriana:** There are so many Malvasias in Italy that keeping track of them gets confusing even for Italians. Bear in mind that Malvasia from Friuli-Venezia-Giulia is always a dry wine, with nuances of pear, apricot, peach, and minerals.
- **Tocai Friulano:** This grape actually belongs to the Sauvignon family, and the wine, always dry, exhibits qualities similar to the better-known Sauvignon Blanc.
- **Picolit:** A delicately sweet late-harvest wine reminiscent of acacia, honey, peach, and citrus fruits. Some air-dried examples can be much more concentrated, with date and fig flavors.
- **Garganega:** The main grape from which Soave is made, Garganega can give simple, light, dry whites or, in the hands of better producers, much more serious wines with real longevity. Recioto di Soave is a sweet wine made from air-dried grapes, with flavors of apricot jam, dried peach, pineapple, honey, and grapefruit.
- **Prosecco:** A lightly aromatic grape from which Italy's national aperitif wine is made—a delicate, thirst-quenching, and often slightly sweet sparkling wine that can be great fun when made by a good producer. Peach and pear are the typical fragrances, and well-made examples offer creamy texture (poor ones are thin and tart). The moniker "di Conegliano-Valdobbiadene" on the label guarantees that the wine comes from grapes grown in the best area.

BANG FOR THE BUCK. Due to high labor costs, the better white wines of Friuli-Venezia-Giulia can be expensive. Some of the top buys in Italy's northeast are nonoak-aged Ribolla, Malvasia. and Tocai from FVG, and similarly made Pinot Bianco and Pinot Grigio from Alto Adige, as well as aromatic varieties like Sylvaner.

2005 ★★★+   2004 ★★★   2003 ★★★–

RECOMMENDED PRODUCERS

Abbazia di Novacella. The abbey has been around for centuries, and its wines have always been famous. A great source for vibrant, well-made aromatic varieties—as well as a very good Pinot Nero (Pinot Noir).

Kerner Alto Adige Valle Isarco		**05** 04	$$
Pinot Grigio Alto Adige Valle Isarco		05 04	$$

Anselmi. One of the most famous of all producers of Soave, Anselmi's wines are notably dense and concentrated. The San Vincenzo bottling is a perennial value. There's also a particularly rich and viscous dessert bottling.

San Vincenzo		04	$
Capitel Croce Veneto	04	03	$$
Capitel Foscarino Veneto		**04**	$$
Passito I Capitelli Veneto		03	$$$$

Bastianich. Joseph Bastianich is a partner in a restaurant empire in New York City, and also makes very successful, typical wines in his family's native Friuli. The Vespa Bianco has been a structured, creamy, deep white wine from its inception, while the Tocai is consistently one of the best, with its typical aromas of hazelnut, almond, and freshly cut grass.

Tocai Collio		**04** 03	$
Tocai Plus Collio		03	$$
Vespa Bianco IGT		03	$$

Key to Vintage Ratings	Key to Assessments of Specific Wines
★★★★★ Outstanding	**03** An excellent to outstanding example *of that wine*
★★★★ Excellent	03 A good to very good example *of that wine*
★★★ Good to very good	03 A disappointing effort (often due to a
★★ Fair to average	difficult vintage)
★ Poor	

Bisol. Perhaps Italy's best producer of Prosecco. The Crede is quintessentially creamy, fresh Prosecco oozing with white pear and green apple flavor. The benchmark Cartizze is wonderfully complex.

NV Prosecco di Valdobbiadene Crede Brut	$$
NV Prosecco Superiore di Valdobbiadene di Cartizze Dry	$$$

Gini. Gini's Soave Classico Superiore and La Frosca bottlings are made entirely from Garganega, planted in some of the best hillside sites of the appellation. Their wines are concentrated, crisp, and minerally, with enticing aromatic character. The rich, barrel-aged Salvarenza, which includes a bit of Chardonnay, is made from 30-year-old vines in a tiny plot within the La Frosca vineyard.

Soave Classico Superiore	04	$
Soave Classico Superiore La Frosca	04	$$
Soave Classico Superiore Salvarenza Vecchie Vigne	03	$$$

Giulio Ferrari. The Giulio Ferrari Riserva del Fondatore is a world-class sparkling wine in a more fruity and less yeasty style than Champagne.

Brut Perlé Talento Metodo Classico Trento	01	00	$$
NV Perlé Rosé Brut Talento Metodo Classico Trento			$$
Brut Riserva del Fondatore Giulio Ferrari Trento		96	$$$$

Gravner. One of Italy's most important winemakers, Josko Gravner makes use of a technique that dates back to Georgia (formerly part of the U.S.S.R.) 4,000 years ago, allowing his wines to macerate on the grape skins for several months in large terracotta amphorae before transferring them to oak casks for two years or more of further aging. Gravner's idiosyncratic white wines are almost like reds in their chewy texture (he also makes red wines from Cabernet and Merlot). The Breg is a blend of Sauvignon Blanc, Chardonnay, Pinot Grigio, and Riesling Italico.

Ribolla Gialla Anfora Venezia Giulia	01	$$$$
Breg Anfora Venezia Giulia	01	$$$$

Hofstätter. One of the finest producers in Alto Adige, Hofstätter's Gewürztraminer Kolbenhof is one of the most minerally and age-worthy wines in its category. Excellent Pinot Nero and Lagrein, too.

Müller Thurgau Alto Adige	05	04	$
Gewürztraminer Kolbenhof Alto Adige	04	03	$$$
Gewürztraminer VT Joseph Alto Adige		03	$$$

Jermann. For many people in Italy, Silvio Jermann is the country's most notable and best white wine producer. Certainly very few estates offer three whites at the level of Vintage Tunina (mainly Chardonnay and Sauvignon blended with local grapes), Capo Martino (mainly Tocai and Picolit), and Dreams, a world-class barrel-fermented Chardonnay. The best buy here, though, is Vinnae, a delightful, deceptively light and refreshing Ribolla-based white.

Vinnae IGT	04	$$
Vintage Tunina IGT	03	$$$
Capo Martino IGT	03	$$$$
Dreams IGT (2003)	03	$$$$

Livio Felluga. One of the historic wine producers of Italy, Livio Felluga makes one of the country's best sweet wines, the Picolit, and one of its most important whites, the Terre Alte. A name you can count on.

Pinot Grigio Colli Orientali del Friuli	04	03	$$
Tocai Colli Orientali del Friuli	04	03	$$
Terre Alte Colli Orientali del Friuli	03	01	$$
Picolit Colli Orientali del Friuli	03	01	$$$$

Maculan. One of Italy's most dependable producers, with a strong lineup of dry whites, reds, and sweet wines. The Fratta is an elegant, Bordeaux-like Cabernet-Merlot blend that has never been better, the Dindarello a lightly sweet, refreshing Muscat, and the Torcolato a fine, very rich dessert wine.

Dindarello Moscato del Veneto		04	$$$
Torcolato Breganze		03	$$$$
Fratta Rosso del Veneto	03	01	$$$$$

Pieropan. A top name in Soave; the minerally, stainless steel–aged Calvarino can easily age for a decade, while the more modern La Rocca bottling has the fruit to stand up to its clever use of toasty oak.

Soave Classico Calvarino	04	03	$$
Soave Classico La Rocca		03	$$$

Prà. Another excellent Soave producer, with a consistently fresh entry-level wine and a wonderfully ripe and concentrated yet delicate Monte Grande bottling. The Prà brothers age their Colle Sant'Antonio in small oak barrels.

Soave Classico	04	$
Soave Classico Superiore Monte Grande	04	$$

Produttori Termeno. One of Italy's first-rate sources of white wine, and this is a producers' cooperative! Quality is exceptional, especially in light of the quantity of wine made. Home of some of the country's best Gewürztraminers, this producer also offers fine Pinot Grigio and some outstanding sweet wines.

Pinot Grigio Unterebner Alto Adige	04	03	$$
Gewürztraminer Nussbaumer Alto Adige	04	03	$$
Roan Passito Gewürztraminer Alto Adige		03	$$$
Terminum Passito Gewürztraminer Alto Adige		03	$$$

Ronco del Gelso. Classy, minerally, rigorously made wines, led by one of Italy's best Rieslings and an excellent Pinot Grigio.

Riesling Isonzo del Friuli	04	$$
Pinot Grigio Sot Lis Rivis Isonzo del Friuli	04	$$
Tocai Isonzo del Friul	04	$$

Mario Schiopetto. The late Mario Schiopetto was partly responsible for modernizing white wine in Italy, and this estate carries on with many superbly made bottlings, including a benchmark Tocai.

Pinot Bianco Collio		04	$$$
Tocai Friulano Collio		04	$$$
Mario Schiopetto Bianco Collio		04	$$$

Vie di Romans. Owner/winemaker Gianfranco Gallo favors a rich, high-octane style of wine. Stars here include the Dessimis Pinot Grigio, at times quite oaky, and the Sauvignons—the Vieris barrel-aged and the Pieré done in a combination of wood and steel.

Dessimis Pinot Grigio Isonzo del Friuli		03	$$$
Vieris Sauvignon Isonzo del Friuli		03	$$$
Pieré Sauvignon Blanc Isonzo del Friuli		03	$$$
Flor de Uis Isonzo del Friuli		03	$$$

Villa Russiz. Varietally accurate Sauvignon and very good Ribolla and Pinot Bianco, with an emphasis on vibrant floral and citric aromas and flavors.

Ribolla Gialla Collio	04	03	$$
Pinot Bianco Collio		04	$$
Sauvignon Graf de la Tour Collio	03	01	$$$

OTHER PRODUCERS TO LOOK FOR: Adami (Veneto), Borgo del Tiglio (Alto Adige), Cantina Nalles-Magré (Alto Adige), Castel Juval (Alto Adige), Cesconi (Trentino), Eugenio Collavini (FVG), Girolamo Dorigo (FVG), Drius (FVG), Ermacora (FVG), Falkenstein (Alto Adige), Marco Felluga (FVG), Josko Gravner (FVG), Inama (Veneto), Edi Kante (FVG), Edi Keber (FVG), Renato Keber (FVG), Kuenhof-Peter Pliger (Alto Adige), La Castellada (Friuli), Alois Lageder (Alto Adige), Lis Neris (FVG), Miani (FVG), Manni Nossing (Alto Adige), Pierpaolo Pecorari (FVG), Pojer e Sandri (Veneto), Produttori Colterenzio (Alto Adige), Produttori Cortaccia (Alto Adige), Produttori San Michele Appiano (Alto Adige), Produttori Terlano, Produttori Valle Isarco (Alto Adige), Dario Raccaro (FVG), Radikon (FVG), Ronchi di Cialla (FVG), Ronco del Gnemiz (FVG), Tiefenbrunner (Alto Adige), Franco Toros (FVG), Vignalta (Veneto), Volpe Pasini (FVG), Le Vigne di Zamò (FVG), Elena Walch (Alto Adige), Zidarich (FVG).

RED WINES

Both Alto Adige and Friuli-Venezia-Giulia produce numerous very good cooler-climate Cabernets and Merlots, as well as some more idiosyncratic red wines worth seeking out. Not many years ago, Cabernets and Merlots in Northeast Italy tended to be excessively vegetal, but today more producers are making consistently ripe wines that are at the same time less jammy and alcoholic than wines from the same grapes made in Sicily and parts of Tuscany. Two of Italy's best—and most famous—red wines are made in Trentino, one a Cabernet-Merlot blend from San Leonardo, the other produced from the native grape Teroldego at Foradori. Although Veneto is best known for Soave, it's also the source of Amarone, a very rich, concentrated, high-alcohol, dry red wine made from air-dried grapes pressed weeks or months after the harvest. And don't forget the luscious, port-like Recioto della Valpolicella made in Veneto, perfect with any chocolate dessert.

BANG FOR THE BUCK. Amarone is always an expensive wine, but many other northeast Italian reds are considerably more affordable, not to mention quite flexible at the dinner table. But these wines are rarely cheap.

2004 ★★★   2003 ★★★–   2004 ★★★★

RECOMMENDED PRODUCERS

Stefano Accordini. A modern approach to Amarone yields elegant, fruit-driven but almost austere wines that avoid overripeness and excessive alcohol.

Acinatico Recioto della Valpolicella	03	02	$$$
Acinatico Amarone della Valpolicella	**03**	01	$$$

Allegrini. A popular producer of Valpolicella and Amarone, with a lighter Palazzo della Torre bottling (local grapes plus Sangiovese); a fine, age-worthy, 100 percent Corvina wine called La Poja, and a rich Amarone.

Palazzo della Torre Rosso del Veronese		03	$
La Poja Corvina Veronese		**01**	$$$
Amarone della Valpolicella Classico	01	00	$$$$

Tommaso Bussola. One of the top three producers of Amarone today. The TB bottlings are amazingly powerful and concentrated, the BG versions also impressive and somewhat more approachable. Bussola may be the best make of Recioto today.

TB Valpolicella Classico Superiore	03	01	$$$
BG Amarone della Valpolicella		02	$$$
BG Recioto della Valpolicella Classico		**03**	$$$$

Foradori. The Granato is one of Italy's 50 best red wines every year and a splendid example of what the Teroldego variety can do in the right hands. Firm acidity gives the wine elegance.

Teroldego Rotaliano		03	$$
Granato IGT	03	02	$$$

Masi. Masi's Mazzano is quintessential large-framed Amarone, while the Campolongo di Torbe is softer and more approachable. Both are first-rate.

Costasera Amarone della Valpolicella	**03**	01	$$$
Serego Alighieri Vaio Armaron Amarone della Valpolicella	00	99	$$$$
Campolongo di Torbe Amarone della Valpolicella	00	99	$$$$
Mazzano Amarone della Valpolicella	**00**	**99**	$$$$

DISTINCTIVE RED GRAPES OF NORTHEAST ITALY

- **Corvina, Corvinone, Rondinella, and Molinara:** These four grapes form the basis of Amarone and Valpolicella in the Veneto, with each contributing something to the final blend. Corvina gives silkiness, Corvinone tannic backbone, Rondinella an herbal/spicy touch, and Molinara an easy drinkability, but producers seeking to make bigger, richer wines are beginning to phase out this last variety.
- **Lagrein:** This variety is the source of inky, tannic behemoths made in Alto Adige and named after the grape. The best offer aromas and flavors of rich black fruits, dark chocolate, and coffee, but poorer efforts can be vegetal.
- **Marzemino:** This variety yields light-bodied, somewhat herbaceous, strawberry-infused wines with some charm; best served lightly chilled.
- **Pignolo:** These are tannic wines with loads of black fruits, along with coffee and chocolate notes that are a bit more subtle than those of Refosco. Pignolo has come into vogue only in the past decade or so, and thus the considerable potential of this variety is still largely untapped.
- **Refosco del Peduncolo Rosso:** Peduncolo Rosso refers to the stalk leading to the grape cluster, which turns red when the grapes are ripe. Fuller-bodied than Schioppettino (see below), these wines typically exhibit more structure and fat, with pronounced coffee and chocolate flavors amidst the black fruits.
- **Schiava:** Often labeled as Lago di Caldaro or St. Magdalener, for the areas of Alto Adige and Trentino in which this grape is grown, Schiava gives light-bodied, faintly colored wines perfect for drinking chilled in the warm months. With their strawberry and raspberry aromas and enticing freshness, they can accompany some fish preparations in much the same way as Pinot Noir.
- **Schioppettino:** Medium-bodied wines with notes of peppery black and red berries.
- **Teroldego:** Native to Trentino, this fascinating grape is difficult to grow anywhere else. In the hands of the better producers, Teroldego yields full-bodied, age-worthy reds characterized by red fruits, game, truffle, and leather.

Roberto Mazzi. Mazzi produces modern, smooth wines that emphasize the fruity rather than tannic nature of Valpolicella; even the classically dry Amarone can give pleasure in its youth. The Valpolicella Poiega is midway between Valpolicella and Amarone in style, as the grapes are dried for three or four weeks.

Valpolicella Classico Superiore		03	$
Valpolicella Classico Superiore Vigneto Poiega	03	01	$$
Amarone della Valpolicella Punta di Villa	01	00	$$$$

Ronchi di Cialla. The Rapuzzi family single-handedly saved Schioppettino from extinction and was one of the first to use barriques to age sweet wines in Italy. Ronchi di Cialla's Schioppettino is a medium-bodied wine with compelling perfume of blackberry and green pepper, while the Refosco is somewhat more plummy and rich.

Schioppettino di Cialla COF	02	01	$$$
Refosco dal Peduncolo Rosso di Cialla	02	01	$$$

San Leonardo. The flagship wine, San Leonardo, is one of Italy's best Cabernet-Merlot blends; other wines are competently made but not at the same lofty level.

Merlot Trentino	02	01	$$
Villa Gresti Vigneti delle Dolomiti Rosso	01	00	$$$
San Leonardo Rosso delle Dolomiti	01	00	$$$$

Tenuta Sant'Antonio. A future star of Amarone, with numerous excellent bottlings that are highly concentrated without being exaggerated. Try also their superb Valpolicella.

Valpolicella Superiore La Bandina	00	99	$$$
Amarone della Valpolicella Selezione Antonio Castagnedi		02	$$$
Amarone della Valpolicella Campo dei Gigli	00	99	$$$$

OTHER PRODUCERS TO LOOK FOR: Brigaldara (Veneto), Giorgio Cecchetto (Veneto), Cesconi (Trentino), Produttori Colterenzio (Alto Adige), Dorigati (Trentino), Franz Gojer-Glög-glhof (Alto Adige), Gottardi (Alto Adige), Roccolo Grassi (Veneto), Franz Haas (Alto Adige), Hofstätter (Alto Adige), Maculan (Veneto), Marion (Veneto), Davide Moschioni (FVG), Santa Maddalena (Alto Adige), Fratelli Tedeschi (Veneto), Ronchi di Cialla.

EXTRAORDINARY AND VERY EXPENSIVE: Quintarelli (Veneto), Romano Dal Forno (Veneto).

CENTRAL ITALY

Italy's central regions (Emilia-Romagna, Tuscany, Umbria, Marche, Lazio, Abruzzo, and Molise) produce some of the country's most impressive age-worthy reds (such as Brunello di Montalcino and Vino Nobile di Montepulciano), tasty everyday reds, and remarkably dense sweet wines (Tuscany's Vin Santo). On the other hand, these regions also churn out dishearteningly huge volumes of rustic, boring reds and whites that are either neutral, overoaked, or acid-deficient. That said, central Italy represents a dynamic viticultural zone in which excellent new producers and wines are springing up all the time. Many of the most exciting wines are bottled as IGT (Indicazione Geografica Tipica), a designation that allows producers greater flexibility, both to use varieties that are not permitted for DOC or DOCG wines, and to include up to 20 percent of grapes from outside the delimited area as long as the wines do not lose their "typical" character.

Central Italy is geographically marked by the Apennine ridge, a low-lying range that runs roughly northeast to southwest, thereby effectively splitting central Italy into two halves: Emilia, Tuscany, Umbria, and Lazio in the western part, and Romagna, Marche, Abruzzo, and Molise in the east. Climate and soils vary greatly from area to area, as do the prevalent grape varieties. But there is no doubt that, with a few very high-quality exceptions, central Italy is red wine country, and Sangiovese dominates. Sangiovese is rarely bottled on its own, however; varying percentages of just about any grape variety are added to it nowadays. As Sangiovese is a fairly delicate variety in terms of the fragrances and flavors it offers, what ends up being added makes a huge difference in the final profile of the wine. Climate and altitude are also important in explaining the key differences among central Italy's Sangiovese-based wines. Wines made in the hotter, drier portions of southern Tuscany or in the drier areas of Romagna are much fleshier than Sangiovese-based wines made in Chianti and other distinctly cooler areas, where vineyards may be located as high as 1,600 to 1,800 feet above sea level.

In Tuscany and Emilia-Romagna, international red grapes have also proven highly successful: Italy's best Merlots are all made in Tuscany, and some fine Cabernet Sauvignons, Cabernet Francs, and Syrahs are produced there as well. These varieties also do well in Umbria and Lazio, with the wines of the latter region much less familiar to consumers than those of the former, even if Lazio holds out considerable potential. The rather full-bodied, spicy Sagrantino, a very tannic red wine unique to Umbria, is worth special mention. Marche, located on the Adriatic coast and often referred to as the elbow of Italy (one look at the map will explain why), also makes solid reds called Rosso Conero and Rosso Piceno, which are blends based on the native grapes Sangiovese and Montepulciano. But this region is especially renowned for what may well be Italy's best indigenous white variety, Verdicchio. Abruzzo and Molise are home to the red Montepulciano and the white Trebbiano d'Abruzzo varieties.

TUSCANY

Along with the Piedmont, Tuscany is Italy's most important wine-producing area. Chianti, Brunello, Vino Nobile, and Vin Santo are known all over the world, as are the so-called Supertuscans, a large group of important, high-quality reds born in the early 1970s and now representing some of Italy's best wines. Back then, producers began chafing under the restrictive regulations of the DOC (Denominazione di Origin Controllata). Some sought to avoid using certain legally recommended grape varieties, such as the white grapes that were considered an integral part of Chianti; others started blending Cabernet and Merlot, which at the time were proscribed, with native grape varieties.

Tuscany is about red wine: its white wines are fairly nondescript, although the simple, fresh Vermentino and Ansonica of the coast are charming, and a few examples of Vernaccia di San Gimignano can be interesting and age worthy, developing an uncanny resemblance to aged Chablis. Vin Santo, usually very rich and decadently sweet, can be among the world's greatest sweet wines, but the best bottlings are very expensive.

While Tuscany offers a plethora of riches to the wine lover, some of its most famous wines, especially Chianti and even Brunello, are experiencing a real slump in sales. There are many reasons for this, beginning with a steep rise in prices over the last five or ten years, which has greatly dampened demand for these wines. But there has also been a wave of new, moneyed owners who have not let their lack of winemaking experience get in the way of buying a piece of this beautiful region. This has opened the floodgate for enological consultants, many of whom work for numerous estates in the same area but routinely apply their tried-and-true recipe to winemaking, leading to the production of wines that resemble one another to a dismaying degree. Add to this the insistence on making deeply colored wines that are often overconcentrated, overoaked, and charmless—not to mention overbearing at the dinner table—and you begin to have a good idea of why Chianti and some other Tuscan red wines don't sell all that well anymore. Fortunately, producers have begun to recognize these errors, prices have finally stopped rising, and, mercifully, more trees are being allowed to live as less importance is afforded to new oak barrels.

2004 ★★★★+   2003 ★★★−   2002 ★   2001 ★★★★   2000 ★★★

CHIANTI

Perhaps Italy's best-known wine, Chianti has historically been associated with straw-covered flasks and checkered tablecloths. The flask is rarely seen nowadays (certainly no serious high-quality producer uses it) and Chianti has generally moved upscale. Today, many serious, full-bodied, and expensive wines are made, in addition to the hearty, simpler versions meant to be drunk within a year or two after bottling. Chianti is based on the Sangiovese grape, with up to 20 percent of other grape varieties allowed. Traditionally, white grapes were allowed in Chianti blends, but they have steadily been eliminated in an effort to produce bigger, more age-worthy reds. A good Chianti typically exhibits violet on the nose, together with slightly underripe, fresh red fruits, and a hint of licorice. It should always taste vibrant, as Sangiovese is a high-acid, late-ripening variety; not surprisingly, vintages are important when picking Chianti, much as they are when selecting Burgundy or Barolo, for a cool summer or harvest-time rain can relegate a vintage to mediocrity.

The best Chiantis are widely thought to come from the Classico zone, a small area with four small towns at its core: Greve, Castellina, Radda, and Gaiole. In 1932, six other Chianti subzones were added (Chianti Colli Aretini, Chianti Colli Senesi, Chianti Colli Pisani, Chianti Colli Fiorentini, Chianti Montalbano, Chianti Rùfina), with Chianti Montespertoli being a more recent addition. All are located immediately around the Classico area, and each, in theory at least, should present its own fragrance and flavor profile. Some recognizable differences do exist: the wines of Rùfina, situated to the northeast of Classico, are more elegant, higher in acidity, and longer-aging, while those of the Colli Senesi, located southeast of Classico right next to Montalcino, are the biggest, richest Chiantis. However, too many of today's Chiantis offer limited sense of place, for two main reasons: the ubiquitous presence of the consulting enologist and the rather generous percentages of foreign varieties added to Sangiovese (legal up to 20 percent of the blend), which can easily mask the delicate qualities of Sangiovese.

BANG FOR THE BUCK. Most Chianti is expensive but entry-level bottlings from solid producers can still be a wonderful buy. Stick to reputable names.

RECOMMENDED PRODUCERS

Antinori. This is Italy's best-known wine producer, and rightfully so, with more than 600 years of history making fine wine. Textbook entry-level Chianti and two excellent Chianti Classico Riserva bottlings. Antinori's Solaia blend is one of Italy's greatest wines nearly every year.

Pèppoli Chianti Classico	**03**	**01**	$$
Badia a Passignano Chianti Classico Riserva	**01**	**00**	$$$
Solaia Toscana Rosso	02	**01**	$$$$$

Capannelle. From the start, this has been one of the most forward-thinking operations in Chianti, yet the wines are among the most traditional and true to their terroir. The 50 & 50 (a Sangiovese-Merlot blend) is a joint venture with Montepulciano's Avignonesi estate, which supplies the Merlot.

Chianti Classico Riserva	**01**	**00**	$$$$
50 & 50 Toscana Rosso	**01**	**00**	$$$$$

Castellare. Another producer of very good, traditional, high-acid Chianti, as well as a top Supertuscan, I Sodi di San Niccolò, that eschews foreign varieties in favor of the classic Sangiovese–Malvasia Nera mix.

Chianti Classico BG Recioto della Valpolicella Classico			**03**	$$
Il Poggiale Chianti Classico Riserva		02	**01**	$$$
Sodi di San Niccolò Toscana Rosso	**01**	00	**99**	$$$$

Castello di Ama. Arguably the single most elegant Chianti of all, with more than a passing resemblance to Pinot Noir in some vintages. The two single-vineyard bottlings, Bellavista and La Casuccia, are also top-notch. L'Apparita is Italy's most refined Merlot and is particularly outstanding in weak vintages.

Chianti Classico	**03**	02	**01**	$$$
Vigna Casuccia Chianti Classico		**01**	00	$$$$$
L'Apparita Toscana Rosso		**01**	00	$$$$$

Castello dei Rampolla. Owners of one of the choicest vineyard sites in all of Chianti, in the perfectly exposed amphitheater of Panzano. The best wines here are the two Supertuscans, Sammarco (made with Cabernet Sauvignon, Merlot, and Sangiovese) and La Vigna d'Alceo (made with Cabernet Sauvignon and Petit Verdot).

Sammarco Toscana Rosso	**03**	**01**	$$$$$
La Vigna d'Alceo Toscana Rosso	**03**	**01**	$$$$$

Castello di Fonterutoli. One of Chianti's oldest families (an ancestor of the current owners is the first person documented to have used the term Chianti) is also one of its most modern in outlook: their wines are profoundly dark, tannic, and low in acidity, crammed with ripe black fruit.

Castello di Fonterutoli Chianti Classico	**01**	**00**	$$$
Siepi Toscana Rosso	**03**	02	$$$$

Felsina. Year in and year out, Felsina makes some of Tuscany's greatest wines. The wines of Giuseppe Mazzocolin, who has been at the helm for more than 20 years, are benchmarks for the region, from the Rancia Riserva to the Fontalloro, a pure, lush Sangiovese Supertuscan. The Vin Santo is also one of the best in Chianti.

Rancia Berardenga Chianti Classico Riserva	03	**01**	$$$
Fontalloro Sangiovese di Toscana	**01**	00	$$$
Maestro Raro Cabernet Sauvignon di Toscana	00	99	$$$$

Fontodi. This producer's top-drawer Vigna del Sorbo Chianti Riserva (with ten percent Cabernet Sauvignon) ages spectacularly well, as does the Flaccianello, one of Italy's first and still best Supertuscans. Also made here are interesting attempts at Pinot Noir and Syrah, as well as a solid Vin Santo.

Vigna del Sorbo Chianti Classico Riserva	03	**01**	$$$
Flaccianello della Pieve Colli della Toscana Centrale	03	**01**	$$$$
Case Via Syrah Colli della Toscana Centrale	03	01	$$$

Frescobaldi. Their Montesodi bottling is one of the best Chianti Rùfinas, aging spectacularly well. In addition, they make some interesting wines from the Pomino DOC, including one of the few successfully oaked Tuscan Chardonnays.

Nipozzano Chianti Rùfina Riserva	03	02	$$
Montesodi Chianti Rùfina	03	**01**	$$$

Isole e Olena. Paolo De Marchi is justly considered one of Italy's best and most dedicated producers, offering excellent entry-level Chianti, one of the best Supertuscans (all Sangiovese Cepparello), and two of the greatest Cabernets and Syrahs made anywhere in Italy.

Chianti Classico	03	02	$$
Cepparello Toscana Rosso	02	**01**	$$$
Collezione De Marchi Syrah	01	00	$$$

La Massa. Giampaolo Motta recently decided to opt out of the Chianti Classico consortium, so his Giorgio Primo is no longer labeled as such. Still, it remains a solidly made blend of Sangiovese and Merlot, while the simpler La Massa also contains a dollop of Cabernet.

La Massa Toscana Rosso	03	02	01	$$
Giorgio Primo Toscana Rosso	**03**	02	01	$$$$

Monsanto. Fabrizio Bianchi is one of the old sages of Chianti, and his Il Poggio Riserva still ranks among the very best. Also remarkably good is the Chardonnay that carries his name.

Fabrizio Bianchi Chardonnay Toscana Bianco		03	$$
Chianti Classico Riserva	01	00	$$$

Montevertine. One of the historic names in Tuscany, where the late Sergio Manetti led the Renaissance of Tuscan wine in the 1970s and 1980s. Le Pergole Torte is one of the top Supertuscans, and the Montevertine Rosso is among the most enjoyable Chiantis made today, even if Manetti stopped using the Chianti appellation after 1981 due to his desire to make a 100 percent Sangiovese wine, without any white grapes in the blend.

Montevertine Toscana Rosso	03	02	**01** $$$
Le Pergole Torte Toscana Rosso	03	**01**	$$$$

Rocca di Montegrossi. Here you'll find dark, rich, well-made Chiantis with considerable appeal for consumers, as well as a highly successful Merlot and one of the best Vin Santos made in Chianti.

Chianti Classico	03	02	$$
Geremia Toscana Rosso	03	01	$$
Vin Santo del Chianti Classico	98	97	$$$$

Ruffino. The Romitorio Supertuscan (Merlot and Colorino) is fine, but Ruffino's Riserva Ducale Oro is one of Italy's best wines for the money, and a great find on any restaurant wine list. Recent vintages seem to be moving toward a more international taste.

Chianti Classico Riserva Ducale Oro		01	$$
Romitorio di Santadame Toscana Rosso	01	00	$$$$

Selvapiana. Chianti Rùfina doesn't get any better than these elegant, tightly wound examples, the charms of which may be lost on those who chase chewy, tannic fruit bombs in the belief that bigger is better. The Bucerchiale Riserva ages for eons, with bottles from the 1950s still full of life.

Chianti Rùfina	03	02	$$
Bucerchiale Chianti Rùfina Riserva	01	00	$$$

OTHER PRODUCERS TO LOOK FOR: Badia a Coltibuono, Brolio, Casale Falchini, Castell'in Villa, Frascole, La Sala, Livernano, Palagetto, Giovanni Panizzi, Il Palazzino, Poggerino, Querciabella, Riecine, San Felice, San Fabiano Calcinaia, San Giusto a Rentennano, Savignola Paolina, Vecchie Terre di Montefili, Villa Cafaggio.

CARMIGNANO

These wines, from a small DOCG west of Florence, could actually be sold as Chianti Montalbano, but most producers prefer to continue to label them as Carmignano in recognition of the region's historic significance as a high-quality wine-producing area. A Tuscan wine based on a minimum of 50 percent Sangiovese, Carmignano differs from other Tuscan reds in two ways: first, Sangiovese grown here tends to give softer, less acidic wine; second, Cabernet Sauvignon and Franc, which typically comprise 10 to 20 percent of the blend, are fairly ubiquitous and important in Carmignano. The wines undoubtedly benefit from the added backbone and complexity of these varieties. After having fallen by the wayside in the 1960s and 1970s, the wines of Carmignano are making a comeback thanks to the hard work of the Contini Bonacossi family, who own the Tenuta di Capezzana, still one of the best estates. Another DOC wine of the area, Barco Reale, is essentially the second wine of Carmignano. Carmignano normally enjoys drier conditions than most of the Chianti area, so this appellation often performs reasonably well in rain-plagued years like 2002.

BANG FOR THE BUCK. A relatively good buy among the better-known Tuscan wines, especially compared to the more expensive Brunello or Nobile, but the number of high-quality producers is limited.

RECOMMENDED PRODUCERS

Ambra. A reliable producer of typical Carmignano. The Santa Cristina is usually the better of the entry-level wines, while the Riserva Montalbiolo is a consistently serious example from clay-rich soil. Look for this estate's rosato, too.

Carmignano Vigna di Santa Cristina	03	02	$$
Riserva Vigne Alte Montalbiolo Carmignano		01	$$$

Piaggia. Mauro Vannucci's wines have recently become more muscular yet retain their customary elegance. Il Sasso is a solid Sangiovese-Cabernet-Merlot blend.

Il Sasso Toscana Rosso	03	02	$$$
Carmignano Riserva	02	01	$$$

Tenuta di Capezzana. Carmignano's most important producer makes fine reds, but the top wines are much better than the basic bottlings. The Ghiaie della Furba can be a fine Cabernet-Merlot-Syrah blend. And look for their Vin Santo, one of the better examples of this wine made in Tuscany.

Villa di Capezzana Carmignano		03	$$
Ghiaie della Furba Toscana Rosso	02	01	$$$
Vin Santo Carmignano Riserva	99	98	$$$$

TUSCAN COAST

This is one of Italy's most exciting wine regions today, offering the astute consumer wines to suit just about any budget or taste. The "Tuscan Coast" monicker is a relatively new one, as is the subzone itself, where differences in soil and microclimate are only recently becoming apparent. The area referred to as the Tuscan Coast spans a large coastal as well as inland portion of southern Tuscany. It can be roughly divided into two areas: the northern section, known as Costa degli Etruschi, which is actually northern Maremma, extending from Leghorn to Suvereto; and a southern section, or Maremma proper, extending from the town of Grosseto down to the border with Lazio, the region immediately south of Tuscany. In the northern part of the area, international varieties have found an accommodating home, and some of Italy's most famous wines, such as Sassicaia and Masseto, are made there. The southern section, which is much hotter and drier, is particularly suited for Sangiovese; some of the fleshiest and fruitiest versions of the variety are made here. Among the numerous up-and-coming wines, Morellino di Scansano is a particularly enjoyable and relatively inexpensive Sangiovese-based wine that gives many pricier Chiantis a run for their money. The arrival of a number of important Italian wine families such as Biondi Santi, Cecchi, Mazzei, Moretti, Gaja, and others, all of whom have established estates here, is a testament to the bright future of the zone.

The Tuscan Coast is also the area where Tuscany's few decent dry white wines are made, including the Vernaccia di San Gimignano (Italy's first-ever DOC, back in 1966) and the refreshingly clean, herbal, and citrusy Vermentino and Ansonica of the coastline. The latter two wines are typical of the island of Elba, one of Italy's loveliest tourist destinations and the source of Aleatico, a delectable, light-bodied, sweet red wine that will leave you wanting more.

BANG FOR THE BUCK. The white wines and the Aleatico of the coast and the island of Elba are delicious and extremely cheap. Morellino can also be a remarkably good buy, and even the riservas are not expensive by Tuscan standards.

RECOMMENDED PRODUCERS

Castello del Terriccio. One of the hot names in Supertuscan wines, wildly expensive but extremely well made. The best of the lot are the Castello del Terriccio, a blend of Syrah, Petit Verdot, and Mourvèdre, and Lupicaia, from Cabernet Sauvignon and Merlot.

	03	02	01	
Tassinaia	03	02	01	$$$
Castello del Terriccio			01	$$$$$
Lupicaia		03	**01**	$$$$$

Ca' Marcanda. Piedmont giant Angelo Gaja's estate in the Bolgheri area is remarkably improved in recent years. The wines have very smooth tannins and are easy to drink, with the Magari (Merlot, Cabernet Sauvignon, and Cabernet Franc) not far in quality behind the Ca' Marcanda namesake wine.

	03	02	00	
Promis Toscana Rosso	03			$$$
Magari Toscana Rosso	**03**	02		$$$$
Ca' Marcanda Bolgheri Rosso			00	$$$$$

Grattamacco. One of Tuscany's historically great wines, the Grattamacco red (Sangiovese, Cabernet Sauvignion, and Merlot) is always pure and precise, reaching its peak about ten years after the vintage. There is also a solid but expensive Vermentino.

	03	02	01	
Grattamacco Bolgheri Rosso Superiore	**03**	02	**01**	$$$

Tenuta Guado al Tasso. Antinori's Bolgheri estate, from which the flagship wine of the same name has quickly become an icon bottling in Italy. No 2002 was made, although in the past lesser vintages gave wonderful results. Interesting and affordable Vermentino and rosé are also made here.

	04	01	00	
Bolgheri Vermentino	04			$$
Guado al Tasso Bolgheri Rosso Superiore		**01**	00	$$$$

Le Macchiole. This estate today produces three of Italy's best wines: Paleo (Cabernet Franc), Scrio (Syrah), and Messorio (Merlot), the latter two a bit heftier in style.

Paleo Toscana Rosso	`01`	`00`	$$$$
Scrio Toscana Rosso	`01`	`00`	$$$$$
Messorio Toscana Rosso	`01`	`00`	$$$$$

Moris Farms. One of the best producers of Morellino di Scansano, with a Supertuscan called Avvoltore that is one of the best.

Morellino di Scansano	`04`	`03`	$$
Morellino di Scansano Riserva		`01`	$$$
Avvoltore Maremma Toscana	`03`	`02`	$$$

Tenuta di Ornellaia. Two of Italy's greatest wines are Ornellaia, a Bordeaux blend based on Cabernet Sauvignon, and this estate's all-Merlot Masseto. These richly fruity, silky, long-aging wines rank among the world's best, even in lesser vintages.

Ornellaia Bolgheri Rosso Superiore	`03`	`02`	$$$$$
Masseto Toscana Rosso	`03`	`02`	$$$$$

Le Pupille. Perhaps the best overall producer of Morellino di Scansano; certainly the estate's Poggio Valente bottling has no rivals. The Supertuscan Saffredi is a paragon of silkiness and power.

Morellino di Scansano Elisabetta Geppetti	`04`		$$
Poggio Valente Morellino di Scansano	`03`		$$$
Saffredi Maremma Toscana Rosso	`03`	`02`	$$$$$

Tenuta San Guido. Sassicia is one of Italy's most celebrated wines, with the 1985 probably one of the ten greatest Italian wines of all time. This Cabernet Sauvignon–dominated blend needs many years in bottle to show its mettle, and can often be underwhelming in its youth. The second wine, Guidalberto, is also remarkably fine.

Guidalberto IGT Toscana Rosso	`03`		$$$
Sassicaia Bolgheri	`03`	02	$$$$

Tua Rita. Tua Rita produces some of Italy's most interesting wines, a couple of which have achieved cult status. The Redigaffi is a Merlot in the same quality league as Masseto and L'Apparita, the Giusto di Notri blend is top-notch, and the Syrah is one of the best in Italy. Quantities are limited and prices are high.

Syrah Toscana Rosso		`03`	`01`	$$$$
Giusto di Notri Toscana Rosso	`03`	02	`01`	$$$$
Redigaffi Toscana Rosso	`03`	`02`	`01`	$$$$$

OTHER PRODUCERS TO LOOK FOR: Acquabona, Badia a Morrone, Campo alla Sughera, Fattoria di Magliano, Mantellassi, Montepeloso, Petra, Poggio Argentiera, La Regola, Sassotondo, Michele Satta, Sorbaiano, Tenuta di Ghizzano, Tenuta di Valgiano.

MONTALCINO

A pretty medieval hilltop town only 25 miles south of Siena, Montalcino is home to one of Italy's most famous red wines, Brunello di Montalcino. Brunello may also be Italy's longest-lived table wine (though producers of Barolo might take exception to the statement); wines from the 1888 and 1891 vintages are still alive and kicking in the cellars of the producer who started it all, Biondi Santi. Ferruccio Biondi Santi was singlehandedly responsible for creating Brunello at the end of the 19th century, but the area has exploded onto the international scene in just the past 30 years. The list of producers has grown from not many more than 20 in the 1950s to well over 100 today, with prices, especially for the more desirable bottlings, growing exponentially over time. Brunello is 100 percent Sangiovese, but the Sangiovese of the area is a particular clone, known as Sangiovese Grosso, that tends to fuller-bodied, richer, more age-worthy wines. Brunello typically displays aromas and flavors of red cherry and leather, with riper examples also exhibiting plum and chocolate.

Much as in Bordeaux, where the wines of Pauillac are quite different—or at least ought to be—from those of Margaux, soils and climates vary considerably in Montalcino according to the individual subzone. For instance, soils can be rich in chalky clay, *tufa* (a volcanic soil), gravel, sand, or a combination thereof. Vineyards exposed to the north give leaner, higher-acid, more perfumed wines that are completely different from those that come from vineyards grown on the southern side of the Montalcino hill. Still, some producers feel that the best Brunellos are those made from a blend of grapes from both sides of the hill. The wine called Rosso di Montalcino is often in essence a baby Brunello that has been aged for only one year prior to being released and is the equivalent of a simpler, entry-level Chianti. Indeed, in many instances it is declassified Brunello—those barrels of wine that the producer deems not good enough to become Brunello, which cannot be released until the fifth January after the harvest.

BANG FOR THE BUCK. Only the Rosso di Montalcino can be considered a good buy here, as Brunello is always expensive and sometimes exorbitantly so. But the better examples of Rosso are satisfying, full-bodied wines that deserve more attention.

RECOMMENDED PRODUCERS

Argiano. A rather traditionally styled Brunello that has steadily improved in recent vintages. But Argiano's Supertuscan Solengo, a blend of Cabernet, Syrah, and Merlot, remains firmly established as the best wine of the estate.

Brunello di Montalcino	01	00	99	$$$
Solengo Toscana Rosso	03	02	01	$$$$

Biondi Santi. Extremely long-lived wines that are tight and lean in their youth and often disappoint when compared in blind tastings with fleshier, juicier wines. The Riserva is much better than the regular Brunello, though.

Brunello di Montalcino	00	99	$$$$$
Brunello di Montalcino Riserva		99	$$$$$

Caparzo. A solid if rather one-dimensional entry-level Brunello, and an outstanding riserva called La Casa, made in a traditional style, avoiding overly jammy fruit and capable of long aging.

Brunello di Montalcino	01	00	99	$$$$
Brunello di Montalcino La Casa	01	00	99	$$$$$

Ciacci Piccolomini d'Aragona. Among the suavest, most velvety Brunellos, with vibrant fruit character, enticing perfume, and very supple tannins. Unlike many other top wines of the zone, this stylish Brunello does not normally require lengthy cellaring to show its charms. The estate also makes a popular blend of Sangiovese, Cabernet, and Merlot called Ateo.

Rosso di Montalcino	04	03		$$
Pianrosso Brunello di Montalcino Pianrosso	01	00	99	$$$$

Col d'Orcia. Each year this estate produces one of the best basic Brunello bottlings, with ripe red fruit flavors complicated by hints of leather and tobacco. The riserva is also good, but best of all is the single-vineyard Poggio al Vento. The Supertuscan Olmaia (Cabernet) is also top-notch.

Brunello di Montalcino	01	00	99	$$$
Brunello di Montalcino Poggio al Vento			98	$$$$$
Olmaia Toscana IGT		01	00	$$$$

Costanti. Elegant, structured Brunellos with enticing floral lift to their focused red fruit fla-
v   o   r   s   .

Brunello di Montalcino	01	00	99	$$$$

Lisini. A solid producer of traditional Brunello with excellent vineyard sites in the warmer parts of Montalcino. The Ugolaia bottling is frequently one of the top ten wines of Montalcino.

Brunello di Montalcino	01	00	$$$$
Brunello di Montalcino Ugolaia		99	$$$$$

Silvio Nardi. Emilia Nardi uses clonal selections and vinification of small lots to make the best wine possible. While the basic Brunello is only average, Nardi's Manachiara bottling is first-rate, in a smoother and less tannic style than some other top Brunellos.

Brunello di Montalcino Manachiara	01	00	99	$$$$

Pertimali/Livio Sassetti. Consistently rich, deep Brunellos with the silky texture of Burgundy. Look also for the estate's Sangiovese-Cabernet Supertuscan Vigna Fili di Seta.

Vigna Fili di Seta Rosso di Toscana			03	$$$
Brunello di Montalcino	01	00	99	$$$$

Piancornello. Silvana Pieri is a small producer of excellent Brunello and very good Rosso that are worth a special search.

Rosso di Montalcino		04	03	$$
Brunello di Montalcino	01	00	99	$$$

Pian delle Vigne. This estate is producing high-quality Brunellos following its purchase by Antinori in 1995. Its especially silky tannins give it a very smooth finish.

Brunello di Montalcino	01	00	99	$$$$

Pieve Santa Restituta. Owned by Angelo Gaja, who makes some of Italy's greatest red wines in Piedmont, this estate's Brunellos have surged to the top since the latter half of the 1990s. The wines have the telltale fine tannins and glossy texture of all of Gaja's wines, in addition to the firm grip of Brunello.

Brunello di Montalcino Rennina	00	99	$$$$$
Brunello di Montalcino Sugarille	01	99	$$$$$

Poggio di Sotto. Piero Palmucci makes some of the best traditional Brunellos (the riserva is usually spectacular), even if these somewhat lean, high-acid, pale-colored wines often confuse tasters looking for outsized examples. But pure Sangiovese should never be black, and besides, Palmucci's Brunello ages marvelously. The Rosso is one of the very best of Montalcino.

Rosso di Montalcino		03	02	$$$
Brunello di Montalcino	01	00	99	$$$$

Il Poggione. This estate's riserva bottling of Brunello is one of the great wines of Montalcino, but both Brunellos made here are typical large-framed wines that show Sangiovese at its best, with fragrant violet and red cherry aromas, chewy tannins, and strong acidity adding welcome lift.

Rosso di Montalcino			03	$$
Brunello di Montalcino	01	00	99	$$$$
Brunello di Montalcino Riserva		99	98	$$$$$

Salvioni/Le Cerbaiola. Ever since its first vintage in 1985, this estate has been considered one of the top sources of Brunello, with a tendency toward producing superripe wines with impressive richness.

Brunello di Montalcino La Cerbaiola	01	00	99	$$$$$

Siro Pacenti. Older vintages here often showed overly generous use of oak, but Giancarlo Pacenti has managed to reign in the tannins of his Brunellos. Today, even wines from weaker years such as 2000 are impressively concentrated, silky-smooth and elegant.

Rosso di Montalcino		04	03	$$
Brunello di Montalcino	01	00	99	$$$$

OTHER PRODUCERS TO LOOK FOR: Agostina Pieri, Altesino, Banfi, Canalicchio, Canalicchio di Sopra, Capanna, Casanova di Neri, Castelgiocondo, Cerbaiona, Fuligni, Lambardi, La Poderina, La Torre, Le Macioche, Le Presi, Mastrojanni, Poggio Antico, Romitorio, Salicutti, San Felice, Soldera, Talenti, Ucceliera, Vasco Sassetti, Sesti, Valdicava, Val di Suga.

MONTEPULCIANO

Another scenic medieval hilltop town, Montepulciano's most famous wine is Vino Nobile, so-called because it was long a favorite of popes and of the nobility (in fact, most of its earliest producers were members of aristocratic families of the area). Vino Nobile is also made with Sangiovese, or rather a particular subvariety known as Prugnolo Gentile. Gentile refers to genteel or noble, not to gentle or soft; in fact, Prugnolo Gentile is one of the harshest and most tannic subvarieties of Sangiovese. Vino Nobile is a blend of 60 to 80 percent Sangiovese, with most of the rest accounted for by any number of other varieties, although historically local grapes such as Colorino and Mammolo were used. As in other parts of Tuscany, Cabernet and Merlot have gained followings of late, much to the dismay of those who feel that Mammolo, especially, gave Nobile its distinctive violet perfume. As in Montalcino, there is also a user-friendly, more quickly accessible red wine, here called Rosso di Montepulciano.

BANG FOR THE BUCK. Rosso di Montepulciano can be a very good buy, but Vino Nobile itself is also a reasonable value in the context of the world's important red wines, as prices are normally much lower than those of equivalent big, age-worthy reds from California, Australia, and France.

RECOMMENDED PRODUCERS

Avignonesi. Though the Nobile made here is fine, the estate's decadently rich, unctuous, and extremely expensive Vin Santo and Vin Santo Occhio di Pernice are even better, numbering among Italy's finest sweet wines.

Vino Nobile di Montepulciano Riserva Grandi Annate	99	$$$
Vin Santo	93	$$$$$
Vin Santo Occhio di Pernice	94	$$$$$

Boscarelli. The estate vineyards are located in one of the best subzones of Montepulciano, that of Cervognano, and the wines are smooth, stylish, and structured to age, but rarely hard in their youth.

Vino Nobile di Montepulciano	03	02	$$$
Vino Nobile di Montepulciano Nocio dei Boscarelli	01	00	$$$$

Dei. A reliable name for supple, elegantly styled wines with vibrant fruit and silky texture. Dei's wines are among the most accessible of the Montepulciano zone but have good depth too.

Rosso di Montepulciano		04	03	$$
Vino Nobile di Montepulciano	03	02	01	$

Poliziano. The top Nobile bottling here, Asinone, is often the best version of the vintage, a paragon of elegance, with rich red fruits, silky tannins, and considerable aging potential. The Cabernet-Merlot blend Le Stanze is also quite good.

Rosso di Montepulciano	04	03	$

Vino Nobile di Montepulciano Asinone	03	01	$$
Le Stanze del Poliziano Toscana Rosso	03	02	$$$

Valdipiatta. Although established in the 1970s, Valdipiatta only became a high-quality producer of Nobile in 1990 with the arrival of new owner Giulio Caporali, who immediately began investing in his vineyards, reorganizing and replanting them, and greatly reducing yields.

Rosso di Montepulciano	04	03	$$
Vino Nobile di Montepulciano Riserva	99	98	$$$
Vino Nobile di Montepulciano Vigna d'Alfiero		01	$$$

OTHER PRODUCERS TO LOOK FOR: Il Macchione, La Braccesca, La Calonica, Fattoria del Cerro, Lodola Nuova, Poggio alla Sala, Romeo, Salcheto, Villa S. Anna.

OTHER RED WINES OF CENTRAL ITALY

The other regions of central Italy have been endowed with a patchwork of soils and climatic conditions, many of which are ideal for the production of high-quality wines. Marche, Umbria, and Lazio are blessed with hilly terrain, lakes that effectively moderate temperatures, and a wide range of vineyard exposures. It follows that great wines should be commonplace here, as they were in antiquity, right? Unfortunately, only a few passionate producers make outstanding wines in these regions today. Lately, however, a new commitment to serious viticulture has produced some stunning wines in areas that had long been dormant.

Emilia-Romagna is the land best known for Lambrusco, some examples of which are actually quite enjoyable, with good depth of fruit and an attractive acid/tannin balance, but much of which is painfully tart and tannic. Much better is Sangiovese di Romagna, even if most of these wines show limited individuality. The Marche is best known for two blends of Sangiovese and Montepulciano—Rosso Piceno and Rosso Conero—both of which can be juicy and interesting. Rosso Piceno is usually the more food-friendly and approachable of the two. In Umbria, few red wines communicate much sense of place, and there are many nondescript Sangiovese or Sangiovese-Cabernet-Merlot blends made. One notable exception is Lungarotti's deservedly famous Rubesco Riserva. Sagrantino di Montefalco does have real personality; these highly alcoholic, tannic behemoths can also age for decades. And the air-dried version, a Passito not unlike Recioto della Valpolicella, can be fascinating.

In Abruzzo, Montepulciano is capable of being one of Italy's lushest, fruitiest red wines, with a satisfyingly mouthfilling texture and very soft tannins. When made with care and reasonably low vine yields, it can be the ultimate everyday food wine of Italy, but only the best producers make more serious and age-worthy versions. Lazio is the home of a difficult native variety, Cesanese, that has only recently been tamed, but current results are encouraging. Cesanese del Piglio and Cesanese di Olevano Romano, two wines made from various manifestations of the Cesanese grape, can be a revelation when competently made. Especially in hot years like 2003, they offer plenty of red fruit and old leather notes. All of these regions of central Italy have also planted Cabernet, Merlot, and other international varieties (Petit Verdot is attracting increasing attention in Lazio), with the best results coming from Umbria and northern Lazio.

BANG FOR THE BUCK. Montepulciano d'Abruzzo, when well made, is a yummy, food-friendly wine that costs very little. Cesanese from a reputable producer can be excellent but the top bottlings are already dismayingly expensive. Rosso Piceno represents an excellent low-cost alternative to Chianti and the Rossos of Montalcino and Montepulciano.

2004 ★★★+   2002 ★★★

RECOMMENDED PRODUCERS

Paolo Bea. One of the oldest names in Montefalco wine, with a history dating back to the 16th century. The ultratraditional winemaking practiced here yields highly individual wines that are quite wild, even rustic, but rich, concentrated, and powerful.

Montefalco Rosso	01	00	$$
Montefalco Rosso Riserva Vigna Pipparello	01	00	$$$
Sagrantino di Montefalco Secco Pagliaro	00	99	$$$$

Arnaldo Caprai. The most famous producer of Sagrantino di Montefalco; Caprai's 25 Anni Riserva is considered the best of them all, year in and year out. But Collepiano, the far less expensive midlevel Sagrantino, is actually much more drinkable in its youth.

Collepiano Sagrantino Montefalco	02	01	$$$
25 Anni Sagrantino Montefalco	03	01	$$$$$

Còlpetrone. Very good, powerfully spicy Sagrantino and perhaps an even better Passito version.

Rosso di Montefalco			03	$$
Sagrantino di Montefalco	03	02	01	$$$
Passito Sagrantino di Montefalco		02	01	$$$

Lungarotti. Lungarotti singlehandedly put the small town of Forgiano on the wine map. The estate is worth a visit for its wine museum, the excellent and beautiful Tre Vaselle restaurant, and a Riserva Monticchio bottling that ages forever. There's also a very good Cabernet-Sangiovese-Canaiolo blend called San Giorgio.

Rubesco Torgiano Rosso	03	02	$$
Vigna Monticchio Torgiano Rosso Riserva	01	00	$$$
San Giorgio Rosso dell'Umbria	01	00	$$$$

Masciarelli. Fat, soft, pleasing Montepulciano. The impressive Villa Gemma will appeal to those who like huge, superconcentrated wines.

Montepulciano d'Abruzzo	03	02	01	$
Villa Gemma Montepulciano d'Abruzzo		00	99	$$$$

OTHER PRODUCERS TO LOOK FOR: Antonelli San Marco (Umbria), Borgo di Colloredo (Molise), Casale della Ioria (Lazio), Castellucio (Emilia-Romagna), Cavicchioli (Emilia-Romagna), Umberto Cesari (Emilia-Romagna), Ciccio Zaccagnini (Abruzzo), Di Majo Norante (Molise), Drei Donà (Emilia-Romagna), Emidio Pepe (Abruzzo), Falesco (Lazio), Illuminati (Abruzzo), La Carraia (Umbria), La Fiorita (Umbria), Marramiero (Abruzzo), Orlando Contucci Ponno (Abruzzo), Pallavicini (Lazio), San Patrignano (Emilia-Romagna), Tabarrini (Umbria), Terragens (Emilia-Romagna), Venturini Baldini (Emilia-Romagna).

SCARCE BUT WORTH A SEARCH: Valentini (Abruzzo).

WHITE WINES

Central Italy's white wines are often priced at a fraction of better-known bottlings from the north or south. The best white wine made in this part of Italy is Verdicchio, from two different DOCs: the Verdicchio dei Castelli di Jesi and the fuller-bodied Verdicchio di Matelica. Both develop interesting minerality and Riesling-like petrolly nuances over time. Better yet, Verdicchio comes in a range of styles, from lighter, fresh versions, to oak-aged, fuller wines of real depth and layered complexity, to late-harvested examples not unlike better Alsatian wines. Orvieto in Umbria and the wines of the Castelli Romani in Lazio benefit from rich volcanic *tufa* soils that nurture minerality and complexity. Unfortunately, decades of industrial-scale production have ruined their image, and today a handful of serious producers are struggling to emerge from the wreckage.

Some of central Italy's newer white wines are among the most interesting. Most often, they are made from long-forgotten native varieties that had been abandoned in favor of high-volume Trebbiano Toscano and Malvasia di Candia. Grape varieties such as Malvasia Puntinata, Bombino, and Bellone have bright futures, with Puntinata and Bellone capable of giving both outstanding dry and sweet wines. In fact, dessert wines are another thing Lazio and Umbria have in common, as these are two of the few areas in Italy where *Botrytis cinerea* (noble rot) naturally occurs. Other white wines of Central Italy worth considering are the Pignoletto of Emilia (light and fresh, with citrus and herbal nuances) and the Trebbiano d'Abruzzo. The latter can be intensely rich and almost Chardonnay-like when made by Marina Cvetic (at Gianni Masciarelli), or elegant, citrusy, and minerally in the hands of Edoardo Valentini, but is more often neutral plonk.

BANG FOR THE BUCK. Verdicchio can be an excellent buy, but some picking and choosing is necessary as prices have been creeping upward for most of the better versions. The best white wines of Lazio can also offer very good value.

2005 ★★★   2004 ★★★+   2003 ★★+

RECOMMENDED PRODUCERS

Barberani (Umbria). A solid Orvieto producer with an excellent late-harvest wine called Calcaia and good late-harvest Muscat.

Villa Monticelli Moscato Passito Umbria		03	$$$
Calcaia Muffa Nobile Orvieto Classico Superiore Dolce		02	$$$

Castel de Paolis (Lazio). The Malvasia Puntinata–Viognier blend called Vigna Adriana is one of Italy's better white wines, but the Frascati is also quite good, if not as complex.

Campo Vecchio Lazio Bianco		04	$
Vigna Adriana Lazio Bianco		04	$$

Castello della Sala (Umbria). Cervaro is one of Italy's best Chardonnays, even if the wine's toasty oak can dominate in the early going. This Antinori-owned estate also makes a very good late-harvest wine from botrytis-affected grapes called Muffato and a solid Sauvignon Blanc labeled Conte della Vipera.

Conte della Vipera Umbria		02	$$
Cervaro della Sala Umbria	03	02	$$$
Muffato della Sala Umbria		03	$$$

Garofoli (Marche). The best bottlings among this estate's strong lineup of Verdicchios are the elegantly oaked Serra Fiorese and the concentrated, minerally Podium.

Serra Fiorese Verdicchio dei Castelli di Jesi Classico Riserva		02	$$
Podium Verdicchio dei Castelli di Jesi Classico Riserva	04	03	$$

Sartarelli (Marche). The Tralivio is light, fresh Verdicchio at its best, but it's the Balciana that ranks with Italy's finest whites. This late-harvest wine is meant to be dry, but often has a bit of residual sugar and is reminiscent of a top Alsatian white.

Tralivio Verdicchio dei Castelli di Jesi Classico		04	$$
Balciana Verdicchio dei Castelli di Jesi Classico Riserva		03	$$$

Sergio Mottura (Lazio). Even though he's based in Lazio, Mottura is probably the best overall producer of Orvieto. He also makes two dry whites from the Grechetto grape that rank with the best in Italy (the Latour bottling is aged in oak). In addition, there's a very good, sweet late-harvest wine called Muffo.

Vigna Tragugnano Orvieto		04	$$
Poggio della Costa Grechetto di Civitella d'Agliano		04	$$
Latour a Civitella Grechetto di Civitella d'Agliano		03	$$

OTHER PRODUCERS TO LOOK FOR: Belisario (Marche), Cardeto (Umbria), Casale Pilozzo (Lazio), Colle Picchioni (Lazio), Colle Stefano (Marche), Colonnara (Marche), La Monacesca (Marche), La Stoppa (Emilia-Romagna), Luretta (Emilia-Romagna), Montecappone (Marche), Palazzone (Umbria), Cantina Sant'Andrea (Lazio), Vallona (Emilia-Romagna), Cantina Valtidone (Emilia-Romagna), Villa Bucci (Marche).

SCARCE BUT WORTH A SEARCH: Valentini (Abruzzo).

SOUTHERN ITALY

Italy's south—Campania, Puglia, Basilicata, Calabria, and the two islands of Sicily and Sardinia—has attracted considerable attention in the past decade for the improving quality of its wines. Although an ocean of neutral or downright faulty wine is still produced in these provinces (a generation ago most white wines were born tired if not oxidized and the reds were rustic at best), today some of Italy's most captivating, fruit-driven wines come from southern Italy. The single greatest asset that southern Italian producers share, besides a climate ideally suited to viticulture, is a panoply of indigenous grape varieties peculiar to the region. Most of these grapes have been cultivated in the area for centuries. Whereas international varieties such as Merlot, Cabernet Sauvignon, Chardonnay, and even Syrah have done remarkably well in Italy's south, it is the native grape varieties that are generating much of the excitement today.

While Campania, the region that includes Naples and Pompeii, is a tourist destination that usually conjures visions of heat, sun, and sand, its inland, hilltop vineyards enjoy a relatively cool climate that produces some of Italy's most interesting and distinctive white wines, full of mineral nuances and delicate herbal accents. The inland volcanic soils of the Taburno and Taurasi areas are home to the Aglianico grape, which produces red wines that are among the best in Italy. Outstanding Aglianico is also made in Basilicata, Italy's smallest region, tucked between the toe (Calabria) of Italy's boot-shaped peninsula and its heel (Puglia). The extinct volcano called Vulture provides an ideal habitat for this grape, grown in some of the highest and latest-picked red wine vineyards in Europe.

Puglia is home to some of Italy's burliest red wines, with high alcohol levels and lots of ripe fruit. Salice Salentino, produced in the southernmost part of Puglia, is actually the lightest of these, and is a good alternative to wines such as Dolcetto or Chianti. Keep in mind that Puglia, along with Abruzzo, is the best source for rosés in Italy. It also supplies some charming, lightly sweet muscats and highly alcoholic and tannic sweet reds (which are great with chocolate!) made from the Aleatico grape.

There is no question that Sicily has received the lion's share of attention over the last few years, thanks to the presence of numerous marketing-savvy estates, several unique grape varieties, and a host of wines crammed full of ripe fruit, spices, and herbs. Cool-climate areas not far from the city of Catania, in the northeastern part of

SOUTHERN ITALY

the island (where the still-active Etna volcano is located) yield both fresh red wines of real personality and mineral- and citrus-infused white wines that age surprisingly well. The rest of the island excels at big hearty reds that are priced for all budgets. Don't forget about Marsala, a wine normally made in an oxidized style reminiscent of dry sherry, with some versions being extremely sweet. And the smaller islands of Pantelleria and the Lipari, right off Sicily's coastline, are home to some of Italy's best sweet wines—the Moscato and Passito of Pantelleria and the Malvasia delle Lipari.

Last but not least, Sardinia is home to Vermentino (the Rolle of southern France), one of the white wines that Italians love the most: always crisp, lemony, and herbal, it's the ideal soulmate for the many seaside fish preparations typical of the island. The best Vermentinos are labeled di Gallura, as opposed to the more generic di Sardegna. Sardinia's diversity of microclimates and soils, plus the astonishing mix of native grape varieties still found on the island, help explain the great range of red wines available here, with Grenache (called Cannonau in Sardinia) and Carignan being the most dependable.

Key to Vintage Ratings		Key to Assessments of Specific Wines	
★★★★★	Outstanding	**03**	An excellent to outstanding example *of that wine*
★★★★	Excellent	03	A good to very good example *of that wine*
★★★	Good to very good	03	A disappointing effort (often due to a
★★	Fair to average		difficult vintage)
★	Poor		

RED WINES

Although some excellent Merlots and Syrahs are being made in Sicily, most of the interest generated today surrounds native Italian grapes such as Primitivo, Negroamaro, Nero d'Avola, and Aglianico.

BANG FOR THE BUCK. Primitivo and Negroamaro are usually fairly priced hearty reds, but the Nero d'Avola of Sicily has becoming increasingly expensive and good buys are harder to find. The top Aglianico del Vulture wines are hardly cheap, but they can compare in quality with the best Barolos and Brunellos, and they are usually 30 to 40 percent cheaper than those more famous wines.

2005 ★★★★+   **2004** ★★★★   **2003** ★★★   **2002** ★   **2001** ★★★★

RECOMMENDED PRODUCERS

Agricole Vallone. Traditionally made wines that have never been better. The Vigna Flaminio is the archetypical southern Italian red: full-bodied, a touch rustic, yet light enough to go well with your whole meal. The Graticciaia is a knockout, a luscious dead ringer for Amarone.

Vigna Flaminio Brindisi Rosato		04	$
Vigna Flaminio Brindisi Rosso		01	$
Graticciaia Salento Rosso	00	97	$$$$

Antonio Caggiano. Perhaps the best modern-styled Taurasi made in Campania today, the Macchia de Goti is a benchmark for the variety, with heaps of supple, spicy red cherry, and plum fruit. Soft, low-acid wines that are never clumsy.

Taurì Aglianico dell'Irpinia		01	$$
Salae Domini Aglianico dell'Irpinia	03	01	$$$
Macchia de Goti Taurasi	02	01	$$$

Argiolas. Sardinia's quality leader, thanks to a long relationship with star enologist Giacomo Tachis, the winemaker who was responsible for Tuscany's famous Sassicaia.

Perdera Monica di Sardegna	04	03	$
Costera Cannonau di Sardegna	04	03	$
Turriga Isola dei Nuraghi	02	01	$$$$

Cantine del Notaio. Modern, luscious wines that show the potential of the Vulture. La Firma is now firmly entrenched in the stellar category of Italian reds.

Il Rogito Aglianico del Vulture Rosato		04	$$
Il Repertorio Aglianico del Vulture	03	01	$$
La Firma Aglianico del Vulture	03	01	$$$

IMPORTANT RED GRAPES OF SOUTHERN ITALY

- **Aglianico:** Arguably Italy's third-best red variety, following Nebbiolo and San-giovese, Aglianico is capable of producing massive, complex yet elegant wines that age very well. In Campania, the Aglianico of Taurasi and the version of Aglianico that makes Taburno differ slightly: the former normally offers fra-grances of spices and red rose, the latter scents of tobacco and leather. The Aglianico del Vulture of Basilicata is deeply colored and redolent of ripe plum. Aglianico from Vulture and especially Taurasi can age for decades.

- **Negroamaro:** Negroamaro, one of Puglia's main red varieties along with Primitivo, has a tendency to produce huge and monolithic reds, and for that reason it's almost always softened with a touch of another local variety, Malvasia Nera, much as Canaiolo Nero had been used with Sangiovese in Chianti for centuries. When harvested late or even slightly air-dried, Negroamaro can yield a wine not unlike the Amarone of Italy's north: velvety-rich, high in alcohol, and classically dry.

- **Primitivo:** Better known as Zinfandel to North American consumers, Puglia's Primi-tivo is generally less jammy and alcoholic than its American counterpart, and is almost always more earthy and rustic. The finest are labeled Primitivo di Manduria.

- **Uva di Troia.** Puglia's next emerging red grape, the Uva di Troia yields far more elegant wines than Negroamaro or Primitivo, but with serious structure. Top examples show a layered complexity, typically offering blackberry fruit, a deli-cate blond tobacco element, and forest floor nuances.

- **Nero d'Avola:** Sicily's Nero d'Avola is a distant cousin to Syrah, and one can easily recognize black pepper, mushroom, and herbal notes in the wines it pro-duces. When Nero d'Avola is well made, it's a delightfully spicy, luscious, black cherry- and prune-scented wine, but alas, some examples are rustic and green.

- **Carignan:** Carignan from Sardinia is frequently almost too soft for its own good, yielding palate-caressing wines with aromas and flavors of red cherry, nutmeg, and grilled meat.

- **Cannonau:** Cannonau, a grape better known elsewhere as Grenache, is almost always characterized by red fruits, tobacco, and leather in wines from Sardinia, as well as substantial levels of alcohol, with some examples quite earthy or vegetal.

Cantina del Taburno. One of the best cooperatives in Italy, with a bevy of well-priced, high-quality wines. Star winemaker and enology professor Luigi Moio knows Aglianico like nobody else. The Delius and Fidelis wines are excellent values, while the Bue Apis, from a 100-year-old vineyard, is a woody, tannic behemoth that needs time.

Fidelis Aglianico del Beneventano	01	00	$$
Delius Aglianico del Beneventano	03	01	$$$
Bue Apis Aglianico del Beneventano	03	01	$$$$

Donnafugata. One of the best and most reliable all-around producers of Sicily. The Mille e Una Notte, from native grape varieties, is usually soft, layered, and complex.

Tancredi Contessa Entellina Rosso	03	02	$$$
Mille e Una Notte Contessa Entellina Rosso	02	01	$$$$

Elena Fucci. A hot new name in the volcanic soils of the Vulture, with the highest vineyard (the Titolo) at nearly 2,000 feet above sea level. A true grand cru, showing notes of black plum, tobacco, and spice and the elegance that comes from slow ripening of the fruit.

Titolo Aglianico del Vulture	03	02	$$$

Feudi di San Gregorio. The Ercolino brothers have created one of Italy's biggest wine success stories, with a plethora of well-made wines that nod to international tastes. Their ripe, juicy, low-acid reds speak less of terroir than some more traditionally styled wines of Campania, but they are crowd-pleasers, especially the large-scaled Patrimo, made from 100 percent Merlot.

Taurasi Piano di Montevergine	01	99	$$$
Serpico Irpinia Rosso	03	01	$$$$
Patrimo Irpinia Rosso	03	02	$$$$$

Salvatore Molettieri. Molettieri is widely considered to be the best interpreter of traditionally made Taurasi aged in large oak casks. In contrast to wines that essentially deliver gobs of superripe fruit, Molettieri's uncompromising examples are characterized by tobacco and leather and offer considerable aging potential.

Cinque Querce Taurasi	01	00	$$$
Cinque Querce Vigna Riserva Taurasi	01	00	$$$

Mastroberardino. The Mastroberardino family put Taurasi on the map: their 1968 is considered one of the greatest Italian wines ever made, and is still wonderful today. Keep in mind that serious Taurasi needs about five years in bottle before beginning to strut its stuff. The Avalon, from the lighter, tobacco-scented Piedirosso variety, is an ideal everyday table wine.

Avalon Rosso		03	$$
Radici Taurasi	01	00	$$$
Radici Riserva Taurasi	99	98	$$$$
Naturalis Historia Irpinia Rosso	01	00	$$$$

Montevetrano. One of Italy's true cult wines, made with care and passion by Silvia Imparato, who was once one of Rome's most famous photographers.

Montevetrano Colli di Salerno Rosso	03	02	$$$$

Paternoster. Nobody does the Vulture better than Vito Paternoster, who turns out Aglianico in all shapes and sizes, from the bubbly red version known as Barigliott to the traditionally made Don Anselmo to the more modern Rotondo.

Synthesi Aglianico del Vulture	03	02	$$
Don Anselmo Aglianico del Vulture	00	99	$$$
Rotondo Aglianico del Vulture	03	01	$$$

Planeta. Perhaps southern Italy's best-known wine producer, and deservedly so. An amazing array of bottlings that cater mainly to international tastes, from the lighter-styled Cerasuolo to the Bordeaux blend Burdese to a chewy, soft Merlot and spicy Syrah.

Burdese Sicilia Rosso	03	01	$$$
Syrah Sicilia Rosso	03	01	$$$
Merlot Sicilia Rosso	03	01	$$$

Rivera. The De Corato family deserves credit for bringing the native, high-quality grape Uva di Troia back into the limelight. The fleshy, palate-pleasing Il Falcone bottling (70 percent Uva di Troia and 30 percent Montepulciano) is always one of Italy's best buys.

Rosé Castel del Monte		04	$
Il Falcone Rosso Riserva Castel del Monte	01	00	$$$
Puer Apuliae Nero di Troia Castel del Monte	03	02	$$$

Santadi. Arguably the best co-op on the island of Sardinia. The Terre Brune and Rocca Rubia are excellent examples of how well Carignan does in Sardinia with the right winemaker in charge.

Rocca Rubia Riserva Carignano del Sulcis	01	$$
Terre Brune Carignano del Sulcis Superiore	01	$$$

Tasca d'Almerita. Rock-solid wines that speak of the bright sun and heat of the land from which they come, even if it seems that these concentrated reds have become increasingly tannic in recent years. The Rosso del Conte (from Nero d'Avola) has long been one of Italy's best red wines.

Contea di Sclafani Rosso del Conte	01	00	$$$
Contea di Sclafani Cabernet Sauvignon	03	02	$$$

Tormaresca. The Puglia branch of the Antinori wine empire offers two stellar reds—the Bocca di Lupo is an outstanding Aglianico-based wine, while the Masseria Maime is a particularly refined version of Negroamaro.

Masseria Maime Salento Rosso	03	02	$$
Bocca di Lupo Castel del Monte Rosso	03	02	$$

OTHER PRODUCERS TO LOOK FOR: D'Alfonso del Sordo (Puglia), Basilisco (Basilicata), Camerlengo (Basilicata), Conti Zecca (Puglia), Cottanera (Sicily), Feudo Principi di Butera (Sicily), Firriato (Sicily), Gulfi (Sicily), Leone de Castris (Puglia), Macarico (Basilicata), Il Nibbio Grigio (Basilicata), Passopisciaro (Sicily), Tenuta Le Querce (Basilicata), Torre Quarto (Puglia), Zemmer (Sicily).

WHITE WINES

Although southern Italy is mainly red wine country, Campania is the source of some of Italy's best whites. Fiano and Greco produce lovely wines characterized by minerals and citrus fruits in cooler climates and by tropical fruit bombs when grown in warmer areas. The Greco grape usually produces bigger and more alcoholic wines, with more minerality and less obvious fruit. Coda di Volpe offers enticing tropical fruit and honey nuances, while Falanghina is usually fresh, crisp, and minerally.

Sicily also offers some interesting whites made from the Inzolia and Cataratto varieties (the former more floral, the latter frequently resembling warm-climate Chardonnay), but the best variety is Grillo, which can pack lots of alcohol and structure into a wine with a decidedly herbal, somewhat Sauvignon-like aroma. Chardonnay and Viognier have been planted in Sicily, but the former variety often yields blowzy caricatures with little grace. Viognier appears to hold promise but the vines are too young for growers to make a definitive judgment on the future of this variety on the island.

Finally, southern Italy has always been home to Passito-style wines—sweet wines made from grapes left to dry on straw mats or the like (passito in Italian means dehydrated). Although some of these wines can be a bit deficient in acidity, the best of them are wonderful. Among the finest are numerous white Muscats and especially Muscat of Alexandria (Zibibbo) from Sicily, as well as some excellent dessert wines made from native grape varieties in Sardinia.

BANG FOR THE BUCK. Most southern Italian white wines are still relatively good buys, but stick to producers with track records for quality. From Campania, whites such as Falanghina and Coda di Volpe can be wonderfully fresh—and they're always less expensive than the more famous Fiano and Greco. The Vermentino from Sardinia is a similarly good deal.

2005 ★★★+   2004 ★★★★   2003 ★★

RECOMMENDED PRODUCERS

Benanti. This pioneering winery in Sicily produces one of Italy's most interesting and age-worthy white wines, Pietramarina, made at high altitude in rocky, volcanic soil in the Etna appellation from the native Carricante variety—not unlike a dry Riesling, with unfolding layers of lemon, minerals, and herbs.

Pietramarina Etna Bianco Superiore	01	00	99	$$$
Moscato Passito di Pantelleria Coste di Mueggen			02	$$$

Benito Ferrara. A source of some of the best Fianos and Grecos made, especially the Vigna Cicogna bottling, which shows just what Greco can do on mineral-rich soil when vine yields are reasonable.

Fiano di Avellino		04	$$
Greco di Tufo		04	$$
Greco di Tufo Vigna Cicogna		**04**	$$

Cantina del Taburno. Falangina and especially Coda di Volpe don't get any better. These light, fresh, honey- and citrus-scented wines are a joy to drink.

Aminea Coda di Volpe del Taburno	05	04	$$
Falanghina del Taburno	05	04	$$

Capichera. High-quality Vermentino of real structure, depth, and length, though a bit more expensive than most.

Capichera Classico Vermentino	04	03	$$$
Vigna n'Gena Vermentino di Gallura	04	03	$$$

Clelia Romano/Colli di Lapio. Maybe the best Fiano in all of Campania, with fresh aromas of flowers, mint, chalk dust, and gin, and surprising aging potential.

Fiano di Avellino	**04**	03	$$

Attilio Contini. Contini's Antico Gregori, a multivintage blend of the best Vernaccia components of the past 50 years, is by far the best example of Vernaccia di Oristano, a wine not unlike a dry sherry.

NV Antico Gregori Vernaccia di Oristano	$$$$

Donnafugata. In addition to its brilliant dry reds and whites, Donnafugata makes one of Sicily's best sweet wines as well.

Ben Ryé Passito di Pantelleria	03	02	$$$

Marco de Bartoli. The top producer of Marsala, another wine made in an oxidized style reminiscent of sherry and not in favor today. But these wines, wonderful as aperitifs or as after-dinner companions, deserve to be better known.

NV Marsala Superiore	$$
NV Marsala 10 Anni Riserva	$$$
NV Bukkuram Moscato di Pantelleria Passito	$$$$

Salvatore Murana. Renowned producer of sweet wines from the Muscat of Alexandria grape, offering a number of different cru bottlings.

Khamma Passito di Pantelleria	01	$$$$
Martingala Passito di Pantelleria	00	$$$$

OTHER PRODUCERS TO LOOK FOR: D'Ambra (Campania), Cantina Sociale del Vermentino (Sardinia), Cantina Sociale di Gallura (Sardinia), De Conciliis (Campania), Gran Furore/Marisa Cuomo (Campania), Leone de Castris (Puglia), Rosa del Golfo (Puglia), Villa Raiano (Campania).

SPAIN

S pain has more acres under vine than any other country and ranks third in production behind Italy and France. Much of this output continues to be hot-country jug wine made to satisfy the everyday thirsts of the domestic and greater European markets. But even at the low end, Spain's wines are of increasing interest to export markets. The explanation is simple: many inexpensive Spanish wines that once were rustic, tired, or dried out have been replaced by bottlings that are lush, round, ripe, and, above all else, cleanly made. Regions that previously made blending wines that were virtually too strong to be bottled on their own— such as Tarragona, Valencia, Yecla, Jumilla, Toro, and numerous hot spots along the Mediterranean coast—are now firmly in the table wine business, even if these wines can be alarmingly high in alcohol. While individual wines can be hot, shapeless, and lacking in freshness, their competently made counterparts rank among the world's greatest wine bargains.

At the high end, and avidly pursued by international collectors, are exciting new bottlings from the historically important Rioja and Ribera del Duero regions in north-central Spain and from the wild, hilly Priorat in Cataluña, in the northeast corner of the country. A new generation of winemakers has further stimulated interest in Spain by crafting wines in a distinctly modern international style, sometimes referred to as *alta expresión* in Spain: deeply colored, very ripe, and high in alcohol, generally aged in a high percentage of new French oak, and often quite pricey. The majority of these wines are based on Tempranillo, Spain's most distinguished red variety. While the ultimate quality and longevity of these wines are yet to be proven, these new bottlings have unquestionably captured the attention of wine drinkers both inside and outside Spain.

Although much of Spain bakes in the sun for at least half the year, the country actually covers a vast range of climates—from the cooler and much wetter Atlantic-influenced northwest, to the arid, blazing Mediterranean south and southeast—so vintage generalizations are tricky. Moreover, the majority of Spain's better vineyards lie at relatively high altitude, where summer nights are cool even when afternoons are stifling. Except for along the northern coast of Spain, drought is a constant danger, and vines are usually widely spaced to minimize competition for scarce water reserves. It's worth noting that, like most of Europe, Spain suffered through an incredibly hot summer in 2003, and the wines in almost all regions show the effects of relentless sunshine. The best red wines are even richer than usual but many betray a distinctly roasted character, and 2003 in general was a difficult year for making vibrant whites. On the other

hand, 2004 was a superb year across much of the country, and reports on the drought year of 2005 are highly positive as well.

Spain's wine-producing regions are classified in a hierarchy quite similar to those of France's AOC and Italy's DOC and DOCG. As in these countries, many of Spain's most exciting wines today are being made outside the DO (Denominación de Origen) system, due to objections over required or prohibited varieties or the amount of time a wine must be aged in barrel or bottle prior to release. (To date, Spain's top wine distinction, DOCa—Denominación de Origen Calificada—has only been granted to Rioja.) On the other hand, the Spanish authorities have given their wine producers a freer rein, thus nurturing an atmosphere of creativity virtually unmatched in other European countries.

RIOJA

Located in north central Spain, Rioja is the country's most famous wine-producing region. Until the mid-1980s, Rioja was the only category other than sherry and the wines of Miguel Torres with a serious presence in international markets. Some of the greatest wineries in the region, such as CVNE (Compañía Vinícola del Norte de España), La Rioja Alta, López de Heredia, and Marqués de Murrieta are more than a century old and continue to use modified traditional winemaking techniques, even if most of these large old firms have recently constructed high-tech vinification facilities. The relatively long growing season enables the fruit to ripen thoroughly without undue loss of acidity, permitting intensely flavored, complex wines with medium weight, moderate alcohol, and plenty of structure for aging. The finest Riojas—blends based on Tempranillo, with some jammy Garnacha included for alcoholic strength, Mazuelo for acidity, and Graciano for aromatic delicacy—have always been easier on the head and stomach than most of the world's other serious reds, with more flavor and complexity than would seem possible from wines carrying a relatively low 12 to 13 percent alcohol. But the movement here today—as virtually everywhere else in the wine world—is toward riper, bigger, and darker wines, and alcohol levels over 13 percent have become commonplace.

Rioja is divided into three zones. Rioja Alta and Rioja Alavesa, which comprise the western half of the greater Rioja area, are relatively cool, although protected from the coldest Atlantic winds by the Sierra de Cantabria mountain range. This is Tempranillo country par excellence. Farther to the east and south is the warmer, drier Rioja Baja, an area with a distinctly Mediterranean climate conducive to the softer, lower-acid, higher-alcohol Garnacha (Grenache), which marries well with Tempranillo. Most Riojas are blends from vineyards within one of these regions, if not from more than one region, but the trend in recent years has been toward wines from more closely defined areas, if not from single sites.

Traditionally, Rioja wines have been vinified and aged in American oak, which often contributes exotic notes of coconut, vanilla, and cedar. In recent years, many producers have increased use of French oak barrels, in some instances to tone down the more aggressive aspects of American wood but in others simply because French oak is more fashionable today. Some have jettisoned American oak entirely.

By and large, Rioja has traditionally been a wine that was released only when deemed ready to drink by its maker. *Reserva* and *gran reserva* Riojas, which spend longer in barrel and bottle before going to market, are especially mellow, aromatically complex wines that combine wood and fruit tones in a particularly harmonious way. They're perfect accompaniments to the excellent country cuisine of the region. But an increasing number of producers, especially the relative newcomers, are making wine from mostly or all Tempranillo grown in favored sites, aging them for a shorter period in smaller, newer barrels (often of French rather than American oak), and releasing them earlier—sometimes too quickly even to qualify as *crianza*, which must be aged in small oak casks for at least a year and cannot leave the winery until the third year after the vintage. These new wines are darker, more robust, and more tannic than traditionally styled wines from the region, and often possess more primary fruit flavors. But many aficionados of old-school Rioja consider the new wines to be heavy-handed.

Traditional white Rioja has mostly fallen below the international wine radar, as wine lovers have turned away from wines they view as too dry, oaky, or austere, if not oxidative in character. But there are also fresher white wines to be found today from the likes of Muga, Marqués de Cáceres, and Finca Allende, not to mention a handful of older-style whites—such as the occasional superstar from López de Heredia—that transcend their category with their sheer structure and minerality.

BANG FOR THE BUCK. Rioja ranges widely in price, with many reserva and gran reserva bottlings now quite expensive. But superb bargains are still to be found in basic Rioja wines from conscientious producers.

2004 ★★★★− **2003** ★★★− **2002** ★★+ **2001** ★★★★+

RECOMMENDED PRODUCERS

Bodegas Artadi. A modernist leader, producing powerful, dense wines that are textbook examples of the *alta expresión* school of Spanish winemaking. For sheer drama, these are among Spain's most impressive wines. The entry-level Viñas de Gain can be a terrific value; the Viña el Pisón is from a single chalky vineyard; and the special Grandes Añadas bottling is only made in the best vintages.

	03	02	01	
Viñas de Gain Rioja	03	02	**01**	$$
Pagos Viejos Rioja		**03**	**01**	$$$$
Viña el Pisón Rioja			**01**	$$$$$

Viñedos del Contino. This estate, partly owned by CVNE, benefits from a protected amphitheater vineyard along the Ebro River in Laserna, where the fruit often ripens even in cooler years. The wines combine the fruitiness of the modern style, a judicious dose of French oak, and the structure and elegance of the old school. The Contino Reserva is the estate's flagship bottling.

	01	99	
Rioja	**01**		$$
Reserva Rioja	**01**	**99**	$$$

CVNE (Cune). This traditional producer makes classic, structured, long-aging Riojas in a high-tech vinification facility. The suppler Viña Real is done in a Burgundy-shaped bottle, while the more firmly built Imperial comes in a Bordeaux bottle. Reservas and gran reservas are offered in the better vintages. Real de Asúa is the top of the line.

	03	02/00	01/98	
Viña Real Crianza Rioja	03	02	**01**	$$
Imperial Reserva Rioja		**00**	**98**	$$$

Finca Allende. Modern producer (established in 1994) of dense, fruit-driven wines with the strength of material to support their spicy French oak character. The special Aurus bottling comes from the estate's oldest vines.

Rioja		`01`	$$
Calvario Rioja	`02`	`01`	$$$$

La Rioja Alta. A great old Rioja producer that is now using younger barrels (the winery has always preferred American oak) and somewhat shorter aging in wood since moving into its state-of-the-art vinification facility in the late 1990s. Still, these are among the most traditional Riojas on the market, with reserva and gran reserva bottlings released after long aging in barrel and bottle.

Viña Alberdi Rioja		`02`	`01`	$$
Viña Arana Reserva		`98`	`97`	$$
Viña Ardanza Rioja	`99`	`98`	`97`	$$$
Gran Reserva 904 Rioja		`95`	`94`	$$$

R. López de Heredia. The damp, cobwebbed cellar of this ultratraditional bodega looks like a relic from the 19th century, and it is. Most wines, including rosé and white Riojas, are released only when the producer feels they're ready, and as a result, some new releases seem old by the time they reach the North American retail market. These are firmly structured, penetrating, and highly idiosyncratic wines, sometimes funky and lacking in freshness, but more often nuanced and ethereal, with captivating floral, red berry, mineral, cedar, and coconut notes.

Viña Bosconia Rioja		`98`	$$$
Viña Tondonia Reserva Rioja	`98`	`97`	$$$

Marqués de Cáceres. This enlightened traditionalist, founded in 1970 by the Forner family, which owned Châteaux Camensac and Larose Trintaudon in Bordeaux, ages its best red wines in a high percentage of French oak. These are supple wines with enticing sweetness of fruit, rarely tough in the early going. The white wines and rosés made here can be among the freshest in Rioja. Pricing is very competitive.

Crianza Rioja	`01`	`00`	$
Reserva Rioja		`98`	$$
Gaudium Rioja	`00`	`98`	$$$

Herederos del Marqués de Riscal. One of the oldest and largest producers in Rioja, established in 1860, Marqués de Riscal offers modernized versions of traditional midweight wines that combine sweet fruit, supple texture, and firm structure. Riscal has a supermodern new vinification facility and a visitors' center designed by Frank Gehry. The dense, generous Barón de Chirel bottling is entirely fermented in large French oak vats and contains some Cabernet Sauvignon. Riscal also offers a consistently excellent Verdejo bottling from its property in Rueda.

Reserva Rioja	`01`	`00`	$
Barón de Chirel Reserva Rioja	`00`	`99`	$$$$

Bodegas Muga. A forward-looking traditionalist, making powerful but fleshy wines with great aromatic complexity and impeccably integrated tannins. The reserva is consistently a world-class red wine at an impossibly low price. The two top bottlings here come from vineyards at higher altitude: the Torre Muga is aged mostly in new French oak, while the Prado Enea, only made in the best years, is a silky, traditional, structured Rioja capable of long aging.

Reserva Rioja	02 01	$$
Torre Muga Rioja	01	$$$$

Bodegas Ostatu. This modern-school producer makes rich, fleshy wines with impressive sweetness of fruit. The superb and rare Gloria de Ostatu, from the estate's best old vines, is made by consultant Hubert de Boüard, proprietor of Château L'Angélus in Bordeaux's Right Bank.

Crianza Rioja	03	$$
Reserva Rioja	01	$$
Gloria de Ostatu Rioja	02 01	$$$$

Viñedos de Páganos. This new producer (the first release was the 2001) makes a wonderfully dense, pliant Rioja in a distinctly modern and very ripe style, from fruit harvested late for maximum ripeness. The 2002 was a great success for the vintage.

El Puntido Rioja	02 01	$$$

Bodegas Palacios Remondo. Superstar winemaker Alvaro Palacios, creator of L'Ermita and Finca Dofí in Priorat, is now extensively involved in the family estate in Rioja. Here, he makes concentrated, lush wines, including two (Herencia Remondo and Propriedad H. Remondo) that are among the greatest wines produced to date from the normally hotter, drier Rioja Baja, which Palacios calls "La Rioja Oriental."

La Vendimia Rioja	05 04 03	$
Herencia Remondo La Montesa Crianza Rioja	04 03	$$
Propriedad H. Remonda Rioja	04 03	$$

Remelluri. This cool, high-altitude estate on the northern banks of the Ebro River in Rioja Alavesa, at the foot of the Sierra Cantabria mountains, produces structured and often distinctly wild wines with uncanny aromatic complexity.

Rioja	02 01	$$

Fernando Remírez de Ganuza. Fernando Remírez spares no expense in making one of the Rioja region's—and Spain's—richest and most individual wines from old estate vines. Methods at this estate highlight all new barrels, a high percentage of French oak, and bottling without filtration.

Reserva Rioja	02 01 00	$$$$

Bodegas Riojanas. Classic, firm, structured wines made in a highly traditional style, with no concessions to modern fashion. The leaner, more understated Viña Albina is done in a Bordeaux bottle, while the fleshier, deeper-pitched Monte Real comes in a Burgundy bottle. These are emphatically not competition wines, but they are wonderful with food.

Viña Albina Reserva Rioja	98	$$
Monte Real Reserva Rioja	98	$$

Bodegas Roda. A relative newcomer (established in 1991), Roda makes some of Rioja's best modern-style wines, aged in French oak, from vines mostly in Rioja Alta. Roda I is a selection made for longevity, while Roda II is a more easygoing wine released a few months earlier. Cirsión is a powerful, deeply colored, all-Tempranillo wine aged in 100 percent new French oak.

Roda II Reserva Rioja	`01`	$$$
Roda I Reserva Rioja	`01`	$$$$
Cirsión Rioja	`03`	$$$$$

Señorio de San Vicente. Made by Marcos Eguren of Bodegas Sierra Cantabria from a single vineyard, this dense, fruit-driven Rioja is a very impressive example of the modern style. Previously made in all American oak but more recently aged in a majority of French barrels.

San Vicente Rioja	`02`	`01`	$$$

Bodegas Sierra Cantabria. Consistently excellent producer of a broad range of modern-styled, fruit-forward wines. These represent exceptional value at the entry level and some of the highest quality of the region at the upper end of the range.

Crianza Rioja		`01`	$
Cuvee Especial Rioja		`01`	$$
Gran Reserva Rioja	`98`	`96`	$$$

Torre de Oña. Under the same ownership as the famed La Rioja Alta, this bodega produces a consistently good reserva bottling in a traditional style, with plum and cedar flavors and a gently tannic structure.

Reserva Rioja	`99`	$$

OTHER PRODUCERS TO LOOK FOR: Barón de Ley, Bodegas Bréton, Faustino Martínez, Viña Izadi, Bodegas Lan, Luis Cañas, Marqués de Griñon, Marqués de Murrieta, Bodegas Martínez Bujanda, Montecillo, Primicia, Bodegas y Viñedos Pujanza, Ramón Bilbao, Viña Salceda, Vinos de Benjamin Romeo, Marqués de Vargas, Finca Valpiedra.

RIBERA DEL DUERO

Despite the fact that the celebrated Ribera del Duero wine Vega Sicilia has been Spain's most sought-after wine for nearly a century, DO status for Ribera del Duero was only granted in 1982, a testament to the fact that the estate was practically going it alone for decades. Located in north-central Spain, to the southwest of Rioja, the high plain of Ribera del Duero is Tempranillo country, with nearly all of the best wines made entirely or almost all from this variety. (Vega Sicilia is a notable exception, as it has a long history of including the Bordeaux varieties Cabernet Sauvignon, Merlot, and Malbec in its flagship wine, Unico.) As in Rioja, the spring comes late here; summer temperatures can be high but drop considerably at night in these altitudes, with the result that the wines from this region normally possess decent acidity and avoid overripe character.

As a region, Ribera del Duero came to prominence in the 1980s by offering more deeply colored, aggressively fruity, alcoholic, and tannic reds from its own more structured and sometimes higher-acid tinta del país, or tinto fino (local names for Tempranillo), occasionally with a bit of Cabernet added. Compared to Rioja, most Ribera del Duero wines are aged for a shorter period of time in small oak barrels—a higher percentage of which are new—and are released earlier. The most powerful of these wines require extended time in bottle to refine their tannins, but there are plenty of lesser wines that offer early appeal. Think of Rioja as more Bordeaux-like and Ribera del Duero as more akin to California Cabernet, even if these two categories are increasingly converging in style.

Ribera del Duero has seen explosive growth in the past decade, and the quality of today's wines varies widely. The best examples are suaver than ever, as gentler handling of the fruit has enabled many producers to make wines of greater class without compromising structure or freshness. The lesser examples—and there are still too many of these—are dilute, rustic, or too dry. Some show signs of unclean barrels, while in other cases young vines are the explanation for a lack of intensity.

BANG FOR THE BUCK. Ribera del Duero was one of Spain's greatest success stories in the 1980s and early 1990s, and prices shot up accordingly. But among the vast number of new wineries in this region, prices for entry-level wines have necessarily become more competitive in the past few years.

2004 ★★★★   2003 ★★+   2002 ★★+   2001 ★★★★–

RECOMMENDED PRODUCERS

Bodegas Aalto. High-extract wines with strong oak tones and flamboyant fruit; their exotic, forward nature ensures early appeal. Bodegas Aalto was renowned winemaker Mariano García's first Ribera del Duero project since leaving Vega Sicilia. But the style here is much more modern. The PS bottling comes from very old vines.

Aalto Ribera del Duero	03	02	01	$$$
Aalto PS Ribera del Duero			01	$$$$

Bodegas Alejandro Fernández. This bodega's rich, dense, lavishly oaked Pesquera, the second important Ribero del Duero wine after Vega Sicilia, helped to draw attention to its region as a source of world-class red wine in the early 1980s. While some new Ribera del Duero wines have skyrocketed in price, Pesquera remains an excellent value.

Tinto Pesquera Ribera del Duero	04	03	02	$$
Tinto Pesquera Reserva Ribera del Duero	03	02	01	$$$

Bodegas y Viñedos Alión. A second project from the owners of Vega Sicilia, who wanted to make a more modern, Bordeaux-styled wine. The wine is made from all Tempranillo and aged entirely in French oak. Recent vintages have been wonderfully complex and fine.

Ribera del Duero	02	01	00	$$$$

Condado de Haza. This large property, established in 1988, was the second Ribera del Duero estate of Alejandro Fernández. The wine is similarly supple, rich, and full, with sweet American oak notes and plenty of early appeal. A special wine called Alenza is offered in the very best years.

Ribera del Duero	**04**	**03**	02		$$
Reserva Ribera del Duero				**00**	$$$

Dominio de Atauta. One of the most exciting new Ribera del Duero estates, this fairly small producer, benefitting from very old vines in a cooler microclimate in the extreme eastern end of the appellation, produces a concentrated, rich wine with solid acid spine and considerable aging potential.

Ribera del Duero	**04**	**03**	**02**	$$$
Valdegatiles Ribera del Duero	**04**	**03**		$$$$

Bodegas y Viñedos Hacienda Monasterio. This is the estate that Danish winemaker Peter Sisseck calls home when he's in Spain. Fans who slaver over his legendary star wine Pingus, which frequently sells for more than $300 a bottle, can experience Sisseck's winemaking talents at a fraction of the price. This is an aromatically complex, dense, and soil-inflected wine. The 2002 bottling was excellent for the vintage.

Ribera del Duero	**02**	**01**	$$$

Hermanos Pérez Pascuas. The wines of the Pérez Pascuas brothers are richer and more concentrated than ever before, thanks to maturing vines, low yields, late harvesting, and strong extraction during vinification. While most of the offerings here are now expensive, the bodega's more affordable entry-level wine is an excellent introduction to the house style.

Viña Pedrosa Crianza Ribera del Duero	**04**	**03**	**02**	**01**	$$
Viña Pedrosa Reserva Ribera del Duero		**03**	**01**	**00**	$$$$

Bodegas Hermanos Sastre. Sastre crafts consistently excellent wines largely from estate-owned old vines, but pricing for the Regina Vides and especially the huge and powerfully oaky Pesus bottling has reached nosebleed levels.

Crianza Ribera del Duero	**02**	**01**	$$
Pago de Santa Cruz Ribera del Duero		**99**	$$$$

Bodegas Vega Sicilia. The first icon wine of Ribera del Duero and historically the most influential producer in Spain. These long-aging, highly complex wines, which bear comparison to the first growths of Bordeaux, have become extremely expensive, thanks to strong international demand and an admirable track record for excellence. The flagship wine, Unico, is a Spanish blue chip, usually selling for $300 and up on release, with prices much higher for the top vintages. Valbuena is Vega Sicilia's second wine.

Valbuena Ribera del Duero	**01**	**00**	**99**	$$$$$
Unico Gran Reserva Ribera del Duero	**95**	**94**	**91**	$$$$$

OTHER PRODUCERS TO LOOK FOR: Viñedos Alonso del Yerro, Arzuaga Navarro, Cillar de Silos, Matarromera, Montebaco, Bodegas Emilio Moro, Pago de Carraovejas, Pago del Los Capellanes, Peñalba-López, Bodegas Reyes, Bodegas Valduero, Valtravieso, Finca Villacreces, Vizcarra Ramos.

SCARCE BUT WORTH A SEARCH: Dominio de Pingus.

SOME TOP SOURCES FOR SPANISH RED WINES

- **Priorat.** Priorat (Priorato in Castilian) is a small, favored area within the greater Tarragona region that benefits from a hot, very dry, sheltered, and hilly microclimate; distinctive, mineral-rich, brown slate soil (*llicorella*); and a good stock of very old Cariñena and Garnacha vines, with the steepest and best sites concentrated around the town of Gratallops. A group of five winemakers led by René Barbier essentially reinvented this area, beginning with their releases from the 1989 vintage. Priorat has been on fire ever since, with a reputation for superconcentrated, high-octane wines from traditional varieties supplemented by mostly new plantings of Syrah, Cabernet Sauvignon, and Merlot.
- **Montsant.** This horseshoe-shaped appellation surrounding Priorat enjoys similar continental climatic conditions but less distinctive soils. The wines, which are blends often based on Garnacha, have less weight, complexity, and class than those from Priorat, but they are also a lot less expensive.
- **Penedès.** The Penedès region, home to the influential Torres concern, has historically combined Spanish and French wine sensibilities. While Garnacha and Tempranillo are grown with success in this warm Mediterranean climate, oak-aged wines intended for cellaring have long been made from Cabernet Sauvignon and Merlot.
- **Navarra.** Lying just northeast of Rioja, Navarra used to be planted mostly to Garnacha, but Tempranillo has made rapid gains here, and there is also considerable Cabernet Sauvignon and even Merlot. As is the case in Rioja, Tempranillo dominates in the more Atlantic-influenced north while Garnacha is more important in the south, making warmer, more alcoholic wines with less aromatic complexity. Navarra is also a source of excellent *rosado* (rosé) wines from red grapes.
- **Toro.** Toro is in the northwest, less than 50 miles from Spain's border with Portugal on the banks of the Duero River. Tempranillo (called Tinto de Toro here) dominates but there are also plantings of Cabernet Sauvignon and Merlot. The wines are powerful and high in alcohol, often with a distinctly roasted, meaty character.
- **Bierzo.** The Bierzo area of northwestern Spain, in a region generally better known for white wines, features a mild climate and substantial plantings of the early-ripening Mencía variety, a grape that produces floral, fruit-driven, and very dry wines with lighter body than most Tempranillos. The most serious wines here come from old vines planted up steep, slate-rich hillsides.
- **Jumilla.** Jumilla, in the arid Murcia region of south-central Spain, is a high desert that has historically produced massive quantities of bulk wine. Recent plantings by quality-minded growers, mostly of Monastrell (Mourvèdre), have yielded wines that combine black fruit flavors and firm tannic structure.

OTHER RED WINES OF SPAIN

Rioja was virtually synonymous with high-quality Spanish red wine until 20 years ago, when Ribera del Duero captured the attention of wine lovers in the late 1980s and 1990s. Today much of the excitement in Spain is coming from new—or, more precisely, resurgent—regions, including some that previously did not ship their rustic wines very far from home. Regions like Priorat, Toro, and, more recently, Bierzo have attracted considerable investment, and the upgrading of existing vineyards and replanting of new vines have already yielded outstanding results. In some areas, Priorat in particular, a new gold rush has driven prices of the top wines to exorbitant levels, but a wealth of red wine values can be found in regions like Somontano in the north and in hot, dry areas like Yecla, Jumilla, and La Mancha. The Penedès region of Cataluña, where Cabernet Sauvignon has long been planted, has been kept viable in the international market by Miguel Torres, while Tarragona, just down the coast, has witnessed heavy planting of French red grapes in recent years. The producers featured on the following pages represent merely a taste of the current wine scene in Spain.

BANG FOR THE BUCK. Prices in such areas as Jumilla, Yecla, and Somontano have not caught up with recent improvements in wine quality.

RECOMMENDED PRODUCERS

Alvaro Palacios. Alvaro Palacios's huge but creamy and refined L'Ermita, from mostly Garnacha vines, some more than a century old, is one of Spain's true cult wines. His far less expensive Finca Dofí is just a step behind L'Ermita in quality, and Les Terrasses makes an excellent and very reasonably priced introduction to Priorat wine.

Les Terrasses Priorat	04	03		$$
Finca Dofí Priorat	04	03	02	$$$$
L'Ermita Velyes Vinyes Priorat	04	03	02	$$$$$

Bodegas Artazu. This Navarra property produces a superb lush-but-sappy wine from old Garnacha vines planted in chalky soil at high altitude. There is also a delightful *rosado* called Artazuri, produced in limited quantities.

Tinto Navarra	04	03	$
Santa Cruz de Artazu Navarra	04	03	$$$

Bodegas Borsao. This large operation, located in the Campo de Borja region in Aragón just southeast of Navarra, is a phenomenal source of outstanding wine values that are widely available in the market. The style here is distinctly user-friendly and unpretentious: fat, lush, and loaded with sweet berry Garnacha fruit.

Borsao Campo de Borja	05	04	$
Reserva Selección Campo de Borja		01	$
Tres Picos Garnacha Campo de Borja	04	03	$

Celler de Capçanes. One of the better producers in Montsant. This means that these wines approach Priorat bottlings for richness and depth at a fraction of the price. The Mas Donis, a blend of 80 percent Garnacha and 20 percent Syrah, is a special bottling done for the American importer, while the Costers del Gravet features a relatively high 50 percent Cabernet Sauvignon.

Mas Donis Barrica Montsant	04	03	$
Costers del Gravet Montsant	03	01	$$

Bodegas Castaño. This large Yecla cooperative is a source of some stunning values, mostly based on Monastrell. The Solanera, made for the North American market, is a blend of 70 percent Monastrell, 20 percent Cabernet Sauvignon, and 10 percent Garnacha.

Monastrell Yecla	04	$
Hecula Yecla	03	$
Solanera Viñas Viejas Yecla	03	$

Clos Erasmus. French-born Daphne Glorian, who was part of the original group of winemakers who set up in Priorat in the late 1980s, makes a limited quantity of one of the best wines of the appellation, a Garnacha-based blend with Cabernet Sauvignon and Syrah. Recent vintages have offered an exhilarating combination of liqueur-like sweetness and finesse.

Clos Erasmus Priorat	03	02	$$$$$

Clos Mogador. René Barbier was the first to see the potential of the rugged Priorat region and its old vines, setting up shop there in 1979. His flagship Clos Mogador is a concentrated, powerful, age-worthy wine based on old plantings of Garnacha, Cabernet Sauvignon, and Syrah.

Clos Mogador Priorat	04	03	02	$$$$

Descendientes de José Palacios. This is the recent Bierzo project of Alvaro Palacios, who offers a series of 100 percent Mencía wines from old vines planted on steep hillsides in this relatively cool area in northwest Spain. There are small quantities of site-designated wines in addition to the early-released, entry-level Petalos and the fuller-bodied, more serious Corullón.

Petalos del Bierzo	05	04	$$
Corullón Bierzo	04	03	$$$

Dominio de Tares. The other top choice in the Bierzo appellation, along with Descendientes de José Palacios. Unusually silky, sappy Mencía wines with sexy, chocolate and coffee notes from new oak.

Exaltos Cepas Viejas Bierzo	04	03		$$
Bembibre Bierzo	04	03	02	$$$

Bodegas y Viñedos Dos Victorias. These are lush, liqueur-like Toro wines that manage to retain enough acidity to leaven their superripe flavors. There is also an enticing, well-made white wine from Rueda.

Elias Mora Toro	04	03	$$
Elias Mora Crianza Toro	03	01	$$
Gran Elias Mora Toro	03	01	$$$$

Bodegas El Nido. This joint venture involving the Gil family (owners of Bodegas Juan Gil), U.S. importers Jorge Ordoñez and Dan Phillips, and Australian winemaker Chris Ringland exploded onto the scene with a couple of superconcentrated, liqueur-like, international-style wines from the 2002 harvest—both blends of Monastrell and Cabernet Sauvignon. These are wines that showcase the potential of the Jumilla region.

Clio Jumilla	02	$$$
El Nido Jumilla	02	$$$$$

Joan d'Anguera. This very old estate, one of the elite producers of Montsant, relies heavily on Syrah to produce velvety, powerful, gripping wines with pronounced mineral character. The entry-level La Planella bottling is especially good value.

La Planella Montsant		04	$$
L'Argata Montsant	03	02	$$
El Bugader Montsant	03	02	$$$$

Mas Gil. Superstar winemaker Peter Sisseck (Pingus, Hacienda Monasterio) consults at this small operation in the Costa Brava region of Spain, not far from the French border. In addition to the almost liqueur-like red blend of Cabernet Sauvignon, Syrah, and Merlot there's an exotically rich and spicy barrel-aged white from Rhône Valley varieties.

Clos d'Agon Tinto Emporda Costa Brava	01	$$$$

Bodegas Mauro. Mariano Garcia, the longtime winemaker for Vega Sicilia, established his bodega in Tudela del Duero, just west of the delimited Ribera del Duero region, in 1980. His wines are rich, suave, and sweetly oaky, with powerful, dense dark fruit flavors and fine-grained texture.

Crianza Vino de la Tierra de Castilla y Léon	04	03	02	$$$
Vendimia Seleccionada Vino de la Tierra de Castilla y Léon	02	01		$$$$$

Miguel Torres. For an earlier generation of North American wine lovers, Torres was Spanish wine. This huge operation, which now spans a number of regions (including California), is based in the Penedès region of Spain. Working largely with Tempranillo and Cabernet Sauvignon, Torres makes a consistently excellent range of wines, mostly in a user-friendly style. The entry-level reds in particular can offer great value, but the high-end bottlings are also superb.

Sangre de Toro Cataluña	03	02	$
Gran Coronas Cabernet Sauvignon Penedès		01	$$
Mas La Plana Cabernet Sauvignon Gran Reserva Penedès	01	00	$$$

Bodegas Nekeas. This large Navarra producer offers a vast range of competently made, fruit-driven wines at shockingly low prices. These are some of the most remarkable wine values in the world.

Vega Sindoa Merlot Navarra	04	03	$
Vega Sindoa Cabernet/Tempranillo Navarra	04	03	$
El Chaparral Old Vine Grenache Navarra	05	03	$

Bodega Numanthia Termes. This new project in Toro is the source of heady, creamy-rich wines with powerful fruit and enough structure to maintain their shape and balance. Even the 2002s here are quite successful, the result of very late harvesting. There's a costly luxury bottling called Termanthia from the estate's oldest vines, but the price is nearly four times as high as the Numanthia.

Termes Toro	03	02	$$
Numanthia Toro	03	02	$$$

Bodegas San Alejandro. This cooperative produces wonderfully sweet, supple Garnacha-based wines at absurdly low prices. In the better vintages, there is an old-vines bottling that can rival many Châteauneuf-du-Papes for power and density of flavor at a fraction of the price.

Las Rocas Garnacha Calatayud	04	03	$

Finca Sandoval. This is the project of Spanish journalist Victor de la Serna, who saw potential for growing Syrah in the forgotten Manchuela area southeast of Madrid, using vine cuttings from Château de Beaucastel in Châteauneuf-du-Pape. He was right, as each vintage of his lush, black fruit- and chocolate-driven wine has been richer and more refined than the one before. (The house blend now includes bits of Mourvèdre, Tempranillo, and Bobal, a local variety.)

Finca Sandoval Manchuela	04	03	$$$

Compañia de Vinos de Telmo Rodríguez. A far-flung collection of rather modern-style wines from the restless Telmo Rodríguez, who originally made the reputation of his family's Rioja estate, Remelluri. The range of offerings includes dry whites, sweet whites, and reds from all over Spain. Many of these wines offer solid value plus early accessibility.

Lanzaga Rioja	04	02	01	$$
Montazo Vino de Mesa			02	$$
Pegaso Vino de la Tierra de Castilla y Léon	02	01	99	$$$
"G" Dehesa Gago Toro		05	03	$
"G" Pago la Jara Toro	03	02	01	$$$

Celler Vall Llach. A modernist Priorat producer of velvety-rich wines that are strikingly concentrated and loaded with sweet, spicy berry fruit, with normally suave tannins.

Embruix Priorat	03	02	$$$
Idus Priorat	03	02	$$$
Vall Llach Priorat	03	02	$$$$

OTHER PRODUCERS TO LOOK FOR: Abadía Retuerta (Sardón de Duero), Bodegas Alto Moncayo (Campo de Borja), Casa Castillo (Jumilla), Celler Bárbara Forés (Terra Alta), Julián Chivite (Navarra), Cims de Porrera (Priorat), Clos Figueras (Priorat), Costers del Siurana (Priorat), Dits del Terra (Priorat), Enate (Somontano), Estefanía (Bierzo), Falset (Montsant), Finca Luzón (Jumilla), Celler Genium (Priorat), Liberalia Enológica (Toro), Celler Mas Doix (Priorat), Mas Igneus (Priorat), Mas Martínet (Priorat), Bodegas Ochoa (Navarra), Bodegas Olivares (Jumilla), Pasanau Germans (Priorat), Quinta de la Quietud (Toro), Rotllan Torra (Priorat), Scala Dei (Priorat), Tómas Cusiné (Costers del Segre), Celler Vinos Piñol (Terra Alta).

WHITE WINES

Not long ago, the white wines of Spain were nonstarters among international wine lovers. Most of these wines were dull, if not simply oxidized, and their appeal was limited to an older generation of drinkers in Spain who had grown up with this style. But substantial investments in modern vinification equipment, and the ability to control the temperature of both stainless steel fermentation tanks and aging cellars, now help protect white wines from destructive oxidation and heat. Cool Atlantic coastal regions account for the lion's share of brisk citrus- and mineral-flavored examples. Albariño, the defining variety of Rías Baixas (as well as the best grape used to produce Portugal's Vinho Verde), is alleged by some to be a descendent of Riesling, brought to Spain by German monks in the 12th century. The Basque wine-growing region of Chacolí (Txakoli), on the Atlantic coast just east of Bilbao, depends on the indigenous Hondarrabi Zuri grape to make high-acid floral/herbal wines that, like Albariño, have a strong affinity for local seafood-based tapas.

Rueda is the most important white wine area of Castilla y León, enjoying a dry yet rather cool climate. The fruity, aromatic Verdejo grape is the most important variety in Rueda, yielding very fresh wines with good body, and the Sauvignon Blanc is also highly successful. And then of course there is Penedès, on Spain's Mediterranean coast. Chardonnay has been cultivated here for generations, alongside other transplanted white varieties like Muscat, Riesling, and Sauvignon Blanc, as well as the native varieties Parellada and Macabeo (the local name for Viura).

2004 ★★★★   2003 ★★–

RECOMMENDED PRODUCERS

Adegas Valmiñor. A producer that makes bright, citric, minerally Albariño from a blend of fruit sources, in a very modern vinification facility.

Albariño Rías Baixas   04 $

Ameztoi. Juicy, gingery fruit bombs with incisive mineral and citrus tones.

Txakolina Getariako Txakolina	`04`	`03`	$$
Txakolina Getariako Upelean Txakolina		`04`	$$

Belondrade y Lurton. Owned by a member of the Lurton clan of Bordeaux, this property produces a rich, smoky, barrel-fermented Verdejo from old vines. The wine can resemble serious white Graves in the best vintages, but the oak can dominate in weaker years.

Verdejo Rueda	`05`	`04`	`03`	$$$

Burgans. Owned by the Martín Códax firm and produced at their winery, this fresh, crisp example of Albariño is also a bit suppler and rounder than most examples—not to mention cheaper.

Albariño Rías Baixas	`05`	`04`	$

Do Ferreiro. Fragrant, spicy Albariños that are loaded with fruit but maintain elegance and balance. The Cepas Vellas is made from a sandy vineyard that reportedly still retains some 200-year-old vines.

Albariño Rías Baixas	`04`	$$
Albariño Rías Baixas Cepas Vellas	`03`	$$$

Huguet de Can Feixes. A very good source of vibrant white wines in a modern style. High-altitude vineyards on the northern edge of Penedès are planted to Chardonnay as well as to the native varieties Parellada and Macabeo (these are also at the core of the house's consistently good vintage-dated Cava bottlings).

Blanc Selecció Penedès	`05`	`04`	$

Bodegas Naia Viña Sila. A new (2002) producer offering superb Verdejo wines (the Las Brisas also contains some Sauvignon Blanc and Viura). The barrel-fermented Naia Des offers uncanny texture and intensity for a white wine from Rueda.

Las Brisas Rueda		`04`	$
Naia Rueda		`04`	$
Naia Des Rueda	`04`	`03`	$$

Palacio de Fefiñanes. One of the top producers in Rías Baixas, with a track record for making fruity, flavorful wines even in difficult vintages.

Albariño de Fefiñanes Rías Baixas	`04`	$$

Pazo de Señorans. In addition to its consistently excellent herbal, minerally basic Albariño bottling (the 2004 was unusually ripe and rich), this superb estate offers an impeccably balanced, rich, and complex wine that has been aged for three years on its lees.

Albariño Rías Baixas	`05`	`04`	$$
Selección de Añada Albariño Rías Baixas		`01`	$$$

Miguel Torres. The Torres family makes some of the fresher white wines of the Penedès region, including a few terrific values. The Viña Esmeralda is Moscatel with Gewürztraminer, while the Viña Sol is Parellada. The more expensive Torres whites are often quite oaky, though.

Viña Sol Penedès	04	$
Viña Esmeralda Catalunya	04	$

OTHER PRODUCERS TO LOOK FOR: Angel Lorenzo Cachazo (Rueda), Condes de Albarei (Rías Baixas), Fillaboa (Rías Baixas), Lusco do Miño (Rías Baixas), Martínsancho (Rueda), Bodegas Emilio Rojo (Ribeiro).

ROSÉS

Many red wine producers in Spain make *rosado*, or rosé wine, and the best examples can be exuberant and lush, with vibrant red berry fruit. Navarra is an especially good source, thanks to its extensive plantings of Garnacha, whose fruity character is perfectly suited to making rosé. Today, almost all Spanish rosé is made in temperature-controlled stainless steel to preserve freshness. These wines should be consumed as soon as possible following the vintage, as their charm lies in their bright, succulent fruit, which can quickly fade with aging. Unfortunately, some of the better rosés from Navarra have had spotty distribution in U.S. in recent years. Some examples worth seeking out are Artazuri from Bodegas Artazu and the rosés from Julian Chivite and Bodegas Ochoa, whose reds are also consistently good. From Rioja, the rosés of Marqués de Cáceres and Bodegas Muga have been recent standouts, and the idiosyncratic, late-released example from López de Heredia can be downright ethereal if it reaches the North American market with its delicate, minerally freshness intact.

CAVA

While Cava is a legally defined term for Spanish sparkling wine made via the Champagne method (called *método tradicional* in Spain), most Cava is produced in Cataluña in the Penedès district. Although some Chardonnay is planted here, mostly in the highest-altitude vineyards, the dominant varieties are Spanish: Xarello, for body; Parellada, for fruitiness and acidity; and Macabeo, for vibrancy and aromatic character. Most Cavas are multivintage blends, like Champagne, although virtually all producers also offer at least small amounts of vintage-dated wines from the best years. As in Champagne, vintage-dated wines are not necessarily superior, as blending across vintages allows producers to take advantage of the best qualities of good years while downplaying the shortcomings of the more difficult ones. Huge producers like Freixenet and

Codorníu make some Cavas that are excellent values, but they also ship vast quantities of strictly commercial-grade wine, so finding fresh, well-handled bottles can be tricky.

BANG FOR THE BUCK. The best Cavas are the world's greatest values in sparkling wine, even if few Cavas approach the complexity of Champagne.

RECOMMENDED PRODUCERS

Avinyó. Round, nutty, dry wines with noteworthy suavity and flavor concentration. There's also a very interesting *rosado* (rosé).

NV Brut Nature Reserva Cava		$$
NV Brut Reserva Cava		$$

Vins El Cep. The American importer brings in a single vintage-dated estate-bottled wine that's fresh, fruit-driven, and pure despite getting three years of aging prior to release. A great value.

Marqués de Gelida Brut Exclusive	01	$

Gramona. The basic Gran Cuvée bottling is unusually rich and complex for a Cava in its price range. Gramona's Grand Reservas, which are held back several years before being released, are among the finest Cavas in the market, albeit at a rather high price.

Gran Cuvée Cava	02	$
Gran Reserva Brut Cava	97	$$$

Llopart. The Brut Nature typically reveals a gingery spice character, while the rosé shows pure, ripe red berry and watermelon notes.

Brut Nature Reserva Cava	99	$$
Brut Rosé Cava	01	$$

U Mes U Fan Tres. The basic nonvintage Cava offers good intensity of flavor and presence on the palate, but the vintage-dated Brut Nature is toastier, nuttier, and fatter.

NV Brut Cava			$
Brut Nature Cava	01	00	$$

OTHER PRODUCERS TO LOOK FOR: Agustí Torelló, Albet i Noya, Codorniu, Freixenet, Jané Ventura, Mont-Marçal, Parxet, Raventós i Blanc, Segura Viudas, Bodegas Sumarroca.

SHERRY

Sherry-style wines are produced in a number of countries, but true sherry comes from the triangle bounded by Jerez de la Frontera, Puerto de Santa María, and Sanlúcar de Barrameda, in Andalucía. The best sherries are made from the white Palomino Fino grape grown on pale chalky soil called albariza. In theory at least, the finest raw materials are reserved for the production of dry sherries—fino, manzanilla, amontillado (see box on page 185). These dry, aperitif-style wines are made possible by a natural yeast, known as *flor*, that grows on the surface of the wine in barrel, protecting it from oxidation and imparting a yeasty, fresh bread smell in classic, unfiltered versions. Dry sherries receive little or no fortification with grape spirits to boost their alcohol levels or hide their flaws, nor are they sweetened via the addition of darker, almost confectionery wines made from Pedro Ximénez or Moscatel grapes. Some wine lovers find the driest sherries a bit too uncompromising, preferring the somewhat less rigorous sweetened olorosos and cream sherries.

With very few exceptions, sherry is an amalgam of vintages, produced through a blending and aging process called the *solera* system, through which more mature barrels are continually topped up with younger wine of the same sort to ensure a continuity of style and quality for the various sherry types offered by each bodega. As is the case with Cava, some of the largest sherry producers turn out vast quantities of innocuous wine but also some limited bottlings that are among the best in their respective categories.

BANG FOR THE BUCK. The best sherries are remarkably complex, and many of them are incredibly underpriced.

RECOMMENDED PRODUCERS

Alvear. Alvear is not technically a sherry producer as their wines are from Montilla-Moriles. But for wine lovers this should be incidental, as these wines are impressively deep and concentrated, not to mention fairly priced. Alvear has recently introduced some single-vintage bottlings, a rarity for this region.

Fino en Rama	`02`	$$
Amontillado Carlos VII		$$$
Pedro Ximénez de Añada	`03`	$$$

Bodegas Dios Baco. Textbook versions of the range of sherry styles, with very good flavor precision and less thickness than many versions. Pricing is very friendly.

Amontillado	$$
Oloroso	$$
Oloroso Baco Imperial	$$
Pedro Ximénez	$$

González Byass. Tio Pepe Fino is perhaps the best-known high-end dry sherry and a consistently fine value. Rapid turnover raises your odds of getting a fresh bottle of this crisp, lemony wine, which is a classic, if distinctly user-friendly, fino. The Amontillado del Duque is a thirty-year-old solera.

Tío Pepe Palomino Fino	$
Amontillado del Duque	$$

SHERRY STYLES

Fino is a light, subtly almond-scented, dry wine generally carrying 16 to 18 percent alcohol. The area around El Puerto de Santa María produces particularly delicate examples, while Jerez itself yields fuller-bodied fino. **Manzanilla** is an even more delicate though bracing aperitif-style sherry aged in the bodegas of the port town of Sanlúcar de Barrameda. **Amontillado** is essentially aged fino that develops over a longer period while its normally thinner layer of *flor* gradually dissipates and controlled oxidation occurs. The relatively rare **palo cortado** combines the nutty aromas of amontillado with the deeper color and fuller body of oloroso; most palo cortados in the North American market are slightly to moderately sweet. Oloroso is made from raw materials that are not quite as refined as those used for fino, but are believed to have greater potential for aging. Like palo cortado, **oloroso** does not develop *flor*; because the wine comes in contact with the air, it is somewhat oxidized in character. Most oloroso is sweetened to some degree with wines made from sugar-laden Pedro Ximénez or Moscatel grapes. **Cream sherries** are also olorosos mellowed by Pedro Ximénez, but these wines tend to be even sweeter. As a general rule, sweetened sherries begin with more heavily fortified base wines, and typically carry alcohol in the heady 18 to 23 percent range. Some supersweet **dessert sherries**, normally better suited for tasting than drinking, are also produced entirely from Pedro Ximénez or Moscatel. **Montilla**, a wine very similar to sherry, is produced in the hill country around the town of Montilla, near Córdoba, from the Pedro Ximénez grape; Montilla comes in the full range of sherry styles.

Bodegas Hidalgo. One of the few sherry producers to rely solely on estate-grown grapes, Hidalgo is justly renowned for their bracing, minerally, saline Manzanillas, especially the ethereal La Gitana. The aged (Viejo) Sherries offer remarkable power and depth, but are quite rare.

La Gitana Manzanilla	$
Napoleón Amontillado	$$
Wellington Palo Cortado	$$
Pastrana Manzanilla Pasada	$$$
Palo Cortado Viejo	$$$$$

Emilio Lustau. A vast range of wines that are all at least very good, and many exceptional—and almost ridiculously inexpensive. Lustau is known for its faithful, vibrant renditions of the classic sherry styles, as well as for limited lots matured by small stockholders—usually doctors, lawyers, or shopkeepers—called *almacenistas*. The designation 1/50, for example, denotes the number of barrels (i.e., one of fifty) in that particular solera.

Light Fino Jarana	$
Puerto Fino	$
Emperatriz Eugenia Very Rare Dry Oloroso	$$
Old East India Solera Reserva	$$
Almacenista Palo Cortado 1/50 Vides	$$$

Bodegas Toro Albalá. A Montilla-Moriles producer of limited-release Pedro Ximénez sherries with remarkable intensity of flavor and molasses-like thickness. These elixirs are difficult to find but worth the search.

Pedro Ximénez Don PX	04	$$
Pedro Ximénez Don PX Gran Reserva	71	$$$

A. R. Valdespino. Very traditionally made sherries from a producer that has been in the business for 700 years. The Fino Inocente is an atypically full-bodied version with outstanding lemony persistence.

Fino Inocente	$$
Amontillado	$$

LARGE PRODUCERS OF NOTE: Pedro Domecq, Osborne.

Key to Vintage Ratings	Key to Assessments of Specific Wines
★★★★★ Outstanding	**03** An excellent to outstanding example *of that wine*
★★★★ Excellent	03 A good to very good example *of that wine*
★★★ Good to very good	03 A disappointing effort (often due to a
★★ Fair to average	difficult vintage)
★ Poor	

PORTUGAL

For most North American wine lovers, Portuguese wine means port, the rich fortified wine made in the hot, dry Douro Valley in the northern part of the country. But the past decade has witnessed a greater flow of high-quality table wines, mostly red, into the North American market—partly as a result of a depressed market for port.

In fact, Portugal has long been a reliable source for somewhat rustic but satisfying red wines that seldom exceeded $15 on American retail shelves. Most wines from Portugal's Dão region, together with Alentejo, the country's deepest source for quality red wines outside the Douro, were under $10 until recently and still seldom exceed $20, even those from the top producers. The majority of today's new Portuguese table wines are made in a more modern, fruit-driven style, with emphasis on ripe dark berry and plum flavors, often complemented (in some instances bullied) by lavish oak spice but less earthy and leathery than more traditional examples. Many of these new wines are priced rather ambitiously, so it remains to be seen how warmly they will be accepted by North American wine drinkers and other export markets.

In the 1980s and early 1990s, international varieties like Cabernet Sauvignon, Merlot, and Chardonnay enjoyed something of a vogue in Portugal. But despite the fact that there are scattered plantings around the country, as well as a handful of successful bottlings from these varieties, they have made limited impact on Portugal's wine scene. On the contrary, today's most interesting wines rely almost exclusively on indigenous grapes or on those of Iberian origin, such as Alvarinho (called Albariño in Spain) and Tinta Roriz (known as Tempranillo in Spain).

One note: In the table wines featured in this chapter, the category of *vinho regional* is less restrictive in terms of permitted grapes and blends than DOC (Denominação de Origem Controlada), as well as less specific geographically. For example, the important DOCs of Bairrada and Dão lie within the larger Beiras area of north-central Portugal, while the DOC Alentejo covers closely defined districts within the large southern area whose wines are labeled vinho regional Alentejano. Terras do Sado is another vinho regional.

RED WINES

Although in recent years the Alentejo region has taken over as Portugal's best source of popularly priced red table wines, the real news for serious enophiles comes from the Douro Valley, where varieties traditionally blended to make Port are now increasingly used to make very good table wines. Many of today's wines are from single varieties, the best among them Touriga Nacional, Portugal's finest red grape. But many insiders continue to believe that the most balanced and complex red table wines, like the best ports, may also be made from blends of two or more varieties.

BANG FOR THE BUCK. Although many top Douro wines, especially varietally labeled Touriga Nacional, have gotten expensive, Portugal remains a superb source of value in red wine.

2003 ★★★★+ 2002 ★★− 2001 ★★★★−

DISTINCTIVE RED GRAPES OF PORTUGAL

- **Baga:** This highly distinctive variety dominates in the Bairrada region of north-central Portugal, where it produces high-acid, slow-to-evolve wines with moderate alcohol but substantial tannins from thick skins. Some examples show a rather exotic grapefruit quality. There have been efforts recently to tame the more brutal qualities of the grape through destemming and shorter, less extractive vinification. Baga is sometimes blended into Dão and Ribatejo wines to give them more backbone.
- **Castelão:** Also called Periquita, especially in the southern half of the country, where the grape is widely planted. The wine it produces is usually lush and fruity, providing wines that can be enjoyed young. The best examples come from Ribatejo, northeast of Lisbon, and on the Setúbal Peninsula east of the capital. Castelão has been described as Merlot to Baga's Cabernet, although in Ribatejo it can also produce firmer wines.
- **Tinta Barroca:** Planted throughout the Douro, where it is one of the main components in port, this large-berried variety produces deeply colored but often somewhat rustic wines with generous alcohol levels. Tinta Barroca is often used to add softness and floral character to port blends.
- **Tinta Roriz:** This is Spain's Tempranillo, producing wines that are fragrant and complex, with good color, body, backbone, and resistance to oxidation despite possessing only moderate acidity. The second most widely planted variety in the Douro, this grape is increasingly popular as a stand-alone variety for dry red wines. (Tinta Roriz is called Aragonez in Alentejo, where the wines it produces are softer and more liqueur-like.)
- **Touriga Franca.** Limited mostly to the Douro, where it's the most widely planted variety (and often called by its former name Touriga Francesa), this grape is a key ingredient in most ports owing to the fleshiness of texture it imparts. This relatively thick-skinned grape has a tendency to overproduction, and sugar levels are generally moderate to low.
- **Touriga Nacional:** The heart of port, and the Douro region's—if not the country's—most complete and most fashionable red grape, even if it still accounts for only a small percentage of production in the Douro. The wine produced from this low-yielding variety, characterized by thick skins and small berries, is deeply colored and concentrated, with excellent tannic and acid spine but also a seductive floral character. Touriga Nacional is also the backbone for most reds from Dão, where it may have originated.
- **Trincadeira Preta.** One of the most widely planted red grapes in Portugal, and at its best in the hot, dry Alentejo, where it produces deeply colored, spicy wines with good body. Trincadeira Preta is known as Tinta Amarela in the Douro.

RECOMMENDED PRODUCERS

Caves Aliança. Bordeaux consultant Michel Rolland has a hand in a number of this far-reaching producer's properties. Not surprisingly, the wines are increasingly modern and accessible but also have structure and show some traditional Old World earthiness.

Quinta da Terrugem "T" Alentejano		01	$$$
Quinta Dos Quatro Ventos Douro	02	01	$$
Quinta das Baceladas Beiras		01	$$

A. A. Ferreira. This producer's red blend Barca Velha, made only in the best vintages, has been Portugal's most famous and expensive wine for decades, analogous to Spain's Vega Sicilia. Slightly less-good vintages are labeled Reserva Ferreirinha. Both are complex, suave wines, released after they've had considerable bottle aging. In recent years, Ferreira has also offered a number of supple, fruit-driven wines that are released earlier.

Vinha Grande Tinto Douro		01	$$
Tinto Reserva Douro		96	$$$
Barca Velha Douro	99	95	$$$$$

J. P. Vinhos. A large producer with holdings in Terras do Sado as well as Alentejo. In its earlier incarnation as João Pires, this firm hired Australian winemaker Peter Bright, who helped to revolutionize white winemaking in Portugal in the early 1980s. Their Quinta da Bacalhoa Cabernet, which includes a bit of Merlot, is decidedly Bordeaux-like in style, with plenty of aromatic complexity.

JP Garrafeira Palmela	00	$
Quinta da Bacalhoa Cabernet Sauvignon Terras do Sado	01	$$

José Maria da Fonseca. A massive producer of a huge range of wines, including the mass-market Lancers. The Setúbal Peninsula southeast of Lisbon, the company's home base and historically known for long-aging, sweet fortified wines from Muscat of Alexandria, is also the source of Fonseca's dry, fresh, fruit-driven Periquita, whose sweet red cherry flavor and smooth texture make it a perennial value at well under $10.

Periquita Terras do Sado	02	$
Periquita Classico Terras do Sado	95	$$

Luís Pato. Concentrated, fruity, spicy single-vineyard wines based on Baga. The Vinha Barrosa and Vinha Barrio are from very old vines. Pato's holdings are in Bairrada but he uses the broader vinho regional Beiras following a disagreement with the Bairrada wine authorities.

Vinha Barrosa Vinha Velha Beiras	01	00	$$
Vinha Barrio Beiras	01	00	$$
Vinha Pan Beiras		01	$$

Niepoort. Dirk Niepoort, whose family has been making port since 1842, plunged into the table wine business in the early 1990s and is now considered one of the top producers of high-end Douro wines. His wines are rich and dense, with considerable oak influence and serious weight.

Vertente Tinto Douro		03	01	$$
Redoma Tinto Douro	04	03	01	$$$
Batuta Tinto Douro	04	03	01	$$$$
Charme Tinto Douro			04	$$$$

Prats & Symington. A joint venture between Bruno Prats (former owner of Château Cos d'Estournel in Bordeaux) and the Symington family, who are among the most important landowners in the Douro region and owners of the Dow, Graham, and Warre port houses. The wines, from a blend of port varieties, are glossy, modern, and suave, with dense fruit and impressive complexity. The Post Scriptum, launched in 2002, is intended for earlier drinking.

Post Scriptum de Chryseia Douro		02	$$
Chryseia Douro	03	01	$$$

Quinta do Carmo. This estate in the Alentejo region is now majority-owned by the Barons de Rothschild, proprietors of Château Lafite-Rothschild in Bordeaux. The lower-level wines are suave and Old World in style, while the upper-end wines are a bit more international and polished, with ample new oak character.

Don Martinho Tinto Alentejano	02	$
Tinto Alentejano	01	$$
Tinto Reserva da Quinta Alentejano	02	$$$

Quinta do Crasto. A leader in the production of superpremium table wines in the Douro, Quinta do Crasto makes wines with richness, concentration, and structured that compare with many New World cult wines.

Reserva Old Vines	04	03	02	$$$
Maria Teresa Douro			03	$$$$

Quinta do Fojo. Both the flagship bottling and the slightly lighter Vinha do Fojo are deeply colored, dense, and powerful wines with big tannic structure and serious heft, based on old plantings of Tinta Francesa and Tinta Roriz.

Vinha do Fojo Douro	01	99	$$$
Fojo Douro		00	$$$$

Quinta de Pancas. Understated, well-balanced wines with deceptive concentration and a track record for improving with age. The Quinta de Parrotes bottling is a lighter style of wine for earlier consumption. Also look for limited-production varietal bottlings labeled Special Selection.

Quinta de Parrotes Alenquer	02	$
Cabernet Sauvignon Estremadura	02	$$

Quinta dos Roques. Rich, fleshy wines with sweet fruit: a modern take on traditional Portuguese wine, but without the new-oak excesses of some examples. Pricing is very fair for the quality. Look also for elegant, fresh wines from Quinta das Maias, under the same ownership.

Quinta dos Roques Tinto Dão		03	02	$
Touriga Nacional Quinta dos Roques Dão	03	02	01	$$
Garrafeira Dão			00	$$$

Quinta do Vale Dona Maria. Under the direction of Cristiano van Zeller, whose family sold the famous Port house Quinta do Noval to the French insurance group AXA in 1993, this is a top source of firmly structured but modern-style red table wines from the Douro, featuring judicious use of new oak.

Tinto Douro	04	03	02	$$$

Quinta do Vale Meão. The flagship wine here is a concentrated, seamless blend based on 60 percent Touriga Nacional, made by Francisco Olazabal, whose father ran Ferreira for 30 years and is a living legend of Portuguese wine.

Vale Meão Douro	04	03	02	$$$

Quinta do Vallado. A new producer with a sizable percentage of young vines—but with the advantage of the talented Francisco Olazabal of Quinta do Vale Meão as winemaker. Raised in small French barrels (the Reserva is aged in 100 percent new oak), these are highly modern wines with sweet, powerful dark berry, spice, and licorice flavors.

Tinto Douro			03	$$
Tinto Reserva Douro	03	00	99	$$$

Quinta de Ventozelo. The new owners of this venerable port-producing property have introduced a line of modern, lush wines with pliant berry fruit and spicy American oak.

Tinto Roriz Douro	03	$$
Touriga Nacional Douro	01	$$

OTHER PRODUCERS TO LOOK FOR: Casa de Casal de Loivos, Casa de Santar, Pintas, Quinta de Chocapalha, Quinta das Maias, Quinta do Mouro, Quinta da Pellada, Ramos Pinto.

WHITE WINES

Aside from port, Portugal's best-known wine is Vinho Verde. This "green wine," with its high acidity, low alcohol (typically well below ten percent), and slight spritz, is intended to be drunk virtually upon release, before its fruit fades. Classic Vinho Verde is bone-dry and lively, even underripe or downright tart, with notes of lemon, lime, minerals, and earth. There are actually hundreds of villages, in six subregions, that are entitled to call their wines Vinho Verde, making this Portugal's largest wine zone. (There is also a widely made red version of Vinho Verde, but this is fairly nasty stuff and rarely exported). Vinho Verde is normally made from a blend of grapes, especially Loureiro, Trajadura, and Alvarinho (Albariño in Spain). The last is generally best, and in recent years a growing number of Vinho Verde bottlings have been made entirely from Alvarinho. Some of these are capable of a year or two of bottle aging.

BANG FOR THE BUCK. Vinho Verde can be an exceptional value, with many very good examples available at single-digit prices.

2004 ★★★★   2003 ★★

DISTINCTIVE WHITE GRAPES OF PORTUGAL

- **Alvarinho:** Grown almost exclusively along the Minho River in the north end of the Vinho Verde region, Alvarinho produces aromatic wines with more alcoholic body and concentration than most other white grapes in this cool area. It's an important element in many Vinhos Verdes and is increasingly bottled on its own.
- **Arinto:** This high-acid variety is responsible for some of the freshest, most fragrant wines of Bucelas, Estremadura, and Alentejo. (In the cooler Vinho Verde region, where it's called Pedernão, it's usually too tart.) The wines are characterized by steely and minerally nuances and brisk citrus fruits.
- **Bical:** Widely planted in Bairrada and Dão, this is another white variety that's coming back into favor and increasingly being bottled on its own. Bical can produce weighty yet fragrant wines with enough acidity to develop gracefully in bottle, becoming more minerally and petrolly (as in Riesling) with age.
- **Encruzado:** This grape, which has long been planted in the Dão region, is being brought back from near-extinction by a handful of producers who are convinced that its sound balance of sugars and acids should enable it to produce complete, full-bodied wines on its own. The wines show a tendency toward exotic, tropical fruits, and are increasingly being fermented and aged in small barrels.
- **Loureiro:** Widely planted in the north, this grape, along with Trajadura, is an important component in many Vinho Verde bottlings. Common characteristics of the variety are high yields and subtle floral and herbal notes.
- **Trajadura:** A base variety for most Vinho Verde, this grape has lower acidity but higher potential alcohol than the other important varieties used to make these wines. Not surprisingly, this early-ripening, very productive grape adds body to Vinho Verde.

RECOMMENDED PRODUCERS

Quinta da Aveleda. Outstanding values in textbook Vinho Verde. The Quinta da Aveleda bottling is classic austere, green-appley Vinho Verde, while the wine simply labeled Aveleda is a bit more user-friendly and less serious. Quinta da Aveleda offers varietal bottlings from Alvarinho, Loureiro, and Trajadura, all of them extremely inexpensive.

Quinta da Aveleda Vinho Verde	`05`	`04`	$
Alvarinho Vinho Verde		`05`	$

Niepoort. This producer's Redoma Branco, from local white varieties, offers a flamboyantly leesy, vanillin character but has the richness of fruit to support its barrel fermentation and aging in oak. (The scarcer Redoma Reserva Branco is one of Portugal's elite white wines.)

Redoma Branco Douro	`04`	$$$

Provam. A small cooperative venture in Monção producing exuberant, firmly built wines with more concentration and thrust than standard-issue Vinho Verde.

Portal do Fidalgo Alvarinho Vinho Verde	`04`	$
Varanda do Conde Alvarinho-Trajadura Vinho Verde	`04`	$

Quinta do Feital. A leading producer of pristine, concentrated Alvarinhos from low-yielding old vines. Winemaker Marcial Dorado puts his wines through malolactic fermentation and ages them on their lees for greater complexity and richness, but they never lack freshness.

Auratus Alvarinho-Trajadura Vinho Verde	`05`	`04`	$$
Dorado Alvarinho Vinho Verde	`04`	`03`	$$

Quinta do Minho. The light, minerally, and slightly off-dry wine labeled Vinha Verde (green vine) is one of the most consistent widely available basic bottlings of Vinho Verde in the market.

Vinha Verde Vinho Verde	`04`	$

Quinta dos Roques. Highly regarded for rich, fruit-driven red wines, Quinta dos Roques also produces a fleshy, exuberant, barrel-fermented white from the rare Encruzado variety. Also look for wines from their sister property, Quinta das Maias.

Branco Encruzado Dão	`04`	$$

OTHER PRODUCERS TO LOOK FOR: Casa de Cello, Quinta dos Carvalhais, Porta dos Cavaleiros, Quinta do Correio, Quinta das Maias, Quinta da Murta.

PORT

Although port-style wines are produced in many countries, the real article is made from a blend of indigenous grape varieties planted on terraced vineyards in Portugal's hot, dry Douro Valley. Port's name comes from Oporto, the Portuguese coastal town from which the wine has been shipped since the 17th century. Port is a fortified wine made by adding neutral grape spirits to stop fermentation. The result is a wine with significant residual sweetness and high alcohol (normally in the 18 to 20 percent range, but slightly lower for white port, which constitutes a tiny percentage of port production and is consumed mostly in Portugal).

For generations, vintage port has been one of the world's great collectible wines. A vintage port is only "declared" three or four years out of ten, when a producer believes that that year's harvest has yielded an outstanding wine. Vintage ports from the best port houses in the best years normally require ten to twenty years of addi-

WOOD-AGED PORT VS. BOTTLE-AGED PORT

The two basic types of port are defined by the medium in which the wines reach maturity. **Wood ports** are, in theory, aged in wooden casks, but nowadays are in fact frequently aged in cement tanks. They are decanted off their sediment at the time of bottling, and are considered ready to drink upon their release. The two most common types of wood port are rubies and tawnies. Rubies are bottled young, after just two or three years in wood; they are very dark in color, and usually quite sweet, with an aggressive, almost peppery fruitiness. Tawnies, many of which have generally spent much longer in wood (20- and 30-year-old tawnies are widely available in the retail market), are less relentlessly fruity and considerably mellower, offering notes of nuts, dried fruits, and vanilla, and silkier texture. A colheita is a tawny port from a single vintage.

Bottle ports, in contrast, spend a relatively short time in barrel prior to bottling, and can require many years of bottle aging to harmonize, soften, and express themselves fully. "Classic" vintage port is the apotheosis of bottle port. These are wines from a single vintage, usually made from superior grapes grown in the finest vineyards owned by the producer. They are made in years whose raw materials have the depth and structure to benefit from early bottling and to reward aging in bottle rather than cask. As these wines are generally bottled without filtration, uncorking a maturing port many years later will require careful decanting of its heavy sediment, or crust. Late-bottled vintage (LBV) ports, which share some characteristics of both bottle and wood ports, are relatively affordable wines from a single vintage—usually a good but unexceptional one—bottled four to six years after the harvest. The best traditional LBVs are bottled without filtration, using corks rather than stoppers, and show some of the fruit concentration and backbone of true vintage port. While these LBVs also call for decanting, they generally require considerably less time to reach full maturity.

tional bottle aging before their initially brutal black fruit flavors, often fiery alcohol, and powerful tannins have harmonized. Although true vintage port attracts a disproportionate share of the North American market's interest in port, these bottlings represent only a tiny fraction of total port production. Note that the last two vintages declared by a majority of port producers, 2003 and 2000, are both among the greatest port vintages of the past 40 years.

BANG FOR THE BUCK. Prices for classic vintage port are generally high. Other types of port, especially mellower tawnies, offer the major advantages of lower prices and immediate drinkability.

RECOMMENDED PRODUCERS

Dow. A great traditional port shipper, producing firmly structured ports, typically drier than the wines from most other houses, with emphasis on balance and elegance rather than power and sweet fruit.

Boardroom Tawny Port			$$
20-Year-Old Tawny Port			$$
Vintage Port	03	02	$$$$

Fonseca. Renowned as one of the great port producers, Fonseca's vintage wine is among the best in virtually every widely declared vintage. The house style is flamboyantly rich, even exotic, and the wines are usually sweeter and fuller in body than those from most other producers.

Bin 27 Port			$$
20-Year-Old Tawny Port			$$$$
Vintage Port	03	02	$$$$$

Graham. Along with Fonseca, Graham is known for producing the sweetest ports. Graham's vintage wines are often approachable on the early side owing to their layered dark berry flavors but have the density for long aging. The fresh, floral Six Grapes bottling is one of the finest port values, and the Quinta dos Malvedos one of the top vineyards in the region.

Six Grapes Port			$$
Quinta dos Malvedos		96	$$$
20-Year-Old Tawny Port			$$$
Vintage Port	03	00	$$$$

Niepoort. This family-owned firm has been revitalized in recent years by Dirk Niepoort, who has improved its vintage ports and is also a leader in the table wine movement in the Douro Valley.

Senior Tawny Port			$$
10-Year-Old Tawny Port			$$
Vintage Port	03	00	$$$$

Porto Rocha. A specialist in very old, aged tawny and colheita ports. One of the rare sources of wood ports over 40 years of age, offering a rare but relatively affordable glimpse at the complex, seductive character of very old port. The Three Centuries bottling is a blend of old tawnies dating back to 1900, while the Glorious 50th is a blend of tawnies averaging about 50 years of age.

20-Year-Old Tawny Port	$$$
Three Centuries Tawny Port	$$$$$
The Glorious 50th Old Tawny Port	$$$$$

Quinta do Noval. Owner of the famed Nacional vineyard, whose vines were not attacked during the phylloxera epidemic of the 1870s and 1880s and thus were never grafted onto American rootstock. This rare collectible is by far the most expensive port, at over $600 a bottle, but Quinta do Noval's "regular" bottling has been significantly upgraded in recent years by managing director Christian Seely and is now among the handful of elite vintage ports, wonderfully creamy and stylish, and featuring a high percentage of Touriga Nacional. Silval, which is intended to be drinkable earlier, is an excellent value in vintage port.

			$
Special Ruby Port			$
LBV Port	99	98	$$
Silval Vintage Port	03	00	$$$
Vintage Port	03	00	$$$$

Ramos Pinto. Best known for aged tawnies that are widely available and offer a good introduction to aged port at attractive prices.

	$
Tawny Port	$
Collector Reserve Port	$$
10-Year Old Tawny Quinta de Ervamoira	$$$
20-Year Old Tawny Quinta do Bom Retiro	$$$$

Taylor, Fladgate & Yeatman. Perhaps the single greatest port house, producing powerful, dense, firmly structured vintage wines that require long bottle aging, while the aged tawny bottlings are usually among the finest on the market, with outstanding aromatic complexity and depth of flavor. Their Quinta de Vargellas has been one of the most famous single-quinta wines in recent decades.

Quinta de Vargellas	99	95	$$$
30-Year Old Tawny Port			$$$$
40-Year Old Tawny Port			$$$$$
Vintage Port	03	00	$$$$$

OTHER PRODUCERS TO LOOK FOR: Churchill, Cockburn, Croft, Delaforce, Ferreira, Gould Campbell, Kopke (colheitas), Offley, Poças Junior, Quarles Harris, Quinta do Infantado, Quinta do Portal, Quinta de Roriz, Quinta do Vesuvio, Romariz, Sandeman, Smith Woodhouse, Warre.

MADEIRA

Madeira, made on the volcanic Portuguese-owned island of the same name off the coast of Morocco, was originally an unfortified wine. In the 18th century, it was discovered that wine shipped to the U.S. was changed and actually improved by the heat and constant movement of the long sea voyage. To make Madeira today, neutral grape spirits (i.e., pure alcohol) are added to stop the fermentation with the targeted amount of residual sugar and to stabilize the wine. Following this semi-pasteurization, the wine may be designated as vintage quality or for use in shippers' blends, and is matured accordingly—sometimes for as long as several decades in barrel.

The process of *estufagem* was developed to simulate the conditions of an extended journey by sea. Madeira's distinctive character—its notes of raisin, toffee, caramel, nuts, and smoke—comes from the fact that the wine has literally been cooked: heated over a period of months in casks or other vessels inside *estufas*, or "hot-houses," at temperatures as high as 130 degrees. This unique process makes Madeira virtually indestructible, as the wine is effectively preoxidized: 200-year-old wines can be full of life, and bottles can be recorked for weeks or even months with little or no ill effect. Madeira's very high acidity also contributes to the ageability of what is often called the world's longest-lived wine.

Consumption of Madeira in this country has fallen in recent years, making this one of the great underappreciated wines in the market. Madeira marries high-toned aromas and flavors of burnt caramel, dried fruits, and chocolate with a pungent acidity that keeps even the sweetest versions from cloying. The sweetest Madeira types, made from Malmsey (Malvasia) and Bual, are perfect endings to a meal. The driest style of Madeira, Sercial, is a lighter, quite penetrating, high-acid wine that makes an excellent aperitif. Madeira made from Verdelho is also dry but has more body and richer flavor than Sercial. Rainwater is a fairly dry and distinctly light style of Madeira. Generic Madeira, usually simply labeled dry, medium, sweet, or rich, as well as wines called Bual-style or Malmsey-style, are usually made from the prolific and coarser Tinta Mole grape, and are best suited for sauce making.

BANG FOR THE BUCK. Vintage Madeira is extremely rare and priced accordingly. From time to time tiny quantities of wines from the 19th and early 20th centuries become available, at prices generally over $200 per bottle, and sometimes much higher. Far better value for most consumers are the five-year-old bottlings or, better yet, the suaver and more harmonious ten- and fifteen-year-old versions.

RECOMMENDED PRODUCERS

Blandy's. A vast range of wines, from three-year-olds through assorted five-, ten-, and fifteen-year-old versions of different varieties, to old vintage bottlings. Established in 1811, Blandy's is now the largest exporter of Madeira. Their wines tend to be richer and heavier than most.

5-Year-Old Verdelho	$
Alvada Rich 5-Year-Old Madeira	$$
10-Year-Old Malmsey	$$
15-Year-Old Malmsey	$$$

Broadbent. A collection of Madeiras made by Justinho Henriques and selected by noted wine writer Michael Broadbent for Broadbent Selections, his son Bartholomew's U.S. import company. There are also limited bottlings of rare vintage wines available.

Broadbent Rainwater	$
Broadbent 5-Year-Old Reserve	$$
Broadbent 10-Year-Old Malmsey	$$$

Cossart Gordon. The oldest Madeira firm, established in 1745, Cossart Gordon is noted for their colheita bottlings: wines made from a single vintage but released earlier than the 22 years required for vintage Madeira. The most widely seen Cossart Gordon wines are their Bual bottlings, ranging from five-year-old to colheita. Cossart's wines have a reputation for being fruitier and more elegant than most.

Rainwater	$
10-Year-Old Bual	$$
1995 Bual Colheita	$$$

Leacock's. Produces the full range of Madeira, with a tendency toward extra sweetness in each category, but best known in North America for Rainwater. Founded in 1760, Leacock's combined their interests with Blandy's and joined the Madeira Wine Company in 1925.

Rainwater	$
5-Year-Old Sercial	$$
10-Year-Old Bual	$$

Rare Wine Company. This American importer offers a range of Madeiras made by the Barbeito firm. Called the Historic Series, they are made from older and younger wines that are blended to produce a "vintage character" bottling that replicates the style of an aged wine. Prices are very reasonable for the quality offered.

Charleston Sercial Special Reserve	$$$
Boston Bual Special Reserve	$$$
New York Malmsey Special Reserve	$$$

OTHER PRODUCERS TO LOOK FOR: D'Oliveira, Henriques & Henriques, Justinho Henriques, Barbeito.

Key to Vintage Ratings		Key to Assessments of Specific Wines
★★★★★	Outstanding	**03** An excellent to outstanding example *of that wine*
★★★★	Excellent	03 A good to very good example *of that wine*
★★★	Good to very good	03 A disappointing effort (often due to a
★★	Fair to average	difficult vintage)
★	Poor	

GERMANY

German vintners and Germany's wine law have often been their own worst enemies, and consumers understandably bemoan the unintelligibility of the labels as well as the mediocre quality of so many commercial-grade wines. It is a shame if this situation acts as a barrier to appreciating some of the world's most distinctive and versatile wines. In fact, an excellent case can be made that no other class of wine offers the stylistic diversity, nuanced expression of site and climate, and versatility at the table of German Riesling. These wines can be adamantly dry, off-dry, or downright sweet. They can be complex and satisfyingly complete at a mere seven percent alcohol, yet can also avoid coming off as heavy at over 14 percent.

The tradition of Riesling excellence in Germany makes two important presuppositions, over and beyond the talents of the individual vintner. First, in a generally cool environment incorporating Europe's northernmost significant vineyards, the microclimatic conditions of a given vineyard site—its exposure to the sun, shelter from wind, proximity to water, geological underpinnings, and other environmental factors—are of paramount importance. Second, to get the most out of Riesling's potential in a good site, the grapes in any given parcel are generally harvested in multiple passes, at times weeks apart, in a process that often involves the selection of particular bunches or occasionally even of individual berries. These factors explain why most of the best German Rieslings preserve their vineyard identity and are labeled to reflect this. They also reflect the many pickings of a given vineyard through labeling with different designations of *prädikat* (Kabinett, Spätlese, etc.) or taste (Trocken, Halbtrocken), as is explained in the box on page 202.

The finest German Rieslings can age at a slower pace and with greater gustatory rewards than practically any other type of wine, white or red. In only three of Germany's 13 growing regions does Riesling represent more than 50 percent of vineyard plantings, but its importance as a source for most of Germany's finest wines as well as of Germany's historic wine-growing reputation is far out of proportion to its acreage. In the classic Riesling regions such as the Mittelrhein, Mosel-Saar-Ruwer, Nahe, Rheingau, Rheinhessen, and Pfalz, much of what is not Riesling is of lower quality. That said, there are some excellent wines made in these regions from other traditional varieties such as Pinot Blanc (Weissburgunder) and Silvaner, as well as from a few of the most interesting grape crossings. The dominant red variety of Germany, particularly in Riesling-growing regions, is Pinot Noir (Spätburgunder), though Germany's red wines are rarely sighted in the North American market.

The best guarantee of wine quality from Germany is naturally a conscientious, skilled grower with good vineyard sites. The membership of Germany's most prestigious growers' association, the VDP, includes a high percentage of the country's best vintners, all of them practicing controlled yields and otherwise responsible farming of excellent sites. So looking on a label or capsule for those initials and the stylized eagle that is the VDP's symbol is an excellent course to follow, although one risks missing a few rising stars or political renegades.

Deciphering German Wine Labels

The basis of the German wine law and labeling is the amount of sugar in the grapes at harvest. A wine that has been chaptalized (i.e., has had sugar added to the grape must prior to fermentation) is known as a QbA (Qualitätswein bestimmter Anbaugebiete, or quality wine from a particular growing region). Any wine that meets certain minimum standards of sugar in the grapes at harvest is known as QmP (Qualitätswein mit Prädikat, or quality wine with predicate). The predicates in question, each pegged to an increasingly high minimum of grape sugar, are, from least to most sugar, known as Kabinett, Spätlese, Auslese, Beerenauslese, and Trockenbeerenauslese.

Effectively, Kabinett wines are lighter than Spätlese, while Auslese and above are wines of very ripe or overripe character. Wines of Kabinett, Spätlese, and Auslese level can be dry (labeled Trocken), which will mean, since most of their sugar has been converted, that they are higher in alcohol than a corresponding wine labeled Halbtrocken, or half dry. Halbtrocken Rieslings, given the high natural acidity normally exhibited by this variety, usually taste dry, while those labeled Trocken often taste austerely dry. A German wine that is not labeled either Trocken or Halbtrocken is apt to exhibit noticeable sweetness, but ideally this will be integrated into the overall personality of the wine, and be balanced by bright acidity and fresh fruit. At the levels of grape ripeness stipulated by Beerenauslese or Trockenbeerenauslese (as well as for Eiswein, a category reserved for grapes harvested in naturally frozen condition), a wine will have significant levels of residual sweetness and be appropriate for serving with very rich or sweet dishes—or simply by themselves.

What all this amounts to is that a typical wine name would be Monzinger Frühlingsplätzchen Riesling Spätlese Halbtrocken: i.e, Village Name + Vineyard Name + Grape Variety + Predicate + Indication of Taste. Even this much information is not always enough to satisfy the grower's demand for a unique descriptor. There might, for example, be more than one wine to which the five-word description above applies. In such a case, the fact that there are two or more different wines will be signified by the next-to-last pair of digits on the registration number (known officially as A.P. number) in tiny print on the label. As a further means of identifying or calling attention to differences between wines, German growers are fond of resorting to devices such as a gold capsule for a wine of special quality, or one or more stars on the label.

MOSEL-SAAR-RUWER

The river Mosel and its tributaries are home to some of the country's best-known wines—almost entirely Riesling and packaged in tall green bottles. While the dominant environment here is steep slate slopes, even small variations in mineral content of the slate, subsoil, exposure, and other factors can make for quite dramatic and systematic variations in the resulting wines. Take for instance the top vineyards of neighboring Erden, Ürzig, Zeltingen, and Wehlen, to the eye each just another towering wall of slate. Erden Rieslings are nearly always dominated by aromas and flavors of citrus, particularly lemon and tangerine. Rieslings from Ürzig evince red berries, usually strawberry. And those from the top sites in Zeltingen and Wehlen are nearly always redolent of apple, vanilla, and nut oils.

Besides the Upper and Middle Mosel areas—from Koblenz upstream to Trier—this large official growing region takes in the tributaries of Saar and Ruwer, which flow into the Mosel near Trier. Rieslings from the Ruwer and Saar have reputations for being harvested even later than on the Middle Mosel and being even more of a challenge to ripen.

BANG FOR THE BUCK. The Mosel-Saar-Ruwer is essentially the high-priced neighborhood of Germany, but Rieslings at lower predicate levels can offer excellent quality/ price rapport.

2004 ★★★–   2003 ★★★+   2002 ★★★★–

RECOMMENDED PRODUCERS

Fritz Haag. Owner-winemaker Wilhelm Haag, long a leader in Mosel quality and wine politics, owns some of the choicest parcels in the great wall of slate known as the Brauneberg, and makes the most of it with many different bottlings, the best of which are auctioned, frequently setting price records.

Brauneberger Juffer-Sonnenuhr Riesling Spätlese	04	03	$$$
Brauneberger Juffer-Sonnenuhr Riesling Auslese	04	03	$$$$

Reinhold Haart. Theo Haart is the foremost proponent of Piesport's famous terroir, with unabashedly sweet Rieslings that stand the test of time.

Piesporter Goldtröpfchen Riesling Kabinett	04	03	$$
Piesporter Goldtröpfchen Riesling Spätlese	04	03	$$$

Von Hövel. Eberhard von Künow, whose top property is his *monopole* (a vineyard with just a single owner) Oberemmeler Hütte, is also well known as the longtime auctioneer of the prestigious Trier auction each September. This has not kept him from pricing many of his own offerings at bargain levels.

Oberemmeler Hütte Riesling Spätlese	04	**03**	$$

Karlsmühle. In the late 1980s, proprietor Peter Geiben took it upon himself to propel this estate into the top echelons of quality. The excellent dry wines are seldom exported. Eiswein is harvested here with regularity.

Lorenzhöfer Mäuerchen Riesling Kabinett	04	03	$$
Kaseler Nies'chen Riesling Spätlese	04	03	$$$

Karthäuserhof. In the 1980s, Christoph Tyrell rescued the reputation of his family's estate and its *monopole* vineyards. Bottling is generally by style rather than by individual parcel, and excellent dry wines form a significant part of the lineup. The list of Auslese bottlings, each differing on the label only by A.P. registration number, is often long.

Eitelsbacher Karthäuserhofberg Riesling Spätlese	04	03	$$$

Schloss Lieser. Thomas Haag is crafting unabashedly rich and opulent Rieslings from superb but largely forgotten terroirs. In most years, there are multiple bottles of Auslese from the same site.

Lieser Niederberg-Helden Riesling Auslese	04	03	$$$

Dr. Loosen. Ernst Loosen revived his family's estate beginning in the late 1980s and does justice to famous vineyards in Erden, Ürzig, and Wehlen. As at many Mosel estates, Auslese bottlings designated "gold capsule" or "long gold capsule" are frequently offered, usually at auction.

Ürziger Würzgarten Riesling Spätlese	04	03	$$
Erdener Prälat Riesling Auslese	04	03	$$$$

Egon Müller. Owners of most of the great Scharzhofberg vineyard since Napoleon's time, the Müllers are famous for a wide range of sweet, selectively picked Riesling bottlings, the best of which are sold at auction, often at record prices. One usually gets what one pays for: the more expensive a given Scharzhofberger bottling at any given predicate level, the better.

Scharzhofberger Riesling Spätlese	04	03	$$$$

Joh. Jos. Prüm. This signature Mosel estate's wines, with their low alcohol, high residual sugar, and considerable retention of CO_2, age at a glacial pace. In addition to the wines noted below, Prüm's less frequently seen Rieslings from Bernkastel and Zeltinger can be consistently recommended.

Wehlener Sonnenuhr Riesling Kabinett	04	03	$$$
Graacher Himmelreich Riesling Spätlese	04	03	$$$
Wehlener Sonnenuhr Riesling Spätlese	04	03	$$$
Wehlener Sonnenuhr Riesling Auslese	04	03	$$$

St. Urbans-Hof. Ambitious owner Nik Weis and his young team have recently taken this estate, with its increasingly widespread vineyard holdings, to new levels of excellence.

Piesporter Goldtröpfchen Riesling Auslese	04	03	$$$
Ockfener Bockstein Riesling Auslese	04	03	$$$

Selbach-Oster. Under the direction of Hans and son Johannes Selbach, this winery has showcased Zeltingen's Himmelreich, Schlossberg, and Sonnenuhr vineyards while gradually acquiring outstanding properties in nearby Wehlen, Graach, and Bernkastel. A plethora of sites as well as degrees of dryness and numerous "star"-labeled bottlings make for a vast and consistently excellent menu that can only be hinted at below.

Zeltinger Himmelreich Riesling Kabinett Halbtrocken		03	$$
Zeltinger Sonnenuhr Riesling Spätlese	04	03	$$$
Zeltinger Sonnenuhr Riesling Auslese	04	03	$$$$

Zilliken–Forstmeister Geltz. Hanno Zilliken's small estate, known for steep-slope Rieslings that successfully pit enormous sweetness against vibrant acids, sells much of its production in North America.

Riesling	04	03	$
Saarburger Rausch Riesling Spätlese	04	03	$$$

OTHER PRODUCERS TO LOOK FOR: Von Beulwitz, Joh. Jos. Christoffel Erben, Grans-Fassian, Heymann-Löwenstein, Markus Molitor, Maximilian von Othegraven, Schloss Saarstein, Willi Schaefer, Von Schubert, Von Volxem.

THE RHINE

The wines of the Mittelrhein, Nahe, Rheingau, Rheinhessen, and Pfalz, while diverse in microclimate and tradition, all feature the Riesling grape in their best sites and are all bottled in tall brown flutes. The Mittelrhein, which runs from just south of Bonn, past the confluence of the Rhine and Mosel, to just north of the confluence of the Rhine and Nahe, is dominated by slate slopes and wines with certain similarities to those of the Mosel. The Nahe is geologically diverse, with three distinct major subregions plus many interesting outlying towns. At their best, Nahe Rieslings are incredibly complex, with distinct floral, fruit, and mineral elements. Across the Rhine from its intersection with the Nahe begins the Rheingau, a stretch of river running east to west and exposing gentle riverside slopes and steep hillsides farther back, both of which generate some of Germany's most famous wines.

The Rheinhessen, south of the Nahe region and across the Rhine from the Rheingau, is still better known for its high volume of interesting wines from flatlands and grape crossings than it is for its handful of top Riesling sites. But the latter—particularly the steep red shale slopes down to the Rhine—are justly famous. The Pfalz, which begins south of Rheinhessen and is, in effect, the northward extension of Alsace's Vosges foothills, is the warmest and driest of Germany's Riesling regions, supporting fuller-bodied wines that are typically dry. Like the Rheinhessen better known until recently for quantity than for quality, the Pfalz's handful of top villages and vineyards have nevertheless always been among Germany's most cherished, and the entire region has undergone a substantial turnabout in reputation over the last two decades.

2004 ★★★+   **2003** ★★★   **2002** ★★★★

BANG FOR THE BUCK. Prices are generally more reasonable for German wines in brown bottles than for Mosel-Saar-Ruwer wines from steep slopes, as production levels—especially in the more fertile soils of the Pfalz and Rheinhessen—are typically higher. Then, too, the top estates outside the M-S-R are lesser known even within Germany.

RECOMMENDED PRODUCERS

Von Bassermann-Jordan. The Bassermanns recently sold a majority share in this historical estate, but quality under the winemaking guidance of Ulrich Mell continues to be fully worthy of their incredible string of vineyard pearls.

Forster Pechstein Riesling Spätlese Trocken	04	03	$$$
Forster Jesuitengarten Riesling Spätlese		03	$$$
Deidesheimer Hohenmorgen Riesling Auslese		03	$$$

Georg Breuer. The late Bernhard Breuer was a leader in the return by Rheingau vintners to a dry, full-bodied, and at times austerely mineral style. The estate's best dry Rieslings are bottled simply with the name of the vineyard.

Riesling Berg Schlossberg	04	03	$$$$

Von Buhl. One of the Pfalz's venerable estates, Von Buhl has had an up-and-down track record for much of the last quarter-century but appears to have regained its footing in the past several years. Having terrific terroir does not hurt.

Forster Pechstein Riesling Trocken	04	03	$$$
Forster Jesuitengarten Riesling Spätlese	04	03	$$$

Schlossgut Diel. The foremost producer of the Lower Nahe, Armin Diel is also well known in Germany as a wine critic and author. His model for off-dry Riesling is the exhilarating sugar/acid balance and subtle mineral nuances of the Mosel, but his full-bodied dry wines are impressive too. Eiswein is also a specialty here.

Dorsheimer Goldloch Riesling Spätlese	04	03	$$$$

Hermann Dönnhoff. Probably the single most revered wine grower in Germany today, Helmut Dönnhoff has assembled a collection of the Middle Nahe's best vineyards and achieves consistently outstanding, site-inflected results. Any Dönnhoff wines are worth buying (when they can be found), and the list below is merely representative.

Oberhäuser Leistenberg Riesling Kabinett	04	03	$$$
Norheimer Dellchen Riesling Spätlese	04	03	$$$$
Oberhäuser Brücke Riesling Spätlese	04	03	$$$$
Niederhäuser Hermannshöhle Riesling Spätlese	04	03	$$$$

Emrich-Schönleber. Werner Schönleber farms little-known but outstanding vineyards at the western edge of Nahe viticulture. This is another estate with such a long list of bottlings that those noted below can only be taken as indicators.

Monzinger Halenberg Riesling Spätlese Halbtrocken	04	03	$$
Monzinger Halenberg Riesling Auslese	04	03	$$$

Gunderloch. Through dedication and fastidiousness, Fritz and Agnes Hasselbach brought this historic riverside estate back to the forefront of Rheinhessen viticulture, where it has remained for the past two decades. The very expensive nobly sweet wines at this estate are delicious.

Jean Baptiste Riesling Kabinett	04	03	$$
Nackenheimer Rothenberg Riesling Auslese	04	03	$$$

Freiherr Heyl zu Herrnsheim. The Ahr family, farming some of the best sites in Nierstein, is working to revive a once-benchmark estate. Their dry Red Slate Riesling—from several top sites on Nierstein's famous Permian red shale—offers consistently good value, and their limited single-vineyard bottlings can be exceptional.

Red Slate Riesling ("Rotschiefer Riesling")	04	03	$$$

Johannishof. Johannes Eser crafts a stylistically wide but consistently age-worthy range of archetypical Rheingau Rieslings and sells them for remarkably affordable prices.

Johannisberger Klaus Riesling Spätlese	04	03	$$
Rüdesheimer Berg Rottland Riesling Spätlese	04	03	$$

Toni Jost. Jost's *monopole* Bacharacher Hahn produces wines of tropical fruit richness yet distinct minerality, the Kabinett frequently weighing in above the legal minimum for Auslese. Justly renowned upper-predicate wines here tend to be very expensive.

Bacharacher Hahn Riesling Spätlese	04	03	$$$

Keller. The young Klaus-Peter Keller has invigorated this estate, which is known for high-quality whites, reds, and botrytized dessert wines. In recent vintages, the dry wines here have been standouts.

Riesling Trocken von der Fels	04	$$
Dalsheimer Hubacker Riesling Spätlese	04	$$$

Koehler-Ruprecht. Bernd Philippi gives both his dry and sweet wines a leisurely upbringing in cask and bottles them late.

Kallstadter Saumagen Riesling Spätlese	04	03	$$$

Künstler. The top vintner in the famous chalk-soil town of Hochheim on the Main, Gunter Künstler bottles excellent full-bodied dry as well as more delicate, sweet Rieslings and increasingly serious Pinot Noirs.

Hochheimer Reichestal Kabinett	04	03	$$
Hochheimer Stielweg Alte Reben Trocken	04	03	$$

Josef Leitz. Johannes Leitz produces several amazingly inexpensive and unabashedly sweet wines in considerable volume for spring release to the North American market; his limited quantities of slow-fermenting dry and nobly sweet wines from the Rüdesheimer Berg are fought over internationally.

Dragonstone Riesling	04	03	$$
Rüdesheimer Klosterlay Riesling Kabinett	04	03	$$
Rüdesheimer Berg Schlossberg Riesling Spätlese	04	03	$$$

Müller-Catoir. Under the direction of longtime cellarmaster Hans-Günter Schwarz and now under young Martin Franzen, this estate boasts a nearly unprecedented streak of stellar quality. Varieties in addition to Riesling—notably the aromatically bold and acid-retentive Rieslaner and Scheurebe—also reach unparalleled heights here. Due to sheer multiplicity of bottlings and to vineyard replanting, it is difficult to pick just a wine or two that best illustrate this estate's consistency and quality.

Haardter Bürgergarten Riesling Spätlese   04   03 $$$

Pfeffingen. Three generations of the family Fuhrmann-Eymael work this estate in Ungstein with admirable attention to detail. Successes often include their sweet Scheurebe and Gewürztraminer bottlings as well as their excellent value dry generic Riesling noted below.

Riesling Trocken   03 $$
Ungsteiner Weilberg Riesling Spätlese Trocken   04   03 $$$

Ratzenberger. The Ratzenbergers craft age-worthy, slate-based Rieslings of riveting clarity and verve, including awesomely intense and expensive Eiswein. Their several nonvineyard-designated bottlings, both dry and off-dry, often represent outstanding value.

Bacharacher Posten Riesling Spätlese Halbtrocken   04   03 $$
Bacharacher Wolfshöhle Riesling Spätlese   04   03 $$

Schäfer-Fröhlich. The Fröhlichs's town and vineyard areas are thus far little known, but that is changing. In recent years they are sending Rieslings of thrilling quality to international markets.

Bockenauer Felseneck Riesling Spätlese   04   03 $$$

Spreitzer. A pair of young brothers has quickly brought a spotlight to the latest generation at this estate, which excels in dry, off-dry, and nobly sweet styles from the unusual *loess* soils of Oestrich.

Oestricher Lenchen Riesling Spätlese   04   03 $$$

Robert Weil. This traditionally great estate of the Rheingau underwent an unprecedented late-20th century renaissance under the majority ownership of Suntory and the directorship of Wilhelm Weil. Having consolidated much of Kiedrich's best acreage, Weil selectively harvests Rieslings of stunning richness with amazing consistency. Only the best small lots are bottled as vineyard-designated Gräfenberg.

Kiedricher Gräfenberg Riesling Spätlese   04   03 $$$$

Florian Weingart. Florian Weingart has made a singular reputation for the steep Bopparder Hamm, just south of the confluence of the Rhine and Mosel. Given the proliferation of bottlings (with labels at times differing only by A.P. registration number) from which a different export selection is made annually, the recommendation below must be taken as merely indicative.

Bacharacher Hamm-Feuerlay Riesling Spätlese   04   03 $$$

OTHER PRODUCERS TO LOOK FOR: Dr. Bürklin-Wolf, A. Christmann, Dr. Crusius, Heymann-Löwenstein, Schloss Johannisberg, Jakob Jung, August Kesseler, Knipser/Johannishof, Peter Jakob Kühn, Herbert Messmer, Theo Minges, Georg Mosbacher, Matthias Müller, Von Othegraven, August and Thomas Perll, Ökonomierat Rebholz, Schloss Schönborn, Walter Strub, Geheimrat J. Wegeler Erben, Dr. Heinz Wehrheim, Wittmann.

AUSTRIA

Austrian wine has rapidly gained in international stature in the past decade, mostly on the strength of the country's dry whites produced within a 20-mile radius of the small city of Krems on the Danube, less than 50 miles west of Vienna. The steep, terraced, riverside vineyards of the Wachau, immediately west of Krems, as well as geologically diverse sites on the edges of the city and to the north in the Kamptal, yield Austria's most brilliant and distinctive wines. Differences among wines from various sites within close proximity to one another can be as dramatic as the region's crumbling volcanic slopes, sandstone buttes, and huge wave-like mounds of ancient glacial dust called *loess*.

Lesser known subregions further from Krems—including the vast Weinviertel, running north to the Czech border and east past Vienna to the border with Slovakia—have wrought increasingly impressive wines, usually at reasonable prices. The city of Vienna itself possesses noteworthy vineyards. Because the city marks a transition from the moderate climate and day-night temperature swings upstream and north of the Danube to the warmer, drier conditions of the Pannonian steppe (Hungary's great plains), Vienna's vintners are able to make rich, full-bodied reds in addition to juicy dry whites. The same can be said of growers in Carnuntum, immediately to Vienna's east, and the Thermenregion, immediately to the south. Burgenland, a long, narrow swath of land running the length of Austria's border with Hungary, is home to the majority of Austria's red wines and botrytis-influenced sweet wines. Northern Burgenland is subdivided into two viticultural regions, the Neusiedlersee and Neusiedlersee-Hügelland, both named for the long, shallow lake that runs between them. To the south, two red wine regions are appropriately known as Mittelburgenland and Südburgenland.

Along Austria's border with Slovenia run the vineyards of Styria. This area offers distinctively bright, dry whites from Sauvignon Blanc, Welschriesling, and Yellow Muscat, as well as Chardonnay and Pinot Blanc in a range of styles.

DRY WHITE WINES

Grüner Veltliner is Austria's most distinctive and widely planted white grape, although it is seldom grown in the extreme east or south. Capable of a wide stylistic range from crisp and light to full and rich, Grüner Veltliner will require a new tasting vocabulary for North American wine drinkers: cress, sweet pea, green bean, beet,

rhubarb, and roasted red pepper, plus a more familiar array of pit fruits, citrus, and flowers. The sum effect is much better than it sounds. Wines from this variety exhibit saline minerality and spicy and peppery pungency, typically with a tactile bite. At the riper end of the spectrum, they can show the corpulence and tannic content of a red wine. Grüner Veltliner is a remarkably food-flexible wine. With bottle age, it often becomes spicier and more exotic, losing much of its green vegetility and developing a potpourri of dried orange and clove scents.

Riesling can offer as much complexity and sensitivity to site in the Danubian regions of Austria as it can in Germany or Alsace. While technically lower in acidity than German Rieslings, Austrian Rieslings are by no means flabby, in part because of an invigorating degree of astringency. Seldom as aromatically effusive as their German counterparts, Austrian Rieslings at their best often finish with a building whiplash of flavor. These wines typically become smoother and rounder as they age, and are perhaps less obviously mineral in character, with emerging floral and honeyed nuances to go with their underlying peach and apricot fruit.

Pinot Blanc, known in Austria (and Germany) as Weissburgunder, appears in all of Austria's growing regions, and the best examples can be dramatic and satisfying. There is also significant acreage of Chardonnay and Sauvignon Blanc, the latter particularly important in Styria. Grapes of the Muscat family and Traminer are common in the east and south, and one also encounters Pinot Gris (Grauburgunder). Austria's most ubiquitous grape, after Grüner Veltliner, is Welschriesling, but this grape achieves nobility only as a bearer of botrytis.

BANG FOR THE BUCK. No Austrian wine is particularly cheap, due to feverish demand for these bottles in Austria's wine-thirsty domestic market, high local labor costs, and the strength of the Euro. Riesling and Grüner Veltliner from the Wachau can be particularly pricey, but sharp-eyed fans of these wines are always able to find excellent, more affordable bottlings.

2005 ★★★+   2004 ★★★−   2003 ★★+

RECOMMENDED PRODUCERS

Willi Bründlmayer. One of the largest and most influential vineyard holders in Austria, Willi Bründlmayer exports a significant percentage of his wines. Bründlmayer bottles several different Rieslings from the terraces of the butte-like Heiligenstein.

Grüner Veltliner Kamptaler Terrassen	04	03	$$
Grüner Veltliner Lamm	04	**03**	$$$
Riesling Heiligenstein Alte Reben	04	**03**	$$$

Schloss Gobelsburg. Michael Moosbrügger has resurrected this formerly ecclesiastical estate, owner of numerous choice vineyards, and is now making some of Austria's best-value dry whites as well as increasingly serious reds.

Grüner Veltliner	04	03	$$
Grüner Veltliner Renner	04	**03**	$$$
Riesling Heiligenstein	04	**03**	$$$

Ludwig Hiedler. Hiedler vinifies sappy, fruit-filled whites from diverse sites, ideal as an introduction to the Kamptal yet satisfying to the most discriminating palate and eminently age worthy. His consistently outstanding Weissburgunder is one of the few top Austrian wines of that variety to be regularly exported.

Grüner Veltliner Thal	04	**03**	$$
Riesling Gaisberg	**04**	**03**	$$$
Weissburgunder Maximum	**04**	**03**	$$$

Hannes Hirsch. An estate with a rapidly rising reputation, based on consistently outstanding Rieslings from the two best sites in the Kamptal. The less expensive Hirsch wines offer outstanding value.

Riesling Heiligenstein	04	03	$$$
Riesling Gaisberg	**04**	**03**	$$$

DECODING AUSTRIAN LABELS

When it comes to dry whites, a few distinctive aspects of Austrian wine labeling must be noted. The word Trocken (dry) is seldom displayed as prominently on Austrian white wine labels as it is on German, simply because it is understood. Should a wine be over the nine-grams-per-liter threshold of Halbtrocken (literally, half-dry), that is also typically buried in small print, because the wine is still unlikely to taste noticeably sweet. In certain regions around Krems, the terms Kabinett and Spätlese are still officially in use to describe a more delicate and a riper, fuller style of wine, respectively. But in practice, these terms are rarely seen on labels anymore, and if they are, they appear in fine print. Nowadays, growers prefer to indicate differences in ripeness, richness, or body through their own winery-internal designations—for example, they may offer "regular" and "reserve" bottlings from the same grape and vineyard. The term Auslese on a label signifies a wine with noticeable sweetness. The Wachau region uses its own set of terms to differentiate degrees of ripeness and to designate styles from delicate to full-bodied dry whites: Steinfeder, Federspiel, and Smaragd. Happily, Austria's red wines are normally labeled by variety, without any unusual terminology, although there are numerous blends labeled with proprietary names.

Franz Hirtzberger. Chairman of the Wachau growers' association, Hirtzberger makes benchmark wines that combine richness and site-specific personalities. It's not only his most expensive wines that are worth cellaring.

Grüner Veltliner Federspiel Rotes Tor	04	03	$$
Grüner Veltliner Smaragd Honivogl	04	03	$$$$
Riesling Smaragd Hochrain	04	03	$$$$
Riesling Smaragd Singerriedel	04	03	$$$$

Josef Jamek. Vintner-restaurateur Jamek did much to define the modern dry wine style of the Wachau, and his son-in-law Hans Altmann has ratcheted up quality in recent years.

Grüner Veltliner Smaragd Achleiten	04	03	$$$
Riesling Smaragd Klaus	04	03	$$$$

Emmerich Knoll. Knoll has for 20 years demonstrated his mastery of a range of styles and Wachau terroirs. In recent years, his best Grüner Veltliner from multiple vineyards has been used to make a "Vinothek" bottling.

Grüner Veltliner Smaragd Loibenberg	04	03	$$$
Grüner Veltliner Smaragd Vinothekfüllung	04	03	$$$$
Riesling Smaragd Loibenberg	04	03	$$$

Familie Nigl. Martin Nigl makes penetrating, crystalline wines with spicy, citric, and floral character.

Grüner Veltliner Freiheit	04	03	$$
Grüner Veltliner Alte Reben	04	**03**	$$$
Riesling Privat	**04**	03	$$$

F. X. Pichler. Austria's most celebrated grower and greatest champion of Grüner Veltliner, "Effix" (as he is known by his initials) makes wines whose richness can overshadow their firm underlying acidity in the early going, yet they are always elegant and built for extended aging. Son Lucas has recently taken over much of the cellar work.

Grüner Veltliner Federspiel Frauenweingarten	04	03	$$
Grüner Veltliner Smaragd Loibnerberg	**04**	**03**	$$$$
Riesling Smaragd Steinertal	**04**	**03**	$$$$
Riesling Smaragd Kellerberg	**04**	**03**	$$$$

Prager. Proprietor Toni Bodenstein offers site-specific Rieslings from a half dozen outstanding vineyards and has recently become a more important source of Grüner Veltliner. Exemplary dry wines for the price, with a good percentage of them exported to the U.S.

Grüner Veltliner Federspiel Hinter der Burg	04	**03**	$$
Grüner Veltliner Smaragd Achleiten	**04**	**03**	$$$
Riesling Federspiel Steinriegl	04	03	$$
Riesling Smaragd Klaus	**04**	**03**	$$$

Heidi Schröck. Schröck vinifies some serious reds and outstanding sweet wines from the shores of Lake Neusiedler, but she is virtually the only vintner in Burgenland whose reputation is based mostly on the quality of her dry whites, including Pinot Blanc, Muscat, and Furmint, as well as a Sauvignon-based blend called Vogelsang.

Weissburgunder	**04**	03	$$

Manfred Tement. The most ambitious and successful vintner in Styria, Sauvignon Blanc proponent Tement is also the only one from this region to have wide availability in North America. His top wines are matured in cask, although he has in recent years backed off somewhat on the use of new oak.

Sauvignon Blanc Steierische Klassik	04	03	$$
Sauvignon Blanc Grassnitzberg	04	03	$$$

OTHER PRODUCERS TO LOOK FOR: Leo Alzinger, Alois Gross, Markus Huber, Jurtschitsch/ Sonnhof, Fred Loimer, Malat, Ludwig Neumayer, Nikolaihof, Bernard Ott, R. & A. Pfaffl, Rudi Pichler, Walter & Erich Polz, Franz Proidl, Salomon/Undhof, Johann Schmelz, Fritz Wieninger.

SWEET WINES

Growers of Riesling and Grüner Veltliner in the regions around Krems are capable of achieving memorable results with selectively harvested, botrytized fruit, as well as with Eiswein, and the same can be said of several vintners in Styria with their diverse varieties. Nonetheless, the total quantity of such wines is very small. The only areas of Austria traditionally known for sweet wines—and in which these wines play a significant role—are the Neusiedlersee and, on the opposite side of the same long, shallow lake, the Neusiedlersee-Hügelland. Still, few of these wines make it to North America, with the extraordinary bottlings of Alois Kracher a notable exception. The production of botrytis wines originated in this area—traditionally part of Hungary—at around the same time as in Tokaj. The town of Rust has revived the use of the traditional term Ausbruch (Hungarian Aszú) for its top botrytis wines, but the terms Auslese, Beerenauslese, Trockenbeereenauslese, and Eiswein are the most frequently used in Burgenland, just as in Germany.

Compared with Germany's botrytized Rieslings, the sweet whites of Burgenland are more opulent and softer in palate impression, with natural alcohol ranging from as low as seven percent to as high as 15 percent. Compared with the sweet wines of Bordeaux, they have a more juicy fruitiness, and more lift and delicacy. The richness and fat of Chardonnay and the fruit acids of Welschriesling frequently figure prominently in the sweet wines that are blends of two or more varieties. In Rust, the Furmint—widely planted in Hungary—is staging a highly localized but impressive comeback.

2004 ★★+   **2003** ★+   **2002** ★★★★★

RECOMMENDED PRODUCERS

Feiler-Artinger. Red wines make up two-thirds of Feiler's production, but this estate is best known internationally for sweet wines.

| Ruster Ausbruch | | 02 | $$$ |

Alois Kracher/Weinlaubenhof. The charismatic Kracher is known internationally as one of the top producers of sweet wine in the world. In the best vintages, Kracher offers a unique, numbered series of Trockenbeerenauslesen from single varieties and blends, some made in tank and some in barrel. Those from Scheurebe and Welschriesling have been consistently outstanding. Kracher's moderately priced Auslese Cuvée is made mostly from Chardonnay and Welschriesling.

| Auslese Cuvée | 04 | 03 | $$$ |

OTHER PRODUCERS TO LOOK FOR: Martin Haider, Josef Lentsch, Josef Pöckl, Peter Schandl, Heidi Schröck, Ernst Triebaumer, Velich.

RED WINES

Austria's red wines are not well known internationally, but the stylistic diversity and quality of the best of them deserve wider recognition. Red wine vinification is more sophisticated than ever in Austria, but overextraction and overoaking still result in many ungraciously tannic wines with little apparent fruit. Austria's most widely planted and distinctive varieties are Zweigelt, Blaufränkisch, and St. Laurent (see box below), but internationally known grapes like Pinot Noir, Cabernet Sauvignon, and Merlot are also found, the latter two typically in blends. Syrah has been infiltrating Burgenland in recent years with occasionally promising results.

BANG FOR THE BUCK. Austria's red wines are generally fully priced, if not downright expensive, in export markets, but good basic bottlings from ripe years can offer reasonable value.

2004 ★★–   **2003** ★★★★+   **2002** ★★★★

RECOMMENDED PRODUCERS

Paul Achs. Achs's vineyard practices are focused on getting ripe fruit early, in order to preserve elegance and avoid excessively high levels of alcohol in the finished wines.

Zweigelt Langer Acker	`04`	$$
St. Laurent	`04`	$$
Blaufränkisch Edelgrund	`04`	$$

AUSTRIA'S DISTINCTIVE RED GRAPES

- **Zweigelt:** Widely planted inside Austria and virtually unknown outside (like the white grape Grüner Veltliner), Zweigelt typically exhibits bright red fruit and spices. Often effusively juicy in its unoaked state, versions raised in barrel show darker flavors and layered complexity.
- **Blaufränkisch:** This grape, associated with Burgenland and neighboring Hungary, typically yields wines with rich black raspberry, white pepper, and forest floor flavors. More concentrated examples are palate staining and complex.
- **St. Laurent:** Said to be a member of the Pinot family and seldom encountered outside Austria, this grape of mysterious origins can give polished, caressing wines with rich red fruit and intriguing meaty nuances.

Walter Glatzer. In the little-known Carnuntum region immediately east of Vienna, Glatzer bottles textbook examples of Austria's two principle red varieties and sells them at reasonable prices.

Blaufränkisch Reserve	`03`	$$$
Zweigelt Dornenvogel	`03`	$$$

Paul Lehrner. Lehrner frequently achieves balanced, age-worthy reds free of exaggerated ripeness, overextraction, and overoaking.

Blaufränkisch Gfanger	`04`	`03`	$$
Blaufränksch Steineiche	`04`	`03`	$$$

Engelbert Prieler. Prieler has an enormous reputation inside Austria, with prices to match. His Blaufränkisch from the Goldberg, bottled only in top vintages, and his Schützner Stein, a blend based on Blaufränkisch, are generally firm in their youth but repay cellaring.

Blaufränkisch Schützner Stein	`04`	`03`	$$$
Blaufränksch Goldberg	`04`	`03`	$$$$$

Ernst Triebaumer. Triebaumer's longstanding reputation for reds makes for high prices, but his formidable Blaufränkisch-based reds have a track record for aging gracefully in bottle.

Blaufränkisch Oberer Wald	`03`	$$$
Blaufränksch Mariental	`02`	$$$$

Josef Umathum. One of several Austrian growers whose local reputation makes for dauntingly high prices but whose wines deserve international attention. Umathum also crafts delicious, inexpensive reds in collaboration with the grower cooperative in Andau under the Zantho label.

Hallebühl	`02`	$$$$

OTHER PRODUCERS TO LOOK FOR: Willi Bründlmayer, Fritsch, Schloss Gobelsburg, Gernot Heinrich, Johann Heinrich, Kollwentz-Römerhof, Krutzler, Paul Lehrner, Josef Pöckl, Franz Weninger.

Key to Vintage Ratings		Key to Assessments of Specific Wines	
★★★★★	Outstanding	`03`	An excellent to outstanding example *of that wine*
★★★★	Excellent	`03`	A good to very good example *of that wine*
★★★	Good to very good	03	A disappointing effort (often due to a
★★	Fair to average		difficult vintage)
★	Poor		

UNITED
STATES

CALIFORNIA

It is remarkable that an industry essentially less than a half-century old could capture the attention of the American wine-buying public to the degree that California has. Powerful consumer interest in California wine is driven by two major factors. The more obvious reason is that California's best wines, which come from grapes grown in a benign climate featuring endless sunshine, very warm summer days, and generally dry harvests, are wonderfully fruity, full, and satisfying, and rarely too austere or tannic to be enjoyed from day one. California is blessed with an extraordinary range of soils and microclimates, allowing for the successful cultivation of many varieties. In at least three out of four years, the best sites produce healthy, ripe fruits that are the envy of European producers in more marginal climates.

The other reason Americans buy so much California wine is that California is the home team. Clearly, a high percentage of domestic wine drinkers are more comfortable buying American wines (and not just those from California) than imports. Then, too, foreign bottles are generally identified by place name, rather than by the more familiar varieties that American wine drinkers have come to know and enjoy. Moreover, in much of North America, outside the top 15 or 20 largest metropolitan markets, consumers have limited access to imported wines even if they wanted to buy them.

The American consumer's hesitance, or inability, to purchase imported wines that can provide drinking pleasure at considerably lower cost is also one of the driving factors behind the high price of California wines. If more wine drinkers were willing and able to try other wines from around the world—not just from France, Italy, and Spain but from Australia and New Zealand, South Africa, and South America—California wine prices for all but the most hotly pursued collectible wines might well be lower than they are today. Compared to many other countries, the U.S. is not protectionist when it comes to taxing imported wines, but the California wine industry is certainly protected by the natural reluctance of consumers to try wines completely alien to them.

For many, Napa Valley is California wine, and Cabernet is king in Napa Valley. Meanwhile, the Burgundy varieties Chardonnay and Pinot Noir have gravitated to cooler areas, generally closer to the Pacific, such as the western stretches of Sonoma County, the Anderson Valley in Mendocino County, and the Santa Maria and Santa Ynez valleys within Santa Barbara County. Syrah vines have yielded interesting wines in a range of styles all over the state, in regions as disparate as Mendocino County, the Sonoma coast, Carneros, Paso Robles, and Santa Maria

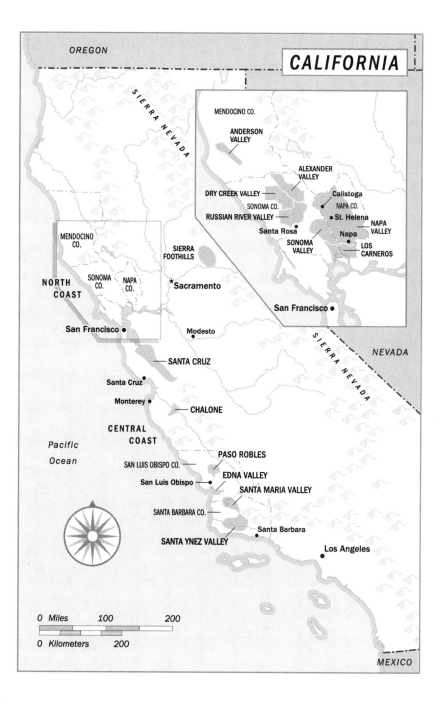

CALIFORNIA

OREGON

SIERRA NEVADA

MENDOCINO CO.

ANDERSON VALLEY

ALEXANDER VALLEY

DRY CREEK VALLEY

SONOMA CO.

RUSSIAN RIVER VALLEY

Calistoga

NAPA CO.

St. Helena

Santa Rosa

SONOMA VALLEY

Napa

NAPA VALLEY

LOS CARNEROS

San Francisco ●

MENDOCINO CO.

NORTH COAST

SONOMA CO.

NAPA CO.

SIERRA FOOTHILLS

★ Sacramento

San Francisco ●

Modesto

SIERRA NEVADA

NEVADA

SANTA CRUZ

Santa Cruz ●

Monterey ●

CHALONE

CENTRAL COAST

Pacific Ocean

PASO ROBLES

SAN LUIS OBISPO CO.

EDNA VALLEY

San Luis Obispo ●

SANTA MARIA VALLEY

SANTA BARBARA CO.

Santa Barbara ●

SANTA YNEZ VALLEY

Los Angeles ●

0   Miles   100   200

0   Kilometers   200

MEXICO

Valley. Very good Zinfandel similarly comes from multiple growing areas, although to date the age-of-vines variable has been almost as important as geography. Zinfandel, though its roots are in Europe, is a true California original and the only California wine imitated abroad. It's also a variety of which there are still significant plantings of very old vines, in some cases dating back to the end of the 19th century.

CABERNET &
CABERNET-DOMINATED BLENDS

Cabernet Sauvignon has been the flagship red grape of the California wine industry for decades, and its popularity shows no sign of abating. Napa Valley is the heart of Cabernet production and is clearly an ideal region for creating world-class wines. If any Cabernet-based wine is capable of giving Bordeaux a run for its money, it is Napa Valley's examples. However, due to the extremely high cost of purchasing and developing vineyards here, and the cachet of Napa Valley on the label, this has largely become a category for the well-heeled wine lover. Those seeking value in California wine generally look elsewhere.

At their best, Napa Valley's Cabernets are characterized by fruit notes of cassis, black cherry, and licorice and sweet oak notes of chocolate, mocha, cedar, and tar. Today, most of the best wines are aged entirely or almost completely in French oak barrels, which tend to produce somewhat more refined wines than do most American barrels. (These latter barrels often introduce exotic and pungent suggestions of scotch, bourbon, tar, coconut, and dill.) But the use of expensive French oak is no guarantee of a good bottle: too many wines today, due to high crop levels or insufficiently ripe fruit, do not have the stuffing to support their oakiness and can quickly be dominated or even dried out by their wood component. The best California Cabernets mellow and soften with five to ten years of bottle aging, developing more complex and less fruit-dominated notes of tobacco, leather, and earth, with mellower wood tones. Compared to the top Bordeaux, however, many California Cabernets merely endure in bottle rather than truly become more interesting. And it remains to be seen if today's outsized showstoppers (see box on page 223), made from super-ripe grapes and undeniably impressive on release, will reward extended bottle aging or will turn out to have been best suited for drinking in their youth.

Many wines labeled Cabernet Sauvignon contain small percentages of other so-called Bordeaux varieties—chiefly Merlot and Cabernet Franc but also Petit Verdot and even Malbec (varietally labeled wines in California must contain at least 75 percent of the variety named). In 1988, the name Meritage was selected to describe

Mailing List Wines & the Issue of Availability

In the dynamic California wine industry, many of the leaders from the 1970s and 1980s have fallen off the radar screens of most serious enophiles, as the attention of consumers has shifted to a new generation of talented young wine-makers. Most of the new generation make small but growing quantities of wine from purchased fruit and do not own their own vines. They tend to specialize in just one or two varieties (Chardonnay and Pinot Noir; Rhône Valley varieties; Cabernet Sauvignon) and offer a number of vineyard-designated wines in very limited quantities—in many instances, as little as 100 to 200 cases of a particular item. Pricing for these wines is often steep, but many of these newcomers begin with reasonable prices to establish their brands in the marketplace. Meanwhile, many large, older wineries struggle to sell their wines, which are increasingly viewed by critics and consumers as generic and interchangeable.

It is often said that there are two kinds of California wines: the ones consumers want but can't find, and the high-production generic wines that collect dust on retailers' shelves. While this is an overstatement, the fact remains that many of California's most in-demand wines are sold partly or even largely via mailing lists. The advantage of mailing-list sales to producers is obvious: they get the full retail price for their wines, rather than the wholesale price they would receive on bottles sold through regular trade channels. Today, there are waiting lists to get onto the most desirable mailing lists. Needless to say, with so many consumers chasing so few wines—and so few bottles of those wines—prices continue to defy gravity.

The issue of availability has implications for this guide. I am hesitant to devote significant space to profiling top producers whose wines are virtually impossible to find for consumers who are not already on their mailing lists. This is a shame, as many of the most exciting wines being made in California today fall in this category. Note that most of these small, high-quality producers, who often work with fruit from California's best vineyards, are listed in this chapter, but generally under the rubric of "Other producers to look for" or, more likely, "Scarce but worth the search." But in all the commotion over these rare objects of desire, it is easy to forget that larger, established wineries also make commercial quantities of excellent wine, and that these bottles can be found on retail shelves.

blends made from the five Bordeaux varieties in which no single variety accounted for 75 percent or more of the blend (there are also white Meritage wines, which are blends of Bordeaux's white grape varieties).

BANG FOR THE BUCK. Napa Valley Cabernet and Cabernet blends are expensive, often exorbitantly so.

2004 ★★★   **2003** ★★★+   **2002** ★★★★+   **2001** ★★★★+

RECOMMENDED PRODUCERS

Araujo Estate. This winery's flagship bottling is dense, powerful, and rich, typically with soil-inflected notes of plum, mocha, tobacco, and smoke, and very suave tannins. The Araujos own the Eisele Vineyard just outside Calistoga, one of California's finest sites for Cabernet Sauvignon, originally made famous in the 1970s and 1980s by Joseph Phelps Vineyards.

Cabernet Sauvignon Eisele Vineyard Napa Valley	**04**	**03**	**02**	$$$$$

Beringer Vineyards. Beringer's Winemaker Emeritus Ed Sbragia has long had a magic touch with Cabernet Sauvignon. This large operation, the oldest continuously operating winery in Napa Valley, offers massive quantities of Cabernet at a number of price points, but even the basic bottlings are way above average for their categories. Beringer's top Cabernets, especially the Private Reserve, are decadently rich and sweet in the early going but have a track record for lasting well in bottle.

Cabernet Sauvignon Knight's Valley	**02**	**01**	$$
Cabernet Sauvignon Napa Valley	**02**	**01**	$$$
Cabernet Sauvignon Private Reserve Napa Valley	**02**	**01**	$$$$$

Caymus Vineyards. Rich, lavishly oaked Cabernet Sauvignon with bold cassis, black cherry, loam, and spice flavors that often verge on sweet; lush texture; and considerable early appeal. The expensive Special Selection is made from the best lots of Cabernet and is aged in a somewhat higher percentage of new French oak than the Napa bottling.

Cabernet Sauvignon Napa Valley	**02**	$$$$
Cabernet Sauvignon Special Selection Napa Valley	**02**	$$$$$

Chateau Montelena. Classic, austere Cabernet Sauvignons with brooding black fruit and earth character, and powerful structure for aging. Winemaker Bo Barrett is not interested in allowing his fruit to bake in the sun in order to make wine with 15 percent alcohol. There's also a suppler Napa Valley Cabernet offering that features a dollop of Merlot.

Cabernet Sauvignon The Montelena Estate Napa Valley	**04**	**03**	**02**	$$$$

Corison Winery. Suave, fresh, harmonious Cabernets with moderate levels of alcohol and captivating floral notes. These are old school in the way they privilege balance, finesse and understatement over extreme ripeness and early sex appeal. Not surprisingly, Cathy Corison's wines have a track record for repaying extended bottle aging.

Cabernet Sauvignon Napa Valley	**04**	**03**	**02**	$$$

SUPERSIZE ME

Today, it is frequently the darkest, richest, and most flamboyantly ripe California wines that attract the highest point scores from influential critics and the buying interest of consumers. While the best-balanced of these supersized bottlings are among California's most impressive wines, those with dangerously low acidity, very high alcohol levels, and raisined fruit may be best suited for rapid consumption before their fruit fades.

According to Wine Business Monthly, the average alcohol level of California wine rose from 12.5 percent in 1971 to 14.8 percent in 2001—and the 2002, 2003, and 2004 vintages were hotter still. Many factors account for this rise, including healthier vines that ripen their fruit earlier, new trellising methods that expose the grapes to more sun, the widespread use of modern yeast strains that are more efficient at converting grape sugars to alcohol, and a succession of unusually warm growing seasons. But perhaps the most powerful influence of all driving producers to vinify everriper fruit has been the apparent taste preferences of a new generation of wine drinkers, many of whom appear unwilling to accept red wines with any "green" elements (such as fresh herbs, mint, olive, tobacco leaf), even though these green elements are often precursors of complex, varietal flavors that evolve with bottle age. Too often, growers who let their fruit hang on the vine in an attempt to banish any hints of underripeness are simply replacing green tastes with brown tastes—of raisins, prunes, and other dried fruits—and may be compromising the likely aging curve of their wines in the process.

Today's most collectible California wines—not just Cabernets but also Merlots, Syrahs, and even Pinot Noirs—frequently have alcohol levels in the 15 percent + range and dangerously low levels of acidity. But only those California wines from the top sites, and from low yields, carefully extracted from perfectly ripe fruit with very few dried berries, are likely to enjoy an extended positive evolution in bottle. With the 2002, 2003, and 2004 vintages, more of the north coast's big red wines than ever before show distinctly roasted, port-like aromas and flavors. As impressive as many of these extreme wines are, however, they can be difficult to drink. Owing to their low acidity, they are less capable of cleansing and refreshing the palate. They may be more appropriate as food substitutes than paired with a meal, unless you happen to be serving rare brontosaurus steak.

Dalla Valle Vineyards. Sappy, dense, flamboyantly rich wines loaded with black fruits, minerals, flowers, and bitter chocolate, with the especially perfumed, avidly sought Maya bottling incorporating 45 percent Cabernet Franc. Though the wines have a serious tannic structure, the tannins are rarely hard or dry. Production has dropped in recent vintages, as a replanting program due to vine maladies has been accelerated. There was no 2003 Maya bottling.

Cabernet Sauvignon Napa Valley	04	03	02	$$$$
Maya Proprietary Red Wine Napa Valley			02	$$$$$

Dominus Estate. This large property is owned by Christian Mouiex, whose family firm in Libourne owns Château Pétrus, and owns, manages, or markets dozens of other Bordeaux châteaux. Moueix makes a decidedly Old World–style red blend from the historic Napanook Vineyard in Yountville. Those looking for jammy California fruit bombs may be puzzled by the Dominus notes of leather, loam, tobacco, licorice, and fresh herbs, but these suave, complex wines age gracefully. The Napanook bottling is a gently priced introduction to the house style.

Napanook Red Wine Napa Valley	04	03	02	$$$
Dominus Estate Red Wine Napa Valley	04	03	02	$$$$$

Dunn Vineyards. Randy Dunn has been crafting chewy, tannic, uncompromising Cabernet Sauvignons of outstanding depth for a quarter of a century. The Napa Valley bottling is typically a bit less forbidding in its youth than the Howell Mountain release, but both are powerful black fruit–dominated Cabernets that need a minimum of seven or eight years of cellaring—and often considerably longer.

Cabernet Sauvignon Napa Valley		03	02	$$$
Cabernet Sauvignon Howell Mountain	04	03	02	$$$$

Forman Winery. In recent years, Ric Forman's Cabernet, which normally incorporates bits of Merlot, Cabernet Franc, and Petit Verdot, has shown added sweetness and silkier tannins than the wines of a decade ago, without any loss of finesse or claret-like complexity. The price is also reasonable by the standards of Napa Valley Cabernet.

Cabernet Sauvignon Napa Valley	04	03	02	$$$$

Harlan Estate. This boldly flavored, multilayered, and expensive red wine, from a choice hillside estate above Oakville, is the product of a dream team consisting of perfectionist proprietor Bill Harlan, winemaker Bob Levy, and French consultant Michel Rolland. Harlan Estate's flagship wine is one of the bluest of California's blue-chip collectibles. (The Maiden is the estate's second wine.) The same team is responsible for an expanding set of outstanding Cabernet-based wines under the Bond label.

The Maiden Red Wine Napa Valley		03	02	$$$$$
Harlan Estate Red Wine Napa Valley	04	03	02	$$$$$

Laurel Glen Vineyard. Powerful yet elegant wines characterized by briary mountain berry aromas complicated by minerals, flowers, and dark chocolate. These are wines that repay extended cellaring, developing great complexity with bottle age. The Counterpoint, made chiefly from lots that miss the cut for the estate's flagship wine, is dependably a terrific value.

Counterpoint Cabernet Sauvignon Sonoma Mountain	04	03	02	$$$
Cabernet Sauvignon Sonoma Mountain	04	03	02	$$$$

Robert Mondavi Winery. Mondavi has long produced an ocean of very good, food-friendly Cabernet at all price levels. Following the sale of the winery to Constellation Brands in 2004, the winemaking team here continues to focus on District wines and Reserve wines, also producing limited quantities of vineyard-designated bottlings. Mondavi's consistently outstanding Cabernet Sauvignon Reserve release is largely based on a major holding in the superb and historic To-Kalon Vineyard in Oakville.

	04	03	02	
Cabernet Sauvignon Napa Valley		03	02	$$
Cabernet Sauvignon Stags Leap District			02	$$$
Cabernet Sauvignon Oakville		03	02	$$$
Cabernet Sauvignon Reserve Napa Valley		03	02	$$$$$

Joseph Phelps Vineyard. A longtime Napa Valley benchmark for densely fruity, ripe Cabernets that are capable of gaining complexity with bottle aging. Backus, from a single steep vineyard in Oakville, is a muscular Cabernet with characteristic dark berry, bitter chocolate, and mint flavors. The lush, highly concentrated flagship Insignia blend is a rarity: a blue-chip Napa Valley collectible that's made in good quantity from a blend of vineyard sources.

	04	03	02	
Cabernet Sauvignon Napa Valley	04	03	02	$$$
Cabernet Sauvignon Backus Napa Valley	04	03	02	$$$$$
Insignia Proprietary Red Wine Napa Valley	04	03	02	$$$$$

Pride Mountain Vineyards. Winemaker Bob Foley's big reds are especially noteworthy for combining powerful, briary flavors of mountain berries with creamy, round texture, and supple tannins. These are some of the most flamboyantly fruit-driven wines being made in northern California.

	03	02	
Cabernet Franc Napa Valley	03	02	$$$
Cabernet Sauvignon Napa Valley	03	02	$$$$
Reserve Claret Napa Valley		02	$$$$$
Cabernet Sauvignon Reserve Napa Valley		02	$$$$$

Ramey Wine Cellars. In addition to his superb Chardonnays, David Ramey offers three extravagantly rich Cabernet-based blends. Recent warm vintages have yielded especially chocolaty, liqueur-like wines.

	04	03	02	
Claret Napa Valley	04	03	02	$$$
Red Wine Diamond Mountain District	04	03	02	$$$$
Red Wine Jericho Canyon Vineyard Napa Valley	04	03	02	$$$$

Ridge Vineyards. Ridge Monte Bello has been one of California's elite collectible wines since the 1970s. Ridge's high-altitude vineyards in the Santa Cruz Mountains ripen late, producing classic, elegant wines with aromatic complexity, structure and an impression of intensity without excess weight. These are more akin to a Bordeaux first growth than to high-octane Cabernets from Napa Valley. Only in recent years have these wines surpassed 13 percent in alcohol.

	04	03	02	
Monte Bello Proprietary Red Wine Santa Cruz Mountain	04	03	02	$$$$$

Rudd Estate. Classic Oakville wines that combine intense dark fruit flavors; mineral, cedar, tobacco, and licorice notes; and firm acid/tannin spine. These restrained wines, which resemble ripe Bordeaux from the Médoc, have the depth and balance to reward aging.

Oakville Estate Cabernet Sauvignon Napa Valley	**04**	03	**02**	$$$$
Oakville Estate Proprietary Red Wine Napa Valley	**04**	03	**02**	$$$$$

Shafer Vineyards. Very rich, deeply fruity wines with notes of currant, tobacco, brown spices, earth, chocolate, and sweet oak. Shafer's Hillside Select bottling, remarkably consistent over the past decade, is a flamboyantly ripe and full-flavored example of Napa Valley Cabernet Sauvignon.

Cabernet Sauvignon Napa Valley	03	02	**01**	$$$
Cabernet Sauvignon Hillside Select Stags Leap District		**01**	00	$$$$

Spottswoode Vineyard. Vibrant, aromatic, firmly structured Cabernet Sauvignons with excellent balance and restraint, offering characteristic notes of boysenberry, cassis, violet, and dark chocolate. One of the most consistent Cabernet producers of California over the past two decades, with a track record for graceful bottle aging.

Cabernet Sauvignon Estate Napa Valley	**04**	**03**	**02**	$$$$

Viader Vineyards & Winery. Viader's flagship blend is an elegant, juicy, harmonious midweight whose sizable Cabernet Franc component contributes blackberry and licorice elements, and a pronounced violet character.

Proprietary Red Wine Napa Valley	**04**	**03**	**02**	$$$$

OTHER PRODUCERS TO LOOK FOR: Anderson's Conn Valley Vineyard, L'Aventure, Cardinale, Chappellet Winery, Diamond Creek Vineyards, Duckhorn Vineyards, Etude, Fisher Vineyards, Gemstone, Hartwell Vineyards, Hess Collection Winery, Juslyn, Kendall-Jackson, Lail Vineyards, Lang & Reid, Larkmead, Lokoya, Mount Eden Vineyards, Opus One, Pahlmeyer Winery, Paul Hobbs Winery, Peter Michael Winery, Reverie, Seavey, Silverado Vineyards, Silver Oak, Staglin Family Vineyard, Stag's Leap Wine Cellars, Switchback Ridge, Philip Togni Vineyard, Von Strasser.

SCARCE BUT WORTH THE SEARCH: Abreu Vineyards, Behrens & Hitchcock, Blankiet Estate, Bond, Bryant Family Vineyard, Buccella, Caldwell Vineyard, Colgin Cellars, Grace Family Vineyard, Hundred Acre, L'Aventure Merus, Metisse, Sbragia Family Vineyards, Schrader Cellars, Screaming Eagle, Sloan, Tor Kenward Family Wines, Vérité, Vineyard 29.

Key to Vintage Ratings		Key to Assessments of Specific Wines	
★★★★★	Outstanding	**03**	An excellent to outstanding example *of that wine*
★★★★	Excellent	03	A good to very good example *of that wine*
★★★	Good to very good	03	A disappointing effort (often due to a
★★	Fair to average		difficult vintage)
★	Poor		

MERLOT

Merlot enjoyed a surge in popularity in the 1990s as consumers suddenly discovered that they could enjoy aromas and flavors similar to those of Cabernet in a fleshier, softer wine with smoother tannins. A wave of Merlot plantings followed, frequently in soils and microclimates completely inappropriate for this variety, and the market was soon flooded with dilute bottles from young vines and high crop levels, and weedy, herbaceous examples from underripe fruit. Many of these undernourished wines were overoaked in attempts to mask their deficiencies. Over the same period, a number of Cabernet producers began picking riper fruit and doing a better job managing their tannins during the making and aging of their wines. The result was an upswing of powerful, satisfying Cabernets that were far less austere in their youth—and a sharp decline in interest in Merlot.

Still, California's best Merlots, some of which predated the vogue for this variety in the 1990s, continue to be some of the finest examples of this variety outside Bordeaux—in the same quality league with wines from Washington State and Italy's Tuscan coast region. Expect to find broad, supple wines with medium to full body, typically with aromas and flavors of black cherry, plum, dark berries, dark chocolate, tobacco, and earth, and suave, fine-grained tannins.

BANG FOR THE BUCK. Merlot is generally fully priced, with very few under-$30 examples offering consistent quality or much personality. Most of the top wines are at least twice that expensive, making them a questionable value.

RECOMMENDED PRODUCERS

Beringer Vineyards. The house style favors sweet, plump, user-friendly wines with considerable early appeal. At their best, these are among the lushest and most satisfying Merlots of the New World. The Alluvium red is a blend based on Merlot, while the creamy-rich, dark berry-dominated Bancroft Ranch bottling has been one of California's top Merlot bottlings for many years.

Merlot Napa Valley	03	02	01	$$
Alluvium Red Wine Napa Valley		02	01	$$
Merlot Bancroft Ranch Howell Mountain		02	01	$$$$

Duckhorn Vineyards. Duckhorn was one of California's standard-setters for Merlot in the early 1980s. These often earthy, gamey, soil-inflected wines generally need some cellaring to unwind and show their potential.

Merlot Napa Valley		03	02	$$$
Merlot Estate Grown Napa Valley		03	02	$$$$
Merlot Three Palms Vineyard Napa Valley	03	02	01	$$$$

Havens Winery. Michael Havens makes Merlot in a distinctly Bordeaux style, with a restrained sweetness and notes of lead pencil, minerals, game, and tobacco leaf. Prices are reasonable.

Merlot Napa Valley			03	$$$
Merlot Reserve Carneros			03	$$$

Pahlmeyer Winery. Flamboyantly ripe and often outsized Merlot from a blend of vineyard sources, typically offering great early appeal.

Merlot Napa Valley	04	03	02	$$$$

Paloma Vineyard. Exotic, showy Merlot that has a rabid following among those who prize sweetness of fruit, creamy texture, and plenty of spicy oak.

Merlot Spring Mountain	03	02	01	$$$$

Shafer Vineyards. Shafer's single Merlot bottling, produced in large quantity, is reliably lush and round, with more personality and soil character than most examples of this variety.

Merlot Napa Valley	03	02	01	$$$

OTHER PRODUCERS TO LOOK FOR: Arrowood Winery, Luna Vineyards, Joseph Phelps Vineyards, Pride Mountain Vineyards, Twomey Cellars.

SCARCE BUT WORTH THE SEARCH: Arietta, Behrens & Hitchcock, Blankiet Estate.

PINOT NOIR

Burgundy snobs will admit the possibility that Oregon's temperate climate suits Pinot Noir, and that cool New Zealand is a prime source for this finicky variety, but they seem unwilling to concede that the relentless sunshine and warmth of California can produce outstanding Pinots. But, in fact, numerous talented California winemakers, mostly working with fruit grown in cooler microclimates, are making world-class wines from this variety. These wines come from a surprisingly wide geographical range, stretching from Mendocino in the north to Santa Barbara County to the south, with many stops in between.

As a general category, California Pinot Noir has been on fire since the movie *Sideways*. In fact, California's Pinot Noirs are increasingly divergent. The state offers Pinots for virtually every taste, running the style gamut from pungent, cool, minerally, and Burgundian to soft, superripe, and chocolaty-sweet. The latter style of wine, often made from grapes harvested at very high sugar levels, is popular among those who prefer extremely ripe, lush wines with strong fruit character and little apparent acidity or tannin. Many of today's new generation of wine drinkers—especially those who did not cut their teeth on European wines—gravitate toward this style. On the other hand, most veteran wine drinkers, especially those whose model for Pinot Noir is red Burgundy, typically find these new-style wines too roasted and high in alcohol, and lacking subtlety and refinement as well as the ability to gain complexity with bottle aging. But today even the drinker with the most extreme Old World leanings can find California examples that will give pleasure. Never before have consumers had so many good California Pinot Noirs to choose from.

BANG FOR THE BUCK. California Pinot Noir is generally fully priced, but then Pinot Noir is never cheap. The best examples in the $20 to $40 range compare favorably to similarly priced Pinots made in Burgundy, Oregon, and New Zealand.

RECOMMENDED PRODUCERS

Arcadian Winery. This winery has emerged as a serious producer of elegant, balanced Pinot Noirs that are capable of developing real complexity with bottle age. Pungently aromatic, spicy and minerally, and possessing firm acidity, they deliver clarity and intensity of flavor at relatively low levels of alcohol. They are much more Burgundian than Californian in style.

Pinot Noir Pisoni Vineyard Santa Lucia Highlands			02	$$$
Pinot Noir Sleepy Hollow Vineyard Monterey	03	02	01	$$$

Au Bon Climat. Tightly wound and slow-to-open Pinot Noirs with noteworthy delicacy of red fruit, spice, and floral flavors, though often dominated by their new oak component in the early going. Decant these on serving or lay them down for a year or two.

Pinot Noir Sanford & Benedict Vineyard Santa Rita Hills	04	03	$$$
Pinot Noir La Bauge Au-dessus Santa Maria Valley	04	03	$$$

Calera Wine Company. One of the earliest proponents of vineyard-designated Pinot Noirs that offer accurate reflections of favored sites, Josh Jensen offers rather restrained wines that combine red fruit, mineral, earth, and floral notes in a particularly Burgundian way. Made in high-altitude limestone-rich vineyards in the Gavilan Mountains east of Monterey, these are dense but lively Pinots that can improve with age.

Pinot Noir Central Coast		03	02	$$
Pinot Noir Jensen Vineyard	03	02	01	$$$
Pinot Noir Mills Vineyard			01	$$$
Pinot Noir Selleck Vineyard			01	$$$

Dehlinger Winery. Tom Dehlinger is entering his third decade as a producer of smooth, broad Pinots from his Russian River Valley vineyards on Goldridge soil (marine sediment of volcanic origin). His wines combine cherry and strawberry fruit with smoky, earthy, and mineral notes.

Pinot Noir Goldridge Vineyard Russian River Valley	03	$$$
Pinot Noir Estate Russian River Valley	03	02	$$$
Pinot Noir Octagon Russian River Valley	02	$$$

Etude Wines. Tony Soter, who also makes excellent Pinot Noir in Oregon under his Soter Vineyards label, is a master of velvety, suave, immediately enjoyable Pinots from Carneros that are characterized by red fruits, spices, forest floor scents, and particularly fine-grained tannins. For years, Etude has been one of America's favorite Pinot Noirs on restaurant wine lists. Look also for Soter's special Heirloom release, made from old Burgundy clones—a step up in intensity and density from the regular bottling without loss of elegance.

	04	03	02	
Pinot Noir Los Carneros North Coast	04	03	02	$$$
Pinot Noir Heirloom Carneros		03	02	$$$$

Patz & Hall Wine Company. Elegant, silky, medium-bodied Pinot Noirs from disparate growing regions of California, with a common thread of captivating red berry and floral perfume. Never wines of power or weight—with the exception of the bottling from Alder Springs Vineyard in Mendocino—they normally show cool restraint and excellent balance.

	04	03	02	
Pinot Noir Sonoma Coast	04	03	02	$$$
Pinot Noir Hyde Vineyard Carneros	04	03	02	$$$$
Pinot Noir Pisoni Vineyard Santa Lucia Highlands	04	03	02	$$$$

Rochioli Vineyards. The Rochioli family makes consistently rich and aromatic Pinot Noirs from their superb vineyards in the heart of the Russian River Valley. In recent years, a growing percentage of Rochioli's fruit has gone into pricier vineyard-designated bottlings sold mostly via mailing list, but the winery's regular release remains a classic example of Russian River Valley Pinot Noir, with dominant red fruit and spice character.

	04	03	02	
Pinot Noir Estate Russian River Valley	04	03	02	$$$

Saintsbury. This groundbreaking Carneros winery was established in 1981 to focus on the Burgundy varieties Pinot Noir and Chardonnay. Today's Pinots are better than ever thanks to the addition in the early 1990s of the rocky, sandy Brown Ranch property. Saintsbury's easygoing Garnet bottling represents consistently strong value, while the Carneros and Carneros Reserve bottlings are deeper, silkier, and more layered.

	04	03	02	
Pinot Noir Garnet Carneros		04	03	$$
Pinot Noir Carneros	04	03	02	$$
Pinot Noir Reserve Carneros			02	$$$

Talley Vineyards. Nicely focused, medium-bodied wines that never lack for fresh fruit flavor; the best releases show subtle wild notes of smoked meat, minerals, mocha, and earth. The Talley family's vineyards are the source of grapes used by several other top Central Coast producers, but some of the best wines are made right here.

	04	03	02	
Pinot Noir Estate Arroyo Grande Valley	04	03	02	$$$
Pinot Noir Rincon Vineyard Arroyo Grande Valley		03	02	$$$
Pinot Noir Rosemary's Vineyard Arroyo Grande Valley		03	02	$$$$

Williams-Selyem. The proprietors of California's original producer of "cult" Pinot Noirs, the early vintages of which were made in a garage, sold the winery in early 1998. Today, the array of wines here is broader than ever and quality remains high. These are lush, extroverted Pinot Noirs, with sappy cherry, raspberry, and spicy oak flavors, showcasing some of the best sites in the Russian River Valley and cooler Sonoma Coast appellations.

	04	03	02	
Pinot Noir Sonoma Coast	04	03	02	$$$
Pinot Noir Russian River Valley	04	03	02	$$$
Pinot Noir Ferrington Vineyard Anderson Valley	04	03	02	$$$
Pinot Noir Allen Vineyard Russian River Valley	04	03	02	$$$$

OTHER PRODUCERS TO LOOK FOR: Acacia Winery, Bonaccorsi Wine Company, DuMol Wine Company, Fiddlehead Cellars, Flowers Vineyard, Freeman Winery, Hartford Family Wines, Kosta Browne Wines, Landmark Vineyards, Loring Wine Company, Martinelli Vineyards, Melville Winery, Meredith Vineyard Estate, Morgan Winery, Mount Eden Vineyards, Ojai Vineyard, Paul Hobbs Winery, Sea Smoke Cellars, Siduri, Walter Hansel Winery.

SCARCE BUT WORTH THE SEARCH: Adrian Fog, Aubert Wines, Copain Wines, Failla, Kalin Cellars, Kistler Vineyards, Littorai, Marcassin, Peter Michael Winery, Radio Coteau.

SYRAH &
OTHER RHÔNE VARIETIES

Syrah, the mainstay grape of the northern Rhône Valley, has become a hot variety in California in recent years. Consumers enjoy its flamboyantly ripe aromas and pliant texture, and growers have learned that Syrah vines can do well in a surprisingly wide range of climatic conditions, ranging from protected sites within distinctly cool regions to more temperate or ocean-influenced microclimates in hot areas. Today, outstanding Syrahs are coming out of such disparate growing regions as Mendocino County, the Sonoma Coast, Russian River Valley, Carneros, Santa Lucia Highlands, Paso Robles, and Santa Barbara County—in short, dispersed from top to bottom of California's prime wine real estate.

Like Pinot Noir in California, Syrah comes in a range of styles: from Rhône-like, with wild aromas of dark berries, black pepper, and gunflint, and firm structure and alcohol levels that are restrained by California standards, to superripe wines in an almost Australian style—creamy, high-octane fruit bombs with ripeness verging on candied and mostly soft tannins.

Some of the most lavishly rich and aromatically expressive examples come from the central coast, where a growing number of vineyard owners are also experimenting with Grenache and even Mourvèdre. In Paso Robles, some of today's most exciting red wines are blends in which some high-quality Grenache or Mourvèdre may be added to the Syrah to contribute aromatic complexity, creaminess of texture, supporting acidity or tannic spine. These are boom times for Paso Robles, but to date many of the best wines are still made in limited quantities.

BANG FOR THE BUCK. The best Syrahs can be pricey, but there are also values to be found in this category by the standards of California wine, especially in the Central Coast.

RECOMMENDED PRODUCERS

Alban Vineyards. John Alban makes some of the most aromatically complex and explosively rich wines in the New World from Syrah and Grenache. He works entirely with fruit from his own superb clonal material, planted on chalk-rich hillside vineyards open to cooling sea breezes. The wines have the exotic yet varietally accurate character and creamy sweetness to provide immediate pleasure but have the balance and structure to age.

Grenache Alban Estate Edna Valley		03	$$$
Syrah Reva Edna Valley	03	02	$$$
Syrah Lorraine Edna Valley	03	02	$$$$

Beckmen Vineyards. Well-priced, bright, balanced wines with varietally expressive aromas and flavors and more restraint than most California examples from red Rhône Valley varieties. The entry-level Cuvée Le Bec, a blend of Grenache, Mourvèdre, Syrah, and Counoise, is consistently an outstanding value in California red wine.

Cuvée Le Bec Red Wine Santa Ynez Valley		04	03	$$
Syrah Purisima Mountain Vineyard Santa Ynez Valley	04	03	02	$$$
Grenache Purisima Mountain Vineyard Santa Ynez Valley		04	03	$$$

Edmunds St. John. Steve Edmunds makes uncompromising Syrah and southern Rhône–inspired blends with no concessions to modern taste. Edmunds' wines begin life with little of the easy sweetness provided by new oak barrels but are aromatically pure and have a track record for midterm aging. Prior to 2002, the Shell and Bone bottling, a blend of southern Rhône varieties, was called Los Robles Viejos.

Rocks and Gravel Red Wine California		03	01	$$
Syrah Wylle-Fenaughty El Dorado County		03	01	$$

Havens Wine Cellars. A pioneer of California Syrah in a distinctly northern Rhône style, typically showing notes of dark fruits, black pepper, and gunflint. The top Havens bottling is made from fruit from Hudson Vineyard in Carneros, one of California's top sources of Syrah.

Syrah Napa Valley		03	02	$$
Syrah Hudson Vineyard Carneros		03	02	$$$

Jade Mountain. La Provençale, a blend in the style of a southern Rhône wine, is a solid value, and the flagship Syrah under this label is also crafted in a French style, with emphasis on understated fruit, gentle earth tones and structure.

La Provençale Red Wine California		03	$$
Syrah Paras Vineyard Mt. Veeder	03	02	$$$

Jaffurs Wine Cellars. This specialist in Rhône Valley varieties, both red and white, offers focused, spicy Syrah and Grenache bottlings, at relatively gentle prices.

Grenache Stolpman Vineyard Santa Barbara County		03	$$
Syrah Santa Barbara County	04	03	$$
Syrah Thompson Vineyard Santa Barbara County	04	03	$$$

Neyers Vineyards. Flamboyantly ripe Syrah from the Hudson Vineyard in Carneros, characterized by lush texture and wild, Old World flavors of pepper, gunflint, and roasted meat.

Syrah Hudson Vineyard Napa Valley	`04`	`03`	$$$

Qupé Cellars. Consistently interesting Syrah, Grenache, and blends, with dark berry flavors perked up by cool floral, herbal, and spice elements. These wines generally need a year or two of bottle aging.

Syrah Bien Nacido Vineyard Santa Maria Valley	`04`	`03`	$$
Syrah Bien Nacido Hillside Estate Santa Maria Valley	`03`	`02`	$$$

Tablas Creek Vineyard. This important estate in Paso Robles, a joint venture between the Perrin family of Châteauneuf-du-Pape and their longtime importer Robert Haas, planted its vineyards in the 1990s with clonal selections taken from the southern Rhône Valley. Today's Tablas Creek wines offer the breadth, complexity of soil character, classic dryness, and suavity of the best French wines while delivering the sweetness of fruit made possible by California sunshine. To date, the top reds have been blends of Syrah, Mourvèdre, Grenache, and Counoise.

Côtes de Tablas Red Wine Paso Robles	`04`	`03`	$$
Esprit de Beaucastel Red Wine Paso Robles	`04`	`03`	$$$

OTHER PRODUCERS TO LOOK FOR: Bonaccorsi Wine Company, Bonny Doon Vineyard, Carlisle Winery, Culler Wines, Dehlinger Winery, A Donkey and Goat, DuMol Wine Company, JC Cellars, L'Aventure, Melville Winery, Ojai Vineyard, Stolpman Vineyards.

SCARCE BUT WORTH THE SEARCH: Araujo Estate, Behrens & Hitchcock, Colgin Cellars, Copain Wines, Failla, Kongsgaard Wines, Linne Calodo, Pax Wine Cellars, Joseph Phelps Vineyards, Saxum Vineyards, Sean Thackrey, Sine Qua Non, Villa Creek Cellars.

ZINFANDEL

Zinfandel is not the rage it was in the 1980s and early 1990s, as there are now too many wines made from overripe fruit or from young vines, or overwhelmed by excessive use of new barrels. Today's Zin styles range from elegant, taut, and claret-like midweights to superripe and porty behemoths, with off-the-charts alcohol levels, distinctly exotic character, and, frequently, noticeable residual sugar. Classic Zinfandels are normally medium to full in body, with fruit-driven aromas and flavors of fresh berries, black pepper, and spices, sometimes with notes of citrus zest, chocolate, and briary underbrush; they are rarely overwhelmed by oak notes. Many of the best producers continue to work largely with very old vines (sometimes with "field blends" that include other grapes such as Petite Sirah and Carignane), which give consistently low crop levels and make wines with atypical creaminess of texture, aromatic complexity, and aging potential.

BANG FOR THE BUCK. Zinfandel is not the bargain it was a decade ago, but relatively few wines are exorbitantly priced.

RECOMMENDED PRODUCERS

Martinelli Vineyards. Extremely rich, exotic Zinfandels from old vines in the Russian River Valley, often with freakishly high (i.e., 16+ percent) alcohol. The Giuseppe & Luisa bottling is the closest thing to a fruit bomb here, while the Jackass Vineyard and scarce Jackass Hill wines are characterized by roasted fruits, game, leather, menthol, and earth.

Zinfandel Giuseppe & Luisa Russian River Valley	04	03	02	$$$$
Zinfandel Jackass Vineyard Russian River Valley	04	03	02	$$$$

Ravenswood Winery. Joel Peterson's full-flavored Zinfandels—"No Wimpy Wines" is the motto of this winery—have displayed an admirable consistency for more than two decades. Peterson was an early proponent of vineyard-designated Zins, and many of his bottlings from the late 1980s and early 1990s are still in excellent condition. The Vintner's Blend, made in enormous quantities, is a reliably supple, fruity wine at a remarkably low price, while the Old Hill Ranch is one of California's most distinctive reds.

Zinfandel Sonoma County	04	03	02	$$
Zinfandel Dickerson Vineyard Napa Valley	04	03	02	$$
Zinfandel Belloni Russian River Valley	04	03	02	$$
Zinfandel Old Hill Ranch Sonoma Valley	04	03	02	$$$

Ridge Vineyards. Veteran winemaker Paul Draper, who began at Ridge in 1969, favors purity of flavor and structure over sheer alcoholic weight and residual sugar, and his Zinfandels have long enjoyed a reputation for graceful aging. Some of these wines do not say Zinfandel on the front label because the percentage of this variety does not always reach the required 75 percent minimum (Draper especially likes to blend in some Petite Sirah and Carignan) and because Ridge considers the site to be more important than the variety.

Zinfandel Paso Robles	04	03	$$
Geyserville Alexander Valley	03	02	$$$
Lytton Springs Dry Creek Valley	04	03	$$$

Rosenblum Cellars. This longtime Zinfandel specialist offers a huge range of rich, extroverted Zinfandels from vineyards all over the state, typically made in a superripe, high-alcohol style. Some wines from recent vintages have shown a lot of new oak and residual sugar. Prices are reasonable.

Zinfandel Hendry Vineyard Reserve Napa Valley		02	$$$
Zinfandel Rockpile Road Vineyard Dry Creek Valley	03	02	$$
Zinfandel Richard Sauret Vineyards Paso Robles		02	$$

Seghesio Family Vineyards. The Seghesio family first planted vineyards in Sonoma County in 1895. Their best wines are classic, pliant Zinfandels, with intense dark berry fruit, hints of black pepper and spices, and oak in the background.

Zinfandel Sonoma County	04	03	$$
Zinfandel Old Vine Sonoma County	03	02	$$$
Zinfandel Home Ranch Sonoma County	04	03	$$$

Turley Wine Cellars. Larry Turley produces some of California's richest, most powerful, and most exotic Zinfandels, often with head-spinning alcohol and a bit of residual sugar.

Zinfandel Juveniles California	04	03	02	$$
Zinfandel Old Vines California	04	03	02	$$
Zinfandel Moore Earthquake Vineyard Napa Valley		03	02	$$$
Zinfandel Hayne Vineyard Napa Valley		03	02	$$$$

OTHER PRODUCERS TO LOOK FOR: Robert Biale Vineyards, Brown Estate, Chateau Montelena, Cline Cellars, DeLoach Vineyards, Elyse Winery, Green & Red Vineyard, Hartford Family Wines, Howell Mountain Vineyards, JC Cellars, Kuleto Estate, Nalle Winery, Neyers Vineyards, Quivira Vineyards, A. Rafanelli Winery, Saxon Brown Wines, Storybook Mountain Vineyards, Tobias Vineyard.

SCARCE BUT WORTH THE SEARCH: Carlisle Winery, Radio Coteau, Schrader Cellars, Williams-Selyem.

CHARDONNAY

As recently as ten years ago, the American market had an unquenchable thirst for Chardonnay, particularly for examples from California. Today, although Chardonnay is still the most widely planted variety in California in terms of acreage, serious wine aficionados rarely talk about Chardonnays other than those from a handful of specialist producers. Even at the level of the mass market, many consumers have tired of overly alcoholic, overoaked, and clumsy wines, not to mention neutral, technically correct but soulless examples. Many wine drinkers have moved on to fresher, less oak-influenced white wines such as Sauvignon Blanc. This is a shame, as the trend has turned toward brighter, better-balanced Chardonnays from cooler sites, with crisper fruit aromas, more soil character, and less reliance on new barrels for flavor.

Still, it's a two-tier market. A relative handful of producers make wonderfully layered, complex wines that can easily hold their own against more expensive white Burgundies, at least in their early years in bottle. These wines, which can be richer than dry whites have any right to be, are among the most impressive wines made in California today and continue to be hotly pursued by collectors. The rest of California's Chardonnay producers compete for the attention of consumers who are no longer obsessed with this grape. But there are now many excellent choices available, many from cooler areas. Lower elevations of Napa Valley have virtually been abandoned as appropriate sites for Chardonnay, so that now the best wines come almost exclusively from the Russian River Valley and further west in Sonoma County; Carneros, the Anderson Valley to the north; and the south Central Coast, especially the windy western portion of Santa Barbara County. Today, there are fewer blowsy, tropical-fruity Chardonnays with the alcohol levels and flavors of a piña colada and many more wines with fresher stone and citrus fruit elements; mineral and earth notes from the soil; and restrained oak spice.

While most California Chardonnays should be consumed within two or three years of their release, the top examples can give pleasure for four to eight years, although it is debatable whether these wines gain more in texture and complexity than they lose in early fruitiness.

BANG FOR THE BUCK. Most of California's best Chardonnays are in the $40 to $75 range, where they are rather richly priced unless one prefers these wines to premier cru bottlings from Burgundy. But relative bargains can be found for less, particularly from the south Central Coast.

2004 ★★★★   2003 ★★★★-

RECOMMENDED PRODUCERS

Au Bon Climat. Jim Clendenen was a pioneer of Burgundy-inspired Chardonnays as well as Pinot Noirs. His wines are minerally, focused, and restrained in the early going, and sometimes quite oaky. Lay them down for a year or two, or pour them into a decanter if you plan to drink them young.

Chardonnay Santa Barbara County		03	$$
Chardonnay Sanford & Benedict Vineyard Santa Ynez Valley	03		$$$

Beringer Vineyards. Beringer makes a solid, taut basic bottling that is widely available and very reasonably priced. Their Private Reserve is a considerably richer and more exotic wine, combining stone fruits with spicy oak, honey, and butterscotch.

Chardonnay Napa Valley	04	03	$$
Chardonnay Private Reserve Napa Valley	04	**03**	$$$

Forman Vineyards. Ric Forman makes a single Napa Valley Chardonnay with the bracing acidity and cool minerality of a Chablis, blocking the malolactic fermentation to preserve freshness. The wine may be out of step with today's flamboyant, tropical-fruity, and immediately accessible California Chardonnays, but it has established a long track record for positive evolution in bottle.

Chardonnay Napa Valley	04	03	$$$

Kistler Vineyards. Steve Kistler's rich, leesy, Burgundy-style Chardonnays, from a series of ideally situated vineyards all around Sonoma County, have long been favorites among collectors and restaurant clients. Quality has remained high even as production has grown, and the wines have proven to be excellent midterm agers. The best Kistler bottlings are among the richest and most complex Chardonnays made anywhere.

Chardonnay Dutton Ranch Russian River Valley	03	02	$$$
Chardonnay Durell Vineyard Sonoma Valley	03	02	$$$$
Chardonnay Vine Hill Vineyard Russian River Valley	03	02	$$$$
Chardonnay Hudson Vineyard Carneros	03	02	$$$$

Landmark Vineyards. Consistently rich, complex Chardonnays that are underpriced for their quality—and perhaps underappreciated as a result.

Chardonnay Damaris Reserve California	04	03	$$
Chardonnay Lorenzo Vineyard Russian River Valley	04	03	$$$

Peter Michael Winery. For many years among the New World's finest Chardonnays, the Peter Michael wines feature wonderfully deep, layered flavors and outstanding clarity and verve. These wines are routinely mistaken for top white Burgundies in blind tastings.

Chardonnay Mon Plaisir Sonoma County	04	03	$$$$
Chardonnay Belle Côte Sonoma County	04	03	$$$$
Chardonnay Cuvée Indigène Sonoma County	04	03	$$$$$

Mount Eden Vineyards. One of California's elite Chardonnays, Mount Eden's estate bottling has been made since the 1970s from vines planted at an altitude of 2,000 feet in the Santa Cruz Mountains south of San Francisco. The wine is tightly wound, minerally, and emphatically Old World in style, blossoming with age and usually at its best between five and fifteen years after the vintage, making this one of the best California Chardonnays to cellar.

Chardonnay Estate Santa Cruz Mountains	02	$$$

Patz & Hall Wine Company. Working closely with grape growers across a broad range of appellations and mostly cooler sites, this company offers numerous dense, complex, stylish wines that generally offer considerable early appeal.

Chardonnay Dutton Ranch Russian River Valley	04	03	$$$
Chardonnay Durell Vineyard Sonoma Valley	04	03	$$$
Chardonnay Hyde Vineyard Carneros	04	03	$$$

Ramey Wine Cellars. Veteran winemaker David Ramey (ex-Matanzas Creek, Chalk Hill, Dominus, Rudd Estate) crafts dense, layered, highly nuanced Chardonnays from purchased fruit under his own label. There are appellation bottlings and vineyard-designated wines, which Ramey describes as "village wines" and "premier crus," both made in quantities large enough that they can actually be found in the marketplace.

Chardonnay Russian River Valley	04	03	$$$
Chardonnay Carneros District	04	03	$$$
Chardonnay Hyde Vineyard Carneros		03	$$$
Chardonnay Hudson Vineyard Carneros		03	$$$

Talley Vineyards. This sprawling family estate, most of whose vineyards are in Arroyo Grande Valley, offers suave, elegant, and consistently lively Chardonnays characterized by stone fruits, minerals, and spices.

Chardonnay Arroyo Grande Valley	04	03	$$
Chardonnay Rincon Vineyard Arroyo Grande Valley	04	03	$$$
Chardonnay Rosemary's Vineyard Arroyo Grande Valley	04	03	$$$

OTHER PRODUCERS TO LOOK FOR: L'Angevin, Brewer-Clifton, Chateau Montelena, Dehlinger Winery, DuMol Wine Company, Hartford Family Wines, HdV Wines, Martinelli Vineyards, Melville Winery, Robert Mondavi Winery, Newton Vineyard, Neyers Vineyards, Qupé Cellars, Paul Hobbs Winery, Saintsbury, Sbragia Family Vineyards, Shafer Vineyards, Stonestreet, Tor Kenward Family Wines, Varner Winery.

SCARCE BUT WORTH THE SEARCH: Aubert Wines, Kalin Cellars, Kongsgaard Wines, Littorai, Marcassin, Pahlmeyer Winery, Rochioli Vineyards.

SAUVIGNON BLANC

California Sauvignon Blanc ranges in style from minerally, grassy, and citric wines (more akin to examples made in the Loire Valley or New Zealand) to opulent, tropical-fruity wines fermented and aged in barrels and often including a percentage of Sémillon à la white Graves. Some of these latter Chardonnay wannabees seem to miss the point of Sauvignon, which is to be refreshing rather than overbearing. In recent years the brisk, citrusy style of Sauvignon has enjoyed steadily growing popularity on restaurant lists, and today there are many new plantings of Sauvignon Blanc in cooler regions—as opposed to the valley floor of Napa Valley, where Cabernet grapes fetch a higher price anyway. Prices for Sauvignon Blanc have escalated as demand for these wines has grown. (Incidentally, Fumé Blanc is used on the label by a number of producers, usually to signify a wine made in a richer barrel-fermented, oak-aged style.)

Although some examples have proven that they can last in bottle, there's little if anything to be gained by cellaring these wines, and the overwhelming majority of California's Sauvignon Blancs are best consumed in the two or three years following the harvest.

BANG FOR THE BUCK. Prices for these wines have risen sharply in the past five years, but there are still some good values to be found.

RECOMMENDED PRODUCERS

Brander Vineyard. This Sauvignon Blanc specialist offers a range of wines, all racy and minerally. The basic bottling is generally terrific value, the Cuvée Nicolas incorporates some Semillon, while the pungent Au Naturel, fermented with wild yeasts, often shows the grapefruit skin and chalk dust qualities of a Sancerre grown on limestone.

Sauvignon Blanc Santa Ynez Valley		05	$
Sauvignon Au Naturel Santa Ynez Valley		04	$$

Geyser Peak Winery. This winery's crisp, almost New Zealand–style entry-level Sauvignon Blanc, made in stainless steel, is a terrific value in good vintages, while their limited single-vineyard release from a cool, foggy Russian River Valley vineyard offers varietally accurate flavors of grapefruit, gooseberry, and flowers in a more concentrated and dense presentation.

Sauvignon Blanc California	05	04	$
Sauvignon Blanc River Road Ranch Russian River Valley	05	04	$$

Groth Vineyards & Winery. Groth uses a blend of vineyards to craft a consistently satisfying Sauvignon Blanc with melon and citrus fruit flavors, supple texture, and firm backbone.

Sauvignon Blanc Napa Valley	`04`	$$

Honig Vineyard. A consistent best buy in Sauvignon Blanc and a popular restaurant wine: minerally and racy but also round, fruity, and easygoing.

Sauvignon Blanc Napa Valley	`04`	$

Robert Mondavi Winery. Mondavi has made some of California's richest and most serious Sauvignon Blanc bottlings, aged in varying degrees of new oak, for well over a quarter of a century. The Reserve bottling is especially broad and rich, often with suggestions of exotic fruits.

Fumé Blanc Napa Valley	`04`	`03`	$$
Fumé Blanc Reserve Napa Valley	`04`	`03`	$$$

Rochioli Vineyards. Although better known for his Pinot Noirs, Tom Rochioli offers a delightfully brisk and gripping Sauvignon Blanc with penetrating citrus skin and dusty stone character.

Sauvignon Blanc Estate Russian River Valley	`05`	`04`	$$

Spottswoode Winery. One of California's most consistently vibrant, minerally examples of Sauvignon Blanc, with a touch of oak influence and classic cool varietal flavors of lemon, lime, gooseberry, and cut grass.

Sauvignon Blanc Napa Valley	`04`	$$

OTHER PRODUCERS TO LOOK FOR: Cakebread Cellars, Duckhorn Vineyards, Fiddlehead Cellars, Margerum Wine Company, Voss Vineyards.

SCARCE BUT WORTH THE SEARCH: Araujo Estate, Kalin Cellars, Peter Michael Winery.

OTHER WHITE WINES OF CALIFORNIA

As is the case with red wine, white Rhône Valley varieties are enjoying a surge of popularity. Viognier exploded onto the California scene in the mid-1990s and has now been joined by a growing number of mostly white blends from Marsanne and Roussanne. Originally, there was a tendency to apply Chardonnay winemaking techniques to these latter blends—or at least to craft wines with substantial weight and flavor impact, even at the cost of losing the more delicate floral and earthy qualities of these grapes. Too many of these wines were dominated by the generic aromas and flavors of oak barrels and lees contact. Today, happily, California's "other white wines" are more aromatically interesting and more widely appreciated by adventurous restaurants as flexible new options at the dinner table. While many California producers still make Riesling, few of these wines are of much interest to cosmopolitan wine lovers who can find superb examples of this variety from so many other regions.

BANG FOR THE BUCK. Viognier is rarely inexpensive, but other California white varieties, such as Pinot Blanc, Gewürztraminer, Marsanne, and Roussanne, can offer good value to consumers who are willing to experiment.

RECOMMENDED PRODUCERS

Alban Vineyards. This master of Rhône varieties makes a thick, chewy, dry Roussanne of remarkable aromatic complexity, with stone fruit and mineral elements supported but not overwhelmed by spicy oak. Barrel-fermented Viognier is also fragrant and rich.

Viognier Alban Vineyard Edna Valley		04	$$$
Roussanne Alban Vineyard Edna Valley	04	03	$$$

Arrowood Winery. Chardonnay and Cabernet are the most important varieties from a commercial standpoint for veteran winemaker Richard Arrowood, but his Viogniers and his unusually rich barrel-aged Pinot Blanc have been consistently excellent for many years, especially the rather full-bodied tropical, honeyed, minerally wines made from Saralee's Vineyard in Russian River Valley.

Pinot Blanc Saralee's Vineyard Russian River Valley	04	$$
Viognier Saralee's Vineyard Russian River Valley	04	$$
Gewürztraminer Saralee's Vineyard Russian River Valley	04	$$

Bonny Doon Vineyard. Iconoclast Randall Grahm makes fresh, energetic, food-friendly, and inexpensive Rieslings with crisp flavors and excellent focus. The dry Pacific Rim bottling is actually a blend of fruit from Washington and Germany, while The Heart Has Its Rieslings, slightly sweet in style, is sourced from Washington.

Riesling Pacific Rim American	05	04	$
Riesling The Heart Has Its Rieslings American		05	$$

Cold Heaven. These are among the freshest, most mineral-driven examples of New World Viognier, made in a style reminiscent of Condrieu. Pricing is very fair for the quality.

Viognier Le Bon Climat Santa Barbara County		05	$$
Viognier Domaine des 2 Mondes Saints & Sinners Santa Maria Valley	05	04	$$

Luna Vineyards. An idiosyncratic, singular Pinot Grigio marked by unusually rich texture, hints of tropical and dried fruits, and leesy complexity—hardly your typical New World example of this variety. (Look too for this winery's exotic barrel-fermented blend of Tocai Friulano, Pinot Grigio, Chardonnay, and Sauvignon Blanc called "Freakout," not to mention their creamy-sweet yet vibrant Sangiovese, consistently one of the most satisfying examples of this variety made outside Tuscany.)

Pinot Grigio Barrel Fermented Napa Valley	04	$$

Navarro Vineyards. Long a California standard-bearer for Gewürztraminer, Navarro's dry version is made in a rich, powerful style reminiscent of Alsace, offering an extroverted personality and lush texture.

Dry Gewürztraminer Anderson Valley	04	$$

Qupé Cellars. Bob Lindquist was an early proponent of Rhône varieties in California, and not just red grapes. His rich, thick Roussanne, often quite uncompromising in the early going, benefits from decanting or short-term cellaring while his early-bottled and considerably less expensive Marsanne is brighter and lighter.

Marsanne Santa Ynez Valley	05	04	$$
Roussanne Bien Nacido Hillside Estate Santa Maria Valley		05	$$$

Tablas Creek Vineyards. These uncompromisingly minerally and sometimes austere white wines would not be out of place in a tasting of Rhône Valley examples. The Tablas Creek whites are the antithesis of stereotypical California wines, emphasizing structure over lush fruit.

Côtes de Tablas Blanc Paso Robles	04	03	$$
Esprit de Beaucastel Blanc Paso Robles	04	03	$$$
Roussanne Paso Robles	04	03	$$

SCARCE BUT WORTH THE SEARCH: Sine Qua Non.

SPARKLING WINES

The best versions of California sparkling wine, generally made from Chardonnay and Pinot Noir grown in cool areas, approach the brightness and freshness of Champagne but rarely attain the same degree of precision and elegance. This is because relatively few sites allow California growers to get the same intensity of flavor at low grape sugars that many Champagne growers are able to obtain from their limestone-rich soils. Certainly, California's sparkling wine industry has gotten a shot in the arm over the past 20 years from high-visibility investments by numerous Champagne houses. But there are still far too many heavily manipulated, angular, overripe, and tired wines that come off as heavy-handed parodies of Champagne.

BANG FOR THE BUCK. As it is always possible to find excellent nonvintage brut Champagne in the $30 range, there's little reason to spend more for sparkling wines from California. But there are values to be found here in the $20 range.

RECOMMENDED PRODUCERS

Domaine Carneros. Champagne Taittinger opened its showplace winery in Carneros in 1989, where it specializes in making sparkling wines that are creamy yet light on their feet. The prestige bottling Le Rêve, one of California's classiest examples, undergoes long aging on its lees and is especially dense and complex, with characteristic chalk, citrus, toast, and mineral elements and good cellaring potential.

Brut Cuvée Carneros	02	01	$$
Le Rêve Blanc de Blancs Carneros	99	98	$$$

Domaine Chandon. Set up by Moët-Hennessy in the 1970s, Domaine Chandon was the first California sparkling wine specialist established by a French house using traditional Champagne methods. These wines are generally refreshing and on the dry side by California sparkling wine standards, with soft finishes. Recent releases appear to be a bit more complex and less austere than earlier bottlings. The Etoile, a blend of 75 percent Chardonnay and 25 percent Pinot Noir, spends at least five years on its lees.

NV Brut Classic California		$$
NV Blanc de Noirs Brut California		$$
NV Etoile Brut Carneros		$$$

Roederer Estate. The Champagne house Louis Roederer went to the cool, foggy Anderson Valley in Mendocino County to plant Chardonnay and Pinot Noir suitable for making California sparkling wines of delicacy and precision. The wines tend to be crisp and austere in a Champagne way, favoring yeasty complexity over simple fruitiness. Roederer Estate uses a significant percentage of older reserve wines to maintain the consistency of its nonvintage wines.

NV Estate Brut Anderson Valley			$$
L'Ermitage Brut Anderson Valley	99	**98**	$$$

Schramsberg. The Davies family was California's first important producer of sparkling wines from Chardonnay and Pinot Noir, after reviving the historic Schramsberg estate outside Calistoga in the 1960s. A range of styles is produced here, from a dry, minerally Blanc de Blancs to a Blanc de Noirs that's surprisingly lively and refined for this style of wine (Schramsberg's version includes some Chardonnay.) J. Schram is the house's prestige bottling.

Blanc de Blancs Brut California	02	**01**	$$
Blanc de Noirs Brut Napa Valley	02	**01**	$$
J. Schram Brut California		**99**	$$$

OTHER PRODUCERS TO LOOK FOR: Iron Horse Vineyards, Mumm Napa.

Key to Vintage Ratings		Key to Assessments of Specific Wines	
★★★★★	Outstanding	**03**	An excellent to outstanding example *of that wine*
★★★★	Excellent	03	A good to very good example *of that wine*
★★★	Good to very good	03	A disappointing effort (often due to a
★★	Fair to average		difficult vintage)
★	Poor		

OREGON

A lthough wine growing in Oregon stretches from the California border to Washington, for most wine lovers Oregon means the Willamette Valley, a temperate, ocean-influenced growing area that extends from Portland south to Eugene, or roughly a hundred miles. The vast majority of the state's best producers are grouped around the towns of McMinnville (the site of the annual International Pinot Noir Celebration), Carlton, Dundee, and Newberg, as well as near the state capital, Salem. This rather compressed area is ideal for winery visits, and tourist-friendly facilities and restaurants featuring the local cuisine have sprouted throughout the region in recent years. While closer in overall feel to the pastoral countryside of Sonoma's Russian River Valley than to Napa Valley's Disneyland, the Willamette Valley is far from the backwater that its wine pioneers found in the late 1960s and early 1970s.

Oregon's past and future reputation as a world-class growing region rests squarely on Pinot Noir. Hyped in the early 1980s, perhaps prematurely, as the New World's answer to red Burgundy, Oregon Pinot Noir has steadily improved since then as local growers have discovered the best sites and done a better job matching clones to microclimates. While Oregon's soils and climate differ in important ways from those of more continental Burgundy, its mild climate on the Pacific side of the Cascade Range allows the fruit to ripen gently, although harvest-time rain is always a possibility. (In contrast, most of Washington State's vineyards are located in the irrigated semidesert east of the mountains.) Today, Oregon's better Pinot producers, with considerable experience under their belts, are more comfortable in their own skin and less concerned about competing with Burgundy.

PINOT NOIR

Oregon's Pinots typically feature exuberant cherry-berry aromas and flavors; varying degrees of spicy oak; medium body; and reasonable tannin levels. They generally carry moderate alcohol in the 12.5 to 14 percent range, lower than those of today's typical Pinots from California, although very warm years can bring wines with higher alcohol and more roasted flavors. Rarely austere or tough on release, the best Oregon Pinots gain in complexity with three to five years of bottle aging, and top wines from the most successful vintages can improve in bottle for a decade or more. "Tender" might be an apt description of the best Oregon Pinot Noirs.

After a couple of challenging growing seasons, the 2002, 2003, and 2004 vintages brought a return to mostly favorable weather conditions. The 2002 vintage yielded many bright, harmonious Pinots that promise to repay cellaring. Even some of Oregon's old-timers, who have been on the scene for 30 years, consider that year to be their most successful vintage to date. Periods of extreme heat in the summer of 2003 and shortly before the harvest yielded the ripest grapes in Oregon's history. While many wines taste distinctly pruney, overripe, or roasted, the best wines from this vintage are wonderfully dense, sweet, and unusually mouth-filling, with the sheer stuffing to stand up to alcohol levels reaching as high as 15 percent. Vintage 2004 is another excellent year for the Willamette Valley, having produced fresh, tangy, classically balanced Pinot Noirs that lead with their red berry fruit and floral characteristics.

BANG FOR THE BUCK. Oregon Pinot Noir became quite expensive in the mid-1990s, but since then prices have been reasonably stable while Pinots from Burgundy, California, and New Zealand have risen sharply. Today, the best examples in the $25 to $50 range are priced in line with high-quality Pinots from elsewhere. Some wines, however, are considerably more expensive.

2004 ★★★★+   2003 ★★★   2002 ★★★★

RECOMMENDED PRODUCERS

Adelsheim Vineyards. An Oregon pioneer in its third decade of producing elegant, vibrant, understated wines of the old school. These are among Oregon's more predictably age-worthy examples of Pinot thanks to their moderate alcohol and sound balance.

	04	03	
Pinot Noir Oregon	04	03	$$
Pinot Noir Elizabeth's Reserve Yamhill County	04	**03**	$$$

Archery Summit Winery. Lavishly oaked, full-throttle Oregon Pinot Noirs with compelling ripeness, sweetness of fruit, and density. Among the most expensive Pinots in Oregon.

	04	03	
Pinot Noir Red Hills Estate	04	03	$$$$
Pinot Noir Archery Summit Estate	**04**	**03**	$$$$

Beaux Frères. Early vintages emphasized ripeness and power but more recent vintages signal a turn toward a more elegant, less extreme style. These are now consistently rich, complex, and balanced New World Pinots. Wine critic Robert Parker is a co-owner of Beaux Frères, with brother-in-law and co-owner Michael Etzel responsible for winemaking.

	04	03	
Pinot Noir Belles Soeurs Willamette Valley	**04**	03	$$$
Pinot Noir The Upper Terrace Willamette Valley	04	03	$$$$
Pinot Noir The Beaux Frères Vineyard Willamette Valley	**04**	03	$$$$

Bergström Winery. An unabashed devotee of the new school of Pinot, Josh Bergström produces dense, flamboyant wines that are not shy in the oak or alcohol departments. A great source for immediate-gratification Pinot Noir, albeit at a price.

	04	03	
Pinot Noir Willamette Valley	04	03	$$
Pinot Noir Bergström Vineyard Willamette Valley	04	**03**	$$$$
Pinot Noir Shea Vineyard Willamette Valley	**04**	**03**	$$$$

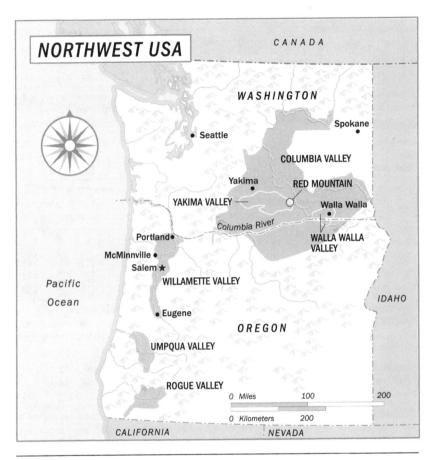

NORTHWEST USA

CANADA

WASHINGTON

Seattle

Spokane

COLUMBIA VALLEY

Yakima

RED MOUNTAIN

YAKIMA VALLEY

Walla Walla

Columbia River

WALLA WALLA
VALLEY

Portland

McMinnville

Salem ★

WILLAMETTE VALLEY

IDAHO

Pacific
Ocean

Eugene

OREGON

UMPQUA VALLEY

ROGUE VALLEY

0 Miles   100   200

0 Kilometers   200

CALIFORNIA   NEVADA

Bethel Heights Winery. The Casteel family has been an industry leader since the winery was founded in 1977, producing deeply flavored wines that are rarely overextracted or out of whack.

Pinot Noir Willamette Valley	04	03	$$
Pinot Noir Southeast Block Reserve Willamette Valley	04	03	$$$
Pinot Noir West Block Reserve Willamette Valley	04	03	$$$

Broadley Vineyards. Highly aromatic, juicy wines with deep red berry flavors and considerable weight. The wines often become more floral with bottle aging.

Pinot Noir Estate Willamette Valley	04	03	$$
Pinot Noir Marcille-Lorraine Willamette Valley		04	$$$
Pinot Noir Claudia's Choice Willamette Valley		02	$$$

Cameron Winery. Owner-winemaker John Paul has a strong following in Oregon for his flagship Clos Electrique bottling, and his regular Pinot Noir is frequently a noteworthy bargain.

Pinot Noir Abbey Ridge Vineyard	03	$$
Pinot Noir Clos Electrique	03	$$$

Chehalem. A producer of consistently stylish, vibrant Pinots with no excess weight. Accessible upon release, the wines also have the balance to reward cellaring.

Pinot Noir 3 Vineyard Willamette Valley	04	03	$$
Pinot Noir Reserve Willamette Valley	04	**03**	$$$

Cristom Vineyards. Veteran winemaker Steve Doerner, who was responsible for some remarkable Pinots at Calera during the late 1980s, has continued to distinguish himself as a master of perfumed, pungently floral, age-worthy Pinot Noir in a distinctly Burgundian style.

Pinot Noir Jessie	**03**	**02**	$$$
Pinot Noir Louise	**03**	**02**	$$$
Pinot Noir Marjorie	**03**	**02**	$$$

Domaine Drouhin. Robert Drouhin, director of Maison Joseph Drouhin in Burgundy, established his Willamette Valley property in 1988, having been convinced by a series of tastings in France of the strong potential of Oregon Pinot Noir. Today, his daughter Véronique oversees production of subtle, restrained, perfumed Pinots with a proven track record of development in bottle—not unlike the family's Burgundies in style.

Pinot Noir Willamette Valley	**04**	03	$$$
Pinot Noir Laurene Willamette Valley	**04**	**03**	$$$$
Pinot Noir Louise Willamette Valley	**03**	**02**	$$$$

Evesham Wood Winery. A broad range of stylish, exceptionally age-worthy Pinots that emphasize aromatic complexity and structure. More Old World in style than most Oregon Pinots, with soil-inflected earth, pepper, spice, and underbrush notes adding complexity to their red fruit.

Pinot Noir Eola Hills	04	03	$
Pinot Noir Le Puits Sec Willamette Valley	04	03	$$
Pinot Noir Cuvée J Willamette Valley		**04**	$$$

Patricia Green Cellars. Patty Green and Jim Anderson, who made their reputation at Torii Mor, purchased the Autumn Wind winery near Newberg in 2002 and have quickly established a reputation here for intense, full-flavored, aromatically complex Pinot Noirs that reward cellaring.

Pinot Noir Oregon	04	03	$$
Pinot Noir Bonshaw Yamhill County	**04**	03	$$$
Pinot Noir Estate Etzel Block Yamhill County		**04**	$$$

Penner-Ash Wine Cellars. Rich, assertive Pinots that nicely balance freshness and palate impact. Lynn Penner-Ash made her name at Rex Hill, crafting some of the most distinctive Oregon Pinot Noirs of the 1980s.

Pinot Noir Willamette Valley	**03**	**02**	$$$
Pinot Noir Seven Springs Vineyard Willamette Valley		**02**	$$$

Ponzi Vineyards. Dick Ponzi established this winery in the earliest days of the Oregon industry, in 1970. Today, Ponzi shares winemaking responsibilities with his daughter Luisa, and the house style continues to emphasize finesse and subtlety, with the Ponzi Reserve bottling adding power and concentration to the equation.

Pinot Noir Willamette Valley	**04**	**03**	$$
Pinot Noir Reserve	**03**	**02**	$$$

St. Innocent Winery. Veteran owner-winemaker Mark Vlossak is a dependable source for restrained, vibrant, food-friendly wines that are solidly structured but rarely overweight and never overoaked.

Pinot Noir Villages Cuvée Willamette Valley	03	02	$$
Pinot Noir White Rose Willamette Valley		03	$$$

Soter Vineyards. Tony Soter made his name with Cabernet Sauvignon in California at Spottswoode, as well as with his own Etude label, but in recent years he has devoted considerable time and energy to his own Oregon property, where he is crafting intensely fruity, layered Pinot Noirs that do not sacrifice balance or focus for power.

Pinot Noir Freedom Hill Yamhill County	03	02	$$$

WillaKenzie Estate. An excellent source for restrained, firm wines with vibrant, sweet fruit, and no excess weight. Look here, too, for an exceptionally good Pinot Meunier, a cousin of Pinot Noir.

Pinot Noir Willamette Valley	04	$$
Pinot Noir Kiana Willamette Valley	02	$$$

Ken Wright Cellars. A leading proponent of vineyard-designated wines, Ken Wright produces sweet, luscious, user-friendly wines from nearly a dozen of Oregon's best sites, with the objective of highlighting the individuality of each vineyard.

Pinot Noir Shea Vineyard Willamette Valley		03	02	$$$
Pinot Noir Canary Hill Vineyard Willamette Valley		03	02	$$$
Pinot Noir Carter Vineyard Willamette Valley	04	03	02	$$$

OTHER PRODUCERS TO LOOK FOR: Amity Vineyards, Belle Pente Wine Cellars, Brick House Wine Company, Domaine Serene, Elk Cove Vineyards, Erath Vineyards, Gypsy Dancer, Hamacher Wines, J. Christopher Wines, J. K. Carriere, King Estate, Lemelson Vineyards, Panther Creek, Raptor Ridge Winery, Rex Hill Vineyards, Siduri Wines, Sineann, Solena Cellars, Stoller Vineyards, Torii Mor Winery.

CONSISTENTLY EXCELLENT BUT SCARCE: Antica Terra, Thomas.

PINOT GRIS

Outside of the cool, hilly Alto Adige region of northeast Italy, no other region produces as many fresh, elegant examples of Pinot Gris (called Pinot Grigio in Italy) as Oregon. Unlike the weightier, spicier, and more flamboyantly ripe examples from Alsace, Oregon Pinot Gris is usually fermented to complete dryness, and few examples see much in the way of oak. Instead, the top producers make brisk, highly aromatic, light- to medium-bodied wines that emphasize clean orchard fruits such as apple, pear, and peach, often with citrus elements as well. These wines are normally best consumed within a couple years of the vintage for their fresh fruit; they are excellent choices with a range of warm-weather fare and go especially well with light, fresh seafood preparations. Pinot Gris rather than Chardonnay is the flagship white wine for many Oregon producers—a smart move in light of the popularity of these wines.

BANG FOR THE BUCK. With few Pinot Gris bottlings surpassing $20, and many of them more like $15, the best of these wines are good value.

2004 ★★★★ **2003** ★★

RECOMMENDED PRODUCERS

Belle Pente Wine Cellars. Round, succulent Pinot Gris in an Alsace mold, emphasizing rich, tropical fruit flavors rather than minerality.

Pinot Gris Willamette Valley	`04`	$$

Elk Cove Vineyards. A very good source for firmly structured, spicy, mineral-tinged wines that favor finesse and precision over weight.

Pinot Gris Willamette Valley	`04`	$$

King Estate. Stainless-steel fermented Pinot Gris in a bright, crisp, minerally style, and a more expensive Domaine bottling that has set a new Oregon standard for its intensity, fullness, and sheer scale.

Pinot Gris Estate Oregon	`04`	$$
Pinot Gris Domaine	`03`	$$

Raptor Ridge. Excellent, structured Pinot Gris with precise, focused, ripe fruit flavors.

Pinot Gris Willamette Valley	`04`	$$

St. Innocent Winery. Based on an Alsace model, the Shea Pinot Gris is partly fermented in barrels to add roundness and texture to its precise, mineral-driven flavors.

Pinot Gris Shea Vineyard Willamette Valley	`03`	$$

Sokol Blosser. Complex, spicy, firm Pinot Gris that is adamantly dry but not at the expense of its vibrant fruit.

Pinot Gris Dundee Hills	`04`	`03`	$$

Solena Cellars. Crisp, bright, highly aromatic Pinot Gris with strong orchard fruit and mineral flavors.

Pinot Gris Oregon	`04`	`03`	$$

WillaKenzie Estate. The estate has a long-standing reputation for producing clean, vibrant Pinot Gris with assertive mineral and citrus qualities.

Pinot Gris	`04`	`03`	$$

Key to Vintage Ratings		Key to Assessments of Specific Wines	
★★★★★	Outstanding	**`03`**	An excellent to outstanding example *of that wine*
★★★★	Excellent	`03`	A good to very good example *of that wine*
★★★	Good to very good	03	A disappointing effort (often due to a
★★	Fair to average		difficult vintage)
★	Poor		

OTHER WHITE WINES OF OREGON

Some producers who offer Pinot Gris are also trying their hands with Pinot Blanc and Riesling, two other varieties also produced in Alsace. Some have even begun to experiment successfully with Gewürztraminer and Viognier, but these are generally oddities rather than truly commercial ventures. Chardonnay continues to be a confusing problem child in Oregon, with many wineries producing exotic, fleshy wines with limited flavor interest and food compatibility. Happily, producers serious about Chardonnay are beginning to settle on a set of clones from Burgundy, which are already beginning to yield more vivid, elegantly styled wines. Rather than attempt to compete with richer Chardonnays from California, Burgundy, and elsewhere, some Oregon producers are raising their wines in stainless steel rather than oak barrels and at least partly blocking the malolactic fermentation to in an attempt to make crisp, fruit-driven wines without the heavier vanilla, clove, and butterscotch manifestations of oak.

2004 ★★★★ 2003 ★★

RECOMMENDED PRODUCERS

Amity Vineyards. Racy, spicy Pinot Blanc that speaks Italian rather than French.

Pinot Blanc Willamette Valley	04	$$

Brick House Wine Company. Smoky, dense, round Chardonnays that resist going blowzy. This estate is now farmed entirely by organic methods.

Chardonnay Willamette Valley		03	$$
Chardonnay Cascadia Willamette Valley	04	03	$$

Chehalem. The house's Chardonnays emphasize vibrant minerality and crisp, focused fruit, although the Ian's bottling is in a distinctly more powerful style.

Chardonnay Inox Willamette Valley	05	04	$$
Chardonnay Ian's Reserve Willamette Valley		03	$$$

Domaine Serene. Well-balanced Chardonnays with deep, ripe fruit, finesse and structure, with a record for aging nicely in bottle.

Chardonnay Clos du Soleil Vineyard Willamette Valley	02	$$$
Chardonnay Etoile Vineyard Willamette Valley	02	$$$

Elk Cove Vineyards. Rich, powerful, smoky Alsace-influenced Pinot Blanc and equally assertive Riesling that's loaded with ripe, even exotic fruit flavors.

Pinot Blanc Willamette Valley	04	$$
Riesling Estate Willamette Valley	04	$$

Evesham Wood Winery. Russ Raney produces creamy, smoky, mineral-laced Chardonnays that reflect his European winemaking sensibility.

Chardonnay Le Puits Sec Willamette Valley	04	03	$$

St. Innocent. Elegant, restrained wines with spine, emphasizing tangy, fresh fruit and sound acidity.

Pinot Blanc Willamette Valley   `04` $$

OTHER PRODUCERS TO LOOK FOR: Adelsheim Vineyards (Auxerrois), J. Christopher Wines (Riesling, Chardonnay), Rex Hill Vineyards (Chardonnay).

WASHINGTON

The proliferation of new wineries in Washington State has slowed in the past couple of years, but the landscape today is radically different from even 15 years ago. As recently as the early 1990s the Washington wine scene was dominated by a few large and well-capitalized players who also owned a high percentage of planted vineyard land. Today, most of the excitement is being generated by small, quality-minded wineries, including a number of new entries, with the industrial-scale producers mostly competing at the low end of the market. In fact, more than half of the wineries recommended in this chapter did not exist in 1995. Many of these players are closely involved in farming the vineyards from which they purchase fruit, and some are even buying land and planting their own vines—the ultimate step for ensuring the best possible raw materials to make consistently good wines.

Cabernet and Merlot are Washington's most serious and successful varieties, with Syrah rapidly increasing in popularity thanks to the efforts of some talented newcomers. Red wine is generally growing as a percentage of total production of premium wines, even if Riesling still has considerable commercial importance.

At the level of the most talented producers, Washington's red wines offer terrific definition of fruit flavor and generally juicy acidity; they are typically more vibrant and less alcoholic than big reds from California—not to mention less pricey—but riper and less obviously soil-driven than wines from Bordeaux. But there are also far too many remarkably bad if not flawed wines that have no place in a civilized society. The fruit-preservation philosophy of many of the University of California/Davis–trained winemakers who founded the Washington wine industry has typically caused them automatically to add acidity in an attempt to make more stable and more age-worthy bottles—even to the extent of making hard, ungenerous wines. Others extract too heavily, making dark and dense but gritty and overly tannic wines—wines that are impressive to taste but not much fun to drink. But an increasing number of younger winemakers are now crafting more graceful, natural wines. They are learning how to tame the

WASHINGTON WINE GEOGRAPHY & CLIMATE CONDITIONS

Don't think of the rain forest of the Olympic peninsula and the drizzle and overcast sky of Seattle when you think of Washington State wine. On the contrary: most of Washington's grapes are grown in the desert east of the Cascade Mountains, in the Columbia and Yakima River valleys, where annual rainfall is so low that the vineyards must be irrigated. The vines in Washington benefit from long daylight hours during the summer, and a longer growing season than California (grapes are usually picked well into October). Although daytime temperatures can be quite hot, frequently surpassing 100 degrees, generally cool September nights allow the grapes to retain healthy acidity, resulting in wines with noteworthy intensity of varietal character. The greatest threat to grape growing in Washington is winter frost, which can sometimes be severe enough to kill vines. Indeed, significant frost damage occurred during the winters of 1996 and 2004.

strong tannins produced by many of the state's most important vineyards, through later harvesting of thoroughly ripe fruit, gentler handling of the grapes, and meticulous *elévage* using top-quality (and usually a high percentage of French) barrels. The best of these wines offer the lusher textures most consumers seek without compromising the wines' ability to age.

CABERNET SAUVIGNON & MERLOT

Merlot and Cabernet Sauvignon clearly perform well in a variety of Washington sites. In recent years, the trend has been to blend these varieties, sometimes with Cabernet Franc and even Petit Verdot and Malbec thrown into the mix. These so-called Bordeaux blends account for a growing percentage of today's most successful Washington reds. While many of these wines come from two or more vineyards, some of the best among them are from a single site. Careful blending of varieties has resulted in better-balanced, more complex, and complete wines, the finest of which can be compared to top wines from California and Bordeaux.

Another trend, and one that may be dangerous in the long run, is the tendency of some producers to try to compete with the superrich cult Cabernets of Napa Valley, which commonly command high prices. But attempting to craft ever-larger, more extracted, and darker wines (often by picking overripe fruit and then being forced to acidify, or even to add water to bring down alcohol levels and finish fermentations) risks sacrificing the features that make Washington's wines so captivating: their combination of ripe tannins, sound acids, moderate alcohol, and intense fresh fruit flavors that avoid going porty or pruney.

BANG FOR THE BUCK. Washington State's wines in general remain reasonably priced. At the high end, the reds are not cheap, but the finest examples match up well against the best Cabernet- and Merlot-based wines from Bordeaux and California.

2004 ★★★+   2003 ★★★   2002 ★★★★–

RECOMMENDED PRODUCERS

Abeja. In just a few years, John Abbott has established a cult following in the local market for his Cabernet. In the best years, there is also a reserve bottling.

	04	03	
Cabernet Sauvignon Columbia Valley	04	03	$$$

Andrew Will. Rich, layered, age-worthy wines from some of the top vineyards in the state. As of the 2002 vintage, veteran winemaker Chris Camarda has switched from varietal to vineyard labeling of his numerous wines, as he believes that he can make more complete wines by blending varieties.

	03	02	
Ciel du Cheval Vineyard Red Wine Red Mountain	03	02	$$$
Champoux Vineyard Red Wine Columbia Valley	03	02	$$$
Sorella Red Wine Columbia Valley	03	02	$$$$

Baer Winery. Consistently lush, ripe Bordeaux blends from Lance Baer, formerly the assistant winemaker at DeLille Cellars.

	04	03	02	
Ursa Red Wine Columbia Valley	04	03	02	$$
Arctos Red Wine Columbia Valley	04	03	02	$$$$

Betz Family Winery. Bob Betz, who spent more than 25 years in a variety of positions for Chateau Ste. Michelle and is one of a handful of American Masters of Wine, makes some of Washington's richest and most complete red wines from Bordeaux varieties. Happily, the construction of a new winery will allow Betz to increase production in the years ahead.

	04	03	
Clos de Betz Red Wine Columbia Valley	04	03	$$$
Père de Famille Cabernet Sauvignon Columbia Valley	04	03	$$$

Cadence Winery. One of the most exciting new Washington red wine ventures of recent years. Working with fruit from some of the state's top sites, husband and wife Ben Smith and Gaye McNutt, formerly a Boeing flight controls analyst and a Microsoft lawyer, respectively, make small quantities of unusually suave, minerally, claret-like wines, with most of their blends featuring a healthy dollop of Cabernet Franc.

	04	03	02	
Ciel du Cheval Vineyard Red Wine Red Mountain	04	03	02	$$$
Tapteil Vineyard Red Wine Red Mountain	04	03	02	$$$
Bel Canto Red Wine Red Mountain	04	03	02	$$$

DeLille Cellars. This winery's flagship red blend, Chaleur Estate, has always been cool, understated, and gripping in the manner of a Médoc wine. Recent vintages have brought more generosity of texture.

Chaleur Estate Red Wine Yakima Valley	03	02	01	$$$$

Januik Winery. Mike Januik is one of Washington State's most consistent winemakers, turning out firm, satisfying, varietally accurate red wines at very reasonable prices.

Red Wine Columbia Valley	04	03	02	$$
Cabernet Sauvignon Columbia Valley	03	02	01	$$
Cabernet Sauvignon Champoux Vineyard Columbia Valley	03	02	01	$$$

Leonetti Cellars. One of Washington's elite sources of red wine since the late 1970s, and as impressive today as ever. Leonetti's Reserve Cabernet, offered in the better years and one of a handful of proven Washington collectibles, is consistently stellar. There's also a fascinating Sangiovese that normally has the sappy fruits, flowers, and spices to support its sizable component of new oak.

Cabernet Sauvignon Walla Walla Valley	03	02	01	$$$$
Cabernet Sauvignon Reserve Walla Walla Valley	03	02	01	$$$$

Northstar. Since the mid-1990s this Merlot specialist has offered remarkably consistent, dense, sweet wines characterized by varietally accurate notes of dark berries, bitter chocolate, and spices.

Merlot Walla Walla Valley	03	02	01	$$$

Owen Roe. David O'Reilly makes big, full-bodied, fruit-driven reds under the Owen Roe (and Sineann) label. Consistently the best of these are his Cabernet Sauvignons from the steep, rocky DuBrul Vineyard in Yakima Valley.

Red Wine Yakima Valley	04	03	02	$$$
Cabernet Sauvignon DuBrul Vineyard Yakima Valley	04	03	02	$$$

Quilceda Creek Vintners. Arguably Washington's most dependably outstanding Cabernet Sauvignon over the past 20 years—with today's fleshier and increasingly refined wines giving Napa Valley cult Cabs a run for their money. The Golitzin family's flagship wine now comes from their portion of the superb Champoux Vineyard. Their Merlot, produced in limited quantities, has also become one of the best in the state.

Cabernet Sauvignon Washington State	04	03	02	$$$$

Ross Andrew Winery. Ross Mickel, who is also assistant winemaker for Betz Family Vineyard, has bottled a typically dense but suave Cabernet Sauvignon under the Ross Andrew label since 1999, usually blended with some Merlot.

Cabernet Sauvignon Columbia Valley	03	02	$$

Woodward Canyon Winery. One of a few Washington wineries that have turned out terrific Cabernet Sauvignon–based wines (and Chardonnays) for more than two decades, although a few recent reds have not been up to past standards. Woodward Canyon's second label, Nelms Road, offers good value in Cabernet and Merlot.

	03	02	01	
Cabernet Sauvignon Artist Series Columbia Valley	03	02	01	$$$
Estate Red Wine Columbia Valley	03	02	01	$$$

OTHER PRODUCERS TO LOOK FOR: Abeja, Basel Cellars, Cayuse Winery, Chateau Ste. Michelle, Côte Bonneville, Dunham Cellars, Isenhower Cellars, L'Ecole No. 41, Matthews Cellars, Sineann, Soos Creek Cellars, Spring Valley Vineyard, Syzygy.

OTHER RED WINES OF WASHINGTON

"Other red wines" in Washington increasingly means Syrah and its Rhône Valley cousins, as these grapes appear to be at home in the climate of the high desert and are enjoying a surge of popularity. Syrah is now the state's third most widely planted premium red grape variety following Cabernet Sauvignon and Merlot. Washington Syrah comes in a range of styles and flavors: from densely packed, superripe, chunky wines aged in a high percentage of American oak barrels to more aromatically perfumed and harmonious bottlings that combine classic northern Rhône notes of black fruits, violet, pepper, and smoked meat, and are made in French oak. The best of these are among the most interesting Syrahs made outside France, and the category appears to offer great potential for Washington State.

BANG FOR THE BUCK. High-quality Washington Syrah is rarely cheap, but the best wines today are at the same level of quality as similarly priced items from California and Australia.

2004 ★★★+   2003 ★★★   2002 ★★★★–

RECOMMENDED PRODUCERS

Basel Cellars. Rich but firm-edged red wines, with Syrah consistently the best of them.

	04	03	02	
Syrah Walla Walla Valley	04	03		$$$
Syrah Lewis Vineyard Reserve Walla Walla Valley	04	03	02	$$$

Betz Family Winery. Bob Betz's Syrahs are at once silky, highly concentrated and wild— and, along with those of Cayuse, more Rhône-like in style than any others in Washington State.

	04	03	02	
La Serenne Syrah Columbia Valley	04	03	02	$$$
La Côte Rousse Syrah Red Mountain	04	03	02	$$$

Cayuse Winery. Frenchman Christophe Baron specializes in compellingly aromatic, layered Syrahs with a distinct Old World flavor, from a rocky vineyard in Walla Walla Valley. He also produces a tiny quantity of Viognier that's a dead ringer for great Condrieu.

Syrah En Cerise Vineyard Walla Walla Valley	`03`	`02`	$$$
Syrah Cailloux Vineyard Walla Walla Valley	`03`	`02`	$$$

K Vintners. Owner-winemaker Charles Smith produces small lots of multiple Syrah bottlings, the finest of which come from vineyards in Walla Walla Valley. These are flamboyant, idiosyncratic wines that combine powerful New World berry fruit with wilder Old World notes of meat and earth.

Cougar Hills Syrah Walla Walla Valley	`03`	`02`	$$$
Morrison Lane Syrah Walla Walla Valley	`03`	02	$$$

McCrea Cellars. Doug McCrea was a Washington State pioneer of Rhône varieties—not just Syrah but also Viognier, Roussanne, Grenache, Mourvèdre, and Counoise—and his wines are still among the state's elite examples. His Amerique bottling, aged in American oak, is his version of a lush, sweet Australian Shiraz, while his Sirocco is a classic blend of southern Rhône grapes.

Syrah Boushey Grand Cote Vineyard Red Mountain		`02`	$$$
Sirocco Red Wine Washington State	`03`	`02`	$$$
Amerique Syrah Amerique Yakima Valley		`02`	$$$

Rulo Winery. A very good source of handcrafted wines, with Syrah, especially from Silo Vineyard, consistently interesting. Very reasonable prices here.

Syrah Columbia Valley	`04`	`03`	`02`	$$
Syrah Silo Columbia Valley		`03`	`02`	$$

OTHER PRODUCERS TO LOOK FOR: Bunnell Family Cellars, DeLille Cellars, Eisenhower Cellars, Januik Winery, Syncline Wine Cellars.

CHARDONNAY

Chardonnay is by a wide margin Washington's most popular white variety in terms of vineyard acreage, yet the number of truly concentrated and consistently excellent wines is limited. Some of the most interesting Chardonnays come from the cooler Columbia Gorge viticultural area, which spills over into Oregon: the Celilo vineyard in particular is the source of some very fresh wines that often show a juicy nectarine component.

BANG FOR THE BUCK. Washington State's better Chardonnays are almost always reasonably priced.

2005 ★★★★+ **2004** ★★★★– **2003** ★★★

RECOMMENDED PRODUCERS

Abeja. Cabernet Sauvignon accounts for the majority of this winery's production, but recent vintages of Chardonnay have been consistently rich, leesy, and satisfying.

Chardonnay Walla Walla Valley	04	03	$$

Chateau Ste. Michelle. New winemaker Bob Bertheau has taken this huge producer's white wines to a higher level in the past couple of vintages. The best news of all is that these Chardonnays are reasonably priced and enjoy wide availability in the retail market.

Chardonnay Canoe Ridge Estate Columbia Valley	04	03	$$
Chardonnay Cold Creek Vineyard Columbia Valley		03	$$

Forgeron Cellars. A very good source of intense, lively Chardonnays with citrus and mineral character and subtle oak spice.

Chardonnay Columbia Valley	04	$$

Januik Winery. Mike Januik, who directed winemaking at Chateau Ste. Michelle through the 1990s, offers spicy, brisk, food-friendly Chardonnays under his eponymous label.

Chardonnay Elerding Vineyard Columbia Valley	04	03	$$
Chardonnay Cold Creek Vineyard Columbia Valley	04	03	$$

Woodward Canyon. Although better known outside the state for its red wines, Woodward Canyon's Chardonnays have been consistently excellent since the 1980s, appearing on the lists of most of Seattle's top restaurants.

Chardonnay Columbia Valley	04	03	$$
Chardonnay Estate Vineyard Walla Walla Valley		03	$$$

Ken Wright Cellars. This first-rate Oregon Pinot Noir producer also offers a consistently dense, expressive, and juicy Chardonnay from the Celilo Vineyard, with characteristic aromas of stone fruits.

Chardonnay Celilo Vineyard Washington State	03	$$

OTHER PRODUCERS TO LOOK FOR: Buty Winery, Harlequin Wine Cellars.

OTHER WHITE WINES OF WASHINGTON

For years, Washington State has specialized in inexpensive, crisp white wines—primarily Riesling but also Sémillon, Sauvignon Blanc, and Chenin Blanc—that offer solid varietal character and food compatibility. Along with the rise in popularity of Syrah in recent years has come growing interest in Viognier, the scented white grape that's at its best in Condrieu, in the northern Rhône Valley.

BANG FOR THE BUCK. Washington's "other white wines" are generally fairly priced, and are often excellent values.

RECOMMENDED PRODUCERS

Buty Winery. This winery offers a consistently interesting white blend in which the honey and fig character of Sémillon is perked up by some crisp, tank-aged Sauvignon Blanc. Buty also offers a very good Chardonnay from the Connor Lee Vineyard.

White Wine Columbia Valley	`04`	`03`	$$

Chateau Ste. Michelle. This winery has a long track record for crisp, juicy Rieslings with noteworthy intensity of flavor. Most savory of all is their Eroica, a slightly off-dry stone-fruit-and-spice-bomb of a Riesling made with the participation of Germany's Ernst Loosen. The less complex, somewhat sweet basic Columbia Valley bottling is hard to beat in its price range.

Riesling Columbia Valley		`04`	$
Eroica Riesling Columbia Valley	`05`	`04`	$$

DeLille Cellars. This winery's Sauvignon Blanc–Sémillon blend has for years been one of Washington's most intriguing white wines, often quite tight and dominated by its oak element upon release but gaining in complexity and richness with a few years of bottle aging.

Chaleur Estate White Wine Columbia Valley	`04`	`03`	$$$

Harlequin Wine Cellars. The lively Viognier from this small family winery offers citrus and peach character lifted by a floral nuance.

Viognier Clifton Vineyard Columbia Valley	`04`	$$

L'Ecole No. 41. This large, established winery in Walla Walla, also a reliable source for Cabernet, Merlot, and Syrah, is one of the few remaining Washington State wineries to offer serious Sémillons with concentration and personality.

Barrel Fermented Semillon Columbia Valley	`03`	$
Semillon Seven Hills Vineyard Estate Walla Walla Valley	`03`	$$

McCrea Cellars. Noteworthy Viognier and Roussanne from this specialist in Rhône varieties.

Viognier Red Mountain	`04`	$$
Roussanne Red Mountain	`04`	$$

Syncline Wine Cellars. Syncline works primarily with Rhône varieties, purchasing fruit from multiple sites around the state. The fruit-driven Viognier always offers early appeal.

Viognier Columbia Valley	`05`	`04`	$$

OTHER PRODUCERS TO LOOK FOR: Abeja (Viognier), Alexandria Nicole Cellars (Viognier and Sauvignon Blanc), Cayuse Winery (Viognier), Chinook Wines (Sémillon and Sauvignon Blanc), Columbia Winery (Riesling).

SOUTHERN

HEMISPHERE

AUSTRALIA

Australian wine experienced explosive growth in the U.S. market during the first years of the new millennium, more than doubling its share of total imported wines between 2000 and 2004 alone. As of the end of 2005, Australia was the second largest category of imported wine in the U.S. (measured by liters), trailing only Italy. Clearly, American wine lovers gravitate toward technically clean, fruit-driven wines that are labeled by variety and in English, and carry gentle price tags. In fact, the overwhelming majority of recent growth in Australian wine has come at the low end of the price spectrum, where Australia offers value that's hard to beat for the mainstream consumer, especially in inexpensive brands with animals on the label, such as Yellow Tail and Black Swan.

Two keys to wine quality in Australia are the continent's mostly hot and dry climate and its great number of technically proficient winemakers. Australia's wine regions are spread across the southern rim of the country, generally close to the sea, from the Hunter Valley, just above Sydney on the east coast, across to the Margaret River, south of Perth on the west coast—a distance of roughly 2,000 miles. (The generic appellation South Eastern Australia is used to describe blended wines from virtually anywhere but Western Australia.) Making blanket statements about Australia's weather in a given growing season would be almost like saying that Southern California and North Carolina experienced the same climatic conditions.

Even within fairly small areas conditions can vary dramatically according to ocean influence, altitude, and type of soil. The often scorchingly hot Barossa Valley in South Australia, for example, can produce red wines that approach vintage port in their dried-fruit flavors and alcoholic heft. But parts of the Clare Valley, less than 50 miles away, are significantly cooler. At the same time, though, Barossa benefits from a high percentage of old vines with deep root systems, which are more likely to be able to get water than younger vines in other regions, which rely heavily on irrigation and scarce water resources. The complicated wine geography of Australia resists easy generalizations.

Key to Vintage Ratings		Key to Assessments of Specific Wines	
★★★★★	Outstanding	**03**	An excellent to outstanding example *of that wine*
★★★★	Excellent	03	A good to very good example *of that wine*
★★★	Good to very good	03	A disappointing effort (often due to a
★★	Fair to average		difficult vintage)
★	Poor		

SHIRAZ & OTHER
RHÔNE VALLEY VARIETIES

Although Australia still ships a huge amount of mostly low-end Chardonnay to North America, Australia's charge in recent years has been led by its signature red grape variety, Shiraz (called Syrah in France). To a great degree, Shiraz, despite a long history in Australia, was a second-class citizen there until the wines were discovered by international markets in the 1990s, and particularly by American wine critics and wine drinkers. The new gold rush was on. Many of the most hotly pursued Shiraz bottlings in the North American market today did not even exist a decade ago.

With its lush, sweet berry profile, Australian Shiraz often bears as much resemblance to California Zinfandel as it does to Syrah from the northern Rhône Valley, but the latter type of wine—less full-bodied, and more spicy, peppery, and floral—can also be found in cooler growing areas of Australia. As proof of this variety's versatility, it is planted in virtually every region of Australia save the coldest; it's found alongside cooler-climate grapes such as Riesling and Sauvignon Blanc as well as in hotter, drier areas with its more traditional companions, notably Grenache and Viognier. Styles of Shiraz range as widely as the variety is planted, from Clare Valley and Margaret River examples that can mimic the northern Rhône to blockbuster bottlings from McLaren Vale and especially Barossa Valley that can make young vintage port seem wimpy. It should be noted that most fans of this variety have a clear preference for one style over the other.

Through the late 1990s and the early years of the new century, the trend was to make bigger and riper Shirazes by letting the fruit hang later into the autumn. Often, however, grape sugars rise more through dehydration of the fruit than from true ripening. The resulting wines, especially from the hottest, driest years, often show aromas and flavors of dried or cooked fruits, extremely low natural acidity, and alcohol of 16 percent or more. Sometimes the flavors are distinctly meaty or salty. These wines, many of which are far more popular in North America than in the local market, can be impressive to taste for their sheer weight and texture but tiring to drink, and some do not have the balance to age gracefully. Many North American wine lovers have apparently caught on, as the market for such wines appears to have passed its peak, and many producers are backing away from this extreme style.

Shiraz's Rhône Valley cousin Grenache has been increasing in popularity, and quality, in the past decade. The best examples are fat, creamy, and loaded with raspberry fruit, with gentle tannins that will not stand in the way of early consumption. And many Grenache-Shiraz-Mourvèdre blends (sometimes simply labeled GSM) are quite popular today, some of them extremely affordable.

RECOMMENDED PRODUCERS

Brokenwood. Luscious, berry-dominated wines offering opulent texture and noteworthy complexity. As ripe as they usually are, they never lack for elegance or precision. These have proven to be age worthy, gaining in complexity but retaining sweet, spicy fruit over the medium term. The Graveyard Shiraz is one of Australia's best.

Shiraz Rayner Vineyard Hunter Valley		02	$$$$
Shiraz Graveyard Vineyard Hunter Valley	03	02	$$$$$

Burge Family Winemakers. This Barossa winery is an excellent source of superripe and aromatically fascinating Rhône blends, mostly from old vines, with Grenache especially favored. The Olive Hill bottling is a blend of Syrah, Grenache, and Mourvèdre.

Garnacha Barossa Valley		03	$$$
Olive Hill Barossa Valley	03	02	$$$

Cape Mentelle. Margaret River Shiraz in a distinctly northern Rhône style, with notes of juicy dark berries, game, pepper, flowers, and spices. Very reasonably priced.

Shiraz Margaret River		`03`	$$

Charles Melton. This top-notch producer of Shiraz and Cabernet Sauvignon also makes a Châteauneuf-du-Pape–styled blend, Nine Popes, with outstanding aromatic complexity and generous fruit. For a wine in great demand in the local market, it's very reasonably priced.

Shiraz Barossa Valley		`02`	$$$
Nine Popes Barossa Valley		`02`	$$$

Clarendon Hills. Roman Bratasiuk's outsized red wines boast explosively ripe, dense berry fruit; thick, velvety texture; and complementary oak. Note that the wines are labeled Syrah rather than Shiraz, partly due to the fact that they are aged in French, not American, oak. (The flagship Syrah Astralis is extremely expensive and rare.) As revered as Bratasiuk's Syrahs are, his flamboyantly fruity Grenache bottlings are also among the most successful examples of the variety in the New World.

Hickinbotham Grenache Clarendon	`04`	`03`	$$$$
Kangarilla Grenache Clarendon	`04`	`03`	$$$$
Liandra Syrah Clarendon	`04`	`03`	$$$$
Hickinbotham Syrah Clarendon	`04`	`03`	$$$$$
Piggott Range Syrah Clarendon	`04`	`03`	$$$$$

Clonakilla. Tangy, Rhône-like Shiraz bottlings, with vibrant berry, pepper, mineral, spice, and mint notes. The winery, which also makes an excellent Viognier, blends a bit of this variety with its Shiraz à la Côte-Rôtie.

Hilltops Shiraz New South Wales		`05`	`04`	$$
Shiraz/Viognier Canberra	`05`	`04`	`03`	$$$

Coriole. This McLaren Vale winery's flagship Shiraz is the Lloyd Reserve, but its basic Shiraz and Lalla Rookh Grenache/Shiraz blend are consistently peppery, shapely, and vibrant wines for the price.

Lalla Rookh Old Vines McLaren Valley		`03`	`02`	$$
Shiraz McLaren Vale	`03`	`02`	`01`	$$$
Lloyd Reserve Shiraz McLaren Vale			`02`	$$$$

D'Arenberg. Enticingly lush, fruit-driven wines that offer early appeal but have the structure for midterm aging. There's a mind-boggling array of both red and white wines here, most with distinctive names, of which those from Rhône Valley grapes are best.

The Footbolt Shiraz McLaren Vale	`04`	`03`	$$
The Laughing Magpie Shiraz/Viognier McClaren Vale		`04`	$$$
The Dead Arm Shiraz McLaren Vale	`04`	`03`	$$$$

Elderton. Flamboyant, fleshy wines that often show exotic American oak tones. The flagship Command Shiraz is a massively rich wine that doesn't quite go over the top.

Shiraz Barossa Valley	`04`	`03`	`02`	$$
Command Shiraz Barossa Valley		`02`	`01`	$$$$

Fox Creek. Bold, full-bodied, accessible wines that deliver a wave of berry and chocolate flavor. The house style ensures satisfying early drinking.

JSM McLaren Vale	03	02	$$
Reserve Shiraz McLaren Vale	04	03	$$$$

Henschke. While the iconic and virtually unobtainable Hill of Grace Shiraz is this venerable winery's most famous bottling, their excellent Mount Edelstone is nearly as good, with great richness and purity and impressive cellaring potential. (The Cyril Henchke Cabernet is a consistent winner too.)

Mount Edelstone Shiraz Eden Valley	03	02	$$$$

Howard Park. Unusually taut, focused Shiraz bottlings in the context of Australia, from the isolated, maritime-influenced southwest corner of the continent. (Note that Howard Park's MadFish label is a reliable source of good inexpensive wine.)

Leston Shiraz Margaret River	04	03	$$
Scotsdale Shiraz Great Southern	04	03	$$

Jim Barry Wines. This large estate in the Clare Valley is best known for its dense, super-ripe, often liqueur-like Armagh Shiraz, but the McRae Wood bottling is nearly as exotic at a fraction the price.

The McRae Wood Shiraz Clare Valley	03	02	$$$
The Armagh Shiraz Clare Valley		02	$$$$$

Kay Brothers Amery. This old winery produces opulent but balanced Shiraz best suited for medium-term drinking. Oak is used judiciously here, allowing the wines' sweet berry fruit to shine. The rare and expensive Block 6 features vines that exceed 100 years of age.

Shiraz Hillside Shiraz McLaren Vale	02	$$$
Block 6 Shiraz McLaren Vale	02	$$$$

Kaesler. A Barossa specialist in full-bodied, exotically fruity Shiraz bottlings and blends: these wines typically avoid the cooked character shown by too many high-alcohol examples from this region. Kaesler also makes the scarce and pricey Old Bastard Shiraz.

Avignon Barossa Valley	04	$$

Leasingham. Sweet, thick Shiraz bottlings that may not be the last word in refinement and vibrancy but are excellent values, especially the Bin 61. Leasingham also makes a good inexpensive Riesling, the Bin 7.

Bin 61 Shiraz Clare Valley	03	02	$$
Classic Clare Shiraz Clare Valley	02	01	$$$

Mitolo. Very intense Shirazes that display the superripe character of many new-wave Australian wines but manage to maintain focus and balance.

The Jester Shiraz McLaren Vale		04	$$
G.A.M. Shiraz McLaren Vale	04	03	$$$

IMPORTANT AUSTRALIAN PLACE NAMES

South Australia: This state dominates production in Australia, accounting for nearly half of all grapes crushed. McLaren Vale, south of Adelaide, enjoys a Mediterranean climate thanks to proximity to the ocean, with warm, dry summers and most of its precipitation concentrated in the winter months. With irrigation necessary but water scarce, the best wines come from low-yielding old vines with deep roots. McLaren Vale is best known for its fleshy, full-flavored Shirazes and Cabernets, but Grenache is on the upswing and there is also a good bit of mostly low-acid Chardonnay. The Adelaide Hills to the east of South Australia's capital offer a coolish climate conducive to making vibrant Sauvignon Blanc and Chardonnay, as well as some finer and more elegant expressions of Merlot and Cabernet Franc. The Adelaide Plains, not surprisingly, is a hotter and drier area that produces rich, powerful reds.

Barossa Valley, Australia's single largest producer of quality wines, makes some of the country's richest, ripest, and most powerful reds, especially from old-vine plantings of Shiraz. Clare Valley, northwest of Barossa and distinctly cooler, yields more precise and sometimes more austere wines with typical minty undertones and more red than dark berry flavors. Just to the east of Barossa Valley but situated high above the valley floor, Eden Valley experiences considerably lower temperatures and higher rainfall. The rocky, well-drained soils here are best for Rieslings with firm acids, brisk citrus flavors, and considerable aging potential, as well as Chardonnays with better acidity than most. Shiraz is the most widely planted red variety, and is generally more aromatic, spicy, and fine-grained, as well as less weighty, than examples from Barossa.

Coonawarra is the best producing area within the mostly flat region midway between Melbourne and Adelaide known as the Limestone Coast, where cooling sea breezes bring down nighttime temperatures during the hot summer months. Coonawarra's famous terra rossa soil (essentially, red loam over porous, quickly draining limestone, with traces of oxidized iron) is prized for producing intensely flavored, elegant wines with firm structure and great aging capacity, especially Cabernet Sauvignon. Padthaway, which also has some terra rossa soil, is best known for its Chardonnays.

Victoria: Heathcote, to the north of Melbourne and generally warm and dry, produces age-worthy Shiraz, with dense, often ultraripe berry fruit character.

The very cool Mornington Peninsula south of the city of Melbourne produces fresh Chardonnay and Pinot Gris, as well as aromatically interesting Pinot Noir, but cool autumn weather normally arrives before Cabernet Sauvignon can ripen fully. Yarra Valley northeast of Melbourne, also reasonably cool and moist, produces a high percentage of Australia's best Pinot Noirs, as well as some elegant, firmly structured examples of Cabernet Sauvignon, typically blended with other red Bordeaux varieties. The cooler climate and slow ripening of the grapes in Yarra Valley allow for wines with excellent flavor intensity and fine tannins.

New South Wales: Hunter Valley, a very warm region north of Sydney that's often rather humid in summer and early fall, has long been the source of outstanding, long-lived Sémillon and juicy, earlier-maturing Chardonnay made in a modern and more oak-influenced style, typically with notes of tobacco and honeydew melon. Medium-weight, spicy and meaty Shiraz, often slow to mature in bottle, is also a specialty of Hunter Valley.

Western Australia: Situated on the extreme southwestern edge of the Australian land mass, the ocean-influenced Margaret River region benefits from a long growing season. Its Chardonnay is typically focused, crisp, and age worthy, while Cabernet Sauvignon has long been the favored red grape of the area, producing wines in a distinctly Bordeaux-like style. Shiraz has been growing in popularity, especially among winemakers and consumers who prefer a more precise Old-World style. The cooler Great Southern region to its south and east is home to a more Germanic expression of Riesling than is usually found in Australia, plus spicy, peppery Shiraz with Rhône-like weight and complexity.

Tasmania: This large island south of the eastern mainland of Australia offers the most temperate growing conditions of all, with slow ripening of the fruit ideal for making vibrant Pinot Noir and Chardonnay, as well as aromatic white varieties like Riesling, Pinot Gris, and Gewürztraminer. Not surprisingly, Tasmania is widely seen as Australia's best source of base material for sparkling wine. Plantings here are relatively tiny compared to South Australia, New South Wales, and Victoria but are increasing rapidly.

Mount Langi Ghiran. Spicy, peppery, cool-climate Shiraz from the western part of Victoria. The top bottling, called Langi Shiraz, is released on the late side, and has a track record for aging well.

Langi Shiraz Victoria	00	**99**	$$$

Penfolds. The most important element of the vast Beringer Blass/Southcorp group, Penfolds is best known for its legendary Grange Shiraz, Australia's most famous wine since it was established in the early 1950s. But Penfolds is a top source for red wines in every price range. (The cheap Koonunga Hill Shiraz/Cabernet, incidentally, is a terrific value in everyday red wine.)

Bin 128 Shiraz Coonawarra	03	**02**		$$
St. Henri Shiraz South Australia	**02**	**01**	00	$$$
Magill Estate Shiraz South Australia	03	02	01	$$$
Grange Shiraz South Australia	**01**	00	99	$$$$$

Rolf Binder Wines. This producer of rich, extroverted wines in a modern vein is also a highly sought-after consultant. Shiraz and Rhône blends are best here. (Binder's venture was formerly known as Veritas.)

Heinrich Shiraz/Mataro/Grenache Barossa Valley	**03**		$$
Halliwell Shiraz/Grenache Barossa Valley	**03**		$$
Hanisch Shiraz Barossa Valley	**03**	02	$$$$$

Rosemount Estate. The McLaren Vale outpost of the vast Rosemount empire produces an outstanding Syrah and one of Australia's best Grenache-Shiraz-Mourvèdre blends.

GSM McLaren Vale	02	**01**	$$
Balmoral Syrah McLaren Vale	**01**	00	$$$

Torbreck. Some of Australia's most successful Shiraz-based bottlings in an opulent, full-bodied style, capturing the extreme ripeness of the Barossa Valley but rarely veering off in a porty direction. The flagship Run Rig, a blend of Shiraz with a smidgeon of Viognier, is one of Australia's cult wines, with the price tag to prove it.

Woodcutter's Shiraz Barossa Valley	**05**	**04**	$$
The Steading Barossa Valley	**03**	**02**	$$$
Descendant Barossa Valley	04	**03**	**02**	$$$$
The Factor Shiraz Barossa Valley	**03**	**02**	$$$$

Two Hands Wines. Emphatically modern-style wines, with lavish but harmonious oak and deep, rich fruit combining to offer early accessibility. Michael Twelftree makes wines from several appellations in South Australia and Victoria, at a variety of price points. This négociant firm has targeted the American market, so availability is good in the U.S.

Angel's Share Shiraz McLaren Vale	**05**	04	$$
Lily's Garden Shiraz McLaren Vale	**04**	**03**	$$$
Bad Impersonator Shiraz Barossa Valley	04	**03**	**02**	$$$

Yering Station. A flamboyantly perfumed, silky fruit bomb of a Shiraz-Viognier in a crowd-pleasing style, but with considerable refinement.

Shiraz/Viognier Reserve Yarra Valley	**03**	**02**	$$$

OTHER PRODUCERS TO LOOK FOR: Balgownie Estate, Bowen Estate, Branson Coach House, The Colonial Estate, Giaconda, Jasper Hill, Langmeil Winery, Lengs & Cooter, Peter Lehmann, Pikes, Rockford, Trevor Jones, Vasse Felix, Wolf Blass, Yalumba.

SOLID SOURCES FOR INEXPENSIVE SHIRAZ AND RHÔNE BLENDS: Hardy's, Hill of Content, Jacob's Creek, Marquis Phillips, Woop Woop.

CABERNET SAUVIGNON & BORDEAUX BLENDS

Like its examples of Shiraz, Australia's Cabernet Sauvignon–based wines run a gamut of styles, from classic, Old World versions with spice, herb, and tobacco leaf character to flashier, more modern expressions of this variety. Not long ago, much of Australia's Cabernet Sauvignon was weedy or herbaceous (as most of its Merlot continues to be today). For a while, winemakers figured that if they could throw enough sweet American oak (or oak chips, or oak extract) into the mix, they might cover the absence of fruit ripeness. More often than not, though, the result was wines that resembled chocolate-covered dill pickles, and some of these wines, unfortunately, can still be found. But by doing a much better job matching the variety to the proper climate and soils, conscientious producers today are making thoroughly ripe and infinitely more complex wines that retain varietal Cabernet complexity while showing off their purity of fruit. And there is even some evidence that local drinkers who are tired of outsized Shirazes are once again seeking out top Cabernets whose ripeness is a bit less flamboyant.

Coonawarra has been Australia's leading Cabernet region for decades and enjoys the greatest concentration of older vines, but Margaret River has an equally high reputation for Cabernet. In both of these regions, Cabernet benefits from reasonably long maturation on the vine, which is generally necessary to produce wines that avoid a distinctly green, underripe streak.

RECOMMENDED PRODUCERS

Balgownie Estate. Now back in private hands following its sale by Mildara Blass in 1999, this estate is once again a solid source for restrained, concentrated Cabernet in an Old World style.

Cabernet Sauvignon Bendigo	04	03	02	$$$

Cullen. Diana Madeline is the new name for Cullen's flagship Bordeaux blend, one of Australia's handful of elite wines: claret-like, suave, and lush, with compelling aromatic complexity and unusually fine-grained tannins. This one is worth a special search of the marketplace.

Diana Madeline Cabernet Sauvignon/Merlot Margaret River	03	02	$$$$

Moss Wood. Moss Wood's brooding, complex Cabernet, with its notes of dark berries and tobacco, can mimic top-tier Bordeaux. Although it has proven to be long-lived, it's rarely hard in its youth.

Cabernet Sauvignon Margaret River	02 01	$$$

Mount Mary. The flagship Quintet bottling, a blend of Bordeaux varieties, is one of Australia's most refined and complex red wines, from the cooler Yarra Valley, best known for its Chardonnays and Pinot Noirs. Give this very expensive wine at least six to eight years in the cellar.

Quintet Yarra Valley	03 02	$$$$$

Penfolds. The Penfolds Cabernets are sometimes overshadowed by the producer's Shiraz bottlings, but they are flamboyantly rich, structured wines that need time to absorb their tannins and reveal their underlying fruit. The often exotically oaky but slow-aging Bin 707 has long been an Australian collectible, while the Bin 407 shows the dark-fruit-and-cedary-vanillin-oak Penfolds style at a much gentler price.

Bin 407 Cabernet Sauvignon South Australia	03 02	$$
Cabernet Sauvignon Bin 707 South Australia	02	$$$$

Vasse Felix. The first vineyard and winery established in the Margaret River region has long been known for its intense, elegant, slow-aging Cabernet-based wines from soils rich in gravel and loam. The Heytesbury Bordeaux blend is the winery's top bottling.

Heytesbury Cabernet Sauvignon Margaret River	02 01	$$$

Wynn's Coonawarra Estate. This important Coonawarra winery produces an impressively rich flagship Cabernet Sauvignon called John Riddoch as well as a basic Cabernet that can offer stunning value.

Cabernet Sauvignon Coonawarra	02 01	$
John Riddoch Cabernet Sauvignon Coonawarra	03 99	$$$$

Yarra Yering. Yarra Yering is a red wine specialist best known for its Dry Red Wine No. 1 and Dry Red Wine No. 2, the former a Cabernet Sauvignon–dominated Bordeaux blend, the latter a Shiraz with bits of Viognier and Marsanne. Both are consistently superb, and worth a search.

Dry Red Wine No. 1 Yarra Valley	04 02 01	$$$$

OTHER PRODUCERS TO LOOK FOR: Charles Melton, Clarendon Hills, Grosset, Howard Park, Henschke, Lake's Folly, Leeuwin Estate, Lindemans, Mount Mary, Parker Coonawarra Estate, Petaluma, Yeringberg.

SOLID SOURCES FOR INEXPENSIVE CABERNET: Brown Brothers, Grant Burge, Lindemans, Peter Lehmann, Seppelt, Wolf Blass, Yalumba.

OTHER RED WINES
OF AUSTRALIA

Pinot Noir has met with mixed results in Australia save for isolated examples. These are Pinots that come from relatively cool regions, where one or two years out of three an extended and moderate growing season allows the grapes to gain enough flavor before reaching excessive sugar levels. The problem for North American wine drinkers, however, is availability: the handful of truly interesting Australian Pinots, such as Coldstream Hills Reserve, Bindi Wine Growers, Bass Phillip, Kooyong, and Yering Station Reserve, are quite scarce in this market. Recent plantings of Zinfandel have turned out some interesting wines that in many cases are quite similar to ripe, powerful Shiraz, but these wines too are rarely sighted in North America.

CHARDONNAY

The export market for Australian Chardonnay was driven in the 1980s by what is called the Show Reserve style—attention-getting wines made for competitive tastings, usually marked by lavish oak spice, superripe tropical flavors, thick textures due to high alcohol, and sometimes even a bit of residual sugar to seduce early tasters. These wines can be difficult to take, either at the table or on their own. For better or worse, though, this is the style that defines Australian Chardonnay for many North American wine lovers. Fortunately, many producers have adjusted their wine-making regimens to make fresher, more vibrant, and energetic Chardonnays. The most obvious strategy has been to plant Chardonnay in regions and in microclimates better suited to making elegant wines with real flavor intensity than those with brute strength. Western Australia, particularly the Margaret River region, has emerged as a top growing area for Chardonnay, with superb wines also being produced in Victoria and the Adelaide Hills. Tasmania is showing promise as well.

Note that the list of featured wines in this section, as in the other sections of this chapter, does not include items that are produced in industrial quantities. But there is little question that Australia's best under-$10 bottles are perfectly acceptable.

RECOMMENDED PRODUCERS

Cullen. Intensely flavored Chardonnay that combines elegance and complexity with understated power and age worthiness. Here's proof that Australia can produce truly world-class Chardonnay.

Chardonnay Margaret River   `04` `03` $$$$

Leeuwin Estate. Leeuwin's Art Series Chardonnay is one of Australia's top collectible wines, in a distinctly Burgundian style: generous, powerful, and deep without being over the top, and capable of long and graceful development in bottle. The Prelude bottling is a more gently priced introduction to the style.

Prelude Vineyards Chardonnay Margaret River	04	03	02	$$
Art Series Chardonnay Margaret River	03	02	01	$$$$

Penfolds. This huge vineyard owner and producer has improved the quality of its entire white wine portfolio as a side benefit of its Yattarna project. Yattarna is a consistently outstanding Chardonnay that's often referred to as the white wine equivalent of the legendary Penfolds Grange Shiraz.

Yattarna Chardonnay South Eastern Australia	03	02	01	$$$$

Petaluma. Broad, rich, spicy Chardonnays with hazelnut and stone fruit nuances. Best is the single-vineyard Tiers bottling.

Chardonnay Adelaide Hills		03	$$
Tiers Chardonnay Piccadilly Valley	02	01	$$$

Vasse Felix. Classic examples of Margaret River Chardonnay: delineated and bright, with noteworthy intensity and, in the case of the Heytesbury, real complexity and breadth.

Chardonnay Adams Road Western Australia	05	04	03	$$
Chardonnay Heytesbury Margaret River	04	03	02	$$$

OTHER PRODUCERS TO LOOK FOR: Bannockburn, Bindi Wine Growers, Cape Mentelle, Coldstream Hills, Giaconda, Katnook Estate, Moss Wood, Mount Mary, Pierro, Rosemount Estate, Yering Station.

SOLID SOURCES FOR INEXPENSIVE CHARDONNAY: Houghton, Lindemans, Oxford Landing, Seppelt, Tyrrell's, Wyndham Estate.

OTHER WHITE WINES OF AUSTRALIA

Roughly 90 percent of Australian white wine shipped to America is Chardonnay. But the overwhelming majority of these exported bottles are plump, oaky, tropical-fruity wines that sell for less than $15. Today, Australia's other white varieties provide at least as many distinctive wines for serious wine lovers, if not the same volume of bottles. In recent years, there has been a surge of interest in cool-climate wines from Sauvignon Blanc, Riesling, and Viognier, mostly made in a crisp, refreshing style with little or no oak influence.

Riesling may be Australia's most undervalued wine in export markets. This variety thrives in cooler, marginal climates, and many producers in Western Australia as well as in the Clare and Eden valleys make dry, taut wines that display sharply delineated citrus and mineral flavors. Some of these wines are capable of slow and positive evolution in bottle, often developing petrol and earth notes like examples from Germany.

Sémillon has a long history in Hunter Valley, where it produces structured, individual wines with a track record for positive evolution in bottle. The emphatically dry nature of these wines as well as a general lack of sweetening oak has meant that these offbeat Sémillons were an acquired taste. Today this distinctly old-fashioned style is increasingly being supplanted by riper wines that are fermented in barrel like Chardonnay.

Sauvignon Blanc is increasing in popularity, no doubt riding the coattails of New Zealand's success with the variety in the export market. It is usually planted in cooler regions, such as Clare Valley, Eden Valley, and Margaret River, and is often blended with Sémillon. The normally unwooded, fresh style of these wines emphasizes bright citrus fruit and vibrancy. With rare exceptions, Australia's Sauvignons and Sauvignon-based blends are best enjoyed within a couple years of the vintage.

McLaren Vale and Barossa Valley are proving to be as hospitable to the white varieties of the Rhône Valley as they are to the reds. Cooler spots such as Yarra Valley are producing fresh, clean Viogniers that can represent the best value for that variety in the world. Trial plantings of other white Rhône varieties are being made across much of Australia.

BANG FOR THE BUCK. The best Australian Chardonnays are rarely cheap, but other Australian white wines are generally reasonably priced.

RECOMMENDED PRODUCERS

Brokenwood. This producer, which also offers top-notch Shiraz, makes a firm, dry, minerally version of Sémillon from Hunter Valley fruit, with penetrating citrus flavors.

Semillon Hunter Valley	05	04	$$

Cape Mentelle. A firm-edged, brisk blend of pungent, minerally, pepper-and-citrus Sauvignon and figgy Sémillon that showcases the incisive Margaret River style. Also good, rich Chardonnay.

Sauvignon/Semillon Margaret River	04	03	$$

Cullen. A consistently stunning Sauvignon Blanc–based blend, with tropical fruit and mineral notes given an extra dimension by some use of oak.

Sauvignon Blanc/Semillon Margaret River	04	03	$$$

D'Arenberg. The house style for white wines, including those from Rhône Valley varieties, emphasizes ripe but crisp flavors and intense fruitiness.

The Dry Dam Riesling McLaren Valey	05	04	$$
The Hermit Crab Viognier/Marsanne McLaren Vale	05	04	$$
The Money Spider Roussanne McLaren Vale	05	04	$$

Grosset. Juicy, stylish Clare Valley Rieslings that combine citrus fruits and bracing minerality. Chardonnay, Pinot Noir, and a Bordeaux blend called Gaia are also consistently excellent.

Watervale Riesling Clare Valley	05	04		$$
Polish Hill Riesling Clare Valley	05	04		$$

Henschke. The Eden Valley winery responsible for the revered Hill of Grace Shiraz also makes a consistently penetrating, ripe, and very persistent Riesling that combines notes of soft citrus fruits and powdered stone.

Julius Riesling Eden Valley	04	03	$$

Leeuwin Estate. Well-structured, energetic Riesling from one Australia's best white wine producers. This light-to-medium-bodied wine consistently combines wonderful fruit and firm, minerally acidity.

Art Series Riesling Margaret River	05	04	03	$$

Margan. This family-owned winery produces well-priced Sémillon with sweet orchard fruit and melon character, as well as an excellent example of Verdelho—a Portuguese variety enjoying growing popularity in Australia as an alternative to Chardonnay.

Semillon Hunter Valley	04	03	$$
Verdelho Hunter Valley	04	03	$

Mesh. Elegant, penetrating, heady dry Riesling with strong mineral, citrus, and stone fruit character. A joint venture between Riesling specialist Jeffrey Grosset and Robert Hill-Smith.

Riesling Eden Valley	05	04	$$

Mount Horrocks. Consistently excellent and compelling Rieslings from Clare Valley. The Cordon Cut Riesling, with multidimensional notes of high-toned tropical fruits, spices, and exotic herbs, is generally quite sweet, even when not affected by botrytis.

Riesling Watervale	05	04	$$
Cordon Cut Riesling Clare Valley	05	04	$$$

Pikes. The Pike Brothers are a superb source for concentrated, tangy, taut Clare Valley Rieslings that offer considerable early appeal but are capable of aging. The winery's other whites are also priced very reasonably.

Riesling Clare Valley	05	04	$$

Pipers Brook. A major venture in chilly Tasmania, Pipers Brook has done best to date with Alsace varieties like Riesling, Pinot Gris, and Gewürztraminer.

Riesling Tasmania	04	$$
Gewürztraminer Tasmania	04	$$

Plantagenet. Flavorful, elegant white wines, especially Riesling and Chardonnay. The winery's Omrah range is typically very good value.

Riesling Great Southern	05	04	03	$$

Tahbilk. Idiosyncratic, uncompromising Marsanne with nutty, honeyed, mineral complexity that needs time in bottle to unwind; a steal for the price.

Marsanne Central Victoria 05 03 02 $$

Yalumba. This large company is an excellent source for reasonably priced, elegant Rieslings and fragrant Viogniers with focus and restraint to their spicy floral and citrus qualities. The Y Series Riesling and Viognier offer outstanding value.

Riesling Y Series South Australia 05 04 $
Viognier Y Series South Australia 05 04 $
Viognier Eden Valley 05 04 $$
The Virgilius Viognier Eden Valley 04 03 $$$

OTHER PRODUCERS TO LOOK FOR: Alkoomie (Riesling and Sauvignon Blanc), Frankland Estate (Riesling), Leo Buring (Riesling), Moss Wood (Sémillon), Mount Langi Ghiran (Riesling), Pike & Joyce (Riesling), Stringy Brae (Riesling), Tim Adams (Riesling, Sémillon), Torbreck Vintners (Sémillon), Two Hands (Riesling).

SOLID SOURCES OF OTHER INEXPENSIVE AUSTRALIAN WHITE WINES: Mitchelton (Riesling), Penfolds (Riesling), Peter Lehmann (Sémillon and Riesling), Tyrrell's (Sémillon), Wolf Blass (Riesling).

SWEET & FORTIFIED WINES

Until the 1970s, when the table wine boom began in Australia, the local industry generally relied on fortified wines for survival in the export market. Even today, fortified, port-style wines from the Rutherglen region in northeast Victoria can be among the most profound examples of their kind made anywhere in the world. Based primarily on old stocks of Muscat and "Tokay," the latter actually the Muscadelle of Sauternes, these golden-brown elixirs offer remarkable complexity, although rare examples that include a high percentage of very old juice can soar well into $$$$$ territory. Rutherglen's fortified wines are normally made via a blending and aging process called the *solera* system (this is how most sherries are made), through which more mature barrels are continually topped up with younger wine of the same sort to ensure a continuity of house style and quality. Because Rutherglen Muscats and Tokays are blends of multiple vintages, they are not vintage-dated. The advantage, though, is that they are remarkably consistent. These extremely sweet, thick fortified wines typically carry between 18 and 20 percent alcohol, and show aromas and flavors of maple syrup, toffee, caramel, fruitcake, orange peel, and exotic spices.

Sauternes-style and late-harvest Rieslings are appreciated in the local Australian market, but few of these dessert wines are sent to North America in more than homeopathic quantities.

RECOMMENDED PRODUCERS

R. L. Buller & Sons. The scarce and very expensive Calliope Rare Muscat and Rare Tokay bottlings are best, but the Premium lineup, with off-the-charts levels of residual sugar, offers great value. The Calliope Rare Tokay contains some juice from the 1921 vintage, the year the winery was founded.

NV Premium Fine Muscat Rutherglen	$$
NV Premium Fine Tokay Rutherglen	$$
NV Calliope Rare Tokay Rutherglen	$$$$$

Campbells. Classic nutty-sweet, toffeed elixirs with more elegance and a bit less thickness than many fortified wines from Rutherglen. Here, too, there's a much more expensive "Rare" line, blends of component wines averaging over 60 years of age.

NV Tokay Rutherglen	$$$
NV Muscat Rutherglen	$$$

Chambers Rosewood. The "Rare" and "Grand" fortified wines of this revered family firm, founded in 1858, are priced like liquid gold (the Rare Muscat and Rare Muscadelle are $300 for 375 ml.). But the lush and thick entry-level wines, which have been aging for far less time, are consistently satisfying at a tiny fraction of the price.

NV Muscat Rutherglen	$$
NV Muscadelle Rutherglen	$$
NV Rare Muscat Rutherglen	$$$$$

DeBortoli Wines. A luscious, marmaladey dessert wine that has consistently been among Australia's best examples of the category for two decades. Bracing balancing acidity keeps the honeyed flavors from cloying.

Noble One Botrytis Semillon New South Wales	03	02	$$$

Key to Vintage Ratings		Key to Assessments of Specific Wines	
★★★★★	Outstanding	**03**	An excellent to outstanding example *of that wine*
★★★★	Excellent	03	A good to very good example *of that wine*
★★★	Good to very good	03	A disappointing effort (often due to a
★★	Fair to average		difficult vintage)
★	Poor		

NEW ZEALAND

New Zealand's ocean-influenced climate—markedly cooler than that of its neighbor, Australia—yields wines with admirable fruit intensity and crisp acidity. Fully two-thirds of New Zealand's wine production is white, and more than half of the wine it ships to America is Sauvignon Blanc. The North American market has developed a major thirst for these juicy, fresh Sauvignons, which are mostly free of oak influence. But New Zealand Pinot Noir, too, is growing rapidly in popularity here, thanks in large part to the emergence of the Central Otago growing region, which has exploded onto the world wine scene in the past five or six years with some stunning, fruit-driven Pinots.

High labor costs, considerable recent investment in frost-protection measures, and the strong New Zealand dollar are just three of the reasons why the average bottle of New Zealand wine is relatively high—significantly higher, for example, than the average bottle from Italy, Spain, Australia, Chile, and Argentina. There's virtually no dirt-cheap wine produced in New Zealand. On the other hand, very little New Zealand wine sells for more than $40—just a handful of bottlings from Bordeaux varieties or Pinot Noir—and white wine prices are mostly moderate.

SAUVIGNON BLANC

Sauvignon Blancs from New Zealand are generally sharply focused, unoaked wines, with bracing acidity, excellent fruit intensity and "cut," and a pungent citrus/grassy/herbal/peppery character not unlike Sauvignon Blancs from France's Loire Valley. Whereas the French versions (Sancerre and Pouilly-Fumé) tend to lead with their flinty mineral and soil tones, New Zealand's are more likely to privilege clean, fresh fruit. But the similarities between these two styles of Sauvignon are more important than the differences. The hub of Sauvignon Blanc production is the cool Marlborough region of New Zealand's South Island, the country's most important wine-producing area, with extensive plantings of Sauvignon vines.

While the brisk, steely style of Sauvignon Blanc has been much in demand with restaurant goers in America for the past several years, and while this is the style that put New Zealand Sauvignon on the world map, there is a somewhat worrying trend today toward bigger, riper, and softer examples of Sauvignon. This trend is especially noticeable in Marlborough, where large producers with high crop levels may have little choice but to let their fruit hang in the hope of making wines with less pungent bell pepper and jalapeño notes, not to mention asparagus and other strong vegetal

qualities. The result is wines with more tropical aromas and flavors—sometimes almost Chardonnay-like in character—plus, of course, some residual sugar. It remains to be seen if this approach succeeds in the marketplace. This issue is an important one for New Zealand because Sauvignon Blanc in recent years has accounted for 35 to 40 percent of total production and an even higher percentage of exports.

BANG FOR THE BUCK. New Zealand Sauvignon Blanc is generally well priced, with many large wineries offering solid examples in the $12 range. Note that a $$ wine is much more likely to cost $16 than $25.

2005 ★★★+   2004 ★★★–

RECOMMENDED PRODUCERS

Ata Rangi. This Martinborough winery may be better known for its Pinot Noir and Craighall Chardonnay, but its Sauvignon Blancs have been among New Zealand's purest and most satisfying in recent vintages.

Sauvignon Blanc Martinborough   `04` $$

Cloudy Bay. This winery has been New Zealand's most famous source of Sauvignon Blanc since the late 1980s, even if the competition is stiffer now. In cool years, Cloudy Bay's rather uncompromising wine can be distinctly peppery and herbaceous, but in a varietally accurate way. Recent vintages have been somewhat softer, riper, and less rigorous. Winemaker Kevin Judd also turns out some of New Zealand's best sparkling wine, called Pelorus.

Sauvignon Blanc Marlborough   `05` `04` $$

Dog Point Vineyard. For years, the superb Sauvignon Blanc grapes from this Marlborough vineyard were sold to Goldwater Estate, but the owners of this property launched their own superb Sauvignon with vintage 2002.

Sauvignon Blanc Marlborough   `05` `04` $$

Foxes Island. Sauvignon Blanc is a newcomer to the portfolio of this winery, previously a specialist in Pinot Noir and Chardonnay, but the 2004 vintage was an attention grabber.

Sauvignon Blanc Marlborough   `04` $$

Goldwater Estate. This producer's excellent Sauvignon Blanc was formerly called Dog Point Vineyard but is now New Dog, as the owners of the Dog Point Vineyard in Marlborough have insisted on sole use of the name. Goldwater Estate is based on the protected Waiheke Island, near Auckland, and has long been known for its expensive, oaky Cabernet and Merlot bottlings, which can be very good when vintage conditions are right.

Sauvignon Blanc New Dog Marlborough   `04` $$

Kim Crawford Wines. Dry, juicy Sauvignon Blancs, with perfumed notes of grapefruit, pineapple, and tarragon. There's also a somewhat weightier oak-aged version, but the wood can get in the way of the wine's varietal purity.

Sauvignon Blanc Marlborough   `05` $$

Matua Valley Wines. This winery, part of the huge Fosters group, has offered Sauvignon Blanc since the mid-1970s. Its basic bottling is always a terrific value.

Sauvignon Blanc Marlborough   `05` $
Paretai Sauvignon Blanc Marlborough   `04` `05` $$

Palliser Estate. Consistently one of the very best New Zealand Sauvignon Blancs made outside Marlborough—or anywhere in the country. The second label, Pencarrow, is especially good value.

Pencarrow Sauvignon Blanc Marlborough   `04` $
Sauvignon Blanc Marlborough   `04` $$

Pegasus Bay. This Waipara Valley producer makes one of New Zealand's most distinctive white wines, a gamey, minerally, layered, complex blend that combines Sauvignon Blanc with a sizable component of barrel-fermented Sémillon that goes through malolactic fermentation.

Sauvignon Blanc Waipara	04	$$

Seresin Estate. This producer's special Marama bottling is vinified with wild yeasts and aged on its lees in small oak barrels for more than a year. The result is one of New Zealand's densest, nuttiest, and most distinctive Sauvignons, in the style of a white Graves but with even more soil character than most of today's examples. The basic Sauvignon here also includes a bit of Sémillon and offers more typical notes of grapefruit, lime, pepper, and powdered stone.

Sauvignon Blanc Marlborough	04	$$
Marama Sauvignon Blanc Marlborough	04	$$$

Villa Maria. This large producer offers Sauvignon Blancs at multiple price points, and all of them offer considerable value. The Clifford Bay Reserve is spicy and stuffed with fruit, but the Cellar Selection is a bit more pliant and accessible earlier. Even the inexpensive Private Bin Sauvignon is consistently well made.

Private Bin Sauvignon Blanc Marlborough	05	$
Cellar Selection Sauvignon Blanc Marlborough	04	$$
Sauvignon Blanc Reserve Clifford Bay Marlborough	04	$$

OTHER PRODUCERS TO LOOK FOR: Babich, Forrest Estate, Jackson Estate, Kumeu River Wines, Mt. Difficulty, Nautilus Estate, Nobilo, Sileni Estates Winery, Te Mata Estate Winery.

CHARDONNAY & OTHER WHITE WINES OF NEW ZEALAND

Even if it is the country's second most important variety in terms of production, Chardonnay in New Zealand is of limited interest to international markets. Few sites appear capable of producing truly distinctive wines, and full crop levels and a high percentage of young vines further limit the grower's ability to transmit soil character into the bottle. Some wineries slap a lot of oak on their Chardonnays, with the result that the wines can be more about wood than about the variety. But fresh, unoaked Chardonnays made in a Sauvignon style have attracted a following in North America, especially where prices are reasonable.

New Zealand's Rieslings can be quite delicious. Despite their normally brisk acidity, they are rarely austere or difficult to enjoy in their youth; in fact, some of these wines are softened by a touch of residual sugar. Other Alsatian grapes like Gewürztraminer and Pinot Gris are gaining in popularity in New Zealand. Some New Zealand producers offer small quantities of late-harvest wines from botrytis-affected varieties such as Riesling, Sauvignon Blanc, and Sémillon. Thanks in large part to strong natural acidity to balance their extreme sweetness, these relatively scarce bottlings can be superb.

BANG FOR THE BUCK. A number of succulent, food-friendly Chardonnays, especially from larger, more export-minded producers, can be found in the $10 to $18 range and offer good value. Rieslings are reasonably priced, but rarely bargains.

2005 ★★★+   2004 ★★★–

RECOMMENDED PRODUCERS

Amisfield. In addition to its tangy, structured Pinot Noir, Amisfield offers excellent white wines, in particular a broad, serious, more or less dry Pinot Gris and one of New Zealand's most penetrating dessert Rieslings.

Pinot Gris Central Otago		04	$$
Noble Riesling Central Otago	04	03	$$$

Felton Road. This top producer of Pinot Noir also offers bracing but subtle dry Riesling from light schist soil in Central Otago.

Dry Riesling Central Otago	04	$$

Forrest Estate. The majority of this winery's production is Sauvignon Blanc but it also produces numerous Riesling bottlings each year, including a superb sticky wine from thoroughly botrytized fruit.

Riesling Marlborough	05	04	$$
Botrytized Riesling Marlborough		04	$$$$

Kumeu River. This important winery in the relatively warm, humid Auckland area made its reputation with New Zealand's richest and most exotic Chardonnays, some of which carry a heavy load of oak. The Pinot Gris is sappy and delicious.

Pinot Gris Kumeu	05	04	$$
Chardonnay Kumeu		04	$$$
Chardonnay Maté's Vineyard Kumeu	05	04	$$$

Lawson's Dry Hills. Of particular note here is a fat but dry Gewürztraminer from clay-rich soil in a vineyard on the southern edge of the Wairau Valley. It consistently ranks among New Zealand's elite examples of this variety.

Gewürztraminer Marlborough	04	$

Mt. Difficulty. This Central Otago producer, which also makes very good Pinot Noir, produces ripe, dusty Pinot Gris and substantial Chardonnay with harmonious acidity.

Pinot Gris Central Otago	04	$$
Chardonnay Central Otago	04	$$

Neudorf Vineyards. Serious, broad, minerally Riesling from clay-rich soils in the Moutere Hills area of Nelson, on the northern tip of the South Island. Very good Pinots here too.

Riesling Moutere	`03`	$$

Palliser Estate. The largest producer in the Martinborough area, Palliser Estate excels with opulent Chardonnay and Pinot Gris in addition to the standbys Sauvignon Blanc and Pinot Noir.

Pinot Gris Martinborough	`04`	$$
Chardonnay Martinborough	`03`	$$

Pegasus Bay. This producer's dense, bracing Riesling, whose exotic spice character perfectly suits it to Asian cuisines, has a track record for repaying bottle aging. There's sometimes a moderate amount of residual sugar that is slowly absorbed as the wine matures.

Riesling Waipara	`04`	$$

Seifried Estate. The oldest and largest estate in Nelson, Seifried does well with a range of white varieties.

Unoaked Chardonnay Nelson	`05`	$
Pinot Gris Nelson	`05`	$

Spy Valley Wines. This relatively recent entrant (2000 was Spy Valley's first vintage) in a comparatively dry, high area of Marlborough, offers a range of supple, fruit-driven and distinctly user-friendly wines that offer considerable early appeal, although the Dry Riesling stands out as more bracing and uncompromising.

Dry Riesling Marlborough	`04`	$
Riesling Marlborough	`04`	$$
Pinot Gris Marlborough	`04`	$
Chardonnay Marlborough	`03`	$$

OTHER PRODUCERS TO LOOK FOR: Ata Rangi (Chardonnay, Pinot Gris), Carrick (Riesling), Craggy Range, Huia (Pinot Gris, Riesling), Konrad & Co. (late-harvest Riesling), The Millton (Riesling), Vineyard (Chenin Blanc), Daniel Schuster Wines (Riesling), Seresin Estate (Riesling, Pinot Gris), Trinity Hill (Chardonnay), Vinoptima (Gewürztraminer).

PINOT NOIR

Pinot Noir has emphatically found a home in New Zealand's temperate climate, where the variety benefits tremendously from an extended growing season. The soil-inflected Pinots of Martinborough, on New Zealand's North Island, where the harvest can last well into May (the Southern Hemisphere equivalant of November), have proven their quality and ageability over the past 20 years. Much more recently, Central Otago, a spectacular inland region of lakes, alpine meadows, and steep mountains and valleys (this is where *Lord of the Rings* was filmed) located in the middle of the South Island, has exploded onto the world wine scene in the past five or six years with some stunning wines. With their rich dark fruit aromas and flavors, intriguing floral and mineral nuances, and ripe, harmonious acidity—not to mention their often considerable heft (typically 13 to 14 percent alcohol)—these Pinots may be better suited to today's wine drinkers than the earthier Pinots of Martinborough, which, despite their often greater complexity, can come off as dry and lean in comparison. Incidentally, beginning with the 2003 vintage, most of the best Central Otago Pinots are bottled under screw cap, which further emphasizes the fresh, clean fruit of these wines.

BANG FOR THE BUCK. Pinot Noir in New Zealand is rarely cheap, but prices for these wines are in line with Pinots of similar quality from elsewhere.

2004 ★★★+   2003 ★★★★–

RECOMMENDED PRODUCERS

Ata Rangi. This Martinborough winery, which has been making Pinot Noir for 25 years, bottles one of the best examples from this region, a wine usually at its best with three or four years of bottle aging.

Pinot Noir Martinborough	`03`	$$$

Carrick. Perfumed, dense, cool-climate Pinot Noirs with dark fruit, floral, and spice notes reminiscent of red Burgundy.

Pinot Noir Central Otago	`03`	`02`	$$$

Daniel Schuster. Prague-born Daniel Schuster, who has also done wine consulting in California and Italy, makes minerally, aromatic Pinot Noirs from the Waipara region in Canterbury. His top Pinot is made in the best years from favored portions of his limestone-rich Omihi Hills Vineyard.

Pinot Noir Twin Vineyards Canterbury		`04`	$$
Pinot Noir Omihi Hills Vineyard Selection	`02`	`01`	$$$

Escarpment. This is the new venture of veteran winemaker Larry McKenna, a Martinborough pioneer who was responsible for some stunning Pinot Noirs at Martinborough Vineyard from the mid-1980s through the late-1990s. His style continues to favor vibrancy and structure over sheer fruitiness. The Kupe bottling is from a single densely planted parcel of young vines.

Pinot Noir Martinborough	`03`	$$$
Kupe Pinot Noir Martinborough	`03`	$$$

Felton Road. Best known for its single-block Pinot Noirs, this is one of the elite wineries of Central Otago, producing wines that are at once gripping and silky. The Block 3 and Block 5 bottlings come from Felton Road's home vineyard.

Pinot Noir Central Otago	`03`	$$$
Pinot Noir Block 3 Central Otago	`03`	$$$
Pinot Noir Block 5 Central Otago	`02`	$$$$

Palliser Estate. This winery's broad, sappy Pinot Noir, one of New Zealand's best values in this variety, is built for midterm aging.

Pinot Noir Martinborough	03	$$

Pegasus Bay. In addition to its superb and highly individual white wines, Pegasus Bay offers an unusually rich, layered yet sappy Pinot Noir from sheltered vineyards that frequently experience summer hot spells. In the best years, there is also a small quantity of a special Prima Donna bottling.

Pinot Noir Waipara	03	$$$

Seresin Estate. Though best known for its white wines, Seresin's Pinot Noirs are unusually pure and penetrating, in a distinctly Burgundian style and capable of developing in bottle for six to eight years.

Leah Pinot Noir Marlborough	03	02	$$$

Villa Maria. The parent company is based in Auckland, but some of this huge producer's best wines come from vineyards in and around Marlborough. Its Taylors Pass Pinot Noir comes from a single vineyard in Awatere Valley.

Pinot Noir Reserve Marlborough	03	$$
Pinot Noir Taylors Pass Marlborough	03	$$$

OTHER PRODUCERS TO LOOK FOR: Akarua, Amisfield, Craggy Range Vineyards, Foxes Island, Fromm Winery, Herzog Winery, Martinborough Vineyard, Mt. Difficulty, Neudorf Vineyards, Quartz Reef, Rippon, TerraVin Wines, Voss Estate Vineyard.

OTHER RED WINES OF NEW ZEALAND

Cabernet Sauvignon and other reds from Bordeaux grapes continue to be a very difficult sell in the North American market, and for good reason. Although it's always possible to find wines that are well made in a rather lean way, few producers have demonstrated an ability to produce consistently satisfying, ripe reds that avoid showing an intrusively herbaceous character. New Zealand's Cabernet Sauvignons and Merlots can be lean, green, and mean in cooler or wetter vintages—and a shock to wine lovers weaned on superripe California reds. Increasingly, however, red grapes are being planted in more protected and better-drained spots, and vine vigor is more carefully managed, with the result that today's red wines show riper aromas and flavors and a bit more flesh on their bones.

Syrah, a versatile grape that frequently does well in cooler microclimates within warm areas or protected spots within cooler regions, appears to have a bright future in New Zealand. Currently available examples are more likely to be in a peppery, medium-bodied, Old World style than full-bodied, superripe, and high in alcohol like Australian Shiraz.

BANG FOR THE BUCK. Red wines from Bordeaux varieties generally offer poor value in export markets.

RECOMMENDED PRODUCERS

Craggy Range. One of the best portfolios of wine from New Zealand, with unusually rich and ripe reds from the Gimblett Gravels area, a particularly warm spot within the greater Hawke's Bay area.

LeSol Syrah Gimblett Gravels Hawke's Bay	02	$$$
Merlot Gimblett Gravels Vineyard Hawke's Bay	02	$$$
Sophia Gimblett Gravels Vineyard Merlot/Cabernet Franc Hawke's Bay	02	$$$

Te Mata Estate Winery. This winery benefits from a warm inland site on well-drained alluvial soils in Hawke's Bay, protected from cool ocean breezes. In addition to their flagship Coleraine blend of Cabernet and Merlot, Te Mata makes very good Syrah.

Coleraine Cabernet/Merlot Hawke's Bay	02	$$$
Bullnose Syrah Hawke's Bay	04	$$

Trinity Hill. This cutting-edge winery in the Gimblett Gravels section of Hawke's Bay has experimented with Tempranillo and white Rhône Valley grapes in recent years. But Trinity Hill believes that Syrah will be the variety that ultimately puts Hawke's Bay on the red wine map.

Syrah Gimblett Road Hawke's Bay	02	01	$$

Unison Vineyard. The winery's top wine, a blend of Cabernet Sauvignon, Merlot, and Syrah from the Gimblett Gravels, is aged for a full two years in barrel and intended for serious bottle aging. Very good varietal Syrah here as well.

Selection Red Wine Hawke's Bay	02	01	$$$

OTHER PRODUCERS TO LOOK FOR: Matariki Wines (Quintology), Mills Reef (Elspeth One), Newton Forrest Estate (Cornerstone), Te Awa Winery (Bordeaux red varieties).

SOUTH AFRICA

South Africa has produced wines in the area of Cape Town since the 17th century, but the country's significant place in the U.S. market is far more recent. During the era of apartheid, trade sanctions imposed on imports from South Africa kept these wines out of the U.S. and many other markets, with the effect that local South African winemakers had little incentive to produce wines that could compete in a global setting, and had limited experience with new developments in the world of wine. In fact, during apartheid most of the country's grape growers sold their fruit to co-ops, who turned it into distilled alcohol on the one hand, sherry and port on the other. With the end of sanctions in 1991, the U.S. market was suddenly flooded with mostly low-end and decidedly mediocre wine from South Africa.

Little more than a decade later, the quality of South African wine has soared, thanks in large part to widespread replanting of virused vines or grafting over new vines onto virus-free rootstock. Replacing virus-weakened vines has enabled grape growers to produce riper fruit less likely to show the green or tea-like flavors that plagued South Africa's wines in the past. Then, too, a new generation of winemakers has benefited from more extensive contact with the outside world, and the country's producers now know what they must do to compete in an international arena. Today, South Africa is the world's eighth-largest producer of wine, supplying everything from crisp, vibrant Sauvignon Blancs and Chenin Blancs to structured, serious Cabernet Sauvignons, Syrahs, and red blends. The best of these are satisfying and characterful wines that are midway between Old and New World in style.

Key to Vintage Ratings		Key to Assessments of Specific Wines	
★★★★★	Outstanding	**03**	An excellent to outstanding example *of that wine*
★★★★	Excellent	03	A good to very good example *of that wine*
★★★	Good to very good	03	A disappointing effort (often due to a
★★	Fair to average		difficult vintage)
★	Poor		

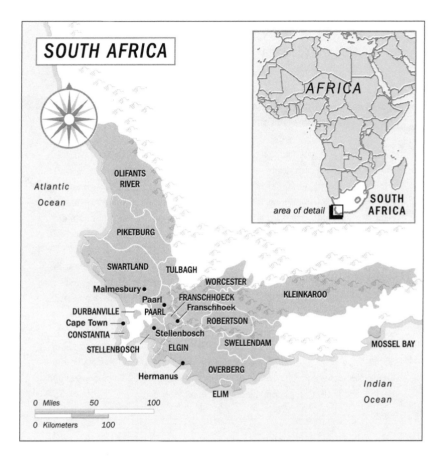

RED WINES

Among red varieties, Cabernet Sauvignon and Syrah, more commonly called Shiraz in South Africa, are the most widely planted and the most interesting. Cabernet Sauvignon is frequently blended with other Bordeaux varieties—in fact, many of the most renowned Cape reds are classic Bordeaux blends. Shiraz is the country's fastest-expanding red grape in terms of acres under vine, and may also be its most exciting variety these days, with many new entries coming onstream, including some boutique wines made in limited quantities. The classic style was dry and refined, with moderate alcohol, noteworthy aromatic complexity, and sound structure, but today some winemakers are picking ever-riper fruit and using more extractive winemaking techniques and a lot of new oak to build bigger, darker, and more powerful wines.

WINE GEOGRAPHY IN SOUTH AFRICA

South Africa's wine-producing areas are located in the extreme southwestern tip of the continent, close to Cape Town. A warm, dry Mediterranean climate, with moderating sea breezes and normally clement weather during the summer and harvest, provides favorable conditions for growing traditional European varieties. A drawn-out growing season is ideal for producing wines with flavor intensity, elegance, and complexity rather than merely size and power.

The spectacularly beautiful Stellenbosch region, which lies barely a half-hour east of Cape Town by car and surrounds the old university town of the same name, features South Africa's greatest concentration of serious wine estates and produces many of the country's best red blends. Paarl, just to the north, is home to a growing number of quality-minded producers and is currently positioning itself as a specialist in big, brawny Syrahs (more often called Shiraz in South Africa, and especially here). The cooler and wetter Constantia region, which was where South Africa's first vines were planted and which is now part of southern Cape Town, is best for white wines, thanks to cooling southeasterly breezes off False Bay. Other areas producing very good wines include Robertson, where the grapes are mostly white; Walker Bay, a maritime climate southeast of Cape Town that produces admirable Chardonnays and Pinot Noirs in a Burgundian style; and Elgin, a coolish valley located between Stellenbosch and Walker Bay that features more cloud cover during the summer.

Pinotage, a unique South African variety created in the 1920s from a crossing of Cinsaut and Pinot Noir, is still widely planted, even if it has been in slow decline in recent years. Pinotage yields a range of styles, from old-fashioned, dry, and somewhat baked to sweeter, spicy, and more obviously fruity. Merlot is in the ascendancy, but few examples to date can be described as exceptional. The category called Cape Blends was dreamed up to showcase Pinotage in combination with so-called noble red grapes like Cabernet Sauvignon, Merlot, Cabernet Franc, and Syrah, but active debate continues within South Africa over the role that Pinotage should play in these blends.

BANG FOR THE BUCK. Despite the sharp appreciation of the South African rand against the U.S. dollar in recent years, South African wine prices remain reasonable. You'll find everything from extraordinary values under $20 to truly world-class wines at very attractive prices.

2004 ★★★+   2003 ★★★★–

RECOMMENDED PRODUCERS

Boekenhoutskloof. Rich, round, intensely flavored wines, with Syrah and Rhône blends best and Cabernet Sauvignon consistently claret-like and focused. Boekenhoutskloof's Porcupine Ridge label offers solid quality at a very low price.

Porcupine Ridge Syrah Coastal	**05**	03	$
The Chocolate Block Western Cape	**04**	**03**	$$$
Syrah Coastal	03	02	$$$
Cabernet Sauvignon Franschhoek	**03**	02	**01**	$$$

De Trafford Wines. A small producer of deeply colored, densely packed wines in a distinctly New World style, with noteworthy power and often high alcohol levels. The Elevation 393 is a blend of Cabernet, Shiraz, Merlot, and Cabernet Franc, aged in a high percentage of new French oak.

Cabernet Sauvignon Stellenbosch	**03**	02	$$
Shiraz Stellenbosch	04	**03**	$$$
Elevation 393 Red Wine Stellenbosch	**03**	01	$$$

Ernie Els Wines. This is a joint venture between Jean Engelbrecht and golfer Ernie Els, specializing in vibrant and distinctly claret-like red blends, mostly from Bordeaux varieties. When Engelbrecht left his family's estate (Rust en Vrede), he took the reliably good and bargain-priced Guardian Peak range of wines with him, along with talented winemaker Louis Strydom.

Engelbrecht-Els Proprietor's Blend Stellenbosch	04	**03**	$$$
Ernie Els Red Wine Stellenbosch	04	**03**	$$$$

Fairview. Charles Back, the owner of Fairview as well as Spice Route Wine Company, is one of the most influential and marketing-savvy producers in South Africa. His Goats do Roam lineup under the Fairview label, wines made in a Rhône Valley style, is aggressively priced and highly popular in the North American market. Fairview's top wines are serious, concentrated, and age worthy, made in an updated traditional style.

Goats do Roam Western Cape	**05**		$
Primo Pinotage Paarl	03	02	$$
The Beacon Shiraz Paarl	03	**02**	$$

Hamilton Russell Vineyards. Elegant, silky, highly nuanced wines with noteworthy minerality and balance, from the temperate, ocean-influenced Walker Bay region just west of the southern tip of the African continent. In the best vintages, Anthony Hamilton-Russell makes South Africa's best Pinot Noir and Chardonnay.

Pinot Noir Walker Bay	04	**03**	$$$

Kanonkop Estate. Veteran winemaker Beyers Truter, source of some of South Africa's greatest Pinotage bottlings here over the past 20 years, has moved on to his own project. But superb, ideally situated Stellenbosch winery continues to produce rich, smoky, and concentrated Pinotage with powerful, dark fruit character and unusual depth. The entry-level Pinotage-based Kadette is a great buy, while the high-end Paul Sauer, a Bordeaux blend, is one of South Africa's greatest wines.

Kadette Stellenbosch	**04**	03	$
Pinotage Stellenbosch	**03**	02	$$$
Paul Sauer Stellenbosch	02	**01**	$$$

Morgenster Estate. A spectacular new Stellenbosch property under Italian ownership, with Pierre Lurton of Châteaux Cheval Blanc and Yquem consulting. In Bordeaux fashion, there is a flagship estate blend and a second label, Lourens River Valley. The style is rich and lush but succulent and firmly mineral in character, incorporating Merlot, Cabernet Sauvignon, and Cabernet Franc; the first wines were released in 2004.

Lourens River Valley Red Wine Stellenbosch	**03**	02	$$
Morgenster Estate Red Wine Stellenbosch	03	**01**	$$

Neil Ellis Wines. This veteran winemaker offers a broad range of consistently excellent wines, made in a fruit-driven and often opulent style but also built to last. Ellis does equally well with red and white wines.

Pinotage Stellenbosch		**03**	02	$$
Cabernet Sauvignon Vineyard Selection Jonkershoek Valley	**03**	02	**01**	$$
Shiraz Vineyard Selection Jonkershoek Valley			**03**	$$

Rupert & Rothschild. This partnership involving the Rothschild family and the consulting assistance of enologist Michel Rolland produces supple, concentrated Bordeaux blends with no shortage of definition or tannic spine. The second wine, labeled Classique, is a terrific value. Rupert & Rothschild's Baroness Nadine Chardonnay is also excellent, and well priced.

Classique Coastal Region	03	**02**	$$
Baron Edmond Coastal Region	02	**01**	$$$

Rustenberg Wines. Winemaker Adi Badenhorst crafts two of South Africa's most serious and complex red wines, the flagship Peter Barlow from all Cabernet Sauvignon and the John X Merriman, a Bordeaux blend.

John X Merriman Red Wine Stellenbosch	**03**	02	$$
Peter Barlow Stellenbosch	**03**	02	$$$

Rust en Vrede Estate. The Engelbrecht family has made some of South Africa's densest, most concentrated and vibrant red wines since the 1980s, and is now moving steadily in the direction of producing just a single proprietary estate blend based on Cabernet Sauvignon.

Estate Red Wine Stellenbosch	02	**01**	$$$

Thelema. Co-owner Gyles Webb, who is also cellarmaster at the important new Tokara Winery, makes suave, structured wines with admirable concentration, balance, and structure—not to mention longevity. He's one of a relative handful of South African winemakers who excel with both red and white wines.

Cabernet Sauvignon Stellenbosch	03	02	$$
Merlot Stellenbosch		02	$$

Vergelegen. In my notebook, this winery, located in the breezy Somerset West area of the Stellenbosch region, is South Africa's single finest producer. Winemaker André van Rensburg backs up his brash talk with consistently brilliant wines across numerous varieties.

Cabernet Sauvignon Stellenbosch	03	01	$$$
Premium Red Stellenbosch	02	01	$$$

Warwick Estate. Located in the favored Simonsberg section of Stellenbosch, Warwick Estate makes concentrated, structured wines in a traditional style, with the whites here in the same quality league as the reds. There are actually two flagship wines, the Estate Reserve (labeled Trilogy everywhere but in the U.S. market) and Three Cape Ladies, consistently one of South Africa's top "Cape Blends." Managing director Mike Ratcliffe is also a partner in the new high-end Vilafonté venture with husband-and-wife Phil Freese (viticulturalist) and Zelma Long (winemaker), veterans of the California wine scene.

Pinotage Old Bush Vines Simonsberg	04	03	$$
Three Cape Ladies Cape Blend Simonsberg	03	02	$$
Estate Reserve Simonsberg	03	02	$$$

OTHER PRODUCERS TO LOOK FOR: Delheim Estate (Shiraz), Dornier Wines (red blends), Ken Forrester Wines (Rhône blends), Meinert Wines (Bordeaux blends), Morgenhof Estate (Merlot, Cabernet), Sadie Family (Syrah), Simonsig Family Vineyards (Shiraz, red blends), Spice Route Wine Company (Syrah, Rhône blends), The Foundry (Syrah), Tokara Winery (Bordeaux blend), Vilafonté (Bordeaux blends), Waterford Estate (Cabernet, Shiraz).

WHITE WINES

The best white wines today are the Cape's solid, fresh, and typically unoaked Sauvignon Blancs and some surprisingly good Chardonnays, the latter especially vibrant and satisfying when made from fruit in cooler spots like Elgin and Walker Bay. As a rule, South Africa's Sauvignons are more classically dry—and a bit less tropical—than New Zealand's. Chenin Blanc represented 34 percent of land under vine as recently as 1990 but less than half that percentage today, as it has rapidly been supplanted by red and white varieties with greater international appeal. Although production of sweet wines has been limited, there is growing evidence that the Cape is a promising region for late-harvest bottlings from Sauvignon Blanc and Sémillon as well as from Chenin Blanc.

BANG FOR THE BUCK. Although a few Sauvignon Blanc bottlings command serious prices, most of these wines still offer excellent value, as do South Africa's Chenin Blancs. It's hard to find better and more varietally accurate Chardonnays anywhere else in the $10 to $20 range.

2005 ★★★★– **2004** ★★★–

RECOMMENDED PRODUCERS

Bouchard Finlayson. Cool-climate, European-styled wines, with crisp, focused flavors and very good balance. These are understated, precise wines that may prove too subtle for those weaned on New World wines of extraction and heft.

Missionvale Chardonnay Walker Bay	04	03	$$
Crocodile's Lair Chardonnay Kaaimansgat Overberg	04	03	$$

Buitenverwachting. Delicate but gripping cooler-climate Sauvignon Blancs. Great pricing for the quality here.

Sauvignon Blanc Constantia	05	04	$
Sauvignon Blanc Hussey's Vlei Constantia	05	04	$$

Hamilton Russell. Vineyards. South Africa's most consistently outstanding Chardonnay, made in a distinctly Burgundian style: silky, spicy, minerally, and fresh, with the structure to develop greater nuance in bottle.

Chardonnay Walker Bay	05	04	03	$$$

Ken Forrester Wines. Ken Forrester's red wines are supple and user-friendly, but his whites are the standouts—especially his splendid and underpriced Chenin Blanc bottlings. In years conducive to the appearance of noble rot, Forrester makes a wonderfully opulent, tropical-fruity late-harvest wine.

Petit Chenin Stellenbosch	06	05	$
Chenin Blanc Stellenbosch	05	04	$

Klein Constantia Estate. Klein Constantia has made South Africa's most famous dessert wine for over two centuries; the winery describes the current wine as a "re-creation" of the famous Constantia wine made in the 18th and 19th centuries. From raisined Muscat de Frontignan grapes, the Vin de Constance is unfortified, fascinating, and exotic, with deep, earthy complexity and long aging potential.

Vin de Constance Muscat de Frontignan Constantia	00	99	$$$

Mulderbosch Vineyards. For years, South Africa's most famous producer of pungently precise citrus-and-gooseberry-scented Sauvignon Blancs that can stand up to the best examples of this variety from anywhere. Chardonnay is also impressive here, including a full but lively version done in new French oak.

Sauvignon Blanc Stellenbosch	05	04	$$
Chardonnay Stellenbosch		03	$$

Raats Family Wines. Bruwer Raats, a lover of Loire Valley wines, specializes in Chenin Blanc and Cabernet Franc. His vibrant, sharply delineated Chenins—there's an unwooded version and one aged in oak—boast intriguing stony, herbal, and floral nuances along with pure orchard and citrus fruit flavors.

Chenin Blanc Stellenbosch	04	03	$
Original Chenin Blanc Unwooded Coastal Region	05	04	$$

Rustenberg Wines. In addition to its impressive reds, Rustenberg also makes world-class Chardonnay—not to mention competent and accessible white wines under its inexpensive second label, Brampton. Rustenberg's Five Soldiers Chardonnay is dense and mineral-rich, one of the three or four best in South Africa.

Brampton Viognier Coastal Region	05	04	$
Chardonnay Stellenbosch	04	03	$$
Chardonnay Five Soldiers Stellenbosch	03	02	$$$

Signal Hill. The idiosyncratic late-harvest wines made here range in style from pungently penetrating to unctuous and liqueur-like, with many stops along the way. Made in limited quantities, these sweet wines are worth a special search.

Straw Wine Paarl	02	$$$
Crème de Tête Muscat d'Alexandrie Noble Late Harvest Paarl	03	$$$

Thelema. Gyles Webb makes varietally accurate, nuanced white wines in a traditional style, with more intensity than most in South Africa. In the better vintages, Thelema's vibrant, limey Rhine Riesling rewards a decade of aging.

Sauvignon Blanc Stellenbosch		04	$$
Chardonnay Stellenbosch	04	03	$$
Rhine Riesling Stellenbosch		03	$$

Vergelegen. Like his reds, André van Rensburg's uncompromising white wines are as good as these wines get in South Africa. Vergelegen's flagship Premium White blend (Sémillon and Sauvignon Blanc) is a house specialty, but the Sauvignon Blancs from the windswept Schaapenberg Vineyard are every bit as distinctive.

Sauvignon Blanc Reserve Stellenbosch		04	$$$
Chardonnay Reserve Stellenbosch	04	03	$$$
Vergelegen Premium White Stellenbosch	04	03	$$$

OTHER PRODUCERS TO LOOK FOR: Neil Ellis Wines (Chardonnay and Sauvignon Blanc), Rupert & Rothschild (Chardonnay), Southern Right (Sauvignon Blanc), Springfield Estate (Sauvignon Blanc), Warwick Estate (Chardonnay and Sauvignon Blanc), Waterford Estate (Chardonnay).

CHILE

Chile is an excellent source of user-friendly, fruit-driven red and white wines, often at bargain-basement prices. Savvy North American buyers have been finding value in Chile's wines for two decades. Due to a stable political environment, Chile's wine-growing regions have steadily attracted foreign interest and investment since the 1970s. At the same time, Chile has benefitted from association with large and established trading companies with powerful networks that have helped to raise the profile and expand distribution of Chilean wines in major export markets such as the U.S. and the U.K. It is worth noting that two of the top twenty imported wine brands by volume in the U.S. are Chilean: Concha y Toro and Walnut Crest.

Yet Chile today is at a crossroads, and it remains to be seen just how competitive the country's wines will remain. The country is a solid source of correct if for the most part commercial-grade wines made from internationally known varieties, especially Cabernet Sauvignon, Chardonnay, and Sauvignon Blanc. But in recent years Chile has faced growing competition in the under-$15 range from its neighbor Argentina, as well as from Spain, Portugal, Australia, and South Africa. Despite the fact that Chile exports a majority of its wine production, the country's share of imported wine in the American market has steadily declined in recent years. At the same time, however, a growing number of producers in Chile are attempting to capitalize on the ideal growing conditions in their country by cutting vine yields and attempting to make more serious and concentrated wines that can bear comparison to the best of the New World. From a marketing standpoint, escaping the "cheap and cheerful" category in which Chile initially established its foothold in the North American market may be essential. But with only a few exceptions these ambitions have not yet become marketplace reality.

The Chilean wine region is an idyllic zone for growing grapes. Virtually every wine region in Chile (see box on page 294) benefits from proximity to the Pacific Ocean and the cooling Humboldt Current that flows up from the South Pole. But although Chile is a narrow strip of land extending more than 2,000 miles from north to south, its grape-growing regions are clustered in the center of the country, where rainfall is concentrated during the winter months, and where an absence of fungal diseases makes for relatively carefree grape farming. The towering Andes Mountains that run down Chile's eastern border block wind and rain from the east, but, more important, trap cool air from the Pacific, with the result that nighttime temperatures even in most of Chile's warmest vineyards typically descend into the 50s. This diurnal variation enables Chile's vineyards

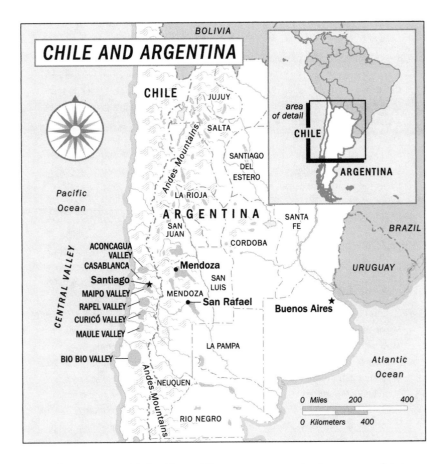

to produce grapes with healthy acidity, strong aromatic character, and intense varietal flavors. And of course melting snow from the Andes is essential for irrigating vineyards in spots that can receive next to no rainfall during the spring, summer, and early autumn.

RED WINES

Cabernet Sauvignon rules the Chilean wine world, accounting for a majority of the country's red wine exports. In most cases these wines are varietally correct and ready to drink on release, with light to medium body. At the low end, however, many wines are dilute and herbaceous, as high crop levels—perhaps partly due to excessive irrigation—prevent the fruit from ripening thoroughly. Recent releases of some

CHILE'S MOST IMPORTANT WINE VALLEYS

- **Casablanca Valley.** This rapidly emerging region north of Maipo and close to the Pacific coast enjoys a climate tempered by the ocean, with frequent sea mist moderating the strength of the sun and extending the growing season. This has become an important source of fresh, elegant Chardonnay and Sauvignon Blanc, but appears to have a promising future for red varieties as well. The Casablanca Valley is in the Aconcagua region, located just to the north of the vast Central Valley region, which includes the Maipo, Rapel, Curicó, and Maule valleys.

- **Maipo Valley.** The first plantings of vinifera grapes (*Vitis vinifera* is the species of grapes used to make wine) in Chile were here, in the mid-1800s. With its Mediterranean climate featuring hot days and cool nights, and the protective effect of the Coastal Range along the Pacific coast, the climate is perfect for a wide range of grapes, but Cabernet Sauvignon is still king in Chile's most important growing region. The Maipo Valley's proximity to Chile's capital city, Santiago (some of the earliest vineyards are now within the city itself), has always ensured a ready market for its wines.

- **Rapel Valley.** Located south of the Maipo Valley, with a climate that provides wide temperature swings between hot days and cool nights, the Rapel Valley actually consists of two distinct areas. The Cachapoal Valley to the north, which includes the hottest part of the Central Valley (around Rapel Lake), shows a strong bias toward red varieties. The larger Colchagua Valley area to the south is more open to Pacific Ocean influence and rainfall as the Coastal Range here is considerably lower, yet this area still favors Cabernet Sauvignon, Merlot, and Carmenère. Chile's most exciting Carmenères and Carmenère blends come from this region.

- **Curicó Valley.** Some of the country's oldest plantings are located in Chile's second-largest wine-growing area in terms of vineyard acreage. A classic temperate Mediterranean climate, with typically dry weather from late spring to early autumn, allows nearly ideal conditions for a wide range of varieties. Cabernet Sauvignon is the most widely planted variety here, but cooler microclimates are better for white grapes, especially Sauvignon Blanc.

- **Maule Valley.** Chile's largest wine region in terms of acres under vine, the Maule Valley offers great climatic diversity as well as a wide range of soils. The Maule Valley is a prime source for fresh, crisp Chardonnay but it's also one of the country's most significant producers of Cabernet Sauvignon, Merlot, and Carmenère. The Maule, Curico, Rapel, and Maipo valleys are all part of Chile's vast Central Valley region.

high-end examples of Cabernet are encouraging but pricing is a serious issue, as most of these wines come in at $40 or more, and in the higher price range Chile has stiff competition from red wines made all over the world. Merlot is planted in Chile, but many examples show a weedy aspect. This may be largely due to the youth of the vines: most Merlot in Chile has been planted in the last ten years. (Most of what was thought to be Merlot previously is now known to be Carmenère.) Greenness and dilution can also plague Chile's Pinot Noir, few examples of which have made it to North America so far.

Perhaps the most intriguing development in Chilean red wine has been the re-emergence of Carmenère, an old and almost extinct grape originally from Bordeaux that is now virtually unique to Chile. It wound up here by accident, being sold as Merlot, and much of what is called Merlot in Chile's vineyards today is actually Carmenère. These wines can be rich and full, often displaying smoky black fruits but frequently showing a peppery, herbal side as well. To date, relatively few examples have shown more than moderate aging potential.

BANG FOR THE BUCK. Careful wine buyers can find excellent Cabernet Sauvignon values for well under $15, but Chilean red wine remains a minefield, with far too many light, weedy wines.

2004 ★★★+   2003 ★★★   2002 ★★

RECOMMENDED PRODUCERS

Almaviva. The objective of this Maipo Valley joint venture between Baron Philippe de Rothschild (owner of Château Mouton-Rothschild) and Concha y Toro is to create a super-premium Cabernet Sauvignon–based Bordeaux blend. Recent vintages have been very impressive.

Almaviva Puente Alta	03 02	$$$

Altair. An ambitious project by the owners of Château Dassault in St. Émilion, Altair is aiming for an international style, with emphasis on sweet, spicy oak and ripe, lush fruit. The early signs are very promising for this Rapel showcase winery.

Altair Cachapoal Valley	03	$$$$

Casa Lapostolle. With consultation from renowned Bordeaux enologist Michel Rolland, Casa Lapostolle is one of the best sources for rich, full-bodied wines with expressive fruit, lush texture, and better concentration than most Chilean reds. Prices are fair, too.

Cabernet Sauvignon Rapel Valley	03	$
Cabernet Sauvignon Cuvée Alexandre Colchagua Valley	03	$$
Merlot Cuvée Alexandre Colchagua Valley	04	$$

Casa Silva. This old property has invested heavily in new vineyards and a modern winery in recent years. The reds here combine Old World balance and New World fruitiness, and the tannins are supple. The whites are also consistently well balanced and fresh.

Cabernet Sauvignon Reserva Colchagua Valley	04	$
Carmenre Reserva Colchagua Valley	04	$
Quinta Generation Red Wine Colchagua Valley	02	$$

Concha y Toro. This large producer, which bottles one of the most popular imported brands in the U.S., offers a full range of wines, from everyday to cellar worthy. The quality standard is reliable and pricing is friendly.

Carmenère Casillero del Diablo Rapel Valley	04	$
Cabernet Sauvignon Marqués de Casa Concha Maipo Valley	03	$$
Cabernet Sauvignon Don Melchor Maipo Valley	02	$$$

Cousiño Macul. A very consistent producer, founded in 1856 and now run by the sixth generation of the Cousiño family. The wines are elegant and suave, with the house's Antiguas Reservas Cabernet bottling long a favorite in the U.S. market.

Cabernet Sauvignon Maipo Valley	04	$
Cabernet Sauvignon Antiguas Reservas Maipo Valley	03	$

Montes. Dependably among Chile's best producers, making a strong range of well-balanced wines in an elegant Old World style. The top reds at this estate have the structure to improve with cellaring.

Montes Cabernet Sauvignon Reserve Colchagua Valley		04	$
Montes Alpha Cabernet Sauvignon Colchagua Valley		03	$$
Montes Alpha "M" Santa Cruz	03	02	$$$
Montes Alpha Merlot Colchagua Valley		03	$$

Odfjell Vineyards. Suave, modern-style, fruit-driven wines, including a very good Carmenère. The Napa Valley's Paul Hobbs consults here.

Orzada Carmenère Valle Central	03	$$
Aliara Red Wine Chile	01	$$

Undurraga. One of the oldest wineries in Chile, founded in 1885, and a popular name with bargain seekers. This enormous (over 2,500 acres) property makes clean, fresh wines that usually offer very good value and enjoy wide availability.

Cabernet Sauvignon Reserva Maipo Valley	03	$

Los Vascos. Under the ownership of Domaines Barons de Rothschild, proprietors of Château Lafite, this winery makes suave red wines in an Old World style. The high-end bottling called Le Dix, however, offers dubious value so far.

Cabernet Sauvignon Colchagua Valley	04	$
Cabernet Sauvignon Reserve Colchagua Valley	03	$$

OTHER PRODUCERS TO LOOK FOR: Caliterra, Carmen, Château Los Boldos, Casa Silva, Errazuriz, William Fèvre, Jacques & François Lurton, MontGras, Santa Rita, Seña, Miguel Torres, Ventisquero.

WHITE WINES

As in most New World wine regions, Chardonnay dominates the market, but most of these wines provide only modest personality and concentration of flavor. Fortunately for North American wine lovers, the availability of more serious Chardonnays has been on the rise in recent years. Although too many wines are either dilute on account of excessive vine yields or numbingly overoaked, the odds of finding Chilean Chardonnay with balance and genuine varietal character are better today than ever before. Sauvignon Blanc has been highly successful in Chile. The most reliable source has historically been the Central Valley, especially the Curicó Valley, but increasingly the best Sauvignons are coming from the Casablanca and San Antonio valleys a bit farther north. The best bottles are made in a vibrant, unoaked style, with noteworthy intensity of varietal character and ideal for immediate drinking.

BANG FOR THE BUCK. Chile's better wines in the $10 to $15 range are among the greatest white wine values available to North American consumers. Chile's best values are its fresh, lively Sauvignon Blancs, usually priced south of $10. Some solid Chardonnays come in at around $15, but in this price range they have competition from many other countries.

2005 ★★★★   2004 ★★★

RECOMMENDED PRODUCERS

Carmen. This was the first winery established in Chile, in 1850, and is now a huge operation, with more than 1,000 acres planted across the major regions. Carmen offers very good value in bright, focused white wines.

Sauvignon Blanc Reserve Casablanca Valley	05	$
Chardonnay Reserve Casablanca Valley	04	$

Casa Lapostolle. Modern, fruit-forward wines, often showing ample use of spicy oak.

Sauvignon Blanc Casablanca Valley	05	$
Chardonnay Cuvée Alexandre Casablanca Valley	04	$$

Concha y Toro. This large producer ships more Chilean wine to the U.S. market than any other. For the volume, quality is high, as the wines are fresh, clean, and well made. At the entry level, these can be great value.

Sauvignon Blanc Casillero del Diablo Central Valley	05	$
Chardonnay Marques de Casa Concha Maipo Valley	04	$$

William Fèvre. The famed Chablis producer William Fèvre set up shop in the Maipo Valley in 1992 and produces elegant, restrained wines along a French model. Pricing is extremely friendly.

Sauvignon Blanc La Misión Maipo Valley	05	$

Jacques & François Lurton. The Bordeaux-based Lurton family has expanded into Chile from their Argentine outpost and is making dense, fresh wines in a style that combines Old World elegance with vivacious New World fruit.

Sauvignon Blanc Araucano Central Valley	05	$
Sauvignon Blanc Gran Araucano Casablanca Valley	05	$$

Santa Rita. Aggressively priced and widely available, Santa Rita's clean, precise, varietally accurate wines offer some of the world's greatest values, particularly in white wine.

Sauvignon Blanc 120 Lontue Valley	05	$
Chardonnay 120 Casablanca Valley	05	$
Chardonnay Reserva Casablanca Valley	05	$

Los Vascos. This Rothschild-owned property makes silky white wines with energy and strong varietal character.

Sauvignon Blanc Colchagua Valley	05	$
Chardonnay Colchagua Valley	05	$

OTHER PRODUCERS TO LOOK FOR: Arboleda, Casa Marín, Casa Silva, Errazuriz, Montes, MontGras, Morandé, Terra Andina, Terranoble, Undurraga, Veramonte, Viña Siegel, Viña Tabali.

ARGENTINA

Until the early 1990s, Argentina's wine industry was focused inward, as the local market's thirst was sufficient to absorb the huge quantities of everyday drinking wine produced there. But with per-capita consumption in the domestic market in sharp decline since the mid-1970s, Argentina's producers realized that they had to look to export markets to remain in business, and winemaking in Argentina began its transformation.

In just a few short years, Argentina has shifted its emphasis to the production of quality wine and turned its attention to export markets. Vine yields have been reduced dramatically. Large old wood casks have been widely replaced by oak barriques. And a major wave of new planting has taken place in mostly cooler, high-altitude sites that are better suited to producing serious wines, such as the Uco Valley, in the foothills of the Andes, about 80 miles south of the city of Mendoza. Despite the widespread reduction of vine yields, Argentina remains a huge wine producer, ranking number five in the world. Red wines, especially those from Malbec, Cabernet Sauvignon, and blends incorporating these two varieties, represent the lion's share of the best bottles.

Many of today's finest Argentine wines have barely five years of history. Consulting winemakers from California and Europe have brought their technical expertise to Argentina, as well as their knowledge of what is necessary to compete in the world wine market. At the same time, there has been an explosion of foreign investment by wealthy wine producers, luxury corporations, and individual investors attracted by inexpensive vineyard land and by Argentina's warm, dry climate. Since the Argentine peso was sharply devalued in late 2001, land prices have been even more attractive to outside investors.

Key to Vintage Ratings		Key to Assessments of Specific Wines	
★★★★★	Outstanding	**03**	An excellent to outstanding example *of that wine*
★★★★	Excellent	03	A good to very good example *of that wine*
★★★	Good to very good	03	A disappointing effort (often due to a
★★	Fair to average		difficult vintage)
★	Poor		

WINE GEOGRAPHY IN ARGENTINA

The province of Mendoza in west-central Argentina, just east of the Andes Mountains that form Argentina's natural border with Chile, dominates the wine industry in Argentina, producing three-quarters of the country's wine. For many wine lovers around the world, Mendoza is Argentine wine. Virtually all photos you're likely to see of the vineyards of Mendoza show in the background the towering snow-capped Andes, the highest peaks of which dwarf the tallest mountains in the western United States.

Mendoza is a semidesert with hot daytime temperatures, cool nights, and a cold winter. Depending on the site, rainfall is generally barely eight to ten inches a year, falling mainly during the summer months, as the high Andes range blocks moist air coming from the western, Pacific coast of South America. The greatest weather threats in Mendoza are spring frost and sporadic but sometimes devastating hailstorms. Harvest rains are rarely a problem, although it should be noted that the summer and harvest of 1998 were a disaster due to conditions caused by El Niño.

The effects of heat are partly mitigated by planting at high altitude, with Mendoza's best vineyards at 3,000 to 5,000 feet. The best sites are not far east of the Andes. Farther to the east, as the land slopes gently down from the mountains, temperatures are considerably hotter, soils are more fertile, and wine quality is lower. Irrigation is necessary throughout the Mendoza region. Happily, Mendoza's growers are able to rely on an ingenious and extensive system of hundreds, if not thousands, of irrigation canals that were originally dug by natives of the area in the 16th century to bring pure, frigid water from the Andes. On the horizon for North American wine lovers are more bottles from the province of Salta to the far north of Argentina, home to some of the highest-altitude grape vines in the world, as well as brisk, sappy wines from Patagonia to the south.

RED WINES

Argentina's signature red variety, Malbec, is a grape that came from Europe prior to the outbreak of the phylloxera epidemic, which nearly wiped out Europe's vineyards in the last decades of the 19th century and ultimately required them to be grafted over to rootstocks resistant to the root-eating aphid, the pest responsible for phylloxera. Malbec, which makes the opaque and often quite tannic Cahors in southwestern France and is still a minor variety in Bordeaux, found a home in Argentina, where it yields red wines in a wide range of styles: from light, fruity, and immediately drinkable to more complex, serious, structured, and age worthy, though rarely with hard tannins. Serious Malbecs are characterized by aromas and flavors of blackberry, dark plum, violet, leather, tobacco, and pepper; medium to full body; and pliant, chewy texture. Bonarda is a widely planted variety that produces some good everyday drinking wines with aromas and flavors of black fruits, tobacco, herbs, and earth, often with more obvious acidity than tannins. Cabernet Sauvignon also does well in Argentina, where it is often blended with Malbec, Bonarda, and Syrah. As in so many other warm climates, Syrah is gaining in popularity in Argentina today.

BANG FOR THE BUCK. Entry-level wines retailing for $10 or less are often commercial and soulless, or even dilute or rustic, but Argentina offers a wealth of nuanced, structured, and satisfying reds in the $15 to $25 range. You can pay $50 or more for an outstanding bottle of red wine from Argentina, but you don't have to.

2005 ★★★★   2004 ★★★+   2003 ★★★−   2002 ★★★★−

RECOMMENDED PRODUCERS

Achával Ferrer. Italian enologist Roberto Cipresso, a partner in this venture and in charge of winemaking, has been instrumental in creating single-vineyard Malbec bottlings that show how this variety expresses its terroir in various sites. Cleanly made wines in an updated Old World style.

Quimera Red Table Wine Mendoza	03	$$$
Finca Altamira Malbec Mendoza	03	$$$$

Altos Los Hormigas. A recent Italian/Argentine joint venture that produces excellent Malbec bottlings at shockingly affordable prices.

Malbec Mendoza	04	$
Malbec Reserve Mendoza	04	$$

BenMarco. Veteran viticulturalist Pedro Marchevsky, who was previously vineyard manager at Catena for many years, now has his own range of concentrated reds that emphasize pure, intense primary fruits and offer considerable early appeal. The Expresivo blend was previously bottled under the name of V.M.S.

Malbec Mendoza	04	03	$
Expresivo Mendoza		03	$$

Carlos Pulenta. Carlos Pulenta, a descendant of one of Argentina's oldest winemaking families, was the former president of the large Salentein Family Wines operation before starting his own venture several years ago. In his elegant new winery in Vistalba he makes the fruit-driven yet surprisingly complex Tomero range of wines and three serious red blends called Vistalba Corte C, B, and A.

Tomero Petit Verdot Mendoza	04	$$
Vistalba Corte B	03	$$
Vistalba Corte A	03	$$$

Catena Zapata. Nicolas Catena has been Argentina's undisputed leader in exporting high-quality wine to international markets since the mid-1990s and is also a major owner of choice vineyards around Mendoza. He offers white and red wines at a variety of price points, all of them concentrated, harmonious, complex, and fresh, with considerable early appeal but also structured to develop in bottle.

Catena Cabernet Sauvignon Mendoza		03	$$
Catena Alta Malbec Mendoza		02	$$$
Nicolas Catena Alta Red Table Wine Mendoza	02	01	$$$$

Clos de los Siete. The flagship Argentine wine of world-famous enologist Michel Rolland, one of seven French partners in the huge Clos de los Siete project in the Uco Valley at the foot of the Andes. Rolland also consults for the other members of this venture, including Monteviejo and Flecha de los Andes, and has a hand in several other top wines in Argentina. Early vintages of Clos de los Siete have been blends of Malbec, Cabernet Sauvignon, Merlot, and Syrah.

Clos de los Siete	04	03	$$

Luca. The label of Laura Catena, daughter of Nicolas Catena. Concentrated, classy wines with supple, fleshy textures, and superb sweetness of fruit. The flagship Beso de Dante is a blend of Cabernet and Malbec.

Malbec Altos de Mendoza		03	$$$
Syrah Altos de Mendoza		03	$$$
Beso de Dante Red Table Wine Altos de Mendoza	02	01	$$$

Dolium. Californian Paul Hobbs, who makes his own Cobos wines in Argentina (see Viña Cobos), is the consulting winemaker at Dolium. The impressively concentrated, structured reds come from vineyards in several top Mendoza sites and are aged for nearly two years in a high percentage of new French and American oak.

Malbec Reserva Mendoza	04	$$
Malbec Gran Reserva Mendoza	03	$$$

Luigi Bosca. The Arizu family bottles wine under more than two dozen labels at a huge former flour mill in the center of downtown Luján de Cuyo. The Luigi Bosca bottlings are updated versions of traditional Argentine wine, with more concentration and personality than most. Gala 1 and 2 are modern-style red blends bottled under the Luigi Bosca umbrella.

Malbec Reserva Luján de Cuyo	02	$$
Syrah Reserva Maipú	02	$$
Gala 2 Red Wine Mendoza	03	$$

Noemía de Patagonia. Highly concentrated, penetrating Malbecs with firm spine and an exhilarating balance of sweet fruit and vibrant acidity, from a high-visibility Italian/Danish venture in Patagonia's Rio Negro Valley.

J. Alberto Malbec Rio Negro Valley	04	03	$$$
Noemía Malbec Rio Negro Valley		03	$$$$$

O. Fournier. The Argentine branch of this multinational collection of wineries applies high-tech methods to high-quality fruit, a large percentage of which is from very old vines. The wines are deeply colored, dense, and chewy, with a sizable new oak component and considerable tannic clout. The B Crux is a blend that features a sizable percentage of Tempranillo.

B Crux Red Wine Valle de Uco Mendoza	`02`	$$
A Crux Malbec Valle de Uco Mendoza	`02`	$$$

Bodega Renacer. A recent start-up, this winery released three impressive full-bodied reds called Punto Final in the fall of 2005, made by Italian enologist Alberto Antonini. The flagship wine is Icono, aged for a full two years in new French oak.

Punto Final Malbec Reserve Mendoza	`04`	$$
Punto Final Icono Malbec Mendoza	`03`	$$

Susana Balbo. Susana Balbo makes her wines in the same new facility (Dominio del Plata) as her husband, Pedro Marchevsky (see BenMarco). Her wines are characteristically drier, more austere, more obviously structured, and less user-friendly at the outset. Her flagship Brioso is a blend of Bordeaux varieties.

Crios de Susana Balbo Cabernet Sauvignon Mendoza	`03`	`02`	$
Susana Balbo Malbec Mendoza	`04`	`03`	$$
Susana Balbo Brioso Mendoza	`03`	`02`	$$

Terrazas de los Andes. The reserva and *afincado* (formerly gran reserva) lineups from this offshoot of Chandon Argentina are impressively concentrated, tannic wines in a modern style, made mostly from the massive vineyard holdings of the parent company. Cheval des Andes, a Cabernet-Malbec blend, is a joint venture between Terrazas and Pierre Lurton, director of Château Cheval Blanc.

Reserva Malbec Mendoza	`04`	`03`	$$
Afincado Cabernet Sauvignon	`02`	`01`	$$$
Cheval des Andes Vistalba Mendoza	`02`	`01`	$$$$

Val de Flores. Just a single outstanding wine is produced from these old Malbec vines adjacent to the Clos de los Siete property. Val de Flores is a French partnership between Philippe Schell and enologists Dany and Michel Rolland.

Val de Flores Mendoza	`04`	`03`	$$$

Viña Alicia. This boutique operation is owned by Alicia Mateu de Arizu, with the wines made by her husband Alberto Arizu, who also directs winemaking at Luigi Bosca. The lineup here features Argentina's best Nebbiolo, the unique Cuarzo (Petit Verdot with Carignan and Grenache), and the rare Brote Negro, made from an old clone of Malbec. These are highly distinctive wines to seek out.

Morena Cabernet Sauvignon Luján de Cuyo	`03`	`02`	$$$
Nebbiolo Luján de Cuyo		`03`	$$$$
Cuarzo Luján de Cuyo		`03`	$$$$

Viña Cobos. Californian Paul Hobbs is partner and winemaker at Viña Cobos, whose Bramare lineup and flagship Cobos number among Argentina's most flamboyantly dense, ripe, and powerful red wines.

Bramare Malbec Marchiori Vineyard Mendoza		`03`	$$$$
Cobos Malbec Marchiori Vineyard Mendoza	`03`	`02`	$$$$$

OTHER PRODUCERS TO LOOK FOR: Alta Vista, Bodegas Banfi, Carmelo Patti, Bodegas Caro, Colomé, Cuvelier de los Andes, Familia Durigutti, Familia Zucardi, Fin del Mundo, Enrique Foster, J. & F. Lurton, Bodega Melipal, Nieto Senetiner, Nómade, Poesia, Pascual Toso, San Pedro de Yacochuya, Finca Sophenia, Tikal, Tomás Achaval, Trapiche, Valentin Bianchi, Bodegas Weinert.

WHITE WINES

Argentina's white wines make a less compelling proposition in export markets than its reds, but good bottles can be found. Of particular interest is Torrontés, an indigenous variety that yields light, scented wines with notes of citrus fruits, peach, floral oils, lichee, and brown spices; perfect as an aperitif or with spicy Asian cuisine. There are solid Sauvignon Blancs, but very few wines with the freshness and cut of examples from the Loire Valley or New Zealand. Chardonnay is widely produced in Argentina, with most examples decidedly tropical in character, not to mention oaky. The Catena family is the source of some of the country's suavest and most complete Chardonnays.

BANG FOR THE BUCK. With the exception of a few high-end Chardonnays, Argentina's white wines are generally cheap, with the best Torrontés bottlings offering very good value.

2005 ★★★★   2004 ★★★

RECOMMENDED PRODUCERS

Alta Vista. In addition to making impressively pliant and deep reds (the winery's special Alto bottling is one of Argentina's finest red blends), this new venture, created in 1997 by the late Jean-Michel Arcaute, who had previously run Château Clinet in Pomerol, also offers Torrontés and Chardonnay with juicy acidity and terrific intensity for their gentle prices.

Premium Torrontés Mendoza	`04`	$
Premium Chardonnay Mendoza	`04`	$

Catena Zapata. Catena's Chardonnays are among the elite examples of this variety from Argentina, as few other producers manage to capture so much freshness of fruit. Even their mass-market Alamos bottling is usually a winner.

Alamos Chardonnay Mendoza	`04`	$
Catena Chardonnay Mendoza	`04`	$$
Catena Alta Adrianna Vineyard Chardonnay Mendoza	`04`	$$$

Luca. Laura Catena's Chardonnay offers exotic but vibrant aromas and flavors of apricot and soft citrus fruits, with judicious use of new oak.

Chardonnay Altos de Mendoza   `04` `03` $$

Luigi Bosca. Among this winery's endless range of wines are one of Argentina's handful of excellent Viogniers and a distinctly Burgundy-style Chardonnay from very old vines. Their Sauvignon Blanc is also a standout.

Finca La Linda Viognier Luján de Cuyo	`04`	$
Sauvignon Blanc Reserva Maipú	`04`	$$
Finca Los Nobles Chardonnay Luján de Cuyo	`04`	$$

Susana Balbo. Balbo's classically dry, understated, floral Torrontés is a ubiquitous favorite in the restaurants of Buenos Aires.

Crios de Susana Balbo Torrontés Cafayate   `05` $

Michel Torino. Consistently delicate spicy-floral Torrontés from vines in the Salta province of Argentina's north.

Don David Torrontés Cafayate Valley   `04` $

OTHER PRODUCERS TO LOOK FOR: Colomé (Torrontés), Doña Paula (Sauvignon Blanc), Etchart (Torrontés), Tapiz (Chardonnay).

WINES OF THE WORLD
BY KEY VARIETY

This buyer's guide is organized geographically, by country and growing region. But if you prefer to select your wines according to variety, following is a list of the best places to look for your favorites. The list includes wine regions where a particular variety is commonly found in its pure form or where it comprises the majority of numerous blends typical to that area.

NOTE: Many consumers don't seem to know the difference between a variety and a varietal. Here in a nutshell is the difference. A grape type (Chardonnay, Cabernet Sauvignon, etc.) is a VARIETY. A wine made entirely from a single variety, or from a sufficiently high percentage of that grape type that it is legally entitled to identify itself by that variety on the label, is a *varietally labeled wine*—for short, a VARIETAL wine. In other words, it is incorrect to say that you prefer wines made from the Chardonnay varietal or that a wine is a blend of several varietals. But you can enjoy the Chardonnay variety, and a wine can be a blend of several varieties.

It should also be noted that if you limit your purchases to varietally labeled wines, you will miss out on the significant percentage of the world's greatest bottles that are blends of two or more varieties.

WHITE GRAPE VARIETIES

CHARDONNAY:
Burgundy (Chablis, Côte d'Or, Côte Chalonnaise, Mâconnais), Northeast Italy (White Wines), California (Chardonnay), Oregon (Other White Wines), Washington (Chardonnay), Australia (Chardonnay), New Zealand (Chardonnay & Other White Wines), South Africa (White Wines), Chile (White Wines), Argentina (White Wines).

SAUVIGNON BLANC:
Bordeaux (Dry White Wines), Loire Valley (Sauvignon Blanc), Northeast Italy (White Wines), Austria (Dry White Wines), California (Sauvignon Blanc), Washington (Other White Wines), Australia (Other White Wines), New Zealand (Sauvignon Blanc), South Africa (White Wines), Chile (White Wines), Argentina (White Wines).

RIESLING:
Alsace (Riesling), Northeast Italy (White Wines), Germany (Mosel-Saar-Ruwer, The Rhine/Other German Wine Regions), Austria (Dry White Wines), Oregon (Other White Wines), Washington (Other White Wines), Australia (Other White Wines), New Zealand (Chardonnay & Other White Wines), South Africa (White Wines).

PINOT GRIS (PINOT GRIGIO):
Alsace (Pinot Gris), Northeast Italy (White Wines), Oregon (Pinot Gris), New Zealand (Chardonnay & Other White Wines).

PINOT BLANC (PINOT BIANCO):
Alsace (Other White Wines), Northeast Italy (White Wines), Oregon (Other White Wines).

CHENIN BLANC:
Loire Valley (Chenin Blanc), South Africa (White Wines).

GEWÜRZTRAMINER:
Alsace (Gewürztraminer), Northeast Italy (White Wines), New Zealand (Chardonnay & Other White Wines).

VIOGNIER:
Rhône Valley (Condrieu), California (Other White Wines), Washington (Other White Wines), Australia (Other White Wines), South Africa (White Wines).

RED GRAPE VARIETIES

CABERNET SAUVIGNON:
Bordeaux (Red Wines/Médoc, Red Wines/Graves), Central Italy (Other Red Wines), California (Cabernet & Cabernet-Dominated Blends), Washington (Cabernet Sauvignon & Merlot), Australia (Cabernet Sauvignon & Bordeaux Blends), New Zealand (Other Red Wines), South Africa (Red Wines), Chile (Red Wines), Argentina (Red Wines).

MERLOT:
Bordeaux (Red Wines/Right Bank), Central Italy (Other Red Wines), California (Merlot), Washington (Cabernet Sauvignon and Merlot), Australia (Cabernet Sauvignon and Bordeaux Blends), South Africa (Red Wines), Chile (Red Wines).

CABERNET FRANC:
Bordeaux (Red Wines/Right Bank), Loire Valley (Cabernet Franc), California (Cabernet & Cabernet-Dominated Blends).

PINOT NOIR:
Burgundy (Côte d'Or, Côte Chalonnaise), California (Pinot Noir), Oregon (Pinot Noir), New Zealand (Pinot Noir), South Africa (Red Wines).

SYRAH (SHIRAZ):
Rhône Valley (northern Rhône Reds), Languedoc-Roussillon (Coteaux du Languedoc, Corbières & Minervois, Other Red Wines), California (Syrah & Other Rhône Varieties), Washington (Other Red Wines), Australia (Shiraz & Other Rhône Valley Varieties), New Zealand (Other Red Wines), South Africa (Red Wines).

GRENACHE (GARNACHA):
Rhône Valley (southern Rhône Reds), Languedoc-Roussillon (Coteaux du Languedoc, Other Red Wines), Provence (Other Red Wines), Spain (Other Red Wines), California (Syrah & Other Rhône Varieties), Australia (Shiraz & Other Rhône Valley Varieties).

SOME IMPORTANT WINE TERMS & CONCEPTS

Acidity: A wine's acidity (principally tartaric, malic, and lactic) provides liveliness, longevity, and balance. Excessive acidity gives a sour or tart impression, while insufficient acidity can result in a flabby, shapeless wine. One could say that if tannin provides a wine's backbone, acidity is its nervous system. Generally speaking, the sweeter a wine is, the more acidity it needs to communicate an impression of balance.

Acidification (or Acidulation)**:** Acid, usually tartaric or citric, is often added during the winemaking process, especially in hot climates where grapes tend toward overripeness or are deficient in natural acidity. On the other hand, in some colder wine regions or in years when fruit does not ripen properly and acidity levels remain high, some wineries may make chemical corrections to deacidify their wines.

Appellation Contrôlée: A system designed in France in the 1930s that controls the kinds of grapes that can be planted in what areas, vineyard practices and permitted yields, the kinds of wines that can be made from permitted varieties and by what methods, and the way the wines must be labeled. The main objective of this system, which is administered by France's National Institute for Appellations and Origins (INAO), is to guarantee the authenticity of wines and to protect consumers from fraud. France's *appellation contrôlée* (AC) system is the model around which many other countries, particularly in Europe, have regulated their wine industries. It should be noted that the trend in recent years, especially in Europe, has been to ease up on restrictions in order to grant greater flexibility to producers attempting to make wines with broader appeal in export markets. Increasingly, prestigious wines are being made outside the restrictions of the AC and sold under less restrictive regional rubrics or as table wine.

Carbonic maceration: A fermentation technique designed to extract fruit rather than tannins from the grapes, generally used to make wines that are bottled early and intended to give immediate pleasure. The most famous example of wine often made via carbonic maceration is Beaujolais. Grapes go into the fermentation vat unbroken, and some or most of the fermentation takes place within the uncrushed berries. The minimal contact between the fermenting juice and the grape skins brings lower tannin levels and emphasizes the fruity character of the grape. Wines made this way are virtually always meant for early consumption.

Cask/Barrel: Most of the world's greatest wines, especially reds, are at least partially aged in barrels, usually made from French or American oak or, increasingly, oak from Eastern Europe. A barrique is the standard Bordeaux barrel, holding 225 liters, or the equivalent of about 300 bottles of wine. (The standard Burgundy barrel, often called a *pièce*, holds 228 liters.) But wood casks may be as large as 100 hectoliters (i.e., 10,000 liters) or more. Barrels are a key element in the *élevage* (maturing, or raising) of a wine and in creating a structured, harmonious wine capable of further development in bottle. The right barrels used skillfully can go a long way toward adding early appeal to a wine by sweetening and framing its aromas and flavors. Too high a percentage of new barrels, poor-quality barrels, or used barrels that have not been properly cleaned can also dominate a wine, dry out its fruit, or introduce dirty aromas. High-quality barrels are quite expensive, with the finest French barriques now costing as much as $1,000 in export markets. One result of this major expense, other than higher prices for wines, is that many producers who believe their customers prefer wines with aromas and tastes of oak are saving money by using oak chips or oak extract simply as a flavoring agent.

Chaptalization: The addition of sugar during fermentation to increase a wine's alcoholic strength. Many winemakers use strategic additions of sugar to extend their fermentations in the belief that this gives more complexity and richness to the resulting wines. While chaptalization is often illegal in warm regions in which growers normally have no difficulty ripening their fruit, it is frequently employed in marginal climates.

Corked: Between four and eight percent of wines bottled with cork stoppers are affected to one degree or another by a mold known as TCA (2,4,6-Trichloroanisole), a naturally occurring, harmless compound that imparts a musty aroma (think wet cardboard or mildewed shower curtain) to a wine. In less obvious cases, a defective cork may simply stunt the aromas and flavors of a wine and dry its finish. The unacceptably high failure rate of corks is the reason so much experimentation continues to go on with alternate bottle closures. The most successful of these to date have been screw caps, which are now widely used in New Zealand and Australia and by forward-thinking producers in many other regions, particularly for white wines meant to be consumed quickly.

Cru: Literally, a French word meaning "growth." When applied to wine, this normally refers to a system of classifying vineyards either by geography or by reputation established over decades or even centuries of production. Systems of classification differ by region. For example, Bordeaux has crus classés (classified growths), while Burgundy has grands crus and premiers crus (great growths and, just under this category, first growths). While geographic appellations have been established in most New World growing areas, creating more specific hierarchies of wine quality has generally been difficult due to the relative youth of many of these regions and to the politics involved in deciding which vineyards are superior to others.

Fermentation: The conversion of grape juice into wine through the action of yeasts present in the juice, which through its enzymes transform the grapes' sugars into alcohol and carbon dioxide. This alcoholic fermentation is also known as primary fermentation.

Filtration: A method of clarifying and stabilizing wine, by passing it through a filter, to give it a bright, clear appearance and to remove yeasts, bacteria, or other solid matter that might otherwise cause the wine to spoil after it has been bottled. Excessive filtration, like excessive fining, can strip a wine of aroma, body, texture, and length, but many winemakers believe that a gentle filtration is essential to producing stable wines.

Fining: A method of clarifying wine by adding a coagulant (such as egg whites) to the top of the wine and allowing it to settle to the bottom, carrying suspended particles with it. In general, a fining agent falls through the wine (the sludge is left behind when the clear juice is racked or bottled), while with filtration the wine is generally pumped through a filter.

Lees: Solid residue (mostly dead yeast cells and grape pulp, pips, and skins) that remains in a barrel or tank after the wine has been drawn off. Many white wines and some reds are kept on their lees for a period of time to protect them from oxidation, enrich their texture, and add complexity. Wines protected by their lees often require less addition of the preservative and antioxidant sulfur dioxide (SO_2), but careful technique is essential to ensure that unwanted aromas don't develop.

Malolactic fermentation: A secondary fermentation in which tart malic acid in a wine is converted into softer lactic acid and carbon dioxide either through naturally occurring lactic bacteria or by inoculation with cultured bacteria. Malolactic fermentation, which generally follows the alcoholic fermentation, is nearly always carried out in red wines. Some producers of white wines, especially Chardonnay, encourage malolactic fermentation, while others, particularly those in hot regions that produce grapes naturally low in acidity, avoid it in order to preserve acidity and maximize freshness.

Must: Grape juice or crushed grapes not yet fermented or in the process of being fermented into wine.

Négociant: A négociant is a wine merchant or broker who buys grapes, must, or fermented wine, then ages, blends, bottles, and markets it under his or her own label. In many regions the line between private estate and négociant has been blurred in recent years. More and more of these merchants now own their vineyards, since controlling sources of supply has become increasingly important to making high-quality wines. At the same time, a growing number of family estates, particularly in Burgundy, now conduct small négociant operations, which enable them to increase their production and income without having to make expensive new investments in land. It should be noted that many high-visibility California wineries are technically négociants, as they make wines under their own labels from the produce of vineyards they don't own. In Bordeaux, négociants have traditionally been the middlemen between the châteaux proprietors and the retail merchants, essentially financing each new vintage by purchasing wines from the châteaux the spring after the harvest and in turn selling the wines to retailers and importers as futures—not a bad arrangement for the châteaux owners since they get paid for their wine a year or more before it's bottled.

Noble rot (Botrytis cinerea): Noble rot is a mold that develops under the right climatic conditions (generally alternating humidity and dry heat), shriveling the skins of white grapes and having the beneficent effect of concentrating sugars and acids and imparting a honeyed character as the grape dehydrates. Certain grape varieties—notably Riesling, Chenin Blanc, and Sémillon—are especially prone to noble rot. Wines made from botrytized grapes are generally medium-sweet to very sweet, sometimes downright unctuous, and typically show aromas and flavors of apricot, pineapple, honey, and licorice. (In years when rot runs rampant, the aromas, flavors, and textures of botrytis can be more dominant in the wines than the grape variety itself.) Most of the world's greatest dessert wines are made from white grapes affected by noble rot. It should be noted that badly timed wet weather prior to the harvest can spawn destructive gray rot, noble rot's evil twin, which can quickly ruin grapes that are still on the vine.

Organic viticulture: In Europe, organic refers simply to organically grown grapes—i.e., grapes grown without the use of chemicals in the vineyard—as there are no rules defining organic winemaking. In the U.S., there are three levels of organic wine: 100 percent organic means that the grapes were grown without the use of conventional pesticides, petroleum- or sewage-based fertilizers, bioengineering, ionizing radiation, or added sulfites. Organic means that no less than 95 percent of the grapes comply with the above rules, and made with organic grapes means that at least 70 percent of the grapes used comply with the "100 percent organic" requirements. The most extreme form of organic wine growing is biodynamic viticulture, in which the vineyard is viewed as a living, self-sustaining, closed system that must be kept in proper balance. The soil itself is seen as an organism to which synthetic fertilizers and pesticides are anathema but which can benefit from the addition of certain natural preparations (e.g., cow manure, silica, oak bark, flower heads), done in conjunction with lunar and planetary cycles, to enhance the life of the soil. Most growers who practice biodynamic viticulture have been heavily influenced by a series of lectures, entitled Spiritual Foundations for the Renewal of Agriculture, delivered by the Austrian philosopher-scientist Rudolf Steiner in 1924, though many growers have made refinements to Steiner's methods to meet their own special needs.

Oxidation: The aging of many of the world's great wines in barrel—not just the most serious reds but also some whites—essentially relies on controlled oxidation to allow the wine's aromas and flavors to develop and its components—fruit, acidity, tannins, alcohol—to evolve and harmonize. But too much exposure to air, either while a wine is being made or after it has been bottled, causes wine to oxidize, the immediate effect being a darkening of color in white wines and a loss of freshness and a flattening out of aromas. More oxidation brings aromas of sherry, and, when combined with exposure to heat, maderization. (But note that some wines, such as Oloroso sherry, some Australian dessert wines, and, of course, Madeira, derive much of their unique character from intentional oxidation.) Red wines are generally far more resistant to oxidation than whites because they are protected by their phenolic material. Sulfur dioxide is the most widely used substance to prevent unwanted oxidation.

Phenolics: Also known as polyphenols, these are chemical compounds, occurring mostly in the skins and seeds of the grapes but also in the stems and juice, that include anthocyanins (coloring material, which is far more abundant in red grapes), tannins, and flavor compounds. Phenols are extracted during the fermentation and maceration (the period when the grape juice is in contact with the skins), and play a crucial role in the flavor, color, and ageability of a wine. (Wines can also acquire phenolics from oak barrels, which can contribute complexity and longevity.) The best wines are generally made from grapes that achieve full phenolic maturity—in other words, fully ripe flavors. In cool, marginal regions, grapes can struggle to ripen. But very warm areas present their own challenges: sugar levels in the grapes can skyrocket and acidity literally be cooked out of the grapes by sun before the fruit achieves true phenolic maturity.

Racking: Transferring the wine from one cask to another to separate it from its lees. Racking can be used to aerate a wine, and the process of leaving precipitated matter behind also helps to clarify the wine. Insufficient racking can result in reduction, while excessive racking can strip a wine of some of its richness or introduce oxidative aromas.

Reduction: Too little exposure to oxygen can cause a wine to be reduced, giving it unpleasant vegetal and chemical fermentation aromas. Reduction is essentially the opposite of oxidation. Aromas of reduction can range from musky notes of cassis or smoked meat to more extreme hydrogen sulfide (rotten egg) and mercaptans (skunky or garlicky smells). (These sulfur and nitrogen compounds occur because wine is fermented by yeast through an anaerobic process—i.e., without oxygen.) Many winemakers intentionally keep their wines in a reduced state during *élevage* to preserve their freshness, but largely to eliminate reductive aromas before bottling their wines by racking them or treating them with copper.

Residual sugar: Any unfermented sugar that remains in a finished wine, usually described in terms of percentage by weight or, in Europe, in grams per liter (15 grams of residual sugar per liter equal 1.5 percent). As a general rule, wines with less than 3 grams/liter of r.s. (0.3 percent) are considered to be dry, but even wines with two or three times that much residual sugar can taste dry if they are high in acidity. The sweetest dessert wines, usually made from grapes whose sugars have been concentrated by noble rot, typically feature residual sugar from 8 to 20 percent, and sometimes more.

Sediment: Solid matter deposited in a bottle during the course of the maturation process. While a wine with substantial sediment requires special handling (the bottle is generally stood upright and then decanted off its sediment), sediment is generally a sign that the wine was not excessively filtered prior to bottling (see fining and filtration).

Sulfur: The most common disinfectant for wine. Most winemakers today feel that it is nearly impossible to produce stable, fresh wine without judicious use of sulfur products at one or more stages of vinification: just after the harvest to thwart fermentation by the wrong yeasts, in the cellar to prevent microbial spoilage and oxidation, and at the time of bottling to protect the wine against exposure to air. But as a general rule, the amount of sulfur used in the production of fine wine has never been lower than it is today as winemakers around the world strive to produce natural wines that are expressive in their youth.

Tannin: Bitter, mouth-drying polyphenols found in the skins, stalks, and pips of the grapes-as well as in the wood barrels in which wines are aged. A wine's tannins act as a preservative and can be an important component if the wine is to be aged over a long period. Tannins are frequently harsh in a young wine, but they gradually mellow or dissipate as the wine ages in the bottle. Excessively tannic wines can lose their fruit or dry out before the tannins soften. Red grapes are as a rule far more tannic than whites—and, in any event, white wines are generally made with limited contact with their skins. Some varieties that tend to be especially rich in tannins include Cabernet, Syrah, Nebbiolo, and Mourvèdre.

Terroir: A French concept incorporating all the elements that contribute to the distinctiveness of a particular vineyard site: its soil and subsoil, drainage, slope and elevation, and its microclimate, which includes temperature and precipitation, exposure to the sun, and the like. The term *goût de terroir* simply refers to the distinctive taste thought to be imparted by a variety or varieties grown in a particular place.

Yeast: The various microorganisms that cause fermentation. Wild yeasts are naturally present on grape skins—as well as in wineries—but specially cultured yeasts (often referred to as commercial or artificial yeasts) are frequently used to ensure more predictable, controlled, and complete fermentations.

Individual wine producers are not listed in the index, but they can be found by locating their geographical region in the book and then referring to that section.